ESCAPE VELOCITY

ESCAPE VELOCITY

Cyberculture at the End of the Century

MARK DERY

GROVE PRESS
New York

The author wishes to express his gratitude for permission to quote from the following:

"A Sane Revolution," from *The Complete Poems of D. H. Lawrence,* ©1964, 1971 by Angelo Ravagli
and C. M. Weekley, executors of the estate of Frieda Lawrence Ravagli. Used by permission of Viking
Penguin, a division of Penguin Books USA, Inc.; "All Watched Over by Machines of Loving Grace,"
from *The Pill versus the Springhill Mine Disaster* by Richard Brautigan. Copyright ©1968 by Richard
Brautigan. Reprinted by permission; "New Mother," from *Machinery* by MacKnight Black. Copyright
©1929 by Horace Liveright. Reprinted with the permission of Liveright Publishing Corp.; "Baby
Driver" copyright ©1969 by Paul Simon. Used by permission of the publisher; "Brand New Car"
(M. Jagger / K. Richards): Used by permission of Promopub, B.V.; the lines from "she being Brand"
are reprinted from *Complete Poems: 1904–1962* by E. E. Cummings, edited by George J. Firmage, by
permission of Liveright Publishing Corp. Copyright ©1926, 1954, 1991 by the Trustees for the E. E.
Cummings Trust. Copyright ©1985 by George James Firmage; "Teachers" written by Leonard Cohen. Copyright ©1967 by Leonard Cohen. Used by permission. All rights reserved. "The Becoming"
and "Happiness in Slavery" reprinted with permission of Leaving Hope/TVT Music. "The Becoming"
©1994 Leaving Hope/TVT Music; "Happiness in Slavery" ©1992 Leaving Hope/TVT Music. "Sin"
and "Ringfinger" reprinted with permission of TVT Music, Inc. ©1989 TVT Music, Inc.

Published simultaneously in Canada
Printed in the United States of America
FIRST EDITION

Library of Congress Cataloging-in-Publication Data

Dery, Mark, 1959–
Escape velocity : cyberculture at the end of the century / Mark Dery.
p. cm.
Includes bibliographical references and index.
ISBN 0-8021-1580-2
1. Computers and civilization.   2. Internet (Computer network)–
Social aspects. I. Title.
QA76.9.C66D47 1996
306′.1–dc20 95-40922

DESIGN BY LAURA HAMMOND HOUGH

Grove Press
841 Broadway
New York, NY 10003

10 9 8 7 6 5 4 3 2 1

CONTENTS

ACKNOWLEDGMENTS

Through its long, laborious birth, *Escape Velocity* had many midwives.

My editor, Anton Mueller, hacked his way through the polysyllables to produce a book that was lighter by many pages, and the better for it.

Gareth Branwyn was my virtual Virgil in the trackless wilds of cyberspace; my chapter on sex and technology benefited greatly from his meticulous reading. In our many exhaustive, exhilarating conversations, Scott Bukatman spurred me on to new insights, admonishing me, always, to beware the dreaded "cyberdrool" that turns so much writing about cyberculture to mush. Chris Grigg vastly improved my chapter section on performing robots with his sharp-witted, often hilarious critique. Additionally, the unpublished manuscript for his anti-guidebook, "Negativland Presents the Rex Everything Guides, Volume 1: Disneyland," proved a mother lode of inside information about the Magic Kingdom. My chapter on cyberdelia was the better for Erik Davis's Kurtzian forays into the dark heart of technopaganism. My analyses of Pat Cadigan's novels profited from her keen-eyed reading. Glenn Branca and Elliott Sharp were my Johnny Mnemonics when I was in pursuit of SF trivia; both shared generously of their encyclopedic knowledge and prodigious libraries. Others opened their Rolodexes, rendered assistance in practical matters, or simply offered words of encouragement, foremost among them Mark Pauline and D. A. Therrien, followed closely by William Barg, Sioux Z. of Formula public relations, Kiyo Joo, Jan E. Willey, Christian Waters, Jonathan Shaw, Dr. Burt Brent, Bart Nagel, and Rich Leeds. I am forever grateful to the WELL and ECHO for on-line press passes that proved invaluable, and to electronic correspondents too numerous to name (although Tiffany Lee Brown, Maxwell X. Delysid,

Richard Kadrey, Jon Lebkowsky, Paco Xander Nathan, Rodney Orpheus, Howard Rheingold, R. U. Sirius, Darren Wershler-Henry, Erika Whiteway, and the legions who responded to my electronic questionnaire deserve special mention).

I owe a debt of gratitude to the photographers whose work graces these pages, many of whom accepted far less than their usual rates.

And I am indebted, more generally, to Bill Mullen, a gifted critic, friend of many years, and foeman worthy of the sturdiest steel; my analysis of Donna Haraway's "A Cyborg Manifesto" and my chapter on sex and technology were sharpened by our thrust and parry. As well, conversations with Mike Davis, Stuart Ewen, Claudia Springer, and Andrew Ross helped shape my thinking about culture in general and cyberculture in specific; the echoes of their ideas can be heard throughout these pages.

Finally, this book would have remained a virtual reality were it not for the Herculean labors of my untiring, uncomplaining agents Laurie Fox and Linda Chester, of the Linda Chester Literary Agency.

But it is with Margot Mifflin—sounding board, sparring partner, soul mate, and so much more—that these acknowledgments must close. Her slashing red pen saved me, time and again, from my worst excesses; her unsinkable optimism buoyed me during dark nights of the soul; her support in countless everyday but all-important ways enabled me to attain escape velocity.

INTRODUCTION: ESCAPE VELOCITY

Reprinted with permission from winter 1995 Adbusters Quarterly

WARNING: IN CASE OF RAPTURE, THIS CAR WILL BE UNMANNED.
—*born-again Christian bumper sticker*

Escape velocity is the speed at which a body—a spacecraft, for instance—overcomes the gravitational pull of another body, such as the Earth. More and more, computer culture, or cyberculture, seems as if it is on the verge of attaining escape velocity. Marshall McLuhan's 1967 pronouncement that electronic media have spun us into a blurred, breathless "world of allatonceness" where information "pours upon us, instantaneously and continuously," sometimes overwhelming us, is truer than ever.[1]

The giddy speedup of postwar America is almost entirely a consequence of the computer, the information engine that has wrenched us out of the age of factory capitalism and hurled us into the postindustrial era of transnational corporate capitalism. In America, manufacturing is undergoing what Buckminster Fuller called the "ephemeralization of work"—the reduction of labor to the manipulation, on computers, of symbols that stand in for the manufacturing process. The engines of industrial production have given way to an information economy that produces intangible commodities—Hollywood blockbusters, TV programs, high-tech theme parks, one-minute megatrends, financial transactions that flicker through fiber-optic bundles to computer terminals a world away. "Only 17 percent of working Americans now manufacture anything, down from 22 percent as recently as 1980," wrote Robert B. Reich in 1992.[2] According to the *New York Times*, American films "produce the second largest trade surplus, after airplane sales, of any American industry."[3] Immaterial commodities dominate the domestic market as well: A recent *Business Week* feature reported that "entertainment and recreation–not health care or autos–have provided the biggest boost to consumer spending" since 1991.[4] We are moving, at dizzying speed, from a reassuringly solid age of hardware into a disconcertingly wraithlike age of software, in which circuitry too small to see and code too complex to fully comprehend controls more and more of the world around us.

Although the genealogy of the computer can be traced to Charles Babbage's Analytical Engine, a steam-powered, programmable mechanical computer designed (but never built) in 1833, Colossus was history's first working electronic computer and the immediate ancestor of today's machines. A hulking monstrosity powered by two thousand vacuum tubes and programmed with punched paper tape, Colossus was developed in 1943 by the British to decrypt enemy messages encoded by the German Enigma machine; its success proved invaluable to the Allied war effort.

The runaway pace of postwar innovation has seen room-sized, vacuum tube-powered behemoths such as ENIAC–the first fully electronic programmable computer, officially switched on in 1946–shrink to a transistorized machine in the fifties, a box full of integrated circuits in the sixties, and a chip-driven microcomputer in the seventies, all the while growing exponentially more powerful.

By the late seventies, computers were a fixture in most businesses, and growing numbers of consumers were buying home computers such as the Apple II, the TRS-80, and the Commodore PET. Even so, it has been just over a decade since the computer revolution moved beyond the esoteric subcultures of researchers and hobbyists to become a mass culture phenomenon with the debut of the IBM Personal Computer in late '81 and the Apple Macintosh in early '84. It was only in January '83, when the PC's sales figures had skyrocketed from a mere twenty thousand machines sold during its first year on the market to five hundred thousand, that a *Time* cover story pronounced the personal computer the "machine of the year."[5] Otto Friedrich wrote, "Now, thanks to the transistor and the silicon chip, the computer has been reduced so dramatically in both bulk and price that it is accessible to millions. . . . The 'information revolution' that futurists have long predicted has arrived."[6]

Likewise, the on-line world now frequented by an estimated seven and a half million households was all but unknown to mainstream America as recently as the early nineties. Media awareness of the Internet reached critical mass in 1993: "Suddenly the Internet is the place to be," wrote *Time*'s Philip Elmer-Dewitt; the *New York Times*'s John Markoff confirmed that the global network was "the world's most fashionable rendezvous," a trendy "on-line gathering spot for millions of PC users around the world."[7]

The Internet was born of ARPANet, a decentralized computer network developed at the University of California at Los Angeles in 1969 by the Department of Defense's Advanced Research Projects Agency (ARPA) to ensure military communications in the event of a nuclear attack. By using a technique called packet-switching to disassemble data into addressed parcels, blip them over high-speed lines, and reassemble them just before they reach their destination, ARPANet rendered itself invulnerable to conventional attack; if a portion of the network went down, traffic would automatically be rerouted. In 1983, ARPANet was divided into military and civilian networks (Milnet and Arpa Internet, respectively); shortly thereafter, the U.S. National Science Foundation (NSF) took charge of the administration and maintenance of the lines and equipment that made up the Arpa Internet "backbone." Whereas the Defense Department restricted system access to institutions receiving Pentagon or NSF funding, the NSF made the network available to all faculty and students at member institutions. As universities, R and D companies, and government agencies connected their computers to the NSF's system, what had once been the Arpa Internet mutated into an anarchic global network of networks known, increasingly, as the Internet (from "internetworking").

By 1990, ARPANet had ceased to exist as a discrete entity; the kudzulike growth of the Internet, or Net, as netsurfers have come to call it, had engulfed it. The global metanetwork of today's Net embraces some ten thousand networks, among them nationwide commercial services such as CompuServe, Prodigy, GEnie, and America Online; the private, academic, and government institutions interwoven by NSFNET (the NSF's network); and esoteric regional BBSs (bulletin board systems) such as the Sausalito, California–based WELL (Whole Earth 'Lectronic Link) and New York's ECHO. Mind-bogglingly, the Internet is itself part of a still larger complex of interconnected networks commonly called the Matrix, which also includes UseNet (a buzzing hive of discussion groups called "newsgroups"), FidoNet (a constellation of more than twenty thousand BBSs, scattered over six continents), and BITNET (Because It's Time Network, an academic system), among others.

As this is written, an estimated thirty million Internet users in more than 137 countries traverse the electronic geography of what the science fiction novelist William Gibson has called "cyberspace"—an imaginary space that exists entirely inside a computer—and their ranks are growing by as many as a million a month.[8] Based on the rate at which computer networks are building on-ramps onto the Internet, a 1993 estimate put its growth rate at a staggering 25 percent every three months—a delirious pace that shows no sign of abating.[9]

The ephemeralization of labor and the evanescence of the commodity, in cyberculture, is paralleled by the disembodiment of the human. In growing numbers, we are spending ever greater amounts of our lives in cyberspace; like the sagely cyborg in Bruce Sterling's SF novel *Schismatrix,* we are convinced that "there's a whole world behind this screen."[10] The electronically disembodied are zapping E-mail around the world, typing messages back and forth in real-time "chat," and flocking to BBS discussion topics and UseNet newsgroups. They're lurking and flaming and ROTFLOL (Rolling on the Floor Laughing Out Loud). They're swapping pornographic .GIFs (digitized photos) and swinging in anonymous "text sex" trysts. They're mousing around the Net's latest addition, the World Wide Web, a hypertext-based system that enables users around the globe to point and click from one multimedia site to another, bouncing from digitized video clips to snippets of sound to screenfuls of text without end.

Overwhelmingly, they're convinced that there is a "there" there, after all. As I observed in my introduction to *Flame Wars,* a collection of essays on cyberculture,

> Those who spend an inordinate amount of time connected
> by modem via telephone lines to virtual spaces often report
> a peculiar sensation of "thereness"; prowling from one [elec-
> tronic] conference to another, eavesdropping on discussions
> in progress, bears an uncanny resemblance to wandering the
> hallways of some labyrinthine mansion, poking one's head

into room after room. "One of the most striking features of the WELL," observed a user named loca, "is that it actually creates a feeling of 'place.' I'm staring at a computer screen. But the feeling really is that I'm 'in' something; I'm some 'where.' "[11]

Even as the computer is revolutionizing our immaterial lives through electronic interconnection, it is irretrievably altering our material lives, as well. "Embedded" microprocessors—speck-sized computers mounted on tiny flakes of silicon—make our car engines, microwave ovens, Stairmasters, and sewing machines markedly "smarter" than their precursors. And as those who live the wired life know, the incredible shrinking computer now accompanies the user virtually anywhere, as a laptop, palmtop, or pocket-sized computer/communicator such as the beleaguered Apple Newton Message Pad. Any day now, we are told, such devices will come alive, animated by "intelligent agents"—software programs that act as personal assistants, scheduling meetings, answering E-mail, trolling the Net in search of information.

The computer revolution has made a host of mind-jarring technologies at least theoretically possible. Celebrated in Sunday supplements or *Omni* articles, some exist as hardware or software; others are pure vaporware (Silicon Valley slang for products announced far in advance of a release date that may or may not ever arrive).

The futuristic sheen of virtual reality—a simulation technology that employs TV goggles and quadraphonic sound to immerse users in 3-D, computer-graphic worlds—briefly captured the media's magpie eye in 1991 with the promise of a tomorrow where virtual thrill seekers, like Arnold Schwarzenegger in *Total Recall*, roam the red seas of Mars without leaving their armchairs. Today, virtual reality is a fixed landmark on the popscape, from arcade VR such as Horizon Entertainment's Virtuality games to theme park attractions such as the *Aladdin* ride at Orlando's Walt Disney World to the Fox TV series *VR.5* to the movie *Lawnmower Man*. A San Francisco dentist provides his patients with VR headgear and sets them adrift in computer-animated dreamworlds during surgery; medical students operate on bodies of information through a VR training system developed by Cine-Med; and wheelchair-bound paraplegics in the Bronx Veterans Affairs Medical Center escape their confinement for a fleeting hour or two, stalking monsters in the shadowy dungeons of a VR game called Heretic.[12]

Other technologies hover below the event horizon. K. Eric Drexler, the founding father of nanotechnology, imagines the creation of self-replicating subatomic engines called nanomachines. In theory, these microscopic devices could slurp up oil spills or suck up toxic clouds; remove diseased DNA segments from the cells of AIDS patients, effectively curing them; or repair the ravages of normal aging at a cellular level, affording near immortality.

Even further afield, the artificial intelligence theorist Hans Moravec calmly assures us that we are about to enter a "postbiological" universe in which robotic life forms capable of independent thought and procreation will "mature into entities as complex as ourselves." Soon, he insists, we will download our willing spirits into computer memory or robotic bodies and do away with the weak flesh altogether.

Clearly, cyberculture is approaching escape velocity in the philosophical as well as the technological sense. It resounds with transcendentalist fantasies of breaking free from limits of any sort, metaphysical as well as physical. Ironically, the very scientific worldview and runaway technological acceleration some say have produced the spiritual vacuum and societal fragmentation that are fertile ground for millenarian beliefs are spawning a techno-eschatology of their own—a theology of the ejector seat.

Increasingly, the musings of scientists, science fiction novelists, and futurologists are inflected with a millennial mysticism. Moravec predicts the creation of human-level machine intelligence by 2010, a development he contends will catalyze quantum leaps in robot evolution, leading ultimately to a universe watched over by godlike machines. For old times' sake, these cybergods may choose to digitize the human race and preserve it in a computer-generated world—the virtual reality equivalent of the Kryptonian city-in-a-bottle in Superman's Fortress of Solitude. In a similar vein, the mathematician and SF author Vernor Vinge maintains that cybernetic evolution will give rise to a "greater than human intelligence" between 2005 and 2030, at which point ultra-intelligent machine life will assume control of its own destiny, producing ever smarter progeny at an ever faster pace. The inevitable result, he argues, will be the ascent of a superevolved, technologically enhanced posthumanity.

The physicist Frank J. Tipler goes even further, reconciling physics and metaphysics. In *The Physics of Immortality: Modern Cosmology, God and the Resurrection of the Dead,* he offers nothing less than a "testable physical theory for an omnipresent, omniscient, omnipotent God who will one day in the far future resurrect every single one of us to live forever in an abode which is in all essentials the Judeo-Christian heaven."[13] Tipler posits an Omega Point (a term borrowed from the French theologian Pierre Teilhard de Chardin) of infinite density and temperature toward which the universe will collapse in a backwards Big Bang called the Big Crunch. The energy generated by this implosion could be used, he theorizes, to drive a cosmic computer simulator (think of *Star Trek: The Next Generation*'s Holodeck) with infinite processing power—enough, certainly, to bring back to (virtual) life every creature that ever lived.

Techno-transcendentalist ruminations from the far fringes of physics and artificial intelligence overlap with the millenarian prophecies of New Age visionaries, many of whom speak a sci-fi language appropriate to our age. Timothy Leary's heir apparent, the cyberdelic philosopher Terence McKenna, has produced a software package called Timewave Zero that illustrates his vision of the end of history—on December 12, 2012, to be exact—with the arrival of an ineffable *mysterium tremendum* that he calls "the transcendental object at the end of time." A cross between the enigmatic monolith from *2001: A Space Odyssey* and Teilhard de Chardin's Omega Point (an evolutionary epiphany that marks the arrival of an "Ultra-Humanity"), McKenna's transcendental object is, in his words, a "cosmic singularity"—a term from chaos theory that refers to the transition point, in a dynamical system, between one state and another. He speculates that the coming of this cosmic singularity may usher in a cybernetic Garden of Earthly Delights where

> all of the technological appurtenances of the present world have been shrunk to the point where they have disappeared into [nature] and are scattered as grains of sand along the beaches of this planet and we all live naked in paradise but only a thought

away is all the cybernetic connectedness and ability to deliver manufactured goods and data that this world possesses.[14]

As the millennium draws near, we are witnessing the convergence of what Leo Marx has called "the rhetoric of the technological sublime"— hymns to progress that rise "like froth on a tide of exuberant self-regard, sweeping over all misgivings, problems, and contradictions"—and the eschatology that has structured Western thought throughout history, in one form or another: the Judeo-Christian Second Coming, the capitalist myth of never-ending progress, Marxism's predestined triumph of the proletariat over the bourgeoisie.[15]

America, to which this book confines its scope, is the fountainhead of this techno-eschatology. Since its beginnings, the United States has been Utopia's home—the "city upon a hill" envisioned by John Winthrop, where Christian teleology, free-market visions of boundless expansion, and an abiding faith in technology have intertwined in a secular theology. The machine-age artist Charles Sheeler, famous for his meticulously realistic paintings of American industry, once observed, "Our factories are our substitutes for religious expression."[16]

Here at the end of the twentieth century, the rhetoric of escape velocity seduces us with its promise of deliverance from human history and mortality. Who can resist hoping that McKenna is right when he assures us that we will have front-row seats at doomsday, elevating our brief lives to cosmic significance? "We are to be the generation that witnesses the revelation of the purpose of the cosmos," he predicts. In our transmigration from the mundane world into "hyperspace," "we will be privileged to see the greatest release of concressed change probably since the birth of the universe."[17]

But as Thomas Hine reminds us in *Facing Tomorrow: What the Future Has Been, What the Future Can Be*, futures like McKenna's are stories we tell ourselves about the present—"an attempt to invest our lives with a meaning and a drama that transcend the inevitable decay and death of the individual. We want our stories to lead us somewhere and come to a satisfying conclusion, even though not all do so."[18] Placing our faith in an end-of-the-century deus ex machina that will obviate the need to confront the social, political, economic, and ecological problems clamoring for solutions is a risky endgame. The metaphysical glow that increasingly haloes

the high-tech tomorrows of cyberdelic philosophers, corporate futurologists, pop science programs such as the Discovery Channel's *Beyond 2000,*
or even ads such as AT&T's "You Will" campaign, blinds us to the pressing
concerns all around us.

In AT&T's corporate brand TV spots, all is sweetness and light. "Have you
ever opened doors with the sound of your voice?" asks a familiar voice, over
a countrified jingle that conjures the wide, open territories of the electronic
frontier. "You will." A young woman steps out of an elevator, her arms full,
and her apartment door unlocks at her command. The elevator landing
bears a striking resemblance to Rick Deckard's in *Blade Runner,* but this is a
kinder, gentler future; Tom Selleck's friendly rasp has replaced Harrison
Ford's numb, monotonic voice-over, and *Blade Runner's* Wagnerian twilight
has been thinned out and brightened up.

Brought to you by the mother of all communications companies,
AT&T's future is, in the best tradition of technological Utopias, a luminous
place, not far off. "I can see the future and it's a place about 70 miles east of
here, where it's lighter," intones Laurie Anderson in her song "Let $X = X$."
The golden glow that suffuses the spacious interiors in the spots–light made
gauzy with the aid of fog machines–sentimentalizes corporate dreams of
electronic interconnectedness by premisting the viewer's eyes. Moreover, it
lends AT&T's vision of things to come an almost metaphysical air, drawing
on the long-standing equation of the luminous with the numinous–an
equation that is at least as old as the seventeenth-century poet Henry
Vaughan's evocation of that ultimate virtual reality, the afterlife ("They are
all gone into the world of light!") and as recent as the radiant aliens in *Close
Encounters of the Third Kind.* Finally, it reminds us that technology is being
etherealized, transformed into what the cultural critic Donna Haraway calls
"machines made of sunshine . . . nothing but signals, electromagnetic
waves."[19] Even now, information flashes through fiber-optic cables, coded as
pulses of light, and Bell Lab researchers are laying the groundwork for a
computer technology based on photons, the particles of zero mass that
make up light.

Oddly enough, the transformation of industrial capitalism's dark
satanic mills into postindustrial "machines made of sunshine" seems not to

have lightened our burden as workers. In a world where "we're all connected," to quote New York Telephone, the office intrudes on our vacations,
the workday stretches into our evenings: Video screens, phones, and laptop
jacks convert every seat in the new Boeing 777 into an airborne office; the
pagers and cellular phones provided by one resort in Vail, Colorado, turn
downtime on the ski lifts into worktime.

   "If you don't close the door to your work," says Peter G. Hanson,
the author of *Stress for Success,* "it spills over into other areas of your life,
making it hard to give anything your full attention—particularly leisure."[20] In
the "You Will" spots, a young male executive links up with a videocon-
ference from what appears to be a seaside cabana: "Have you ever attended a
meeting in your bare feet? You will. And the company that will bring it
to you . . . AT&T."

   AT&T has already brought us the videophone and the wireless
personal communicator (a combination computer, fax/modem, and cellular
phone); the dashboard navigator, automated tollbooth, and voice-recognizing
lock are supposedly only a few years away. But the promised Tomorrowland
of eternal leisure that was supposed to follow in the wake of these marvels
has faded into history, supplanted by a corporate future where we are always
at the beeper's beck and perpetually in motion, too pressed for time to stop
for directions or decelerate for tolls. A yuppie mother on a business trip
coos at her baby on a videophone screen: "Have you ever . . . tucked your
baby in from a phone booth? You will." The "time famine" from which
today's sleep-deprived workforce suffers reaches new heights of absurdity in
a future where the quintessential maternal act—tucking baby in—is performed via videophone, with Ma Bell as the surrogate mother.

   Something as flimsy as a TV commercial might seem to creak under
weighty analysis, but the grassroots response to the AT&T campaign suggests that others have divined similar meanings in the ads. The imperious
"You Will," whose peremptory tone forecloses any alternatives to AT&T's
corporate brand future, has clearly hit a raw nerve. *Adbusters,* a Canadian
magazine of media criticism, recently ran a deft parody of one of the "You
Will" ads. Its satirical copy reminds us that monitoring technologies such as
the global positioning system in AT&T's dashboard navigator, which can tell
you where you are anywhere on Earth, could also enable direct marketers or
government agencies to pinpoint your location. "Have you ever felt op-

pressed or manipulated through technology?" smirks the parody. "YOU WILL. In the near future, no matter where you are, marketers, pollsters, and infobots will be close at hand."[21]

On the WELL, users voiced their misgivings about AT&T's wired world. The cyberpunk author Bruce Sterling fired the first round in a fusillade of well-aimed wisecracks:

> HAVE YOU EVER . . . had your nattering co-workers pursue you, without mercy, to the *beach*, where they insist on your making vitally important business decisions even though you're blitzed on kamikazes?? YOU WILL![22]

Ross Stapleton-Gray quipped,

> Have you ever had your . . . babysitter reroute the house inter-video-com into her school's local net and broadcast your "after-noon delight?" Had a bit error cause a turnpike crossbar to come down on the windshield of your [Mazda] Miata at 100 [miles per hour]? YOU WILL![23]

And Mitch Ratcliffe added:

> HAVE YOU EVER tried to live in a world imagined by a major corporation? If you call that living, YOU WILL.[24]

In their tart send-ups of the "You Will" ads, Sterling and his fellow WELL-dwellers restore the missing critical dimension to AT&T's misty future. Vital issues are nestled inside their throwaway one-liners, among them the alarming ease with which privacy is invaded in the digital age and the disastrous consequences of software "bugs" and data entry error in an increasingly computerized culture. Percolating through these comments is a simmering resentment at the tacit assumption that the future will be—is being, even as you read this—hardwired by multinational corporations rather than collectively imagined by everyone who will one day inhabit it.

As the credibility gap widens between the virtual world of light and the palpable facts of economic inequity and environmental depredation, many have begun to question the trickle-down theory of technological empowerment. As Gary Chapman, a former executive director of Computer Professionals for Social Responsibility, points out,

> Zealots of the computer revolution usually explain that they are exploring the leading edge of the most significant transforma-tion of society in our time, and that everybody else will eventu-ally catch up as the results of technological tinkering filter down to the general public in the form of mass-produced commodities or social and economic reorganization . . . [but] there is an obvious disjuncture between the Panglossian pronouncements of people well rewarded or inspired by the computer revolution and the actual adjustment of society to the impact of this technology.[25]

Simultaneously, the theology of the ejector seat, which preaches a seat-of-the-pants escape into an archaic Paradise Lost or a futuristic Paradise Regained, grows more untenable with each passing day. The Arcadias of the eighteenth-century Romantics or the sixties counterculture are not a viable option for the vast majority in cyberculture, who have no desire to return to a pretechnological life of backbreaking labor, chronic scarcity, and unchecked disease. Simultaneously, the gleaming futures of technophilic fantasy—from Norman Bel Geddes's streamlined Futurama at the 1939 New York World's Fair to Disney's space-age Tomorrowland to the techno-eschatology currently in vogue—look increasingly like so much unreal estate.

Taking it as a given that technology is inextricably woven into the warp and woof of our lives, nearly all of the computer-age subcultures profiled in *Escape Velocity* short-circuit the technophile-versus-technophobe debate that inevitably follows that assumption. Most of them regard the computer—a metonymy, at this point, for all technology—as a Janus machine, an engine of liberation *and* an instrument of repression. And all are engaged in the inherently political activity of expropriating technology from the scientists and CEOs, policymakers and opinion-shapers who have traditionally determined the applications, availability, and evolution of the devices that, more and more, shape our lives.

Some subcultures, such as the underground roboticists and the cyber-body artists profiled in chapters 3 ("Waging a Tinkerer's War: Mechanical Spectacle") and 4 ("Ritual Mechanics: Cybernetic Body Art"), enact this dynamic literally, reanimating cast-off or obsolete technology in perverse, often subversive performances that turn a critical eye on the military-industrial-entertainment complex. Others, such as the postmodern primitives examined in chapter 6 ("Cyborging the Body Politic"), who sport "biomechanical" tattoos of machine parts or microcircuitry, retrofit and refunction the signs and symbols, myths and metaphors of cyberculture.

Wittingly or not, all of them constitute living proof of William Gibson's cyberpunk maxim, "THE STREET FINDS ITS OWN USES FOR THINGS"—a leitmotif that reappears throughout this book. Whether literal or metaphorical, their reclamation of technology and the complex, contradictory meanings that swirl around it shifts the focus of public discourse about technology from the corridors of power to Gibson's (figurative) street; from the technopundits, computer industry executives, and Senate subcommittee members who typically dominate that discourse to the disparate voices on the fringes of computer culture.

"We tell ourselves stories in order to live," the opening line of Joan Didion's *White Album,* is one of *Escape Velocity*'s keystone assumptions. This book is less about technology than it is about the stories we tell ourselves about technology, and the ideologies hidden in those stories—the politics of myth. The cyber-hippies, technopagans, and New Age advocates of "consciousness technologies" in chapter 1 ("Turn On, Boot Up, Jack In: Cyberdelia") invest the new machine with a soul, relocating the Sacred in cyberspace. As well, they join the cultural struggle for ownership of the sixties: Rebooting the transcendentalism of the counterculture in nineties cyberculture, they purge it of its Luddism and consecrate it to technology's promise. On a related note, the cyber-rockers and cyberpunk writers in chapter 2 ("Metal Machine Music: Cyberpunk Meets the Black Leather Synth-Rockers") scuffle over the legitimacy of their mutual claims to the torn mantle of adolescent rebellion. In so doing, they highlight the essentially cyberpunk nature of rock music, a form of low-tech insurrection made possible by human-machine interface. The rogue technologists and cyber-body artists mentioned earlier mount techno-spectacles in which amok robots and humans menaced by heavy machinery dramatize popular anxieties over the growing autonomy of intelligent machines, especially "smart" weapons, and the seeming obsolescence of humanity. In chapter 5 ("RoboCopulation: Sex Times Technology Equals the Future"), on-line swingers who engage in text sex and hackers who fantasize about anatomically accurate robo-bimbos cast a revealing light on the gender politics of computer culture, and on our national obsession with the mechanizing of sex and the sexualizing of machines. Lastly, there are the postmodern exponents, in chapter 6, of what David Cronenberg calls "uncontrollable flesh": a self-made "morph" whose body, through avant-garde surgery, is her medium; a male-to-female transsexual who fancies herself the "techno-woman of the '90s"; bodybuilders who Nautilize themselves into machine-age icons; plastic surgeons who dream of human wings; prophets of posthuman evolution. These and others in cyberculture spin millennial fables about the transitional state and uncertain fate of the body, late in the twentieth century.

The subcultures explored in *Escape Velocity* act as prisms, refracting the central themes that shaft through cyberculture, among them the intersection, both literal and metaphorical, of biology and technology, and the growing irrelevance of the body as sensory experience is gradually supplanted by digital simulation. Each, in its own way, makes sense—or nonsense—of the dialectic that pits New Age technophiles, epitomized by the *Wired* editor Kevin Kelly, who believes that technology is "absolutely, 100 percent, positive," against doomsaying technophobes such as John Zerzan, the anarchist theorist who contends that technology is "right at the heart of what is so chronically wrong with society."[26] Each subculture plots a course between escapism and engagement, between techno-transcendentalism and politics on the ground, in everyday cyberculture.

Most important, fringe computer culture relocates our cultural conversation about technology from the there and then to the here and now, wiring it into the power relations and social currents of our historical moment. It keeps us mindful of Donna Haraway's admonition that any "transcendentalist" ideology that promises "a way out of history, a way of . . . denying mortality" contains the seeds of a self-fulfilling apocalypse. What we need, more than ever, she argues, is a deep, inescapable sense of the fragility of the lives that we're leading—that we really do die, that we really do wound each other, that the Earth really is finite, that there aren't any other planets out there that we know of that we can live on, that escape velocity is a deadly fantasy.[27]

The rhetoric of escape velocity crosses cyberpunk science fiction with the Pentecostal belief in an apocalyptic Rapture, in which history ends and the faithful are gathered up into the heavens. Visions of a cyber-Rapture are a fatal seduction, distracting us from the devastation of nature, the unraveling of the social fabric, and the widening chasm between the technocratic elite and the minimum-wage masses. The weight of social, political, and ecological issues brings the posthuman liftoff from biology, gravity, and the twentieth century crashing down to Earth.

As we hurtle toward the millennium, poised between technological Rapture and social rupture, between Tomorrowland and *Blade Runner*, we would do well to remember that—for the foreseeable future, at least—we are here to stay, in these bodies, on this planet. The misguided hope that we will be born again as "bionic angels," to quote *Mondo 2000*, is a deadly misreading of the myth of Icarus. It pins our future to wings of wax and feathers.

1/ TURN ON, BOOT UP, JACK IN

Cyberdelia

Ravers. *Photo: SKID*

Flashback to the Future: The Counterculture, 2.0

"The '90s are just the '60s upside down," says the comedian Philip Proctor.[1]

LSD is in vogue again. The "classic rock" of the sixties rules FM radio. Jimi Hendrix has been trance-channeled by the retrorocker Lenny Kravitz, whose flowered shirts and squalling wah-wah guitar pay devoted homage to Hendrix's style and sound. Oliver Stone has refought the Vietnam war (*Platoon*), resurrected Jim Morrison (*The Doors*), and obsessed on the blurred phantoms of the Zapruder film and the hermetic meanings of the Warren Report (*JFK*). On August 13, 1994, hordes of Generation Xers and an attendant army of hucksters and roving reporters descended on Saugerties, New York, for Woodstock '94, a hyped-to-death attempt to regain paradise at $135 a head.

As with all revisionist fads, the sixties redux is largely a fashion statement, skinning the look of the decade and leaving its stormy politics and troubling contradictions behind. A bell-bottomed naïf gambols across a 1993 Macy's ad: "DON'T WORRY, BE HIPPIE," counsels the caption.[2] A *Details* pictorial from the same year reconciles boomers and Gen Xers in images of longhaired, love-beaded models in fringed vests and paisley-printed jeans: "Counterculture style returns to where it once began. . . . [T]hese hippie-inspired clothes bridge the gap between grunge and glamour."[3] Time travel is a snap and decades can be mixed and matched when history is reduced to a series of frozen poses and kitschy clichés. The politics of style supplant the politics of the generation gap.

But the superficial faddishness of bell-bottoms and baby-doll dresses belies a deeper cultural tug-of-war over the meaning of the sixties. This pitched battle was a subplot of the 1992 presidential campaign. In his campaign ads, Bill Clinton positioned himself as a grown-up exemplar of John F. Kennedy's idealistic "new generation of Americans." Flushed with his Gulf War exorcism of the ghost of Vietnam, George Bush turned Clinton's sixties exploits—dodging the draft, protesting the war, smoking (but not inhaling) dope—into campaign issues. "[T]he GOP has found a new all-purpose enemy: the '60s," observed the *Newsweek* writer Howard Fineman. "The critique is that in a mad, 'permissive' decade the nation threw away its will, its discipline, its faith in the family and the military, in moral absolutes and rightful authority."[4]

The return of the sixties, and the culture war raging around the memory of that turbulent decade, is at the heart of the cyberdelic wing of fringe computer culture. Not surprisingly, many of cyberdelia's media icons are familiar faces from the sixties: No magazine cover story on the phenomenon is complete without the septuagenarian Timothy Leary, admonishing readers to "turn on, boot up, jack in" and proclaiming that the "PC is the LSD of the 1990s," or Stewart Brand, the former Merry Prankster and creator of the back-to-the-land hippie bible, the *Whole Earth Catalogue* (whose prescient motto was "ACCESS TO TOOLS"). Other prominent cyberdelic spokespeople, such as the *Mondo 2000* founders Queen Mu and R. U. Sirius; Howard Rheingold, the author of books on virtual reality and on-line communities; John Perry Barlow, an advocate of computer users' rights; and the virtual reality innovators Brenda Laurel and Jaron Lanier, are steeped in the Northern California counterculture of the sixties.

Rooted in Northern California and rallied around the Berkeley-based quarterly *Mondo 2000*, the cyberdelic phenomenon encompasses a cluster of subcultures, among them Deadhead computer hackers, "ravers" (habitués of all-night electronic dance parties known as "raves"), techno-pagans, and New Age technophiles.

Cyberdelia reconciles the transcendentalist impulses of sixties counterculture with the infomania of the nineties. As well, it nods in passing to the seventies, from which it borrows the millenarian mysticism of the New Age and the apolitical self-absorption of the human potential movement. As the cyberpunk novelist Bruce Sterling points out,

Today, for a surprising number of people all over America, the supposed dividing line between bohemian and technician simply no longer exists. People of this sort may have a set of windchimes and a dog with a knotted kerchief 'round its neck, but they're also quite likely to own a multimegabyte Macintosh running MIDI synthesizer software and trippy fractal simulations. These days, even Timothy Leary himself, prophet of LSD, does virtual-reality computer-graphics demos in his lecture tours.[5]

In his cyber-hippie travelogue, *Cyberia: Life in the Trenches of Hyperspace*, Douglas Rushkoff uses the "trippy fractal simulations" Sterling mentions—intricate, involuted abstractions generated by computers using complex mathematical formulae—as a root metaphor.[6] To Rushkoff, the fractal is emblematic of the cyberdelic subcultures he collectively calls Cyberia (a coinage borrowed from the Autodesk company's Cyberia Project, a virtual reality initiative). It serves as a cyber-hippie yin-yang symbol, signifying the union of the "two cultures"—the scientific and the nonscientific—into which society has been split by the scientific advances of the twentieth century, to use the scientist and essayist C. P. Snow's famous phrase.

In cyberdelia, the values, attitudes, and street styles of the Haight-Ashbury/Berkeley counterculture intersect with the technological innovations and esoteric traditions of Silicon Valley. The cartoon opposites of disheveled, dope-smoking "head" and buttoned-down engineering student, so irreconcilable in the sixties, come together in Sterling's hippie technophile and Rushkoff's cyberians. Increasingly, the media image of the Gen Xers who predominate in high-tech subcultures is that of the cyber-hippie or, in England, the "zippie" ("Zen-inspired pagan professional"). Toby Young, the associate editor of England's *Evolution* magazine, defines zippies as "a combination of sixties flower children and nineties techno-people."

Like his or her sixties predecessor, the archetypal cyber-hippie featured in Sunday supplement articles is largely a media fiction, synthesized from scattered sightings. He or she sports jewelry fashioned from computer parts by San Francisco's Famous Melissa and dresses in "cyberdelic softwear" from the San Francisco designer Ameba—op-arty T-shirts printed with squirming sperm, leggings adorned with scuttling spiders, belled jester caps popular at raves. He or she meditates on cyberdelic mandalas like the *New Electric Acid Experience* video advertised in *Inner Technologies,* a mail-order catalogue of "tools for the expansion of consciousness." "Recreate the Summer of Love with this '90s version of a '60s light show," the blurb entreats.

> There's something for everyone here: soft swatches of moving color, hypnotic, pulsating mandalas, psychedelicized fractals, surreal film imagery, computer animation, and advanced film graphics. A guaranteed mind-warping experience![7]

In addition, cyber-hippies sometimes seek switched-on bliss through Mindlabs, InnerQuests, Alphapacers, Synchro-Energizers, and other "mind machines"—headphone-and-goggle devices that flash stroboscopic pulses at the user's closed eyes, accompanied by synchronized sound patterns and, in some cases, low-level electrical stimulation of the brain. Advocates claim the devices induce trancelike states characterized by deep relaxation, vivid daydreams, and greater receptivity toward autohypnotic suggestions for behavior changes.

Alternately, a cyber-hippie might choose to boost his or her brain power with "smart drugs"—Piracetam, Vasopressin, and other central nervous system stimulants and so-called "cognitive enhancers" that allegedly increase the production of chemicals associated with memory or speed up the rate of information exchange in the brain's synaptic structure.[8]

What distinguishes the cyberdelic culture of the nineties from psychedelic culture, more than anything else, is its ecstatic embrace of technology. In his 1993 *Time* cover story on the phenomenon, Philip Elmer-Dewitt asserts that cyberdelia "is driven by young people trying to come up with a movement they can call their own. As [Howard Rheingold] puts it, 'They're tired of all these old geezers talking about how great the '60s were.' . . . For all their flaws, they have found ways to live with technology, to make it theirs—something the back-to-the-land hippies never accomplished."[9] Similarly, in his introduction to *Mirrorshades,* the 1986 cyberpunk omnibus that brought the SF subgenre into the mainstream, Bruce Sterling argued that cyberpunk signaled "a new alliance . . . an integration of technology and the '80s counterculture."[10] Sixties counterculture, by comparison, was "rural, romanticized, anti-science, anti-tech."[11]

To the extent that they define themselves in opposition to the Woodstock Nation, high-tech subcultures—whether cyberdelic or cyberpunk—insist on this reductive reading of sixties counterculture. Even so, there is more than a grain of truth in the widespread dismissal of sixties counterculture as "a return to nature that ended in disaster," to quote Camille Paglia.[12] Hippiedom inherited the Blakean vision of a return to Eden and the Emersonian notion of a transcendent union with Nature by way of Beat poets such as Gary Snyder, who counseled a tribal, back-to-the-land movement, and Allen Ginsberg, whose "Howl" demonized America as an industrial Moloch "whose mind is pure machinery." Such intellectual currents led, for some, to the antitechnological utopianism expressed in the rural commune. "It was inevitable that hippie values would lead true believers back to nature," the popologists Jane and Michael Stern write in *Sixties People*. "Although virtually all of them were Caucasian, hippies relished their romantic self-image as nouveau red men, living in harmony with the universe, fighting against the white man's perverted society of pollution, war, and greed."[13]

Nonetheless, sixties counterculture simultaneously bore the impress of Zbigniew Brzezinski's technetronic age. As Sterling notes, "[N]o counterculture Earth Mother gave us lysergic acid—it came from a Sandoz lab."[14] A popular button turned the E. I. Du Pont slogan, "BETTER THINGS FOR BETTER LIVING THROUGH CHEMISTRY," into a sly catchphrase for acidheads. At the same time, as Theodore Roszak points out in *The Making of a Counter Culture*, the Learyite article of faith that the key to cosmic consciousness and sweeping societal change could be found in a chemical concoction sprang from a uniquely American faith in technology. In that sense, he argues, the Du Pont slogan on the hippie button

> [wasn't] being used satirically. The wearers [meant] it the way Du Pont means it. The gadget-happy American has always been a figure of fun because of his facile assumption that there exists a technological solution to every human problem. It only took the great psychedelic crusade to perfect the absurdity of proclaiming that personal salvation and the social revolution can be packed into a capsule.[15]

The archetypal hippie experience was not dancing naked in a field of daisies, but tripping at an acid rock concert. The psychedelic sound-and-light show was as much a technological as a Dionysian rite, from the feedback-drenched electric soundtrack to the signature visual effects (created with film, slides, strobes, and overhead projectors) to the LSD that switched on the whole experience.

The emergent computer culture of the sixties overlapped, even then, with the counterculture. "Students were signing up in droves to take courses in computer studies," report the authors of The '60s Reader, "though having a home computer was beyond the wildest imaginings of most of them."[16] Prophetically, one of Ken Kesey's ragtag hippie troupe the Merry Pranksters was a not so distant relative of Sterling's bohemian techie—a computer programmer named Paul Foster whose life "seemed to alternate between good straight computer programming," when he wore the standard-issue suit and tie, and wilder times with the Pranksters, during which he sported a homemade psychedelic jacket festooned with "ribbons and slogan buttons and reflectors and Crackerjack favors."[17]

Similarly, the electrical engineer and hardware hacker Lee Felsenstein "balanced the seemingly incompatible existences of a political activist and a socially reclusive engineer," writes Steven Levy in Hackers: Heroes of the Computer Revolution.[18] Swept up in the political radicalism of the Berkeley-based free speech movement but obsessed with electronics at a time when technology was regarded with deep suspicion by radicals, Felsenstein strove to reconcile his divided loyalties. He and another activist hacker, Efrem Lipkin, went on to create the Bay Area electronic bulletin board Community Memory in 1973. Dedicated to the proposition that alternative networking was inherently empowering, Computer Memory was free to any and all through two public access terminals. "By opening a hands-on computer facility to let people reach each other, a living metaphor would be created," writes Levy, "a testament to the way computer technology could be used as guerrilla warfare for people against bureaucracies."[19]

Felsenstein and Lipkin weren't the only members of the counterculture to champion personal computing as an engine of social change. Bob Albrecht, a longhaired, wild-eyed zealot with a background in computing, founded a newspaper and a computer center, both called the Peoples' Computer Company. The technovisionary Ted Nelson self-published a "counterculture computer book" titled *Computer Lib,* an impassioned manifesto for an imagined movement whose battle cry would be "COMPUTER POWER TO THE PEOPLE!" Intriguingly, Roszak recently countered Newt Gingrich's use of the term "countercultural" to demonize boomer Democrats with the charge that Gingrich is

> more beholden to the '60s than he may know. It was guerrilla computer hackers, whose origins can be discerned in the old *Whole Earth Catalogue,* who invented the personal computer as a means, so they hoped, of fostering dissent and questioning authority. Ironically, this is the same technology on which Mr. Gingrich, the "conservative futurist," is banking to rebuild the economy.[20]

Whole Earth Catalogue founder Stewart Brand, who put the hacker subculture on the map with his 1972 *Rolling Stone* article, "Frantic Life and Symbolic Death among the Computer Bums," has straddled fringe computer culture and the counterculture almost since their inception. "It's all connected," he says. "It's certainly true that psychedelic research, on back to Aldous Huxley in Los Angeles, is very much a Californian phenomenon, as is the personal computer revolution, which is probably reflective of the frontier status of the American West Coast. The early hackers of the sixties were a subset of late beatnik/early hippie culture; they were longhairs, they were academic renegades, they spelled love *l-u-v* and read *The Lord of the Rings* and had a [worldview] that was absolutely the same as the Merry Pranksters' and all the rest of us world-savers.

"But they had a better technology. As it turned out, psychedelic drugs, communes, and Buckminster Fuller domes were a dead end, but computers were an avenue to realms beyond our dreams. The hippies and the revolutionaries blew it, everybody blew it but them, and we didn't even know they existed at the time! They weren't getting on television like Abbie [Hoffman] and blowing their own horn; they were just inventing the future and they did it with an astounding sense of responsibility, which they embodied in their technology, right there in the chips—a complete blending of high technology and down-and-dirty pop culture."

Where Brand sees the PC revolution as the phoenix that rose from the ashes of hippie romanticism and New Left radicalism, Timothy Leary sees it as a vindication of the counterculture; without the psychedelic revolution, he suggests, the personal computer would have been unthinkable. "It's well known that most of the creative impulse in the software industry, and indeed much of the hardware, particularly the Apple Macintosh, derived directly from the sixties consciousness movement," he asserts. "[The Apple cofounder] Steve Jobs went to India, took a lot of acid, studied Buddhism, and came back and said that Edison did more to influence the human race than the Buddha. And [Microsoft founder Bill] Gates was a big psychedelic person at Harvard. It makes perfect sense to me that if you activate your brain with psychedelic drugs, the only way you can describe it is electronically."

Indeed, throughout the sixties, the social effects of psychedelic drugs, electronic technologies, and youth culture were perceived as synergistic. In a 1969 *Playboy* interview, Marshall McLuhan theorized that hallucinogenic drugs were "chemical simulations of our electric environment," a method of "achieving empathy with our penetrating electric environment, an environment that in itself is a drugless inner trip."[21] "Movies That Blitz the Mind," a *Life* article on the wraparound, multiscreen extravaganzas at Expo '67 in Montreal, likened the disorienting whirl of high-tech multimedia to the sensory derangement of psychedelics: Spectators were "deliberately thrown off-balance mentally and even physically" by the LSDlike sensory assault of a "visual blitz" that made "audiences understand more through feeling than through thinking."[22]

In *The Electric Kool-Aid Acid Test*, Tom Wolfe's picaresque chronicle of the novelist Ken Kesey and his Merry Pranksters, Kesey's proto-cyberdelic commune maintained a shaky equilibrium between psychedelics and cybernetics, between the counterculture's back-to-nature folksiness and its neon nowness. *The Electric Kool-Aid Acid Test* is largely an account of the Pranksters' manic, cross-country trip, in which the wackily costumed, acid-addled troupe challenged consensus reality with hit-and-run guerrilla theater. Significantly, the drug-soaked Pranksters employed both psychedelic and electronic technologies in their demolition of square reality. Their refurbished 1939 school bus, hand-painted with a riot of psychedelic Day-Glo motifs, was loaded down with gadgetry, wired for sound from stem to stern:

> Sandy . . . rigged up a system with which they could broadcast
> from inside the bus, with tapes or over microphones, and it

would blast outside over powerful speakers on top of the bus. There were also microphones outside that would pick up sounds along the road and broadcast them inside the bus. There was also a sound system inside the bus so you could broadcast to one another over the roar of the engine and the road.[23]

A Prankster could listen to the various sound sources simultaneously, on headphones, and free-associate into a microphone hooked up to a tape delay system, improvising over layers of his own echoed words. When the Pranksters returned to their headquarters in rural La Honda, California, Kesey created an electronic Arcadia, wiring nature itself: "There were wires running up the hillside into the redwoods and microphones up there that could pick up random sounds . . . [and] huge speakers, theater horns, that could flood the gorge with sound."[24] In *The Sixties: Years of Hope, Days of Rage,* Todd Gitlin describes the Prankster-sponsored acid tests as public mental meltdowns made possible by free acid,

> pulsating colored lights, Prankster movies, barrages of sound and music, weirdly looped tape-recorders, assorted instruments, a flood of amplified talk. For Kesey, like Leary . . . had a vision of "turning on the world," electrifying it courtesy of the most advanced products of American technology.[25]

The slang says it all: The inhabitants of the sixties counterculture exemplified by Kesey and his Pranksters may have dreamed of enlightenment, but theirs was the "plug-and-play" nirvana of the "gadget-happy American"—cosmic consciousness on demand, attained not through long years of Siddharthalike questing but instantaneously, by chemical means, amidst the sensory assault of a high-tech happening. And when the Pranksters and their ilk attempted to go back to the garden, they brought the madcap, sped-up "electric circus" of modern media culture with them, wiring the garden for sound.

To some sixties futurologists, the machine and the garden were not irreconcilable. Writing in the December 1968 *Playboy,* the science fiction author Arthur C. Clarke imagines an "uninhibited, hedonistic society" of cradle-to-grave leisure, made possible by "ultraintelligent" machines. Much of the planet will revert to wilderness, he predicts, and people will spend youthful idylls in this paradise regained "so that they never suffer from that estrangement from nature that is one of the curses of our civilization."[26] Anticipating the techno-eschatology of the nineties, he concludes, "In one sense . . . History will have come to an end. . . . It may be that our role on this planet is not to worship God—but to create him. And then our work will be done. It will be time to play."[27] Yoking the counterculture's Rousseauistic dream of idling away the hours in Elysian Fields to the promise of artificial intelligence, he resolves the atheistic empiricism of modern science with the paternalistic God of Genesis in a clockwork caretaker.

In "All Watched Over by Machines of Loving Grace," the hippie poet Richard Brautigan echoes Clarke's sentiments, auguring a "cybernetic meadow / where mammals and computers / live together in mutually / programming harmony":

> *I like to think*
> *(it has to be!)*
> *of a cybernetic ecology*
> *where we are free of our labors*
> *and joined back to nature,*
> *returned to our mammal*
> *brothers and sisters,*
> *and all watched over*
> *by machines of loving grace.*[28]

Analyses of sixties counterculture that characterize it as intractably antitechnological neglect the cyberdelic motifs that counterpointed its back-to-the-land primitivism: the perception of psychedelics as liberatory technologies and of electronic media as mind-expanding psychedelics; the embrace of the public access computer terminal as an instrument of empowerment ("guerrilla warfare for people *against* bureaucracies"); SF visions of an earthly Elysium made possible by machines of loving grace.

Nonetheless, the reduction of the countercultural attitude toward technology to a retrograde neo-Luddism persists because it serves the needs of conservatives, the Left, and libertarian cyber-hippies alike. Time and again, we are reminded that the difference between the cyberdelic counterculture and its sixties prototype is, as Elmer-Dewitt observes, that the cyber-hippies "have found ways to live with technology, to make it theirs."

In an early *Mondo 2000* editorial, Queen Mu and R. U. Sirius (the magazine's publisher/"Domineditrix" and then editor in chief, respectively) breathlessly promise to report on "the latest in human/technological interactive mutational forms *as* they happen."[29] Significantly, they place the zeitgeist of the nineties in opposition to sixties counterculture, locating cyberculture squarely on the "culture" side of the nature-versus-culture polarity:

> Back in the '60s, Carly Simon's brother wrote a book called
> *What to Do Until the Apocalypse Comes*. It was about going back
> to the land, growing tubers and soybeans, reading by oil lamps.
> Finite possibilities and small is beautiful. It was *boring!*[30]

In the next breath, however, the authors celebrate the decade's bacchanalian side, which they imply lives on in the thrill-a-minute Nintendo futurism ("High-jacking technology for personal empowerment, fun and games") to which *Mondo* is dedicated:

> [T]he pagan innocence and idealism that was the '60s remains
> and continues to exert its fascination on today's kids. Look at old
> footage of *Woodstock* and you wonder: Where have all those
> wide-eyed, ecstatic, orgasm-slurping kids gone? They're all
> across the land, dormant like deeply buried perennials. But their
> mutated nucleotides have given us a whole new generation of
> sharpies, mutants and superbrights.[31]

Mu and Sirius's Nietzschean "superbrights" are synonymous with Rushkoff's cyberians, personified by the cyberpunk surfers in "Probability Pipeline," an SF story by Rudy Rucker and Marc Laidlaw. Rucker and Laidlaw's characters "are riding the wave of chaos purely for pleasure," writes Rushkoff.

> To them, the truth of Cyberia is a sea of waves—chaotic, maybe,
> but a playground more than anything else. The surfer's conclu-
> sions about chaos are absolutely cyberian: sport, pleasure, and

adventure are the only logical responses to a fractal universe . . . a world free of physical constraints, boring predict-
ability, and linear events.[32]

The rhetoric of Rushkoff and the *Mondo* editorialists reveals how
selected intellectual threads have been teased out of sixties counterculture
and woven into the cyber-hippie worldview, while others have been dismissed
as irrelevant to the nineties. The profound disjuncture between political
radicalism (the antiwar movement, the civil rights struggle, black power, the
New Left, feminism) and psychedelic bohemianism created a fault line in sixties youth culture. Gitlin sums up the "freak"-politico dichotomy, circa 1967:

> There were tensions galore between the radical idea of political
> strategy–with discipline, organization, commitment to results *out
> there* at a distance–and the countercultural idea of living life to
> the fullest, *right here*, for oneself, or for the part of the universe
> embodied in oneself, or for the community of the enlightened
> who were capable of loving one another–and the rest of the
> world be damned (which it was already). Radicalism's tradition
> had one of its greatest voices in Marx, whose oeuvre is a series of
> glosses on the theme: change the world! The main battalions of
> the counterculture–Leary, the Pranksters, the *Oracle* [a hippie
> newspaper]–were descended from Emerson, Thoreau, Rimbaud:
> change consciousness, change life![33]

This dichotomy is resolved, in the cyber-hippie subculture, by
jettisoning "the radical idea of political strategy" and updating "the countercultural idea of living life to the fullest, *right here*, for oneself." In cyberdelia,
the victory of the countercultural tradition over political radicalism is all
but complete. As Gitlin notes, countercultural phrasemakers such as Leary
were "antipolitical purists" for whom politics was "game-playing, a bad trip,
a bringdown, a *bummer*. Indeed, all social institutions were games. . . . The
antidote to destructive games was–more playful games."[34] In like fashion,
movement politics or organized activism of virtually any sort are passé
among the cyber-hippies, for whom being boring is *the* cardinal sin and
"high-jacking technology for personal empowerment, fun and games" the

be-all and end-all of human existence. After all, "sport, pleasure, and adventure are the only logical responses to a fractal universe."

The Yippies Take Tomorrowland: Mondo 2000's Brave New Age[35]

Mondo 2000 will introduce you to your tomorrow—and show you how to buy it today!

—publisher's catalogue blurb for
Mondo 2000: A User's Guide to the New Edge[36]

The Future is Fun! The Future is Fair! You may already have won! You may already be there!

—the Firesign Theatre[37]

Coming to grips with *Mondo 2000* is like wrestling the shape-shifting liquid metal android in *Terminator 2*. By turns illuminating and infuriating, the magazine is an in-crowd status symbol, a career vehicle for would-be Warhols, a beacon of utopian hope, and a source of dystopian anxiety. Epitomizing the contradictions of the cyber-hippie phenomenon, *Mondo* ("M2k" to its fans) has one foot in the Aquarian age and the other in a Brave New World. It is pessimistic about political solutions but Panglossian about technological ones; hardened by cyberpunk cynicism but softened by New Age credulity; eager to jettison the body but determined to retain its humanity; obsessed with upgrading brainpower (through smart drugs, mind machines, neural implants, and nanotechnological tinkering) but impatient for the fleshly pleasures of the "Dionysian revival" prophesied by *Mondo's* publisher, Queen Mu.

Mondo's contradictions manifest themselves in the jarring incongruity of its contents. Issue number five is typical: The soft-core pictorial "Bacchic Pleasures," a cyber-Dionysian fantasy acted out by nude models with hunks of circuit board lashed uncomfortably to their privates, makes a strange bedfellow for John Perry Barlow's "Virtual Nintendo," a sobering reflection on the use of electronic media in the Gulf War to "give war a new lease on death—by keeping it at a distance and transposing another, denatured, reality between the electorate and barbecued bodies."[38]

Mondo's brief history has been fraught with internal tensions between the magazine's hippie/New Age lineage and its libertarian/cyberpunk stance; between its *Beavis and Butt-Head* anti-intellectualism and the starstruck attentions it lavishes on academic celebrities; between the swooning, fin de siècle romanticism that flowers in Queen Mu's prose ("Cancer of the penis must be the ultimate in karmic diseases—just too exquisitely perfect for an incarnation of Orpheus. Jim [Morrison] must have pondered the sweet irony.") and the smirking, isn't-it-ironic Gen X cynicism exemplified by Andrew Hultkrans's column, The Slacker Factor ("This is our 15 minutes of fame. Sell out while you still have the chance.").[39]

But *Mondo* turns its contradictions into rebel cool, running up the Jolly Roger of political incorrectness, "social irresponsibility" (Sirius's catch-phrase), adolescent fun, and shameless sellout. It is no coincidence that Sirius, the magazine's former editor and current "Icon-at-Large," frequently sports a photo button of Andy Warhol. In *Mondo*, Warhol's philosophy of brazen self-promotion reaches its zenith: Queen Mu interviews herself under a pseudonym, Sirius's girlfriend is adoringly profiled, Sirius's rock band is interviewed at length, a book is reviewed by its author, a pair of smart-drink manufacturers who advertise extensively in the magazine are the subject of frequent, fawning interviews.[40]

Sirius (aka Ken Goffman), a fortysomething former yippie who likes to toss off calculatedly contrarian zingers, is unruffled by such charges. "Be mercilessly politically incorrect," he exhorts, in *Mondo*'s fourth issue. "Be commercially successful by being pleasingly offensive. Subvert through media, not because you think you can 'change the system' but because successfully tickling America's self-loathing funnybone is an amusing form of foreplay."[41] This is D. H. Lawrence's "revolution for fun," staged by reality hackers who want to upset the apple cart not for lofty principles, but to see which way the apples will roll. In his poem "A Sane Revolution," Lawrence wrote *Mondo*'s position paper:

> *If you make a revolution, make it for fun,*
> *don't do it in ghastly seriousness,*
> *don't do it in deadly earnest,*
> *do it for fun.*[42]

On the BBS (bulletin board system) the WELL, Sirius responds to the cultural critic Vivian Sobchack's charge that "fancy footwork" is required to resolve the tension between *Mondo*'s self-styled "New Edge" futurism and its New Age romanticism, between its sixties social consciousness and its "privileged, selfish, consumer-oriented, and technologically dependent libertarianism."[43] Emphasizing the magazine's use of irony to let the air out of its own hype, Sirius counters that Sobchack takes *Mondo*'s "clearly double-edged, deliberately provocative, and at the same time honest 'embrace' of high-tech consumerism all too literally."[44]

On the other hand, he implies, *Mondo* futurism and sixties-style social consciousness may not be as antithetical as they seem. Sirius refers Sobchack to the manifestos of the Diggers, a Haight-Ashbury-based anarchist collective that harmonized the counterculture's Arcadian longings with the technetronic age. According to Sirius, the Diggers preached the Arthur C. Clarkeian gospel of "a post-scarcity culture where work was obsolete, 'all of [us] watched over by machines of loving grace.' "[45]

In a *Washington Post* interview, Sirius recalled, "We wanted to believe in this cybernetic vision, that the machines would do it for us. And I maintained that vision, somewhere in the back of my head."[46] A fateful acid trip in 1980, days after John Lennon's death, somehow assured him of "the all-rightness of everything"—a revelation that spurred him to leave the sixties behind and catch up with the emerging computer culture around him.[47] Delving into *Scientific American,* he soon concluded that the Diggers' anarchist utopia of universal leisure and infinite abundance lay within reach; the revolution, if it happened, would be brought about not by political radicals but by the high-tech breakthroughs of capitalist visionaries. But why settle for a cybernetic Eden when the promise of prosthetic godhood lay somewhere over the rainbow? Inspired by Timothy Leary's premonitions in the seventies of "space migration" to off-world colonies, Sirius incorporated a high-tech take on the human potential movement into his vision of robotopia.

In 1984, Sirius's heady blend of gadget pornography, guerrilla humor, human potential pep talk, New Age transcendentalism, and libertarian anarcho-capitalism took shape in the typewritten, newsprint version of what would later become *Mondo 2000.* Subtitled *A Space Age Newspaper of Psychedelics, Science, Human Potential, Irreverence and Modern Art,* it was christened *High Frontiers,* a name borrowed from the book that inspired the L-5 Society. The society was founded in 1975 in response to the Princeton physicist Gerard O'Neill's call, in his book *The High Frontier,* for the establishment of an orbital colony equidistant between the Earth and the Moon at a gravitationally stable point known as Lagrange Point 5. According to the SF writer Norman Spinrad, the L-5 colony held forth the promise of "an escape from the ecological pollution, resource depletion, poverty, collectivism, and unseemly, unplanned natural chaos of . . . Earth."[48] *High Frontiers* crossed the L-5 colony with Fun City in a theme park Utopia characterized, in Sirius's words, by "abundance and leisure, self-fulfillment, play, adventure, limitless space, limitless time, [and] limitless pleasure."[49] Sirius's vision recalls a symbolic coup staged by several hundred yippies in 1970 when antiwar demonstrators infiltrated Disneyland, planting a Vietcong flag on Frontierland's Mount Wilderness before Orange County riot cops threw them out. Now, the techno-yippies had taken Tomorrowland!

High Frontiers begat *Reality Hackers,* which begat *Mondo 2000,* an increasingly slick, sumptuously illustrated glossy now in its thirteenth issue. Over the years, *Mondo*'s design—a product of the desktop publishing revolution made possible by Macintosh computers, digital scanners, and software such as QuarkXPress and Adobe Photoshop—has accelerated into a postliterate blur: jumbled fonts that buzz against fluorescent backgrounds, digitally enhanced photos that flow under, over, and around article copy. *Mondo*'s art direction, like that of its competitors *Wired* and *Axcess,* accepts on faith the cybercultural truism that information overload is the operating mode of computer mavens accustomed to surfing the Internet or bouncing around in hypertext programs. The prototypical *Mondo* reader is one of the "Third Wave people" imagined by Alvin Toffler in *The Third Wave,*

> at ease in the midst of this bombardment of blips—the ninety-second newsclip intercut with a thirty-second commercial, a fragment of song and lyric, a headline, a cartoon, a collage, a newspaper item, a computer printout. Insatiable readers of disposable paperbacks and special-interest magazines, they gulp huge amounts of information in short takes.[50]

Gutenbergian throwbacks who attempt to read *Mondo* from cover to cover will suffer from stop-the-mag-I-want-to-get-off vertigo; it is intended to be skimmed, grazed, subliminally absorbed while doing something else, à la MTV, the paradigmatic "blip culture" form. Ironies abound here: *Mondo* is a print medium counterfeiting a virtual one, a cutting-edge nineties "mutazine" whose cyberdelic layout occasionally recalls the pop/op graphic design of the sixties. The Mondoid prose style is likewise an MTV cutup of the slangy, run-on, first-person voice associated with the New Journalism of the sixties.

Sirius describes the magazine's evolution as a "field shift," with the "psychedelic psychoactivity" foregrounded in *High Frontiers* gradually giving way to *Mondo*'s coverage of cyberculture. Its cover line notwithstanding (" '60S INTO '90S: ANTI-NOSTALGIA"), the fourth issue of *High Frontiers* (1987) is a quintessentially Californian mishmash of patchouli-scented nostalgia, New Age kook science, and reefer madness. It features interviews with the LSD manufacturer Captain Clearlight and Allan Cohen, the founding editor of *The Oracle,* a psychedelic newspaper that flourished in the sixties, a news brief on the theoretical use of ultrasound to stimulate "uncharted neural tissue . . . very much like the 'Krell Mind Booster' in *Forbidden Planet*"; and a how-to article on "sexing" crystals that begins with the matter-of-fact query, "Is your quartz crystal male or female?" Though no less blinded by technology's bright promise, *Mondo 2000*'s twelfth issue (1994) is light-years from the faded, Day-Glo zeitgeist of *High Frontiers,* with a guided tour of the Internet, a roundup of virtual reality games, and an article on "nanocyborgs" that augurs the arrival, within five years, of the "ultimate transhuman, who can choose the design, form, and substance of his/her own body."[51]

Even so, *Mondo* cannot entirely escape its countercultural heritage. The left hemisphere of *Mondo*'s political brain may be libertarian, but the right half's politics are the politics of the pleasure principle, founded on a sixties faith in the power of Eros and childlike play to unfetter the civilized ego and return us to the Garden of Earthly Delights. Sirius ends his on-line rebuttal of Sobchack's critique with the declaration, "Revolution through guilt or revolution through desire? I'll stand by my own opposition to these ever-present, dominant, 'Catholic' notions of goodness."[52]

Mondo's universal cure-all for society's ills is a potent brew of hedonism, humor, and play. In a minimanifesto published in *High Frontiers* (1987), Sirius laments humanity's fall into "individual ego-consciousness," out of the "orgiastic, Dionysian, non-differentiating form of intelligence" that supposedly prevailed before the rise of civilization.[53] He counsels the creation of a "humanistic, intuitive" technoculture that will return us to our former state—a cyberdelic gloss on the popular sixties thinker Norman O. Brown's argument, in *Life against Death,* that repressive modern society can only be healed through a return to something resembling the undifferentiated infantile sexuality Freud called "polymorphous perversity."

Mondo essayists have embroidered this thread. In issue number five, the cyberdelic philosopher Hakim Bey theorizes "temporary autonomous zones"—impermanent Utopias—in which the collective libido of "repressed moralistic societies" might obtain brief release. The temporary autonomous zone, or TAZ, "does not engage directly with the State"; rather, it is a "guerrilla operation which liberates an area—of land, of time, of imagination—and then dissolves itself to re-form elsewhere/elsewhen, before the State can crush it."[54] One example of a TAZ, writes Bey, is a party "where for one brief night a republic of gratified desires was attained. Shall we not confess that the politics of that night have more reality and force for us than those of, say, the entire U.S. government?"[55]

In the same issue, the pseudonymous *Mondo* regulars Gracie and Zarkov admonish "*Mondo*'s technoerotic voluptuaries" to

> [c]reate and communicate examples of intense eroticism to
> others! . . . High technology enables us to explore sensuality far
> out on the New Edge. . . . Why settle for passé kinkiness when
> you can actualize techno-aphrodisia from the infosphere?[56]

The obvious problem with a psychopolitics whose challenges to the status quo are a return to Dionysian excess and abandon is that consumer culture eats such challenges for breakfast. The sexually repressed puritanism that is the bane of Mondoids runs deep in the national psyche, to be sure, but it is subverted by a consumer culture that offers instant, oral gratification and a return to adolescent, even infantile, fun—"social irresponsibility" with a vengeance. As William O'Neill points out in *Coming Apart: An Informal History of America in the 1960s,*

> Where consumption was concerned, [capitalism] urged people
> to gratify their slightest wish. . . . It was, after all, part of Aldous

Huxley's genius that he saw how sensual gratification could
enslave men more effectively than Hitler ever could. . . . Sex was
no threat to the Establishment. . . . [T]he shrewder guardians of
established relationships saw hedonism for what it partially was,
a valuable means of social control.[57]

What's more, taking refuge in "republics of gratified desire" diverts
attention from governmental and corporate challenges to personal liberty
right now, all around us. "To 'turn on and drop out' did not weaken the
state," notes O'Neill. "Quite the contrary, it drained off potentially subversive energies."[58]

Finally, it takes only a modicum of class consciousness to see
Mondo's visions of Dionysian liberation and its *Revenge of the Nerds* fantasy of
a high-tech cultural elite of chemically pumped-up megabrains for what
they are: the daydreams of the relatively privileged. According to the *East
Bay Monthly*, Queen Mu (née Alison Kennedy), a self-styled "New Age
Pollyanna" who believes that "fun . . . is going to be the saving grace of our
universe," grew up in a sixteen-bedroom mansion in upscale Palo Alto and
attended boarding school in Switzerland; the "comfortable legacy" she
inherited from her "prominent, eccentric family" provided the seed money
for *Mondo*, which is headquartered in her sprawling Berkeley Hills home.[59]

Similarly, many of *Mondo*'s readers are sufficiently insulated from
the grimmer social realities inside their high-tech comfort zones to contemplate the power of positive hedonism without irony. In a 1990 interview,
Sirius asserts that a "large portion" of *Mondo*'s audience consists of "successful business people in the computer industry."[60] A 1991 advertising brochure claims that the magazine's readers, 80 percent of whom "work in
information or communications fields" and whose median income is sixty-
five thousand dollars, "have the money to indulge their taste for high-end
quality techno-gear."[61]

To its credit, *Mondo* (in its current and previous *High Frontiers*
incarnations) has served a useful purpose as a wake-up call to liberals and
leftists to cut loose the politically correct neopuritanism that is a millstone
around their collective neck. True radicalism, as Ellen Willis points out in
her essay "Let's Get Radical: Why Should the Right Have All the Fun?" must
affirm "the right to freedom and pleasure."[62] As Sirius and his fellow

Mondoids make abundantly clear, the Left and the Right make common cause in their cultural conservatism, specifically in their puritanical fear of unchained desire. In a cogent, thought-provoking *High Frontiers* essay on the failings of Left/liberal politics in the Reagan eighties, Sirius berates "morally priggish, self-righteous" Left/liberal elements for their puritanical mistrust of money and sensual pleasure and their antitechnological bias, which renders them increasingly powerless in an accelerating technoculture.[63] He argues,

> The left (and the liberals . . .) handed America over to the far right by embracing a philosophy of entropy, the "era of limita-tions," *Muddling Towards Frugality, Small Is Beautiful. . . .* The nation desperately needs a politics to capture and reflect the imaginations of the post-Hiroshima generations.[64]

Again, cyberdelia replays the political dynamics of sixties counter-culture. The issues raised by Sirius came to a head twenty years earlier in what Gitlin calls the "comic collision" that shattered the SDS's "Back to the Drawing Boards" conference in 1967. It was a confrontation between the "sobersided" SDS old guard, most of whom were "leery even of marijuana," and three Diggers who crashed the proceedings in a storm of exhortation, castigation, and howl-at-the-moon lunacy. "You haven't got the balls to go mad," jeered Digger ringleader Emmett Grogan.[65]

Unfortunately, *Mondo*'s idea of a political alternative is an end-of-the-century cyborgasm for "technoerotic voluptuaries"—a fantasy of escape from the constraints of time, space, and the human body rather than a reasoned, realistic response to the politics of culture and technology in peoples' everyday lives. "*Mondo 2000* doesn't have an ideology," Sirius confirms.

> The only thing we're pushing is freedom in this new territory. The only way to freedom is not to have an agenda. Protest is not a creative act, really. . . . We're coming from a place of relative social irresponsibility, actually. But we're also offering vision and expansion to those who want it.[66]

"Vision and expansion," here, are shorthand for unbounded per-sonal potential of the sort offered by corporate motivational gurus and self-help evangelists, and for the posthuman evolutionary potential envisioned on the far fringes of artificial intelligence research. True to Sirius's words, social responsibility is left behind on the launchpad as *Mondo*'s posthumanists rocket toward techno-mystical transcendence.

Significantly, *Mondo* readers continue to demand political accountability from the magazine. In a letter to the editor published in issue seven, Jaye C. Beldo demands, "Why don't you start addressing the crucial political/economic and social issues at hand instead of indulging in this infantile escapism?" On the WELL, Laura Fraser writes,

> Mondo 2000 is the same old romance with technology, the gee-whiz boosterism that's been a theme in our culture since the '50s, without any social consciousness. . . . Just new toys. Toys rich people can buy. Toys that solve no problems, just let us escape. Vision in the limited sense of "what's new." But not what can get us out of this mess we've made.[67]

Grokking the "Submolecular Shamanic Visionquest": *Cyberia*

The *Mondo* fantasy of escape velocity has taken root among the ravers, technopagans, hippie hackers, and other cyberdelic subcultures explored by Douglas Rushkoff in *Cyberia*. Actually, Rushkoff doesn't explore, he "groks"—a sixties verb meaning to instantly, intuitively apprehend. It is a method of uncritical inquiry appropriate to the Northern Californian corner of fringe computer culture he traverses, which is nothing if not defiantly antirational. In it, an utterly uncritical embrace of the proto–New Age aspects of sixties counterculture has been freed from the shackles of back-to-nature romanticism and hitched to the liberatory promise of technology (mind machines, smart drugs, BBSs, virtual reality).

Much of *Cyberia* is given over to speculations about the eschatological zero hour, which is scheduled for sometime around the millennium. In the course of these musings, Rushkoff's cyberians give voice to nearly all of cyberdelic culture's received truths, foremost among them the technopagan axiom that rationalism and intuition, materialism and mysticism, science and magic are converging. For example, the "urban Neo-Pagan"

Green Fire believes that "[m]agic from the ancient past and technology from the future" are synonymous. Rushkoff contends that Western reason, with its emphasis on linear, rational thought, is unable to make sense of the "overall fractal equation for the postmodern experience," where the "rules of linear reality no longer apply." In fractals, he finds confirmation of the cherished article of hippie faith that P. J. O'Rourke memorably described in his essay "Second Thoughts on the 1960s" as the notion that there is "a throbbing web of psychic mucus and we [are] all part of it somehow." Now, writes Rushkoff,

> inconsistencies ranging from random interference on phone lines to computer research departments filled with Grateful Deadheads all begin to make perfect sense. . . . The vast computer-communications network is a fractal approach to human consciousness. . . . At the euphoric peak of a [psychedelic] trip, all people, particles, personalities, and planets are seen as part of one great entity or reality—one big fractal.[68]

Bored and disillusioned with political strategies, Rushkoff's cyberians place their faith in a fuzzily defined program for personal and social change that bears a distinct resemblance to Freud's "omnipotence of thoughts," the primitive mode of thought that assumes a magical correspondence between mental life and the external, physical world. Primitives, wrote Freud, "believe they can alter the external world by mere thinking."[69]

So, apparently, do *Cyberia*'s neoprimitive cyber-hippies, who Rushkoff believes are individually as well as collectively engaged in the creation of "designer realities." Writes Rushkoff,

> We may soon conclude that the single most important contribution of the 1960s . . . to popular culture is the notion that we have chosen our reality arbitrarily. The mission of the cyberian counterculture of the 1990s, armed with new technologies, familiar with cyberspace and daring enough to explore unmapped realms of consciousness, is to rechoose reality consciously and purposefully.[70]

According to Rushkoff, cyberian hackers see the computer as "a whole new reality, which they can enter and even change." In some way not entirely clear, their immersion in digital media such as the low-resolution cartoon world of virtual reality casts "further doubt on the existence of any objective physical reality."

The psychedelic experience ("a psychopharmacological virtual reality") likewise leads cyberians to conclude that they "have the ability to reshape the experience of reality and thus—if observer and observed are one—the reality itself." Underground chemists creating illicit designer drugs "decide what they'd like reality to be like, then—in a submolecular shamanic visionquest—compose a chemical that will alter their observations about reality in a specific way. . . . The world changes because it is observed differently."[71]

Citing chaos theory's premise that order can spring from seemingly random phenomena, Rushkoff asserts that "[e]very chaotic system appears to be adhering to an underlying order," then rushes in where angels (and chaos theorists) fear to tread:

> This means that our world is entirely more interdependent than
> we have previously understood. What goes on inside any one
> person's head is reflected, in some manner, on every other level
> of reality. So any individual being, through feedback and itera-
> tion, has the ability to redesign reality at large.[72]

By this logic, we arrive at an implausible cyber-reality where the "omnipotence of thoughts" prevails. Rushkoff uses the Gaia hypothesis as a springboard for his speculation that the planet may become self-aware once it passes through "the galactic time wave of history" (whatever that is). Formulated by the English scientist James Lovelock in 1974, the Gaia hypothesis (after the Greek Earth goddess) proposes that the Earth is a homeostatic system. Lovelock theorizes that the global ecosystem's attempts to maintain its equilibrium may be causing it to shift into a state unfavorable to human life as humanity becomes an ever greater threat to life on this planet. Global warming can be seen as an example of this process. In New Age circles, variations on Lovelock's thesis are used to justify claims for a planetary consciousness.

Rushkoff's belief that the planet is becoming sentient has its roots in the futurist Jerome Clayton Glenn's contention that the Earth will soon have as many human inhabitants as there are neurons in the human brain. At this juncture, he speculates, humanity will somehow form a collective consciousness, causing the planet to "wake up." Overlaying this notion with a New Age McLuhanism, Rushkoff sees the wiring of the world, through digital communications networks, as "the final stage in the development of Gaia."[73]

Precisely how the fiber-optic interconnection of the number of humans equivalent to the number of neurons in the human brain will give birth to a planetary consciousness is left to the reader's imagination. Perhaps it has something to do with the chaos theory Rushkoff often uses as an anchor for his airier musings. Manuel De Landa, a postmodern philosopher whose ruminations have taken him to the far fringes of chaos theory and computer science, has observed that what chaos theorists call *singularities*—the transition points "where order spontaneously emerges out of chaos"—catalyze curiously lifelike behavior in nonliving matter: so-called "chemical clocks," in which billions of molecules oscillate in synchrony, or amoeba colonies, in which cells "cooperate" to form an organism.[74]

Extrapolating from these natural processes, in which "previously disconnected eléments" reach a critical point where they suddenly " 'cooperate' to form a higher-level entity," De Landa conjectures that the out-of-control growth of the decentralized, nonlinear Internet could result in the emergence of a global artificial intelligence.[75] "Past a certain threshold of connectivity," he writes, "the membrane which computer networks are creating over the surface of the planet begins to 'come to life.' Independent software [programs] will soon begin to constitute even more complex computational societies in which [programs] trade with one another, bid and compete for resources, seed and spawn processes spontaneously, and so on."[76] Singularities have given rise to processes of self-organization in the biosphere, he reasons; why not in the computational ecosystem of the Internet? Quoting the computer scientists M. S. Miller and K. Eric Drexler, he concludes, "These systems 'can encourage the development of intelligent [software programs], but there is also a sense in which the systems themselves will become intelligent.' "[77]

* * *

Indebted though it is to ideas of recent vintage such as chaos theory or the Gaia hypothesis, the techno-transcendentalism of Rushkoff's cyberians owes much to sixties counterculture—specifically, to the scientific humanism mythologized by SF writers such as Arthur C. Clarke.

Although it was published in 1953, Clarke's SF classic *Childhood's End* was a reference point for sixties counterculture, as evidenced in *The Electric Kool-Aid Acid Test*. Noting the novel among the "strange, prophetic books on Kesey's shelf," Wolfe links the conviction shared by Kesey and his Merry Pranksters—that they were hurtling toward "that scary void *beyond catastrophe*, where all, supposedly, will be possible"—to Clarke's evocation of "the Total Breakthrough generation" that becomes "part of the Overmind . . . leaving the last remnants of matter behind."[78]

2001: A Space Odyssey (1968), whose screenplay was cowritten by Clarke and the director Stanley Kubrick, takes up the theme of posthuman apotheosis. At once a psychedelic and a technological epiphany, the film evoked a journey to the center of the mind even as it realized the cosmic promise inherent in John F. Kennedy's proclamation that America would head for the "New Frontier," space. Passing through the hallucinogenic, light-streaked "Stargate Corridor" of the "voyage beyond the infinite" at the movie's end, the astronaut protagonist arrives at the place where odysseys into inner and outer space meet—the realm of the numinous, where he transcends humanity altogether, metamorphosing into a godlike "Star-Child."

Childhood's End and, after it, *2001* presage the cyberdelic posthumanism that crops up in *Cyberia*, where the magic mushroom-gobbling philosopher Terence McKenna asserts that evolution is poised to break free of "the chrysalis of matter . . . and then look back on a cast-off mode of being as it rises into a higher dimension."[79]

More profoundly, the cyberians' visions of escape velocity derive from the teleologies of two thinkers whose ideas percolated into sixties counterculture: Marshall McLuhan and Pierre Teilhard de Chardin. McLuhan and Teilhard de Chardin's contributions to the emerging mythos of techno-transcendentalism were, at points, strikingly congruent. McLuhan's concept of a "global village" borne of communications technologies evolved, over time, into a vision of the "[p]sychic communal integration" of all humankind, "made possible at last by the electronic media."[80] This global

cosmic consciousness is not unlike the evolutionary epiphany foretold by
Teilhard de Chardin, who proclaimed the coming of an "ultra-humanity"
destined to converge in an "Omega Point"—a "cosmic Christ" who is the
"consummation of the evolutionary process."[81] McLuhan, a devout Roman
Catholic, once observed that the psychic convergence facilitated by electronic media

> could create the universality of consciousness foreseen by Dante
> when he predicted that men would continue as no more than
> broken fragments until they were unified into an inclusive
> consciousness. In a Christian sense, this is merely a new inter-
> pretation of the mystical body of Christ; and Christ, after all, is
> the ultimate extension of man. . . . I expect to see the coming
> decades transform the planet into an art form; the new man,
> linked in a cosmic harmony that transcends time and space,
> will . . . himself . . . become an organic art form. There is a long
> road ahead, and the stars are only way stations, but we have
> begun the journey.[82]

Likewise, Teilhard de Chardin, a theologian and paleontologist who
predicted the reintegration of science and religion, maintained that

> [w]e are today witnessing a truly explosive growth of technology
> and research, bringing an increasing mastery, both theoretical
> and practical, of the secrets and sources of cosmic energy at
> every level and in every form; and, correlative with this, the
> rapid heightening of what I have called the psychic temperature
> of the Earth. . . . We see a human tide bearing us upward with
> all the force of a contracting star; not a spreading tide, as we
> might suppose, but one that is rising: the ineluctable growth on
> our horizon of a true state of "ultra-humanity."[83]

The McLuhan quote is from his 1969 *Playboy* interview and the
Teilhard de Chardin excerpt is from an essay written in 1950, but their
refrains resound throughout cyberdelia. According to the *New York Times
Magazine*, Louis Rossetto, the editor and publisher of *Wired*, believes that

"society is organized by a 'hive-mind consensus' that allows humanity to evolve into ever higher forms, perhaps even fulfilling McLuhan's prophecy to 'make of the entire globe, and of the human family, a single consciousness.' "[84] *Wired*'s executive editor, Kevin Kelly, who has described his first visit to the Internet as "a religious experience," calls the net and systems like it "exo-nervous systems, things that connect us up beyond–literally, physically–beyond our bodies."[85] He believes that when "enough of us get together this way, we will have created a new life form. It's evolutionary; it's what the human mind was destined to do."[86]

Similarly, Jody Radzik, identified in a *Rolling Stone* feature on smart drugs and rave culture as "one of the [rave] crowd's resident gurus," believes that " '[t]he planet is waking up. . . . Humans are the brain cells. The axons of the nerve cells are the telephone lines.' "[87] R. U. Sirius hitches Radzik's ideas to McLuhan and Teilhard de Chardin's rhetoric of transcendental liftoff. "I think we're going through a process of information linkup toward the building of a global nervous system, a global brain," he says, "which many people have seen as the inevitable first step toward getting off the planet."

It seems only fitting that John Perry Barlow embraces this all-pervasive paradigm. Barlow stands squarely at the junction, in cyberdelic culture, of the sixties and the nineties: A former "poet and SDS mischief-maker" who according to the *New York Times* "helped lead the psychedelic revolution at Wesleyan University," he is a Grateful Dead lyricist, frequent *Mondo 2000* contributor, and cofounder of the Electronic Frontier Foundation, a group concerned with the civil liberties of computer users.[88] A self-described "techno-crank," he is also, like Rushkoff, Sirius, and Radzik, an unrepentant techno-transcendentalist.

"I'll cut right to the chase with you," he told me, in a phone interview. "I think that we–humanity–are engaged in a great work which is and has been, since that moment when we started abstracting reality into information and put cave paintings up in Lascaux, hardwiring collective consciousness. Not the collective unconscious, which is presumably pretty well wired already, but creating the collective organism of the human mind in one coherent simultaneous thing. I don't know why we want to do that but it seems to me that everything we're up to points in that direction. I think about Teilhard de Chardin a lot, [who] used to talk about something called the noosphere, which was the combined field of all [human consciousness], and how that became stronger and stronger as civilization progressed and how what God wanted was to have someone to talk to on its own level and that was what humanity was in the process of creating. That comes as close as I can to describing what I think is going on.

"Have you ever read [the anthropologist and New Age philosopher] Gregory Bateson? A fruitful way of looking at this is the Batesonian model of mind, which simply stated says that you can't tell me where my mind leaves off and yours takes up. There's simply no boundary condition anywhere and there never has been. There's a coterminous nature of human minds to begin with; it's just a matter of making the tacit connections explicit."

In *Cyberia,* ideas related to Barlow's are accompanied by eschatological visions of humankind being drawn inexorably toward "the chaos attractor at the end of time," a teleological endpoint whose arrival will catalyze "the coming hyperdimensional shift into a timeless, nonpersonalized reality." Although much of Rushkoff's cosmic curtain closer is borrowed from the millenarian musings of Terence McKenna, variations on this myth are all around us in SF movies and pop songs about technologically superior alien saviors (*The Day the Earth Stood Still, Close Encounters of the Third Kind,* the Byrds' "Mr. Spaceman," David Bowie's "Starman"). As the critic Hugh Ruppersberg points out, many of these fables rest "on the premise that advanced technology breeds not only miraculous wonders but moral redemption as well."[89]

In like fashion, Rushkoff relocates the Spiritual in the realm of the technological. He accepts on faith the notion that technologies such as psychedelic drugs "are part of the continuing evolution of the human species toward greater intelligence, empathy, and awareness."[90] Conceding the new, digital mysticism's unfortunate "inability to tackle everyday, real-world strife," he is nonetheless confident that its upgrade of sixties beliefs is preparing the way for humankind's "great leap into hyperspace."[91]

This is techno-transcendentalism's version of born-again Christianity's "rapture," in which true believers are lifted out of the mundane, into the parting clouds. Like so many other millenarian prophecies before it, the cyberdelic vision of a techno-mystical apotheosis in the there and then diverts public discourse from the political and socioeconomic inequities of the here and now.

Cyberia provides ample evidence of this dynamic. Rushkoff thrills to cyberian video art in which Gulf War bombing runs are merely another special effect, collaged together with "virtual reality scenes, and even old sitcoms." A *Mondo* groupie who drops acid before undergoing an abortion is applauded for her "unflinching commitment to experiencing and understanding her passage through time." Homeless "mole people" alleged to dwell in the "forgotten tunnels of New York's subway system" are romanticized as an example of the "cyberian ideal" of insurgent subcultures hidden in the cracks of the power structure. And a homeless man dragging a cardboard box isn't foraging for shelter, he's engaged in "social hacking."[92]

Naïve, self-serving pronouncements such as these are commonplaces among cyberians. Their siren song of nineties technophilia and sixties transcendentalism seduces the public imagination with the promise of an end-of-the-century deus ex machina at a time when realistic solutions are urgently needed. The cyberians' otherworldly trapdoor assumes various guises, among them the wiring of the human race into a collective consciousness; the technopagan ability to dream up a "designer reality" through a judicious application of the knowledge that "we have chosen our reality arbitrarily"; and the "chaos attractor at the end of time."

In truth, cyberdelic rhetoric represents what Walter Kirn has called "an eruption of high-tech millenarianism—a fin de siècle schizoid break induced by sitting too long at the screen."[93] Ironically, Kirn is something of a mentor to Rushkoff, who thanks him in *Cyberia*'s acknowledgments. Rushkoff and his fellow cyberians would do well to heed Kirn's admonition that

> [w]hat the [cyberians] appear fated to learn from their ventures
> into pure electronic consciousness is that ultimate detachment
> is not the same as freedom, escape is no substitute for liberation
> and rapture isn't happiness. The sound-and-light show at the end
> of time, longed for by these turned-on nerds, seems bound to
> disappoint.[94]

Deus ex Machina: Technopaganism

Any sufficiently advanced technology is indistinguishable from
magic.

—*Arthur C. Clarke, SF novelist and science writer*[95]

When magic becomes scientific fact we refer to it as medicine
or astronomy.

—*Anton LaVey, occultist*[96]

Technopaganism permeates cyberdelia. And while it informs the
techno-transcendentalism of *Mondo 2000* and Rushkoff's cyberians, it has
other stories to tell, beyond dreams of a designer reality or escape velocity.

Technopaganism can be simply if superficially defined as the convergence of neopaganism (the umbrella term for a host of contemporary
polytheistic nature religions) and the New Age with digital technology and
fringe computer culture.[97] Erik Davis, a critic of cyberculture and "longtime participant-observer in the Pagan community," defines technopagans
as "a small but vital subculture of digital savants who keep one foot in the
emerging technosphere and one foot in the wild and woolly world of
Paganism."[98] He estimates their numbers at roughly one hundred thousand
to three hundred thousand in the United States, made up "almost exclu-
sively" of bohemian or middle-class whites.

Psychologically, technopaganism represents an attempt to come to
existential terms with the philosophical changes wrought by twentieth-
century science. Philosophically, it bespeaks a popular desire to contest the
scientific authorities whose "objective" consensus is the final, irrefutable
verdict, in our culture, on what is true and what is not, despite the fact that
most of us must accept such pronouncements on faith. Finally, it evidences a
widespread yearning to find a place for the sacred in our ever more secular,
technological society.

From the Enlightenment to the present, instrumental reason,
armed with the scientific method, has systematically dismantled much of
the spiritual worldview, replacing it with the cosmology of science. With
rationalism and materialism encroaching on all sides, those who feel impov-

erished by the withering away of the Spiritual have adopted the strategy, consciously or not, of legitimating spiritual beliefs in scientific terms.

Technopaganism is a manifestation of this strategy, although it is many other things, too. Like the other cyberdelic subcultures discussed in this chapter, technopaganism straddles nineties cyberculture and sixties counterculture. Both neopaganism and the nascent New Age entered the mainstream in the sixties through the counterculture's flirtation with Eastern mysticism and the occult—astrology, the tarot, witchcraft, and magick. (Practitioners of ceremonial magick use the archaic spelling in order to distinguish their rituals from stage magic.)

Technopaganism crystalizes most dramatically in the use of the personal computer in neopagan rituals or magical practices. More prosaically, it bubbles up in the UseNet newsgroup Alt.Pagan and on special-interest BBSs given over to neopagan and New Age concerns, such as Deus ex Machina in Glendale, Arizona; the Quill and Inkpot BBS: Ritual Magick Online! in Passaic, New Jersey; Modem Magick in El Cajon, California; the Sacred Grove in Seattle; the Crystal Cave in Colorado Springs; the Magick Lantern in Denver; and Jersey City's BaphoNet (a pun on Baphomet, the satanic goat who presides over the witches' Sabbath).

Many of these systems employ echomail, a technology that links discussion groups on widely dispersed BBSs into a communal conference. BBSs, reports Julian Dibbell in *Spin*, "are showing signs of becoming the new temples of the information age."[99] He notes,

> Throughout history, spirituality has been a site-specific affair. . . . So what's become of the sacred in a time when instantaneous communication makes a joke of the very notion of geography? It turns node-specific, that's what. Nodes are the electronic network's version of places—any spot where two or more lines of communication intersect.[100]

A verse from the New Testament springs to mind: "For where two or three are gathered together in my name, there am I in the midst of them" (Matthew 18:20).

Technopaganism is embodied, too, in Thee Temple ov Psychick Youth (TOPY, with a long *o*), a loosely knit organization that has evolved

since its founding in 1981 from a fan club for the technopagan band Psychic
TV into a cultish anticult. TOPY incorporates William S. Burroughs's ideas
about social control and guerrilla information war, the hermetic teachings
of the English occultists Aleister Crowley and Austin Osman Spare, and,
most important, the complementary notions that magick is a technology
and technology is magick. According to "Lurker Below (ashton)," a technopagan posting an electronic message in one of the WELL's discussion
groups, "Thee Temple ov Psychick Youth . . . [is] dedicated [to] thee establishment ov a functional system ov magick and a modern pagan philosophy
without recourse to mystification, gods, or demons"; it relies, instead, on
"thee implicit powers ov thee human brain" in its explorations of "neuro-
mancy, cybershamanism, information theory, or magick."[101] (The idiosyncratic spellings are a TOPY convention.)

Technopaganism also surfaces in the electro-bacchanalian urges
that animate raves, where conventions are momentarily suspended in the
social centrifuge whipped up by sweaty, seething dancers; punishingly loud,
unrelentingly rhythmic "house" or "techno" electronic dance music; and the
drug ecstasy, widely regarded as an aphrodisiac. Cultured in the British
techno-hippie musical genre known as "acid house" in the summer of 1989
(dubbed the second "Summer of Love" by British journalists), the rave scene
soon spread to California. In San Francisco, the traditions represented by
Haight-Ashbury and Silicon Valley were intermixed by the rave phenomenon, creating what the Psychic TV frontman Genesis P-Orridge calls
"hyperdelic" culture. Its sound track, says P-Orridge, is high-tech

> trance music, where people shake and spin until they reach a
> state of hyperventilation and psychedelic alpha-wave experi-
> ence. . . . They get completely tranced-out . . . from that primal
> and physical excess. So there's this whole pagan energizing thing
> going on as a result of this free-form dancing to this high-tech
> shamanism.[102]

On their record *Boss Drum* (1992), the English techno-trance/
cyberpop duo the Shamen fashion an archaic futurism from rapped vocals,
fizzing synthesizers, hyperactive drum machine, and the ruminations
of Terence McKenna, whose eschatological humor goes over big with

those whose neurons have been permanently cross-wired by psychoactive substances. In the song "Re: Evolution," which features his overdubbed remarks as its vocal track, McKenna offers an illuminating reading of rave culture:

> The emphasis in . . . rave culture on physiologically compatible rhythms is really the rediscovery of the art of natural magic with sound, [the realization] that sound—especially percussive sound—can actually change neurological states. Large groups of people getting together in the presence of this kind of music are creating a telepathic community . . . an end-of-the-millennium culture that is actually summing up Western civilization and pointing us in an entirely different direction. We're going to arrive in the third millennium in the middle of an archaic revival, which will mean . . . a new art, a new social vision, a new relationship to nature and to ego.

Many raves feature "chill-out" rooms where revelers exhausted by the "psychedelic alpha-wave experience" can relax, cocooned in the gauzy, billowing synthesizers of "ambient" electronic instrumental music. Much of this music exudes a technopagan aura: *Ritual Ground* (1993), by Solitaire, features moody instrumentals—waves of shimmering synthesizer washing over didgeridoo and ethnic percussion—with names like "Runes" and "In the Forest of Ancient Light"; *Mystery School* (1994) by the Ambient Temple of Imagination features a booklet covered with flying saucers, illustrations from the Crowley Thoth tarot deck, and songs whose titles—"Magickal Child," "Thelema"—refer to Crowley's teachings. The liner notes, which include references to magick, shamanism, and alchemy, end with the somewhat *Star Trek*ian prediction that "humanity is destined to join the interdimensional Galactic Federation as our planet evolves to a higher level of being."[103]

Technopaganism leaves its stamp on cyber-rock and "industrial" music, too. *Cyberpunx* (1989), by Rodney Orpheus's band the Cassandra Complex, is technopagan cyber-rock. On one hand, Orpheus conjures Crowley's goatish sexuality, saturnalian revelry, and prankish sacrilege (he is, in fact, a member of a Crowleyite occult order). On the other, he evokes the human-machine interface and video game violence of cyberpunk fiction. The cover of *Cyberpunx* features a computer graphic depicting a *Top Gun* hotshot in a futuristic cockpit, his eyes hidden by the insect carapace of a virtual reality helmet; a nearby screen displays a suffering Christ crowned with thorns.

The songs on *Man-Amplified* (1992) by the industrial band Clock DVA consist of minimalist blipmusic soldered together from "mechanical noises and machine language" and welded to visions of "technogeist," the spokesman Adi Newton's term for the anticipated moment when the computer becomes "a parapsychological instrument for the direct projection of thoughts and emotions."[104] In a sense, argues Newton, "[o]ccult technology is already with us. The computer is really a 20th century oracle we employ to forecast the future. . . . Science . . . has always [sought] to simulate the occult, gain control over nature. . . . [S]cience is now discovering what the mystics already knew."[105]

Technopaganism haunts the mainstream, as well, in the computer game Myst, which takes place in what the *New York Times* reporter Edward Rothstein characterizes as "a world in which ordinary objects are the magical products of an advanced technology"—a dreamscape where "archaic machines" make surreal sense in a "pastoral paradise."[106] Myst transports users to an island lush with photorealistic forests (the tree bark was digitally scanned) and lulled by the murmur of wind, water, and atmospheric music. Wandering through exquisitely detailed computer-graphic scenes—a cluster of Greek columns, a planetarium, a wood-paneled library, a spaceship out of a late-night rocket opera, all of them eerily empty—Myst players search for clues to solve a somewhat metaphysical mystery.

Writing in the *Village Voice,* Erik Davis calls Myst "a metafiction that blends technology and magic, tips its hat to Jules Verne, Edgar Rice Burroughs, and Umberto Eco."[107] Ironically, the CD-ROM game was created by two churchgoing Christians whose father is a preacher, a fact that leads Davis to make much of the game's spiritual themes and symbolism, specifically the pivotal role played by magical books. Even so, he argues, the technology that made the game possible invites a Faustian interpretation. To Davis, the computer-graphic sorcery that enabled the creators to conjure worlds within worlds inside a computer is "a clearly demiurgic magic that heretically usurps God's role as creator."[108]

What all of these examples–Dibbell's nodes, TOPY's "cybersha-manism," P-Orridge's "hyperdelic" raves, Newton's vision of the computer as "a 20th-century oracle," Myst's seamless union of mysticism and technology–have in common is the technopagan tendency to relocate the sacred in the technosphere, to populate cyberspace with superhuman agencies. The voodoo cyber-cosmology of William Gibson's novels is a case in point. *Neuromancer,* Gibson's first, stars an outlaw hacker named Case who interfaces neurologically with cyberspace, plugging his nervous system into the global virtual reality where data is stored in the form of palpable illusions. The title is of course a pun on *necromancer,* a sorcerer who raises the dead; Case engages in the cyberpunk equivalent of such conjurations, effectively leaving his body to roam the otherworldly realm of cyberspace, with the computer-generated ghost of a dead hacker as his guide. As Norman Spinrad perceptively notes, Case is a near-future

> magician whose wizardry consists of directly interfacing . . .
> with . . . the computersphere, manipulating it imagistically (and
> being manipulated by it) much as more traditional shamans
> interact imagistically with more traditional mythic realms via
> drugs or trance states.[109]

In Gibson's second and third novels, *Count Zero* and *Mona Lisa Overdrive,* cyberspace is inhabited by artificial intelligence (AI) programs that have evolved into something rich and strange: a pantheon of voodoo deities known as the *loa*. In a technopagan variation on the scenario imagined by De Landa, the interaction of autonomous software programs has given rise to artificial entities that assume the appearances and attributes of voodoo gods. "In all the signs your kind have stored against the night," explains an AI in *Mona Lisa Overdrive*, "the paradigms of *voudou* proved most appropriate."[110] In *Count Zero,* the Finn, a dealer in exotic, often contraband technologies, elaborates:

> The last seven, eight years, there's been funny stuff out there, out
> on the console cowboy circuit. . . . Thrones and dominions . . .
> Yeah, there's things out there. Ghosts, voices. Why not? Oceans
> had mermaids, all that shit, and we had a sea of silicon, see?

Sure, it's just a tailored hallucination we all agreed to have,
cyberspace, but anybody who jacks in knows, fucking *knows* it's a
whole universe.[111]

Even now, some glimpse ghosts in the machine. In his essay
"Techgnosis: Magic, Memory, and the Angels of Information," Erik Davis
writes, "Far beyond Palo Alto and MIT, in the margins and on the nets,
phantasms hover over the technologically mediated information processing
that increasingly constitutes our experience."[112] Information, he asserts,
"crackles with energy, drawing to itself mythologies, metaphysics, hints of
arcane magic."[113]

For real-life technopagans, Gibson's voodoo electronics is more
than science fiction. Maxwell X. Delysid, an active TOPYite who "accepts
the Internet as a spiritual tool" and is investigating "what magick can be
done with it," read *Count Zero* and was galvanized by the notion of voodoo
spirits lurking in the Net. "[*Count Zero*] blew my mind," he writes, in an
E-mail interview.

I began to think, 'Here we have this worldwide network set up,
just like [Gibson's] cyberspace, and there very well could be *loa*
living in the Internet > now <. What would they be like?
Would they be Haitian (as in the book) or would they be more a
product of the [American] culture that CREATED the Net?
What would their religion be? What would their purpose be?
Would they even WANT us to know that they existed? I haven't
found any, as such, yet.[114]

Faint echoes of this notion are audible in popular culture: In *BBS
Callers Digest,* a columnist describes the staticky squall emitted by a user's
computer when it connects to a BBS—the sound of digital data being
converted into analog waves by the user's modem so that it can be piped over
the phone lines—as "the high electronic scream of BBS angels."[115] Stewart
Brand asserts that "when you communicate through a computer, you
communicate like an angel," by which he means that participants in
electronic conferences "communicate as these disembodied intelligences of
great intimacy."[116] And John Perry Barlow believes that humankind's age-old

desire to inhabit the Spiritual" will be fulfilled in cyberculture. A convoca-
tion of disembodied minds who appear to each other on a BBS as screenfuls
of typed conversation is "the flesh made word," he puns.

The growing tendency to conceive of computer-mediated interaction in spiritual as well as spatial terms revives the Teilhard de Chardinian
dream of reconciling metaphysics and materialism in a science "tinged
with mysticism and charged with faith."[117] It is paralleled, among technopagans and New Age technophiles, by the practice of couching metaphysical
convictions in scientific terms, and of seeking plug-in solutions to spiritual needs.

New Age discourse in particular is woven from scientific-sounding
theories of auras, etheric energies, vibrational fields, biomagnetism, tachyon
energy, and "biological electrons" ("pure, bio-available energy" supposed to
exist in light).[118] In the wake of seventies New Age classics such as Fritjof
Capra's *The Tao of Physics* and Gary Zukav's *The Dancing Wu-Li Masters,*
which draw connections between the new physics and Eastern mysticism,
the language of physics and the theoretical musings of physicists have been
used to buttress New Age thought. In *Bridging Science and Spirit: Common
Elements in David Bohm's Physics, the Perennial Philosophy, and Seth,* Norman
Friedman strikes a delicate balance between the quantum physics of Bohm—
best known for his theory that the brain replicates, in microcosm, the
structure of the universe—and the teachings of Seth, the channeled "energy
personality essence" whose revelations about the nature of time, space, and
the self-creation of reality comprise Jane Roberts's *The Seth Material.*

Furthermore, New Age dreams of self-actualization are increasingly tethered to transformational technologies such as the mind machines,
smart drugs, and other "tools for the expansion of consciousness" mentioned earlier. The catalogues of New Age direct mail marketers such as
Tools for Exploration ("YOUR GUIDE TO ADVENTURES IN CONSCIOUSNESS") offer a
variety of "consciousness technologies" that harness advances from "the
cutting edges of neuroscience and electronics" in the service of a vision of
human potential that partakes of self-help, corporate motivational psychology, and New Age mysticism.

The copy in such catalogues keeps the reader mindful of the fact that
such appliances are high-tech upgrades of pretechnological traditions. A mind
machine sold in a 1993 *Tools for Exploration* catalogue is marketed as the "new

shamanic technology," an information-age upgrade of the hypnotic campfire and ritual drumming used in primitive cultures to induce shamanic trances: "Goggles with flickering solid-state lights provide the 'firelight,' and digital stereo synthesized sounds create the 'drumming.' "[119] Such a device represents the best of archaic and future worlds, it is implied, reconnecting the user to a mythic, holistic past even as it incorporates what we are told are the latest breakthroughs in neuroscience and microelectronics.

In one of his catalogues, Terry Patten, the founder of Tools for Exploration, relates a New Age parable that neatly encapsulates the resolution of mysticism and materialism in cyberculture. After recounting how he and his wife had "sold everything: the house, the cars, the furniture" (a ritual renunciation of the secular world familiar from Christian and Eastern mysticism) and traveled extensively, he notes the psychic dislocation he experienced on returning to his former life, that of "a 3-piece suit professional":

> My wife . . . and I had realized that, too often, we become alienated by the very technology designed to make our lives easier. So we went on to uncover a new kind of technology–one created to connect us more deeply to our bodies, minds, emotions and souls. We call it Consciousness Technology, and from this discovery, Tools For Exploration was born.[120]

Patten offers a holistic vision of technology that integrates rather than alienates. In its power to repair our fractured inner selves and help us realize our "unlimited capacity for positive growth and change" (Patten), it is almost godlike. But despite its desire to make room for the sacred in the technosphere, Patten's high-tech theology has the paradoxical effect of secularizing the Spiritual; the higher powers have dissipated into impersonal, pseudoscientific energy fields, accessible through microcircuitry. The focus, as in the human potential movement to which the "mind tech" wing of the New Age owes so much, is on the perfectible self; pilgrim's progress has given way to personal power.

In *Mega Brain Power: Transform Your Life with Mind Machines and Brain Nutrients*, Michael Hutchison elevates "Consciousness Technology" to the status of a divine agency, a saving grace capable of lifting humanity out of the human condition. "To some it may seem odd and paradoxical that machines–the synthetic, hard, material devices of this electronic temporal reality–may serve as gateways to the spirit, tools of transcendence," writes Hutchison. "But in fact this fusion of spirituality, or the 'inner quest,' and science, the 'external quest,' is the central force of the emerging new paradigm."[121]

Of course, neopagan and New Age attempts to validate their beliefs through the use of tools, terms, and conceptual models appropriated from the scientific and technological communities are a pact with the Devil. Such a strategy reaffirms the cultural superiority of empirical science and inductive reasoning as the arbiters of what is admitted into the mainstream and what is banished to the fringes.

But as technopaganism makes clear, there is more to this story than the desire for cultural accreditation. For those in neopagan or New Age subcultures who reject the antitechnology bias traditionally associated with such beliefs, their relationship to science and technology has less to do with a longing for legitimation and more to do with William Gibson's maxim "THE STREET FINDS ITS OWN USES FOR THINGS." Their willful "misuse" of scientific concepts and digital technology in the service of the spiritual, the intuitive, and the irrational parallels, to a degree, the subversions of the outlaw hacker. (Tellingly, one *Tools for Exploration* catalogue refers to mind machine users as "consciousness hackers.")

At the same time, the New Age/neopagan redirection of science and technology to wholly unscientific ends–attaining mystical states, mending the mind/body rupture, reweaving the alienated modern psyche into the fabric of the universe–speaks to the need to make New Age/neopagan beliefs relevant to a technological society whose model of reality is held together by scientific theories. Too, it mirrors the vision, handed down from Teilhard de Chardin to Hutchison, of the holistic healing of the breach between religion and science, the sacred and the mundane.

These impulses are at the heart of technopaganism. To inaugurate "Cybermage," an echomail topic devoted to the relationship between technology and neopaganism, Tony Lane posted an introduction worth quoting at length:

> For too long magick has looked backward. So often I hear about
> "traditional" Native American this and authentic Egyptian/

Celtic/Hunan that. Sorry folks—there are very few "authentic" magickal items/rituals/practices out there. . . . Something might SEEM stronger if it is wrapped in the mystique of . . . bear clan tribal blood, blah blah blah. I have no doubt that this WAS a very powerful spell (and might still be one) for a member of the bear clan. If you are a CPA from Burbank I doubt that there is much there for you. . . . I feel there is a better way. . . . [T]he central idea of CYBERMAGE [is]: MAGICK that uses the current world is more powerful because it is more personal to the magician. In many of the magickal ancient cultures magick and science were often the same thing. Imagine if they could see what our science today can do! They would worship us as GODS. . . . If in our work we could meld science and magick we could [work] wonders. We could cure and create and build things man has never seen nor dreamed of. But first we have to turn away from the . . . traditional ways and branch out into new areas, [exploring] . . . the parallels between a magickal spell and a computer program and the possibility of having an electrical familiar.[122]

A "familiar," according to *The Encyclopedia of Witchcraft & Demonology,* is "a low-ranking demon in the shape of a small domestic animal to advise and perform small malicious errands."[123] Fittingly, the dormant computer programs which, when triggered, engage in low-level decision making and information gathering on many BBSs are called demons. Similarly, "knowbots," or knowledge robots—information-gathering computer programs currently in development—realize Tony Lane's dream of an "electrical familiar." The computer journalist John Markoff, who defines knowbots as "protoartificially intelligent creatures . . . that have the capacity to relentlessly prowl the [Internet] looking for information morsels," has compared them to sorcerer's apprentices.[124]

A long and winding discussion between BBSers all over the States spiraled off of Lane's initial message, or "post." Aga Windwalker (aka J. Palmer) recounted a venture into "CyberCraft" that involved casting a healing spell over phone lines when a friend suffered a grand mal seizure:

One day, I was chatting with [my friend's] boyfriend [on a BBS] when he suddenly typed "GM" (which meant that the girl was going into a seizure and he had to go to her). [T]ouching my monitor, [I] started channeling energy. Through the monitor, down the cable, through the PC, into the modem, across the phone lines, and into her computer. I visualized it surrounding her, helping her. According to both of them, something DID happen. The boyfriend said he heard a sound from the computer, but couldn't figure what it was. About that same moment, the girl stopped shuddering and called out my name. It wasn't a statement, it was almost a confused question. . . . After a few moments . . . she was all right. As she opened her eyes she said she saw me hovering over her, and that I simply faded INTO her computer monitor and disappeared.[125]

Windwalker's spontaneous CyberCraft is an eyebrow-raising example of the magickal use of the computer mentioned earlier, a "user application" undreamed of by PC manufacturers. Less dramatically, technopagans such as Maxwell X. Delysid use computers and computer networks as an integral part of their "ritual work." A self-styled "computer geek," Delysid has experimented with computer applications for the cabala, using his PC "to process cabala inquiries, making connections between phrases."[126]

Though still not seduced by the computer, Genesis P-Orridge has made his peace with the machine by investing it with an animistic aura. He speaks to his PC before switching it on and keeps it swaddled in fur, which he believes maintains its "contact with the animal spirit kingdom." He and other TOPY members have also dabbled in TV magick, converting the glass teat into a crystal ball by tuning it to an empty channel late at night, with the brightness and contrast turned all the way up—transforming an ordinary set, in effect, into a psychic TV. "[G]et close to the screen, switch off all other light sources and stare at the screen," instructs P-Orridge.

First try [to] focus on the tiny dots that will be careering about the screen like microorganisms. . . . Suddenly time will alter along with your perceptions and you will hit a period of trance where the conscious and subconscious mind are triggered in unison by the mantric vibrations of the myriad dots. It's quite possible that the frequency and pulse rates of the TV "snow" are similar to certain ones generated by other rituals (e.g. Dervish dances, Tibetan magick, etc.). What we have here is a contemporary magickal ritual using the medium, in all senses of the word, of television.[127]

Staring fixedly into a crystal ball, mirror, or any reflective surface as a means of inducing an autohypnotic trance—and, it is believed, precognitive visions—is known as "scrying." As Erik Davis notes, P-Orridge's use of the idiot box as a scrying screen is at once goofily banal, eminently practical, and triumphantly redemptive. "On one hand, you think, 'That's so flaky, so pathetic, trying to take this stupid detritus from modern civilization and make magic with it,' " says Davis, "but on the other it doesn't matter because from a practical perspective—practical in the sense of magical practical, spiritually pragmatic—it doesn't really matter. John Dee used a crystal ball to channel the Enochian language [the purported language of the angels] and [scrying] is what TV magick comes out of."

Again, the street finds its own uses for things. As Davis puts it, "The cyberpunk ethos has a spiritual dimension." He calls technopagan practices such as TV magick "poaching," a term borrowed from critical theory. The cultural critic Constance Penley defines poaching as the unsanctioned, idiosyncratic interpretation of books, TV shows, and other cultural "texts"— "an impertinent 'raid' on the literary 'preserve' that takes away only those things that seem useful or pleasurable to the reader."[128] Technopagans poach on cyberculture, suggests Davis, making off with technologies and scientific concepts that are then incorporated into a "resacralized," reenchanted worldview. In Davis's eyes, such poaching "produces a very pragmatic spirituality that involves the immediate experience of life . . . which lends itself much more richly to computers and computer culture [than most belief systems]."

Like cyberpunk's outlaw hacking and punk robotics, technopagan and New Age poaching have obvious political connotations. They act out a subconscious resentment engendered by science's unquestioned cultural authority and give voice to the desire to democratize that endeavor—to make the stitching together of cultural explanations of the nature of the universe a more communal enterprise. "In its embattled attempts to practice a science pirated and reappropriated from the experts," writes the cultural critic Andrew Ross, "the New Age community feeds off the popular desire for more democratic control of information and resources"—a pronouncement that holds equally true for technopagan poaching.[129]

Technopaganism conspires with recent philosophical challenges to scientific authority on the basis that, while supposedly objective, it often aids and abets cultural bias or political ideology. Much of this enterprise has been carried out by feminists, multiculturalists, and poststructuralists under the rubric of what has been called "social constructionism," which states that science, like all cultural phenomena, is socially determined—blinkered by the biases of the society that produced it and dedicated, consciously or not, to the validation of that worldview. In a consummate irony, this critique unwittingly allies itself with "creationism" and other fundamentalist Christian critiques of science as a "secular humanist" conspiracy bent on usurping religion's power to make sense of the world around us.

At the same time, technopaganism is concomitant with science's own demolition of traditional notions of universal truth and objective reality, a process hastened along by Godel's incompleteness theorem, a cornerstone of modern mathematics that the mathematician Godfrey Harold Hardy defines as the assertion that "there exist meaningful mathematical statements that are neither provable nor disprovable, now or ever . . . because the very nature of logic renders them incapable of resolution."[130] The philosophical implications of Godel's theorem are "devastating," according to Hardy. The mathematician and cyberpunk novelist Rudy Rucker, who delights in such bombshells, asserts, "Godel has shown that the fundamental logical notion of 'truth' has no rational definition."[131] What's worse, Heisenberg's uncertainty principle, a precept of quantum mechanics, leads to the inescapable conclusion that the very act of observation affects the state of the phenomenon observed, an axiom that plays havoc with the notion of objective truth. "The age of absolutes, if it ever really existed, is now most definitely and permanently passé," concludes the mathematician John L. Casti. "Einstein's work buried once and for all the concepts of absolute space and time, while Heisenberg shot down the belief in absolutely precise measurement. Godel, of course, stamped paid to the quaint and curious ideas of absolute proof and truth."[132]

Philosophical upheavals such as these, from within and without the scientific community, have radically revised the rationalist/materialist worldview, giving way to a quantum reality in which physics often borders on metaphysics. Technopagans place their faith in the liquid indeterminacy of such a reality, hopeful that it might at least accommodate, and one day even validate, their cosmology.

Ironically, technopaganism simultaneously embodies the pervasive anxiety engendered by a reality rendered increasingly incoherent by science and ever more alienating by technology. In an essay on "Cyber-Superstition," Bruce Sterling considers our relationship to the computer as a "Magic Machine":

> Computers are fearsome creations, redolent of mystery and power. Even to software engineers and hardware designers, computers are, in some deep and basic sense, hopelessly baffling. . . . Machines that perform millions of operations per second are simply far too complex for any human brain to fully comprehend.[133]

Furthermore, notes Gary Chapman, a former executive director of Computer Professionals for Social Responsibility, these unfathomable, mercurial devices have hidden themselves in everything from household appliances to heavy machinery and are rapidly assuming control of the technosphere:

> Embedded microprocessors that help run everything from cars to coffee makers to airliners are even more widespread than personal computers, but they are largely invisible to the casual viewer. Many people probably have a vague idea that there is a computer under the hood of the newer model automobiles, and that it helps run the engine. But how the computer does this, where it is, and how it can malfunction are typically mysteries for most people. . . . The automobile is no longer a 'natural' thing, that is, something that exhibits properties that can be grasped by a person with a reasonable exposure to physics, but is now a kind of 'supernatural' thing, since its operation is governed by invisible changes, embodied in software.[134]

In a world increasingly dependent on digital technologies, the esoteric knowledge and arcane terminology associated with computer science confers on it an almost religious status. To the laity, it seems that the death of God has merely made way for a theology of technology. Tellingly, magico-religious metaphors have swirled around computers almost since their invention. Room-sized, vacuum tube–powered monsters such as ENIAC (the first programmable electronic computer, officially operable in 1946) provided the mythic image of the computer as an intimidating, inscrutable deity, attended by white-smocked priests who bore a disquieting resemblance to the "machine-tickling aphids" Samuel Butler feared humans might one day become, as he cautioned in his novel *Erewhon*. Firmly fixed in the mass imagination through any number of SF films and *Star Trek* episodes, the archetype of the cyber-god is rendered most memorably in the apocryphal story recounted by the mythologist Joseph Campbell in *The Power of Myth*:

> [President] Eisenhower went into a room full of computers. And
> he put the question to these machines, "Is there a God?" And
> they all start up, and the lights flash, and the wheels turn, and
> after a while a voice says, "*Now* there is."[135]

Campbell, who had recently purchased a desktop computer, noted that as "an authority on gods" he was inclined to identify the machine with "an Old Testament god with a lot of rules and no mercy."[136]

Writing on the eve of the PC revolution, the computer scientist and artificial intelligence enthusiast Christopher Evans presents a mirror image of Campbell's reading of the computer as an arrogant, angry tin god. In *The Micro Millennium*, Evans reflects at length on the "ultra-intelligent machines" he speculates will spring from the computer's brow. Like the more benevolent, all-knowing, all-powerful deities of myth and religion, machines such as these, possessed of "theoretically limitless powers," will deliver us from evil. "Even the most optimistic fan of human beings will admit that our world is in a most dangerously muddled state, and Man, unaided, is unlikely to be able to do much to improve it," writes Evans. "[T]he temptation to turn to the computer for assistance will be overwhelming."[137] He concludes, "[T]here . . . remains the real chance that computers will be seen as deities, and if they evolve into Ultra-Intelligent Machines, there may even be an element of truth in the belief."[138]

Of course, if computers are gods, those who intercede between them and mere mortals must be priests. In fact, there is a long-standing folklore of computer programmers as priests. In Tracy Kidder's chronicle of the birth of a microcomputer, *The Soul of a New Machine*, a programmer recalls the thrill of learning the "assembly language" that enabled him to control the computer's operations: "I could . . . talk right to the machine. It was . . . great for me to learn that priestly language. I could talk to God."[139] Steven Levy's *Hackers* teems with religious and occult metaphors—obsessive programmers are "technological monks," members of a "devout religious order," or, to their detractors in the MIT math department, "witches." Intriguingly, occult references outnumber priestly ones in hacker slang: *The New Hacker's Dictionary* gives definitions for "deep magic," "heavy wizardry," "voodoo programming," "cargo cult programming," and "casting the runes."

Moreover, it is a received truth in cyberculture that the computer has, in large degree, collapsed the traditional distance between word and deed. In an on-line roundtable devoted to outlaw computer hacking, Robert Horvitz, the Washington correspondent for the *Whole Earth Review*, notes,

> There's a traditional distinction between words—expressions of opinions, beliefs, and information—and deeds. You can shout "Revolution!" from the rooftops all you want, and the post office will obligingly deliver your recipes for nitroglycerin. But acting on that information exposes you to criminal prosecution. The philosophical problem posed by [outlaw] hacking is that computer programs transcend this distinction: They are pure language that dictates action when read by the device being addressed. . . . Actions result automatically from the machine reading the word.[140]

There is an irresistible tendency, in the face of such a seemingly supernatural medium, to wrap it in occult metaphors. Thus, *Village Voice* writer Julian Dibbell concludes that, in virtual environments, the computer operates on what amounts to

> the pre-Enlightenment principle of the magic word: the commands you type into a computer are a kind of speech that

doesn't so much communicate as *make things happen,* directly and ineluctably. . . . They are incantations, in other words, and anyone at all attuned to the technosocial megatrends of the moment . . . knows that the logic of the incantation is rapidly permeating the fabric of our lives.[141]

It is somehow fitting that technopaganism, with its emphasis on counterbalancing the power of the computer priests, should invert such metaphors. In a world where programming is seen as cybernetic cabalism, conjuration can be understood as magickal programming. "Programs are the 'ritual' for invoking the appropriate action," analogizes Farrell McGovern, a technopagan participating in the "Cybermage" topic. By the same logic, he argues, a magickal ritual is a program:

> [O]nce you have "compiled" and "run" your ritual once, you really don't need to again, since that energy pattern is now in your head. . . . You just invoke the magickal headspace that the original "source" ritual created! This is how I do magick.[142]

To Rodney Orpheus, the ease with which such metaphors are turned upside down underscores his belief that there's nothing oxymoronic about the term *technopagan* in end-of-the-century cyberculture. "People say, 'Pagans sit in the forest, worshiping nature; what are you doing drinking Diet Coke in front of a Macintosh?' " says Orpheus, who in addition to being a card-carrying Crowleyite is a hacker and mind machine aficionado. "But when you use a computer, you're using your imagination to manipulate the computer's reality. Well, that's *exactly* what sorcery is all about—changing the plastic quality of nature on a nuts-and-bolts level. And that's why magickal techniques dating back hundreds of years are totally valid in a cyberpunk age."

Orpheus's rhetoric is bounded by unacknowledged limits. Philosophical challenges to the scientific worldview notwithstanding, many of us are still sufficiently constrained by it to have difficulty accepting Orpheus's faith in the powers of mind over matter. Certainly, postmodern critiques, together with the paradigm-shattering breakthroughs of modern science (relativity, quantum mechanics, chaos theory), have jimmied open the scientific world-view wide enough to admit ideas that would previously have seemed counterintuitive, even "irrational." But that opening does not accommodate technopagan claims of channeling energy over telephone lines or discerning visions of things to come in "the mantric vibrations of the myriad dots" on a snowy TV screen.

Likewise, Dibbell's eyebrow-raising declaration that the computer reduces the "tidy division of the world into the symbolic and the real" to a philosophical mirage merits closer scrutiny.[143] Few would deny Dibbell's premise, a cornerstone of corporate futurology and postmodernism alike, that our interactions with the world around us take place, more and more, in electronically mediated spaces (videoconferences, BBS discussion groups, and the like). Nor would many debate the notion that transnational corporate power is increasingly dependent on, and exercised in, cyberspace. Nor, finally, would anyone deny that word (programming language) and deed (information processing) become one in the computer, a symbol-manipulating machine operated by strings of arbitrary symbols. Then, too, language's ability to act on the virtual world inside the computer via operating code is echoed in computer-mediated human interaction, where description is indistinguishable from action. For example, sexually harassing messages on electronic bulletin boards are experienced by some on-line recipients as "verbal," even "physical" assaults, no less hurtful than the same actions in RL ("Real Life").

In his argument that the computer collapses the difference between the actual and the virtual, Dibbell reaches for occult metaphors, implying in the process that the computer also does away with distinctions between magick and technology. Ironically, ritual magick offers a highly instructive metaphor for the divorce between the symbolic and the real—between cyberspace, where digital incantations "*make things happen,* directly and ineluctably," and the embodied world outside. As Joseph Campbell notes, "When a magician wants to work magic, he puts a circle around himself, and it is within this bounded circle, this hermetically sealed-off area, that powers can be brought into play that are lost outside the circle."[144]

Thus, while the physical workings of the computer inarguably convert symbols into deeds, and while the disembodied sociology of BBSs may treat descriptions as actions, the most significant exchange of symbols in cyberspace–the global, often computer-assisted traffic in currency, junk bonds, information, and other immaterial commodities–*accentuates* rather than eliminates the "division of the world into the symbolic and the real." Breathless evocations of cyberspace as a "hermetically sealed-off area" where wishes are commands forget the world outside the magic circle–an ever more polarized two-tiered society "with an upper tier of high-wage skilled workers and an increasing 'underclass' of low-paid labor" and the unemployed, according to a special commission headed by former Labor Secretary John T. Dunlop.[145] "Ours is a culture in which the symbolic economy, the traffic in 'information' and abstract value (credit, junk bonds, etc.) has accelerated beyond the economy of material goods," writes Stuart Ewen, a critic of consumer culture.

> It operates more and more apart from it, as if an autonomous realm, though we have by no means conquered scarcity. . . . The stock market skyrockets while the material life of the economy is in shambles. . . . The health-care crisis, poverty and unemployment . . . are all ominous symbols of a worsening disintegration of the social fabric on a material level.[146]

Secretary of Labor Robert Reich worries that the warp-drive acceleration of technological progress will exacerbate, rather than ameliorate, this inequity. In his *New York Times* Op-Ed piece, "The Fracturing of the Middle Class," he writes, "While the information highway promises to speed some people to desirable destinations, it may leave others stranded in the technological version of inner-city ghettos."[147]

Dibbell's argument and my rebuttal reiterate, once again, the binary opposition whose fault line runs through this chapter: that of the political versus the transcendental–what Todd Gitlin identifies as the "Change the World!" versus the "Change Consciousness, Change Life!" dichotomy. On one hand sits the thesis that cyberspace is a sociocultural, perhaps even spiritual "empowerment zone"–a magical social space where the breach between thought and deed is healed and technopagans and other on-line communitarians can conjure virtual "societies more decent and free than those mapped onto dirt and concrete and capital" (Dibbell).[148] On the other, there is the antithesis that those who place their faith in the magical possibilities of computer-generated worlds are abandoning all hope of political change in the world "mapped onto dirt and concrete and capital" at a time when their contributions are desperately needed.

Technopagan visions of cyberspace as a magickal circle, of BBSs as "the new temples of the information age" (Dibbell), or of the Internet as a "spiritual tool" (Delysid) can be seen as empowering—a colonization of cyberspace and the technosphere by a subculture marginalized by the scientific world-view. Then again, such beliefs could be seen as evidence of the triumph of what Neil Postman calls "Technopoly," which he defines as "a state of culture" that is also "a state of mind," characterized by

> the deification of technology, which means that the culture seeks its authorization in technology, finds its satisfactions in technology, and takes its orders from technology. This requires the development of a new kind of social order, and of necessity leads to the rapid dissolution of much that is associated with traditional beliefs.[149]

Technopagans are inclined to argue that technology is fast literalizing magickal powers and may one day render this war of metaphors moot. In the WELL topic "Techgnosis: Computers as Magic," the aeronautical engineer and high-tech entrepreneur William Mook offered a cogent, lyrical version of this argument:

> Computers basically take symbolic strings and produce other symbolic strings. As such, they aren't too magical in the root meaning of the word. But, when attached to something that changes the world in a significant way, through robotic action, then computers are magical by definition.
>
> A computer might recognize the verbal symbol, "Ford Taurus." It might then match it against a tag with CNC files to run a robotic factory which in turn manufactures and assembles an automobile according to the specs of a Ford Taurus. So one

symbolic string is matched with a significantly large symbolic string which when executed by the appropriate hardware modifies the world in accordance with the original string. This is precisely what magic always was, the affecting [of] the world through symbolic acts that are interpreted by agents within the world to achieve the desired effects.

Ultimately, we'll have smart smoke powered by sunlight, eating the air, water and soil. It will be present everywhere and always listening for the words that invoke its power to produce goods and services in response to human need. At this point, the equation between technology and magic will be almost complete, but we will not hold it in awe, because awe is not something the magic will require.[150]

Mook's sublime evocation of a world inhabited by demiurgic demons "everywhere and always listening for the words" that will summon them into action sounds like a poetic rendering of the postscarcity technological Utopia imagined by the nanotechnologist K. Eric Drexler.

In *Engines of Creation: The Coming Era of Nanotechnology,* Drexler foretells a future fabricated by *nanomachines*—self-replicating, computerized microassemblers, smaller than a millionth of a meter, that would stack atoms at eye-blurring speed to build complex objects in the twinkling of an eye. He envisions a rocket engine "grown" by invisible assemblers in an industrial vat, spaceships fashioned from the raw materials of "soil, air and sunlight." Nanomachines, writes Drexler, "will be able to make virtually anything from common materials without labor, replacing smoking factories with systems as clean as forests. They will transform technology and the economy at their roots, opening a new world of possibilities."[151]

But whether or not this alchemist's dream come true will be realized within our lifetimes (or ever), we can at least say that, in a late-twentieth-century culture whose worldview is supposedly structured by science, the technosphere has become an ironic repository of teleological visions and transcendentalist myths—all of them testimony to the abiding influence of sixties counterculture on nineties cyberdelia. The mystical raptures and apocalyptic premonitions of the sixties endure in the millenarian prophecies of techno-hippies, technopagans, New Age disciples of human potential, and visionary technologists.

Throughout cyberculture, and especially in cyberspace, we encounter the capitalist goddess of progress, the angels and alien saviors of the New Age, and the animistic spirits of paganism, calling to mind Robert Pirsig's proclamation, in the New Age classic *Zen and the Art of Motorcycle Maintenance,* that "the Godhead resides quite as comfortably in the circuits of a digital computer or the gears of a cycle transmission as he does at the top of a mountain or in the petals of a flower."[152] Whether Pirsig's Godhead, Maxwell Delysid's *loa,* or Tony Lane's electrical familiars are taken literally, as manifestations of the numinous, or metaphorically, as mythic beings that once resided in nature and now inhabit the technosphere, is a matter of individual conviction. But in either case, it seems that reports of the death of God were greatly exaggerated.

Joseph Campbell assumed as much when he told a short parable about peering inside his PC. Campbell, who held that the major religions were all but obsolete and that modern myths were needed, was dazzled by the dizzy mandala of the computer's microcircuitry. "Have you ever looked inside one of those things?" he asked an interviewer. "You can't believe it. It's a whole hierarchy of angels—all on slats."[153] The Sacred, it seems, is alive and well inside the machine.

2/ METAL MACHINE MUSIC

Cyberpunk Meets the Black Leather Synth-Rockers[1]

Billy Idol, Cyberpunk™. © *Gene Kirkland*

"Cyberpunk" began as a literary subgenre—an ear-catching coinage borrowed from Bruce Bethke's 1983 story of the same name and applied, in a 1984 *Washington Post* article by the critic and editor Gardner Dozois, to the "bizarre, hard-edged, high-tech" SF emerging in the eighties. Soon, the term tore loose from its moorings and floated into the mainstream. In their 1991 nonfiction whodunit, *Cyberpunk: Outlaws and Hackers on the Computer Frontier,* Katie Hafner and John Markoff used it to describe "young people for whom computers and computer networks are an obsession, and who have carried their obsession beyond what computer professionals consider ethical and lawmakers consider acceptable."[2]

Pulled in every direction by journalists, SF manifesto-makers, postmodern theorists, netsurfers, and fans, "cyberpunk" has been stretched into strange new shapes. My use of the neologism, in a 1989 cover story for *Keyboard* magazine, as a label for electro-industrial rock with a grungy, sci-fi edge serves as a prism to refract some of cyberculture's recurrent themes: the convergence of human and machine; the supersession of sensory experience by digital simulation; the subcultural "misuse" of high technology in the service of perverse sensibilities or subversive ideologies; and a profound ambivalence, handed down from the sixties, toward computers as engines of liberation and tools of social control, reweavers of the social fabric shredded by industrial modernism and instruments of an even greater atomization.

To Lewis Shiner, one of the genre's founding fathers, the use of the term to describe "guys in black leather who use synthesizers . . . and digital sampling" betokens the co-optation of what began as the literary equivalent

of a terrorist faction.[3] It is emblematic, he contends, of the mainstreaming of
cyberpunk, a trend he laments in his 1991 *New York Times* editorial,
"Confessions of an Ex-Cyberpunk":

> Cyberpunk started out as a fashionable subset of science fiction,
> showing high technology subverted by opportunists on the
> margins of society, for profit or just for fun. . . . But by 1987, [it]
> had become a cliché. . . . Ironically, as the term . . . was losing
> its meaning for us, it was escaping, virus-like, into the main-
> stream, where it continues to thrive.[4]

Instead of speaking truth to power, he argues, mass market cyberpunk "offers power fantasies, the same dead-end thrills we get from video
games and blockbuster movies"; it mythologizes "our obsession with material goods" and reaffirms our faith in "technical, engineered solutions" to
economic ills and moral malaise.[5]

Shiner's worst suspicions about black leather synth-rockers who
call themselves cyberpunks were confirmed in 1993, when Billy Idol–a
onetime punk rocker whose market-savvy makeovers have helped him
outlast the class of '77–released *Cyberpunk,* a bald-faced appropriation of
every cyberpunk cliché that wasn't nailed down.

At the same time, who is more deserving of the "cyberpunk"
moniker than techno-rockers communing with matte black modules through
what one ad called "neon backlit Mega Screens"? Prosthetically enhanced
by a daunting array of samplers, sequencers, synthesizers, signal proces-
sors, and software that turns computers into recording studios, today's
musicians are not far removed from *Neuromancer's* outlaw hackers, their
sensoriums physically interlinked with the cyberspace matrix. More and
more, musicians of all stripes compose and perform patched into cybernetic
nervous systems whose ganglia are "interactive music workstations" such as
the Korg i3, an inscrutable, button-studded machine resembling the instrument panel of a Stealth bomber. "Unlike other workstations," boasts a
magazine ad,

> the i3 is capable of producing musical "ideas" of its own–phrases
> and patterns called *Styles* that can be modified, looped and

combined to block out songs in minutes. The interactive i3
extrapolates or produces chords and patterns from the notes
you play. And with Korg's Full Range Scanning feature, your
chords won't be forced into the simplistic, default versions found
on other instruments.[6]

A cursory browse through *Keyboard,* a technical magazine for
electronic musicians, reveals the extent to which the contemporary musician has been borged and morphed. An ad for E-mu's Morpheus Z-Plane
synthesizer ("the synthesizer to move your music into the next century")
rejoices in "multi-segment function generators for microscopic sound-
sculpting" and "14-pole Z-Plane filters"

capable of modeling virtually any resonant characteristics and
then interpolating (or "morphing") between them in real time.
Imagine sending a saxophone through the body of a violin and
then smoothly morphing it into a distortion guitar. Or send[ing]
a piano through the resonances of the human vocal tract pro-
nouncing a variety of vowels.[7]

In much the same way that virtual personae adrift on the Internet
seem to be floating farther and farther away from the physical bodies to
which they are anchored, virtual instruments are taking leave of their
acoustic bodies—the guitars, pianos, saxophones, drums, and other Renaissance, eighteenth-, and nineteenth-century artifacts that originally produced their characteristic sounds. "Perhaps [virtual] instruments should
feature a wide variety of control interfaces, both traditional and forward-
thinking," muses *Keyboard*'s technical editor Michael Marans. "Given the
vast number of parameters that can be controlled, maybe virtual reality
goggles and a DataGlove are in order."[8]
    In fact, a handful of composers are using DataGlove-style "gestural
interfaces" even now. Tod Machover, the director of the Experimental Media
Facility at MIT's Media Lab, utilizes an Exos Dexterous Hand Master—a cy-
borglike gauntlet with aluminum phalanges and wire nerves—to translate his
conducting gestures into commands for electronic instruments via a computer. "It uses sensors and magnets to measure the movements at each finger

joint," he explains. "This system works fast enough to monitor the most subtle movements of a finger as well as the largest hand gestures, with great precision, accuracy, and speed. . . . [T]he glove movements influence [dynamics], spatial placement, and the overall timbre of the whole piece."[9] In "Bug-Mudra," on Machover's record *Flora,* the composer-performer uses the Hand Master to direct the course of a giddily syncopated figure churned out by electric and acoustic guitarists and an electronic percussionist. The trio is plugged into Machover's computer-based "hyperinstrument" system, in which "intelligent, interactive machines" respond, in real time, to the performances of live instrumentalists. "The piece's entire timbral content– all the sound color of these instruments–is determined by movements of the hand," the composer informs.[10]

Machover's Exos controller bears a $20,000 price tag; meanwhile, in the bargain basement, Mark Trayle employs a Mattel PowerGlove purchased at Toys 'R' Us for $79.95. (The discontinued PowerGlove was originally designed to enable young users to interact with Nintendo video games through gestures, rather than joystick movements.) In *Seven Gates,* "an interactive computer music composition with a touch of virtual reality," the deconstructionist composer uses a PowerGlove to spindle, fold, and mutilate scraps of TV programs, radio broadcasts, and musical quotes stored in the memory of a computer, among them the "Lacrimosa" from Mozart's *Requiem,* Latino radio announcers, Handel's *Water Music,* "the gray-haired guy with glasses on *The Nightly Business Report,*" and "some drumming from the South Pacific." Conceiving of his prearranged samples as sonic oddments arranged on "invisible shelves" behind an "imaginary fence," Trayle plucks sounds out of thin air by reaching through a "gate" in the fence, removing a sonic bauble from the shelf, and brandishing it in a series of high-tech incantations. With a wave of the Glove, he can raise the sample's pitch to a helium squeak, lower it to a Novocain slur, or loop it so that it stammers frantically until cut short by a flick of the wrist. A reviewer reports that some who have watched Trayle perform "tell of actually visualizing the manipulation of sounds as if they were images projected onto a screen."[11]

DataGlove-style controllers are not the only futuristic interfaces currently in use. BioControls' BioMuse uses an eye motion tracker, together with EMG and EEG signals generated by muscle movements and brain waves, to control virtually any aspect of a MIDI instrument–pitch, panning, timbre, volume, and so forth. (MIDI, short for "Musical Instrument Digital Interface," is an industry-standard computer language that facilitates the communication of pitch, duration, and other musical information between electronic instruments, thus allowing them to control each other. For example, MIDI pulses from an electronic drum machine can play back, or "trigger," sounds recorded and stored as digital data by a computerized device called a "sampler.") Sensors embedded in the Bio-Muse's headband and two muscle bands detect and relay bioelectric impulses to a personal computer by means of a specially designed interface. Erik Davis witnessed a performance in which a BioMusician "played air violin, controlling pitch, volume and vibrato with his arms, while producing stereo as he shifted his gaze across the room, and changing the violin sound to a glockenspiel by closing his eyes and lapsing into [an] Alpha [wave] state."[12]

Ultimately, the story goes, human composers will be superseded altogether by artificial intelligence. Tod Machover imagines the evolution of artificial life whose Darwinian struggles make posthuman music. "One of my dreams for a long time has been to have compositions which are like living organisms . . . [comprised of] musical agents," he says, "each of them a musical tendency, a melodic shape or harmonic progression or tone color. The trick would be to set up an environment with some kind of constraint language where you could put those things in motion. You might just push a button and watch it behave."[13]

Clearly, the "cyberpunk" tag is adequately earned in state-of-the-art electronic music, be it pop or avant-garde. Nonetheless, Shiner's point is well taken: There is something suspect about the light-fingered appropriation of a mediagenic label like "cyberpunk" by pop music, a voracious medium that has perfected the pasteurization of underground trends. A buzzword that must be made to fit artists as disparate as Information Society and Sonic Youth ends up stretched to a transparency.

Information Society invites the cyberpunk classification with records such as *Hack*, whose cover features a *Road Warrior*–style scrapmobile festooned with corrugated tubing and whose lyrics are larded with references to cyberculture (a cassette single features "virtual reality" and "phone phreak" versions of a song, a phone phreak being a hacker obsessed with the intricacies of the phone system and skilled in the illegal art of making long-distance calls for free). Paul Robb, who has since left the group, once observed, "We're musical hackers. What we do is similar to computer hackers breaking into sophisticated systems to wreak havoc."[14] But the band's glossy dance tracks, which swaddle funk lite and disco rhythms in swooning vocal harmonies, are more robopop than cyberpunk.

The label seems more appropriate in Sonic Youth's case. Lee Ranaldo, one of the band's two guitarists, has used the *c* word to describe Sonic Youth's avant-garage rock, an eruption of crackling static, clotted feedback, and sweetly dissonant drones. The liner notes to the group's album *Sister* (1987) cite SF novels such as K. W. Jeter's *The Glass Hammer* and Philip K. Dick's *The Owl in Daylight* as influences, and the SF critics Richard Kadrey and Larry McCaffery dubbed Sonic Youth's *Daydream Nation* (1988) the "ultimate cyberpunk musical statement to date," an evocation of "the confusion, pain, and exhilaration of sensory overload, via chaos theory–produced blasts of sound."[15] Says Ranaldo, "The cyberpunk writers all hate the term, so we'll take it."[16]

According to Paul Moore, a software engineer who edits a desktop-published "cyberpunk/electronic/techno/noise fanzine" called *Technology Works*, "cyberpunk" best describes the folk music of cyberculture. "I appropriated the term from science fiction and applied it to this music because, although nobody seemed to be talking about these bands in terms of a movement, there seemed to be a link between cyberpunk's hard-edged writing style and the edgy music made by bands like Clock DVA, Front 242, and Skinny Puppy," he says. "In a musical sense, [cyberpunk] means using electronics to express yourself. You don't have to be a traditional musician to program machines and get some music out of them. Cyberpunk music is about using high technology to express a 'street' sensibility."

The music that Moore and his readers call "cyberpunk" is characterized by pile-driver rhythms, rammed home by drum machines or clanged out with the sampled sounds of heavy industry or the big city. The music's only concession to melody consists of synthesizer arpeggios that sound like a Touch-Tone phone autodialing. The lyrics, hoarsely barked or recited in a future-shocked monotone, are electronically processed to give them a fuzzy, metallic quality that makes them sound as if they've been synthesized by a computer. Hemmed in on all sides by machines, the claustrophobic vocals embody the human condition in technoculture. A tumult of panicked voices sampled from science fiction, horror, or suspense movies evokes the sensory overload of the media landscape and the growingly surreal violence that is a sign of our times. In much of the music, a paranoia about social control is counterweighted by a perverse fascination with masculinist pathologies—the dehumanization of the individual, the discipline and regimentation of the body.

A distant relative of *Metal Machine Music* (1975), Lou Reed's essay in ear-piercing, mind-numbing noise, cyberpunk rock is more immediately descended from the "industrial" movement that rose from punk's ashes in the late seventies. Throbbing Gristle's *Second Annual Report* (1977), a grainy, white-noise sound track for a Ballardian landscape of cloverleafs and concrete high-rises, is the seminal "industrial" album. In the neo-futurist music of Throbbing Gristle, Cabaret Voltaire, and SPK, created with the aid of electronic instruments, power tools, scrap metal, and industrial noise, the journalist Jon Savage heard "the true soundtrack to the final quarter of the 20th century."[17] As TG's Genesis P-Orridge tartly observed, "[U]p till then the music had been . . . based on the blues and slavery, and we thought it was time to update it to at least Victorian times—you know, the Industrial Revolution."[18]

In a similar vein, cyber-rock uses factory clangor as an ironic metaphor for an information society whose technological totem, the computer, resists representation. Sealed in a smooth, inscrutable shell, the computer's inner workings are too complex, too changeable, for the imagination to gain purchase on them; only when it is imaged in the cold, hard boilerplate of the machine age can this postindustrial engine be grasped. At the same time, cyberpunk rockers draw on SF concepts and iconography. In so doing, they take their place alongside David Bowie in his Ziggy Stardust period, the android synth-rocker Gary Numan, and the mohawked, stiletto-heeled cartoon droogs Sigue Sigue Sputnik in the subgenre formed by the confluence of science fiction and rock, both forms of gadget pornography and unbridled power fantasy that speak powerfully to pubescent males.

Front Line Assembly offers a textbook example of cyberpunk rock. The Canadian duo's 1992 release, *Tactical Neural Implant,* is typified by "Mindphaser," a techno-tribal stomp about mind control and mechanical mayhem strewn with references to "implanted brain cells" and "digital murder," along with a sampled voice from *RoboCop 2* talking about "cyborg technologies" and "destructive capability."[19] Another song, the quasi-symphonic "Biomechanical," grew out of Bill Leeb's fascination with H. R. Giger's "necromantic illustrations involving alien females and cyborgian penis machines."

Says Leeb, "I really romanticize the bionic dream of becoming one with technology. What journalists are calling 'cyberpunk' rock stems from the idea of using machines to make music as well as the integration of technology into the human body, like in *The Terminator*." Rhys Fulber adds, "There are similarities between cyberpunk fiction and our music, especially this idea of breaking down the division between human and machine. Most people are afraid of society's obsession with technology, what with pollution and other global crises, whereas [we feel that cyborging] would increase possibilities for individuals."

In FLA's music, a wariness of technology's ability to render the effects of power ubiquitous and instantaneous blurs into a fetishizing of kill technology and military discipline; it's not at all clear whether the band believes a tactical neural implant is a fearful prospect or a seductive one. Even so, like many cyberpunk artists, they espouse the oppositional politics of the appropriation aesthetic. "We're interested in using technology for our own ends rather than being dogmatic military mutants, following orders," says Fulber. "In the same way that the characters in *Road Warrior* weld together whatever usable parts they can find amidst all the garbage, we're stitching together sounds taken from every imaginable media source. We see ourselves as broadcasting information."

By contrast, the electronic musician David Myers italicizes the *cyber* in cyberpunk, emphasizing the eerie sublimity of out-of-body experiences in cyberspace. "There are many musicians who feel that they're making cyberpunk rock, but I would disagree with most of them rather strongly," asserts Myers. "What do mechanical, stomping dance bands have to do with William Gibson's vision of the levels of experience available in the datastream through human-computer interface? I just don't see the relationship between Front 242's 'Neurodancer' and *Neuromancer*. These bands, in my opinion, have simply latched onto a label that only vaguely relates to their music."

Myers is the inventor of the "Feedback Machine"—a black box whose circuitry is wired to generate feedback loops. By fiddling with its knobs, he is able to conjure withering blasts of distortion, banshee wails, volleys of staticky hiccups. In "Penetrating Black Ice" (*Fetish*, 1990), long, sustained rasps unfurl in slow motion, glittering with harmonics; buzzes and beeps bounce weightlessly, like marbles in zero gravity. Listening, one feels like a hacker brain-plugged into his computer, turning victory rolls in utter darkness.

Which is no coincidence, since "Penetrating Black Ice" was inspired by the scene in *Neuromancer* where Case hacks his way through the last, deadliest level of cybernetic security—Black Ice, which Gibson describes, in "Burning Chrome," as "Ice that kills . . . Some kind of neural-feedback weapon, and you connect with it only once . . . Like some hideous Word that eats the mind from the inside out."[20]

Says Myers, "What really turns me on in cyberpunk literature is the idea of a data thief having a virtual reality experience. My music, as a result, is more a swirl of electronic otherworldliness. Sure, some cyberpunk novels incorporate mean, grungy, almost *Road Warrior*–type imagery for which you would probably need a soundtrack of thumping drum machines and unintelligible, screamed vocals, but that isn't what interests me about these books. For me, the cyberpunk sensibility isn't about leather and studs; it's about total immersion in an electronic reality. And, in the same way that virtual reality is created by manipulating electrons, its musical analog has to be created electronically."

Glenn Branca, an avant-garde composer steeped in postmodern SF and computer culture, has contemplated the notion of a cyberpunk music. In a 1992 *Mondo 2000* interview, he told me, "To be honest, I don't think I've ever heard a musical analog for cyberpunk literature. . . . The closest I've come to cyberpunk music is [the composer and music theorist] Dane Rudhyar's description of music that he would have loved to have heard. In *The Magic of Tone and the Art of Music,* he imagines a techno-mystical hyperinstrument called the Cosmophonon. He describes it as a field of energy forces which is 'played' by touching various colored crystals. The music is all-encompassing for the player and the listener—capable of invoking true synesthesia. [But really], what *is* the proper modern music to accompany cyberpunk? I mean, is it some futuristic-sounding electronic beep-boop music, or what?"[21]

Two answers come immediately to mind: Elliott Sharp and Trent Reznor of Nine Inch Nails.

Elliott Sharp: Mindplayer

"They've long known that there was a Professional Irritant at work, an undesignated one."

—John Shirley[22]

"IRRITANT," reads the warning label stuck to Elliott Sharp's battleship-gray metal door. Originally intended for caustic substances, it perfectly describes the composer's self-appointed role in New York's noisy, contentious, Lower East Side music scene and in the larger mediascape.

Of all the musicians mentioned in this chapter, Sharp is perhaps the most deserving of the cyberpunk label. With his bald head, engineer's boots, and standard-issue Gotham wardrobe (it runs the gamut, from black to black), he looks like central casting's idea of one of Gibson's Sprawl dwellers. His cramped East Village apartment is stuffed with computers, samplers, ad hoc instruments, and miscellaneous flotsam: a giant rubber ear of unknown origin, scavenged sewer pipe couplers, and *Road Warrior* noisemakers such as the Pantar (a steel canister lid fitted with a guitar neck and strings) and the Nailimba (a mutant marimba fashioned from "huge nails and pieces of a towel rack I found in the street"). "I'm a pack rat," says Sharp. "These shelves are filled with instruments and carcasses of instruments—junk, just tons of junk."

Sharp invites comparison to Rubin, the avant-garde roboticist who reanimates industrial rubbish in Gibson's story "The Winter Market." Rubin is a *Gomi no sensei*—a "master of junk," a trawler in "the sea of cast-off goods our century floats on."[23] Sharp, too, is looking for meaning in society's Dumpster, but where Rubin makes his manic contraptions out of lithium batteries, breadboards, and the severed heads of Barbie dolls, Sharp fits big-city bedlam, the meshed rhythms of African drumming, the electric shriek of acid blues, and countless other puzzle pieces into a jigsaw music that is much more than the sum of its parts. Gibson has said that his work tends to be "about garbage, the refuse of industrial society" because "my real business has less to do with predicting technological change than making evident its excesses."[24] Thus, to the extent that cyberpunk is synonymous with Gibson's writings, it is about "junk, just tons of junk," by which definition Sharp's pack-rat music is undeniably cyberpunk.

It is cyberpunk, as well, in its reconciliation of science and the street. True to cyberpunk form, Sharp is both closet anarchist and hard-headed rationalist. As a teenaged "suburban science nerd," he "used to blow things up, using timed fuses so that you'd hear these explosions and I'd be about half a mile away." He spent the summer of '68 at Pittsburgh's Carnegie-Mellon University on a National Science Foundation grant, creating spliced-together sound collages and altering his consciousness with a little help from his friends in the chemistry department when he was supposed to be conducting experiments.

Opposition politics, enlivened by an acid wit that is equal parts Jonathan Swift and H. L. Mencken, are a constant in Sharp's music: "Shredded" (*Bone of Contention*, 1987) features the sampled Ollie North on lead vocals, coyly admitting that his "memory's been shredded"; "Free Society" (*Land of the Yahoos*, 1987) uses a particularly ominous quote from the televangelist and former presidential candidate Pat Robertson–"in a free society, the police and the military are God's special envoys"–to flush out the religious right. With his rock band, Carbon, he records brainy, bludgeoning songs–call them "neurocore"–with titles like "A Biblebelt in the Mouth" and "L.A. Law (Not a TV Show)" (*Truthtable*, 1993). An abiding obsession with abuses of power and networks of control runs through Sharp's entire oeuvre; in the liner notes to *Abstract Repressionism 1990–99*, he writes,

> Elements of control (government, police/military, religion, enter-
> tainment/news media, educational institutions, the artistocracy)
> continue to tighten up their absolute ability to shape what
> people think and do–not so much through overt means (al-
> though these are certainly being practiced) but by selecting
> against and undermining the ability of humans to process
> information and [abstract it]. This we must battle.[25]

Even so, Sharp remains as much a "science nerd" as an agent provocateur. In the mid-eighties, the composer wrote dissonant, slam-banging instrumentals whose compositional architecture, tuning systems, and rhythms were generated using the Fibonacci series (mathematical ratios derived by summing a number and its precedent– 0, 1, 1, 2, 3, 5, 8, 13, and so forth). The spiky, swirling music on *Fractal* (1986), which seems to grow like crystals or eddy like currents, was inspired by Benoit Mandlebrot's fractal geometry, in which mathematical formulae are used to generate surprisingly convincing renderings of snowflakes, coastlines, and other natural forms and phenomena. And his computer music sounds like no computer music ever: Consisting, for the most part, of raw scrapes and granitic rumbles, it is as tough and grungy as the works turned out by most academic electronic composers are tidily formalistic.

Much of Sharp's music is colored by his lifelong science fiction fixation, a mania that began with his first visit to a library and continues to this day: Paperbacks by Gibson, Bruce Sterling, Norman Spinrad, Pat Cadigan, and Lucius Shepard, along with virtually "everything that's available" of Philip K. Dick's prodigious output, are crammed into his bookshelves. His fixation is evident in his band names (Scanners, after the Cronenberg movie about telepathic mutants) and in his song titles: "Kipple" and "PKD" allude to Dick, "Mindsuck" to Cadigan's *Mindplayers*, "Dr. Adder" to the K. W. Jeter novel of the same name, and "Cenobites" to Clive Barker's splatterpunk movie, *Hellraiser*.

There is an unexpected humanism at the heart of Sharp's cyberpunk aesthetic, an embrace of the nonlinear dynamics of human intelligence that is ultimately antithetical to cyberpunk's emphasis on the technological half of the cyborg equation. "I called my group Carbon because I'm interested in nonlinear, curved, continuous, carbon thinking, as opposed to squared-off, logical, rigid, silicon consciousness," says Sharp. "Although I tend to be fairly logical, I try to have the tangential, the wild card, the intuitive, always accessible.

"I investigated computer-composed music at one point, but I decided that computers don't make very interesting music, humans do. The mechanical intellect is very stupid; it's artificial stupidity rather than artificial intelligence. It's binary; we're not. There's always a chemical randomness in us. Some things are uniquely suited to humans, and [the] composition of music is one of them. I guess the operative word here is 'soul.' "

Nine Inch Nails: Sex, Death, God, and Technology

Charles Manson called it "getting the fear."

When Trent Reznor lived at the secluded ranch house at the end of Cielo Drive in Beverly Hills, he saw things, late at night: a sudden movement in his peripheral vision, blurred figures on the security monitor that surveilled the front gate. In such moments, says Reznor, you wonder if the knife-wielding midnight ramblers are outside in the dark, trying the locks, or only "in your own head because you know what's happened here." What happened there made a nation deadbolt its doors: 10066 Cielo Drive is better known as Sharon Tate and Roman Polanski's former home, the site of the Manson Family murders.

Reznor has since moved on, but the shadows in his head linger. As the one-man band, Nine Inch Nails, he is the nonpareil exponent of hummable angst-rock. His canny combination of ingrown neuroses, sinewy dance beats, and rusty, barbed melodic hooks landed *The Downward Spiral* (1994) at number two on *Billboard* magazine's album chart. One reviewer called Reznor's music "the unholy mutant offspring of cyberpunk and the pop song"—a fair characterization of art that revels in "the total misuse of technology." For example, Reznor often lowers the pitch of sampled sounds by three octaves to bring out the "great grainy high-end buzz" that adds a pinch of itching powder to his songs.[26]

Rock critics have made much of the teenage spleen and freshman existentialism that suffuses Reznor's lyrics, interpreting them as yet another dispatch from that media fiction Generation X. By and large, journalists have overlooked the cyberpunk themes that pervade his work: mechano-eroticism, body loathing, social control, and the fear of being superseded by machines. Which is curious, since these threads are woven through his lyrics, record cover art, and public statements. NIN's first release, *Pretty Hate Machine* (1989), features an illustration that Reznor has described as "a turbine wheel . . . distorted so that it looks like a spine . . . kind of [a] human-versus-machines-type thing," and he told a *Mondo 2000* interviewer that he "wanted to express a kind of vulnerability—the idea that I was a person trying to keep my head above water, living in this machine which was moving forward."[27]

The Downward Spiral includes "The Becoming," a suffocating song about someone who is gradually being colonized by a machine that functions like a parasitic organism: "the me that you know is now made up of wires."[28] As in so much science fiction, the invulnerability that comes with being borged ("all pain disappears it's the nature of my circuitry") is purchased at the price of the singer's humanity ("even when i'm right with you i'm so far away").[29] Simultaneously, the metamorphosis of human into machine is mirrored by the transformation of dominant into submissive in the song's S and M subtext: "I beat my machine," declares the narrator as the song begins, but by the end he despairs, "i can try to get away but i've strapped myself in."[30]

Incongruously, a religious motif also recurs throughout Reznor's work. On *Pretty Hate Machine* he assumes so many messianic poses that he seems to be acting out the Stations of the Cross: "I gave you my Purity . . . i'm just an effigy to be defaced," he laments in "Sin," and in "Ringfinger" he accuses a lover of leaving him "hanging like Jesus on this cross."[31] There is more than a hint, here, of the union of sadomasochism and religious rapture epitomized by St. Sebastian, the Catholic martyr usually depicted as an androgynous youth in a loincloth, pincushioned by arrows.

All of the themes noted thus far come together, to shattering effect, in the controversial video for "Happiness in Slavery" (*Broken*, 1992). Shot in black and white by Jonathan Reiss, *Happiness* was banned on MTV due to its gore and nudity (a few brief glimpses of a flaccid penis). The five-minute video sits squarely in the tradition of cyber-horror pioneered by H. R. Giger, the British writer-director Clive Barker in his *Hellraiser* movies, and Skinny Puppy, whose songs about torture and vivisection echo with thumps and clangs and gurgles that sound like blood sluicing through hoses.

Set in what a press release describes as "a world in which people willingly submit to ritualized sadomasochistic relationships with devouring machines," *Happiness* begins with blurry tracking shots of lush, labial foliage, intercut with flashes of grease-caked, phallic machinery, camshafts pumping manfully.[32] Seated in a cage, Reznor shrieks about a slave "being beat into submission."[33] A gaunt young man in a suit, played by the body artist Bob Flanagan, enters a grim, decaying chamber that could be an abandoned basement, an S and M dungeon, a torture cell, or a gothic laboratory. Flanagan places a long-stemmed rose and a single white candle in a tiny shrine, undresses, and performs ablutions at a basin. The religious equations—candle $+$ shrine $=$ Stations of the Cross, ritual cleansing $+$ fontlike basin $=$ baptism—are underscored by the tattooed crown of thorns we see twined around Flanagan's penis, in a fleeting close-up.

Happiness's roller-coaster ride into the abyss begins when Flanagan climbs into the stylized chair in the center of the room and, without warning, the mechanized device comes alive. It is a La-Z-Boy recliner designed to Josef Mengele's specifications: metal restraints snap over the armrests, pinning Flanagan's hands in place, and sharp wires shoot out of them, burrowing into his flesh. He grimaces in agony/ecstasy as a three-clawed pincer rips a gooey, wormlike organ out of his chest while a drill arm bores a messy hole nearby. Flanagan's blood rains down on the foliage seen in the opening shot; the garden's fecundity is suggested by a tangle of fat, lively night crawlers. The victim's entrails are processed by the thrusting, lubricated machines seen at the beginning of the video and, for the coup de grâce, the chair transforms itself into a heavy metal sarcophagus, sealing itself shut with Flanagan inside. A sphincter irises open on its underside, and a wad of offal—Flanagan's remains, presumably—plops onto a mass of writhing worms.

On the most obvious level, *Happiness* concretizes cyberculture's recurrent nightmare about the imminent obsolescence of humanity; in the song itself, the narrator is reduced to "human junk," "just some flesh caught in this big broken machine."[34] But there is more here than the obvious. *Happiness* is also machine porn that literalizes the notion of masturbation as "self-abuse." The castration complex—Freud's theory that the infantile fear of losing one's genitals is rooted in guilt over masturbation—is amply in evidence: The mechanical pincers and tongs that fondle/mangle Flanagan's penis enact a symbolic castration, which is shortly followed by a shot of slick, wriggling worms, shown in a close-up that exaggerates their resemblance to severed members.

Happiness brings to mind the philosopher Georges Bataille's theories about the primal darkness inherent in the sex act, its power to return us to the bestial carnality of a time before taboos. In *Erotism: Death and Sensuality,* Bataille forged links between religious sacrifice and the act of love. The deathblow that elevates the sacrificial victim out of the mundane, into the sacred—"into continuity with all being, to the absence of separate individualities"—is closely tied, in Bataille's eyes, to sexual intercourse, which briefly blurs our "separate individualities" through the near merging of our bodies, the borders of our selves.[35] When, as in *Happiness,* a sacrificial victim lies down willingly with a lovemaking machine that is also the instrument of his destruction, sex and death come together in a transgressive act that embodies our love-hate relationship with the machine world.

Additionally, there is the symbiotic relationship between the garden and what Reznor calls the "room-machine"—that is, the torture chamber considered as a disciplinary mechanism. Together, they form a closed circuit: The carnivorous chair's excreta fertilize the garden, which in some obscure way sustains the machinery, according to Reznor. "The idea," he says, "was [that] this machine, this room, lent itself to being like a recycling process—the whole room may be an organism of some sort—where the waste of what was once Bob comes out of the metal sphincter and feeds the garden, which then keeps the room-machine alive in the process." In keeping with the cyborgian logic of cyberculture, the boundary between biology and technology is constantly shifting: The room is a machine, but then again it "may be an organism," just as nature, here, is part of a mechanical process. Moreover, even as the organic body of the human victim is being penetrated by machinery, the teeming vegetation is invading the "room-machine."

The fantasies of cyborg empowerment that made his *Six Million-Dollar Man* doll one of Reznor's favorite toys when he was little—"I would daydream about being bionic and kicking peoples' ass[es] at school, you know?"—live on in some of his songs.[36] Still, most of his music emphasizes an aspect of humanity's Faustian bargain with technology that industrial culture would just as soon forget—namely, that while machines still serve our needs, we are increasingly bent to the demands of their implacable logic. In *Erewhon* (1872), a wary Samuel Butler wrote, "May not man himself become a sort of parasite upon the machines? An affectionate machine-tickling aphid?"[37] Over a century later, a sardonic Reznor snarls, "Take it from me, you can find happiness in slavery."[38]

Origin Stories

Branca's question—"What *is* the proper modern music to accompany cyberpunk?"—is a Mobius strip for the mind. In essence, he is asking what the objective correlative is, in music, of a literary genre that is itself profoundly informed by a sensibility first expressed in music, namely punk. Rob Hardin, who played synthesizer in the cyberpunk novelist John Shirley's band Obsession, holds that cyberpunk "anachronistically embraced proto-punk, punk, and postpunk" and therefore "existed in music *before* it existed in writing."

In their essay "Cyberpunk 101," Kadrey and McCaffery offer a wealth of evidence for Hardin's case, tracing the movement's genealogy through *The Velvet Underground & Nico* (1967), an album-long heroin nod troubled by dreams of cold turkey and rough sex with a "whiplash girl-child"; *Never Mind the Bollocks* (1977), the Sex Pistols' declaration of total war in punk's scorched-earth campaign against normalcy; and Throbbing Gristle's *Second Annual Report* (1977).

The widely held belief, reasserted by Kadrey and McCaffery, that cyberpunk "appropriated punk's confrontational style, its anarchist ener-gies, its crystal-meth pacings, and its central motif of the alienated victim defiantly using technology to blow everyone's fuses" is borne out in *Neuromancer.*[39] Case's mentor, the outlaw hacker Bobby Quine, is named after the protopunk guitarist Robert Quine, whose choked, apoplectic solo on Richard Hell and the Voidoids' "Blank Generation" (1976) gave vent to the pent-up hostility that would explode soon thereafter in punk rock. Molly, who first appears in the short story "Johnny Mnemonic" as "a thin girl with mirrored glasses, her dark hair cut in a rough shag," her black leather jacket "open over a T-shirt slashed diagonally with stripes of red and black," is modeled on the sultry, sneering photo of the Pretenders' singer-guitarist Chrissie Hynde, on the cover of the group's eponymous debut.[40] "The attitude's all there," notes Gibson. "I was just describing that face and giving it a body and fingernails." In *Neuromancer,* Molly confides that she paid for her implanted mirrorshades, retractable claws, and catlike reflexes with money earned as a "meat puppet"—a prostitute whose software-controlled body functions as a sex machine while her semiconscious mind drifts in a twilight sleep that is "like cyberspace, but blank."[41] Gibson borrowed the epithet from the Meat Puppets, a psychedelic cowpunk trio from Phoenix, Arizona.

In *Neuromancer,* sly allusions to rock songs and musicians function as conceptual coordinates, locating Gibson's novel in cultural space. The records Gibson listened to while writing helped not only to establish the book's atmosphere but served as exemplars of innovation, emboldening him in his own experiments. "I needed music to encourage me," he says, "music that suggested a certain world, music that had a sufficiently radical ambience to make me feel it was possible to write something in that direction. I was looking around for things that regular science fiction novels wouldn't touch and I thought, 'Okay, the universe of the Velvet Underground [is] about as esoteric as I [can] get in terms of what science fiction is attuned to.' I was listening to the Velvet Underground, Joy Division, even *Nebraska* by Bruce Springsteen. I needed lyrical stuff, and Springsteen is keyed into a funny kind of folkloric America which I found artistically very useful for doing that book. I wanted something that would help me tie it back into American pop culture. Generally speaking, I use music in my novels as a touchstone to connect [an] imaginary future to our present world."

In an interview with Larry McCaffery, Gibson confides, "I was going to use a quote from an old Velvet Underground song—'Watch out for worlds behind you' ["Sunday Morning," *The Velvet Underground & Nico*]—as an epigraph for *Neuromancer*."[42] He later elaborated, "There are lots of references to Lou Reed [in *Neuromancer*]. Case's girlfriend, Linda Lee, is a character from a Lou Reed song called 'Cool It Down' [The Velvet Underground, *Loaded*], and if you're familiar with that song, you know more about the character in the book than if you [don't] know the song." A collective pop unconscious is presumed; the text is intended to be read *through* the accreted meanings of its intertextual references.

In this regard, Gibson, like the rest of cyberpunk's fortysomething inner circle, is typical of the generation that came of age during the sixties, in a media landscape dominated by television, film, and rock music. The cyberpunks, maintains McCaffery, were

> the first generation of writers . . . who had grown up immersed
> in technology but also in pop culture, in the values and aes-
> thetics of the counterculture associated with the drug culture,
> punk rock, video games, *Heavy Metal* comic books, and the gore-
> and-splatter SF/horror films of George Romero, David Cronen-
> berg, and Ridley Scott.[43]

Of these influences, music looms largest. As Sterling asserts in *Mirrorshades*, cyberpunk "comes from the realm where the computer hacker and the rocker overlap."[44] Looking back on the October 1982 Armadillo-Con SF convention in Austin, Texas, when "the sense of a movement" crystalized in a fractious panel called "Behind the Mirrorshades: A Look at Punk SF," Shiner remarks on the "common themes" that bound the writing of Gibson, Sterling, Shirley, and himself. Granting that the "hacker's attitude toward technology" is a keystone of cyberpunk, he notes,

> More important to me was what Gibson talked about in his introduction to *Heatseeker:* "Sometimes, reading Shirley, I can hear the guitars." This rock-and-roll quality–the young, hip, protagonists, the countercultural attitude (symbolized by the ever-present mirrorshades), the musical references–defined the movement for me.[45]

Cyberpunks–the kind who live in science fiction novels, rather than the kind who write them–are a mythic hybrid of hacker and rocker whose Macs are their "axes." Rock played an important role in the lives of real-life cyberpunks as well: Acid Phreak, a member of a New York cracker organization called the Masters of Deception, took his handle from acid house, a form of techno music characterized by bare-bones rhythm tracks, static harmonies, and samples lifted from other records; Pengo, a member of a German outlaw hacker gang called the Chaos Computer Club, conducted his Internet break-ins to the stiff, twitchy technopop of the German synthesizer band Kraftwerk.

Simultaneously, cyberpunk writers have invested themselves with a rock 'n' roll aura. In their introduction to the anthology *Semiotext(e) SF*, Rudy Rucker and Peter Lamborn Wilson imagine cyberpunk novelists as "crazed computer hackers with green mohawks and decaying leather jackets, stoned on drugs so new the FDA hasn't even heard of them yet, word-processing their necropsychedelic prose to blaring tapes by groups with names like the Crucifucks, Dead Kennedys, Butthole Surfers, Bad Brains . . ."[46]

Gibson, whose "obvious star quality" so impressed Shiner, told me, "I didn't really think of [*Neuromancer*] as a book; I wanted to make a pop artifact"–in other words, a hit single. In like fashion, Sterling, who has sported an earring and a spiky, David Bowie-esque hairstyle, informed a *Mondo 2000* interviewer, "I've got an album to do, as it were."[47] Asked what instrument he played, Sterling explained, "I don't play anything. I just hang out. I talk rock slang, because it's part of the gig."[48] In a *Science Fiction Eye* interview, he speculated that perhaps neither he nor Gibson was forthcoming about biographical details because

> as cyberpunk writers, we consider ourselves in some sense pop stars rather than litterateurs. We want to guard our privacy. . . . Gibson . . . has that classic pop star cool. I also think of myself as being a pop star, rather than a writer with a capital "W.". . . I'm not really interested in writing the Great American Novel. I mean, who cares? . . . It's boring.[49]

Young turks with a fierce allegiance to pop culture, the eighties cyberpunks dreamed not of the urbane repartee of the Algonquin Round Table but of a speedmetal prose whose "visionary intensity" was the literary equivalent of "the sound of feedback blowing out the speakers: I'll show you God" (Sterling).[50]

For John Shirley, "the Lou Reed of cyberpunk" (McCaffery), Sterling's fantasies of "pop star cool" and feedback epiphanies are more than metaphor. The punkiest of the close-knit cabal that founded cyberpunk, Shirley dressed the part, in his earlier days, of a neon night crawler—snakeskin-snug black leather, earrings fashioned from transistors, and, of course, mirrorshades. He "learned to shout rhythmically" and traumatized unprepared audiences in a succession of punk bands with names like Sado Nation and Terror Wrist.[51] Later, he fronted Obsession, whose eponymous LP Shirley describes as "futuristic Funkadelic, but a little punkier." As of this writing, he is in the San Francisco–based Panther Moderns, whose name is taken from a surgically modified teenage gang in *Neuromancer*.

But, while its internalization of the punk zeitgeist made it faster and louder than its predecessors, cyberpunk was by no means the first SF genre to be galvanized by a jolt from the crossed wires of pulp fiction and electric guitars. The British New Wave movement of the sixties introduced rock music into science fiction by way of Michael Moorcock, whose picaresque Jerry Cornelius novels are routinely cited by the cyberpunks as a formative influence. Cornelius is a longhaired, pill-popping sybarite of questionable morality and ambivalent sexuality who inhabits a "multiverse" ruled "by the gun, the guitar, and the needle, sexier than sex."[52] A quantum-leaping superhero who lives in Swinging London, he battles villains whose James Bond redoubts are booby-trapped with LSD gas and throws parties that last for months.

In all four Jerry Cornelius novels, references to sixties bands and snatches of period songs intensify the books' already oversaturated pop art colors in the same way that the brand name–dropping of Don DeLillo or Donald Barthelme lends their novels a hyperreal quality. The climactic scene of the second novel, *A Cure for Cancer* (1971), is a necromantic ritual involving a "chaos machine" that taps the life force of the living to reanimate the dead. Hooking the device up to his dead sister, Cornelius conducts a psychedelic resurrection:

> Swiftly Jerry increased the entropy rate to maximum, preparing himself for the ensuing dissipation. . . . He began to flood through the universe and then through the multiverse, to the sound of the Beatles singing "A Day in the Life," throbbing in time to the cosmic pulse. . . . Faster and faster flew the particles and Jerry hung on. . . . He looked about him and waited as "Helter Skelter" echoed through the infinite. . . . He felt a moment's concern before the switch clicked over, Jimi Hendrix started to play "Are You Experienced?," and things began to come together again. Soon he would know if the experiment had paid off.[53]

If Moorcock attempted to play Beatle-esque psychedelia and Hendrixian black light voodoo on the printed page, the cyberpunks aspired to the buzzsaw strumming and heart attack tempos of punk and heavy metal. In an interview with the SF critic Takayuki Tatsumi, Sterling likens *Schismatrix* to the "thrashing noise" of the band Husker Du, remarking, "I've heard critics compare [it] to hardcore punk. . . . It goes a hundred miles an hour."[54]

Similarly, Shirley's fiction is shot through with the sounds, semiotics, and agitprop of rock. His first novel, the protocyberpunk *Transmaniacon* (1979), is dedicated to the sci-fi biker metal band Blue Oyster Cult, which is a constant presence in the book: The book's title and three of its characters are taken from the BOC song of the same name, and the emblem of the book's occult conspiracy, the Order, is the portentous glyph familiar from Blue Oyster Cult record covers.

Music seeps beneath the surface of the plot, which revolves around the agent provocateur Ben Rackey's insurrectionist use of the stolen Transmaniacon, an infernal machine that facilitates "the telepathic transfer of mania," turning "a street-brawl into a raging mob and a border skirmish into a full-scale war."[55] Rackey is able to steal the device from Dr. Chaldin's high-security palace because his skills as a Professional Irritant are "sufficient to overcome even the universally pacifying influence" of Chaldin's insidious euphonium, whose saccharine Muzak neutralizes "the capacity for rebellion."[56] Rackey is able to counter the euphonium's enervating effects by means of his mental discipline, but his coconspirators must resort to less subtle means:

> They took small black plastic cusps from their pockets and inserted them in their ears. The cusps played tapes of heavy-metal rock 'n' roll, an electric-music art form extinct for a century; extinct—but the only known musical structure capable of countering the euphonium.[57]

Chaldin's pleasure dome is Shirley's caricature of the society of the spectacle: The "social games . . . and contrived, innocuous conflicts which Chaldin's activity schedules and peripheral media stimuli subtly introduced into the crowds," in concert with the subliminally seductive euphonium that keeps partygoers "malleable and ignorant," constitute the "experiment in large-scale crowd manipulation" that is consumer culture, to Shirley.[58] The author prescribes the punk cure-all for its creeping mind rot: "[Rackey] didn't need the cusps. . . . his capacity for hostility was both healthy and intact."[59] Explosive rage, bottled under high pressure, shields Rackey from the brainwashing influence of commodity culture. The cosmic struggle in Shirley's Manichaean moral universe is constituted as a pitched battle between heavy metal and Muzak.

Agitpop

As *Transmaniacon* makes clear, cyberpunk SF often dramatizes its politics in pop music allegories. Here, however, a conflicting story is told: In most cyberpunk fiction, postmodern rock—symbolized by the synthesizer—is portrayed as a joyless, juiceless thing, a taxidermic approximation of an extinct "electric-music art form" by button-pushing technicians. The antipathy that swirls around the image of cyber-rock in cyberpunk fiction—an echo of Shiner's thinly veiled disdain for "guys in black leather who use synthesizers . . . and digital sampling"—reveals a contradiction at the heart of the genre.

Cyberpunk, it turns out, is in part a struggle for the meaning of the sixties, even as it is, by Shirley's reckoning, a survival strategy for "adapting to future shock, a way of dealing with the tsunami of changes coming down on society." Most of the canonical cyberpunks (that is, those anthologized in *Mirrorshades*) were old enough to remember the sixties even as they responded to the technocultural milieu of the eighties—a milieu dominated by MTV, in which the marching music of youthful rebellion and the promotional video clip are resolved in a whirl of junk sex, consumer icons, and kinetic energy that reduces politics and personalities to sensuous surfaces.

Superficially, MTV and cyberpunk were congruent. In his *Mirrorshades* preface-cum-manifesto, Sterling asserts that cyberpunk is the "literary incarnation" of an aesthetic common to rock video and "the synthesizer rock of London and Tokyo."[60] He invokes those MTV-related forms in an attempt to relocate science fiction *in the real world,* distancing it from the technocratic elitism of earlier decades, "when Science was safely enshrined—and confined—in an ivory tower" and "authority still had a comfortable margin of control."[61] To him, rock video, synth-rock, and by implication MTV signify an in-your-face engagement with streetwise technoculture.

Paralleling Sterling's attempts to distance cyberpunk from traditional SF, MTV cast itself as network TV's punky offspring, wrapping itself in the ragged mantle of adolescent rebellion. Of course, MTV's definition of rebellion is fundamentally apolitical. "[T]he underlying message of MTV," asserts Ken Tucker, in *Rock of Ages: The* Rolling Stone *History of Rock & Roll,*

> was that rock and roll was merely entertainment, fun; its endless chains of surrealistic video imagery suggested that rock music had nothing to do with the real world. [Robert Pittman, the executive vice president of MTV's former owner, Warner Amex Satellite Entertainment Company], never one to opt for subtlety, put it succinctly: "In the '60s, politics and rock music fused. But

there are no more political statements [in rock]. The only thing
rock fans have in common is the music—that's the coalition MTV
has gathered."[62]

Of course, there are those who dismiss the notion that "politics and
rock music fused" in the sixties. "Woodstock made it clear that rock would
spark no revolutions," writes the cultural critic Mark Crispin Miller.

> Rock fans are hedonists; they want to luxuriate in fine blasts of
> sound. They may curse and break chairs if the concert doesn't
> start on time, but they do not run outside and embrace wild
> dogmas. Woodstock's (and rock's) defining moment came when
> Abbie Hoffman clambered onstage to address the woozy multi-
> tudes and Pete Townshend of the Who, the act in progress,
> stepped up behind him and kicked him off.[63]

The cultural critic Andrew Goodwin rejects outright the baby
boomer article of faith that MTV skinned the semiotics of rock, leaving the
meat of the matter—the political innards—to rot. MTV is indeed a "master
manipulator," he grants.

> But that is different from making the often-heard complaint that
> music video has 'sold out' the hitherto unblemished soul of rock
> and roll. Such arguments are nonsensical. Rock and pop were
> commodified practices of mass mediation long before the intro-
> duction of music television.[64]

Even so, as Miller points out in his dry-eyed eulogy for rock,
"Where All the Flowers Went," the music "may have been 'co-opted' all
along, handled by shrewd producers from the beginning, but it was exciting
as long as nobody knew this depressing fact."[65] After 1981 (the year MTV
went on the air), "rock and roll, once too wild for television, became . . . a
necessary adjunct of TV's all pervasive ad."[66] He chronicles the refunctioning of rock, from the drumbeat of the electric bacchanal into "the music of
technological enclosure," experienced singly, passively, and, more often
than not, remotely. MTV's decision to inaugurate its first broadcast with

"Video Killed the Radio Star" by the Buggles proves prophetic: Technology ("a pervasive neutralizing medium") is implicated in the domestication of rock, argues Miller. "Like cinema, rock has become dependent on fine gadgetry," he maintains.[67] The music is

> no longer strummed, blown, and banged, but programmed, and then received in solitude by immobile millions watching TV, or driving to work, or "plugged into" Walkmans, or sitting through live performances as 'silent watchers' lost in memory of the video.[68]

As noted earlier, Sterling applauds the very developments (music video, "rock tech") that Miller contends are sapping rock of the rebelliousness cyberpunks hold dear. Noting the supreme irony that "in order to function as a successful service for the delivery of viewers to advertisers and record companies, MTV must promote countercultural and antiestablishment points of view," Goodwin argues that MTV is "simultaneously involved in the incorporation *and* the promotion of dissent."[69]

So, too, is cyberpunk. It speaks the antiauthoritarian language of the sixties, replete with visions of "street-level anarchy" and rapacious multinationals, even as it celebrates the ingenuity of the military-industrial-entertainment complex that enables the "integration of technology and . . . counterculture" (Sterling). It rejects organized politics in favor of a ruggedly individualistic techno-libertarian survivalism while at the same time contemplating, with something approaching relish, the obsolescence of the human being in the coming age of intelligent machines.

Such conundrums are dramatized by cyberpunk's relation to popular music. The "lurking contradiction" Sterling sees at the heart of the "rural, romanticized, anti-science, anti-tech" counterculture of the sixties—an incongruity symbolized, for him, by the electric guitar that was simultaneously a symbol of resistance to a soulless technocracy and a technological artifact—endures in cyberpunk fiction that incorporates "rock tech" and rock mythos. Such writings highlight the unresolved paradoxes at play in cyberculture at large.

"Rock technology was the thin end of the wedge," declares Sterling, in *Mirrorshades:*

As the years have passed, rock tech has grown ever more
accomplished. . . . Slowly, it is turning rebel pop culture inside
out, until the artists at pop's cutting edge are now, quite often,
cutting-edge technicians in the bargain. . . . The contradiction
has become an integration.[70]

But seen from the "street level" that is cyberpunk's supposed
perspective, the contradiction is far less integrated than he suggests.

In "Rock On," Pat Cadigan's contribution to *Mirrorshades*, "cutting-
edge" technology has severed rock's connection to its musical roots in the
deep, dark loam of folk and blues, and to its sociocultural roots in the rough-
and-tumble of street culture. Cadigan's alter ego, Gina, is a "40-year-old
rock 'n' roll sinner" in the literal as well as the punning sense: a worse-for-
wear survivor of the sixties and a brain-socketed Synner whose video
dreams transform even no-talent nonentities into rock gods. On the run
from Man-O-War, a video star whose business acumen far outstrips his
meager abilities as a musician ("He couldn't sing without hurting someone
bad and he couldn't dance, but inside, he rocked. If I rocked him."), Gina is
kidnapped by the aptly named Misbegotten.[71] Ignoring her protestations,
the band wires her for sound and vision in the hope that she can turn them
into hitmakers:

> And then it was flashback time and I was in the pod with all my
> sockets plugged, rocking Man-O-War through the wires, giving
> him the meat and bone that made him Man-O-War and the
> machines picking it up, sound and vision, so all the tube babies
> all around the world could play it on their screens whenever they
> wanted.[72]

A wisecracking parable about rock's fall from grace, into that
postmodern purgatory of pure simulation, MTV, "Rock On" harks back to a
mythic sixties—before soul had been synthesized and the counterculture
commodified, ostensibly. The story is a series of dualisms, counterpoising
the authentic with the synthetic: rib-sticking "real food" served at a greasy
spoon is juxtaposed with "edible polyester that slips clear through you so
you can stay looking like a famine victim"; Gina's memories of "rocking in

my mother's arms" to the Rolling Stones' "Start Me Up" with an elevator
music version of the same song; the I-Want-My-MTV "tube babies" suckling
at the glass teat with Gina, searching for a dive bar where she can "boogie my
brains till they leak out the sockets."[73] But as Man-O-War reminds her,

> "[A]ll the bars are gone and all the bands. Last call was
> years ago; it's all up here, now. All up here." He tapped his
> temple.
>   "It's not the same. It wasn't meant to be put on a tube
> for people to *watch*."
>   "But it's not as though rock 'n' roll is dead, lover."
>   "You're killing it."
>   "Not me. You're trying to bury it alive."[74]

Cadigan's story betrays a mystical humanism that places its faith in
the ghost, rather than the machine: "Rock tech" may have "grown ever more
accomplished," reducing the act of making music to pure cerebration ("up
here"), but even on-line cyber-rock is dependent on the shamanistic Synner's
ability to access "some primal dream spot." Despite McCaffery's thesis that
science fiction, specifically cyberpunk, is the preeminent literature of
postmodern culture, in which "reproduced and simulated realities . . . have
begun subtly to actually *displace* the 'real,' rendering it superfluous," Cadigan is an unregenerate romantic: She accepts no substitutes (Muzak, rock
video, synthesizers) for the inviolate, irreducible real to which all referents
supposedly point.[75] Like Gina, she is a fortysomething "rock 'n' roll sinner"
whose "poor old heart" has been broken by what she perceives to be the
commodification and cybernation of rebellion.
    Published a year after "Rock On," in 1985, John Shirley's *Eclipse* is,
like Cadigan's story, a reexamination of the meaning of rock 'n' roll and the
values of sixties counterculture in the MTV eighties, when videogenic
prettiness became as important as—if not more important than—musical
ability. In his essay "The Eighties," the *Rolling Stone* editor Anthony De-
Curtis writes,

> Videos, video compilations, long-form videos, corporate spon-
> sorships, product endorsements . . . began to envelop what was

once considered a rebel's world. . . . By the mid-1980s . . . [j]oin-
ing a rock band had become a career move like any other, about
as rebellious as taking a business degree and, if you got lucky,
more lucrative.[76]

"Freezone," an excerpt from *Eclipse* included in *Mirrorshades,* is
convulsed by a gag reflex at the artificially sweetened confections of the
eighties: MTV staples such as Culture Club, Thompson Twins, Wham! and,
archetypically, Duran Duran, which owed its success to videos that were
equal parts *Lifestyles of the Rich and Famous,* soft-core porn, and haute
couture fashion ad.

Shirley's protagonist, Rick Rickenharp, is rock's conscience incarnate, the angry, clanging guitar given human form (his comic-book name
crosses the Rickenbacker, a bright, chiming, electric guitar popular with
sixties groups such as the Byrds, with the Orphic harp). A "rock classicist" in
Harley-Davidson boots and a "gratingly unfashionable" black leather jacket
"said to have been worn by John Cale when he was still in the Velvet
Underground," Rickenharp is the singer–lead guitarist for a hard rock act
left high and dry when the nostalgia wave ebbs away. He stands in staunch
opposition to the effete, ersatz fare that passes for rock in the next
millennium: "minimono," short for "minimalist-monochrome," a "canned
music" of "stultifying regularity" that buzzes, gnatlike, at the edge of
Rickenharp's awareness, "a drill-bit vibration" in the spine. (Rickenharp's
tastes run, predictably, to the "collector's-item Velvet Underground tape . . .
capped into his Earmite" blaring the song "White Light/White Heat.")[77] The
technofetishistic minimonos—Shirley's wry send-up of the preening an-
drogynes who populated the high-tech nightclub scene of the eighties—are
deadpan, die-cut conformists who wear "flat-black, flat-gray, monochrome
tunics and jumpsuits" and are "into stringent law-and-order."

Rickenharp's self-named rock band is jarringly out of place at the
Semiconductor, a minimono nightspot on the floating Las Vegas called
Freezone. Wiredancers such as Joel NewHope, the "radical minimono" who
opens the show, are à la mode:

> He was anorexic and surgically sexless. . . . A fact advertised by
> his nudity: he wore only gray and black spray-on sheathing. How

did the guy piss?, Rickenharp wondered. Maybe it was out of that faint crease at his crotch. A dancing mannequin . . . The wires jacked into NewHope's arms and legs and torso fed into impulse-translation pickups on the stage floor. . . . The long, funereal wails pealing from hidden speakers were triggered by the muscular contractions of his arms and legs and torso.[78]

Listening to this epicene BioMusician, Rickenharp musters a half-hearted enthusiasm, allowing, "It's another kind of rock 'n' roll, is all."[79] That said, he quickly adds, "But real rock is better. *Real rock is coming back,* he'd tell almost anyone who'd listen. Almost no one would."[80]

Shirley renders the contest between the real thing, rock, and its uncanny, android double, minimono, in gendered language that comes perilously close to homophobic caricature, in spots, and misogynistic self-parody in others. In an unfortunate resurrection of the Hitlerian trope of the mercurial, "feminine" masses secretly yearning to be mastered, the audience glowers at Rickenharp "with insistent hostility, but [he] liked it when the girl played pretend-to-rape-me."[81] Inevitably, he has his way with the unwilling crowd, his Stratocaster "discharg[ing]" the pent-up, sexual energy in the room, "nailing a climax onto the air."[82] Minimono, by comparison, is emasculated, sapless: no manly jet for Joel NewHope, who must urinate (if he urinates at all) out of a decidedly feminine "crease."

The subculture is not only decadent but dehumanizing as well: While Rickenharp dances "freestyle," the minimonos interlock in "geometrical dance configurations," "Busby Berkeley kaleidoscopings."[83] The clockwork movement of human cogs intermeshed in a flawless geometry is a hallmark of totalitarian spectacle, of course, from Fritz Lang's crypto-fascist *Metropolis* to Leni Riefenstahl's *Triumph of the Will.* The fascist overtones of the minimonos' disco drills are entirely intentional: *Eclipse* is an impassioned tale of rock 'n' roll resistance to a fascist bid for world domination. In the book's climax, Rickenharp meets the fascist onslaught head-on; reborn as the bard of the resistance, he screams his heavy metal swan song from atop the Arc de Triomphe as the enemy bludgeons the monument to rubble.

The cultural critic George Slusser's pronouncement that "rock and roll has lost its soul and doesn't know where to find it" is axiomatic for a body of cyberpunk and post-cyberpunk writings. In the near future of

Norman Spinrad's *Little Heroes* (1987), the megacorporation Muzik, Inc.,
has a virtual monopoly on popular music, which it mass produces with the
aid of "VoxBox wizards who [can] replace bands, orchestras, and even backup vocalists, with a keyboard, a vocoder, and a black box full of wizard-
ware."[84] The company employs

> platoons of shrinks and unemployed former Pentagon psy-war
> spooks to think up best-selling scenarios for their songhacks and
> VoxBox mercenaries to turn into lyrics and music. . . . Muzik,
> Inc., had turned hit-making into a *science.* . . . the psychological
> profiles of the total mass audience had been broken down into
> fine demographic slices.[85]

Muzik, Inc., bombards the benumbed viewers of its unmistakably
MTVish twenty-four-hour rock video channel, MUZIK, with faceless product such as the "dead-ass plastic max metal thing with a ton of swagger and
rubber underwear and a spec sheet for a soul" that Glorianna O'Toole
wrinkles her nose at, early on.[86] Glorianna is described, in the thumbnail
sketches of the novel's main characters at the front of the book, as

> the Crazy Old Lady of Rock and Roll. She remembers Woodstock
> and Altamont and Springsteen. Technology put her out to
> pasture . . . until [she was] hired to create [a] computer-generated
> rock star.[87]

Billy Beldock, president of Musik, Inc., inveigles her into adding the
ineffable intangible missing from Project Superstar's attempt to create a
million-selling AP (Artificial Personality)—a video rock star conjured from
"raw bits and bytes or stock footage" and brought to singing, dancing life by
an "image organ player." He cajoles, "Aw, come on, Glorianna, you *know* that
APs have to be the future of the industry. . . . It's too cost-effective not to be
inevitable."[88] Beldock needs Glorianna to discover why none of Musik,
Inc.'s APs have "shipped gold or cracked the charts with a megahit," a
mystery she unravels posthaste:

> "That soulless crap is to the real thing as white bread is
> to pumpernickel," she declared from the bottom of her heart.
> "It's—"

"I know, I know," Billy sighed, joining her on the
chorus.
"It's just not Rock and Roll."[89]

Which is to say that Musik, Inc., could not by definition counterfeit
"the great voice of that spirit which had now all but vanished from the
world" because *real* rock 'n' roll was "music that kicked their kind of ass"—in
other words, rock and rebellion (whether teen angst or sixties-style radicalism) cannot be disentangled.[90]

Challenging Sterling's assertion that the movement is in every way consonant with the eighties ("an era of . . . old notions shaken loose and rein-
terpreted with a new sophistication"), cyberpunks such as Cadigan, Shirley,
and the New Wave alumnus Norman Spinrad (who deserves the title of
"honorary cyberpunk," at least) betray an unexpectedly reactionary anti-
postmodernism when it comes to the changes wrought by cyberculture on
popular music.[91]

They inveigh against the supersession of the authentic by the
synthetic, of the visceral by the cerebral: the supplanting of human performance by computer-controlled MIDI instruments; of "real" sounds by
digital samples or synthesized substitutes; of traditional musical skills by
computer literacy; of live performance, experienced communally, by rock
video or pay-per-view TV, experienced privately; even of outsized, unwieldy
technology by small, sleek devices (Rickenharp mourns the passing of the
imposing "stacks" of amplifiers that made the twentieth-century guitar god
such an imposing sight). The transcendentalist raptures familiar from
cyberpunk evocations of the insertion of the human into the technosphere
via cyberspace or, conversely, of the invasion of the body by what Sterling
calls "visceral" technologies are nowhere in evidence here.

But while such creeping technophobia is obviously contrary to the
cyber term of the cyberpunk dualism, it is entirely in keeping with its *punk*
aspect. Punk's cynical embrace of modern consumer culture—a Warholian
mockery of hippiedom's failure to build a New Jerusalem among the dark,
satanic mills of industrial modernity—concealed a yearning for a lost
authenticity of its own (that of fifties rockabilly and sixties garage rock) that

was no less romantic simply because it reeked of hot rod exhaust and
jounced to the twang of electric guitars. According to Mary Harron, a
one-time contributor to the New York underground magazine *Punk*, the
phenomenon "was about saying yes to the modern world. Punk, like Warhol,
embraced everything that cultured people, and hippies, detested: plastic,
junk food, B-movies, advertising, making money."[92] Simultaneously, and
contrarily, punk–informed in part by the return of Teddy Boy culture
and the mainstream rock 'n' roll revival of the early seventies (*Grease, That'll
Be the Day, American Graffiti*)–looked back to the raucous, frenzied maver-
icks of fifties rockabilly and the garage rockers of the mid-sixties. In its
own way, punk was no less nostalgic for the fast-receding Real than hippie:
Punks like Tony James, the Generation X bassist who sported an Elvis
T-shirt, or the Ramones, wearing leather jackets in homage to *The Wild One*,
recalled their audiences to a fabled time when rock was lean and hungry,
uncorrupted by the mainstream influences that had made it fat and fatuous
by the late seventies.

It was this investment in authenticity that accounted for punk's
deep-dyed suspicion of "rock tech"–at least, of any technology more
advanced than the electric guitar–even as it said yes to the modern world. It
explains Lewis Shiner's reflexive resistance to "a lot of guys in black leather
who use synthesizers . . . and digital sampling," as well as the instinctive
aversion to the cyborging of rock in the fiction of Shirley, Cadigan, Spinrad,
and others. As Sterling confirms, cyberpunk, "[l]ike punk music . . . is in
some sense a return to roots."[93] Allowing that groups such as Cabaret
Voltaire "used synthesizers, sequencers, and drum machines to produce
rudimentary avant-punk music," Goodwin notes that

> despite the occasional use of machines, the emphasis in punk
> was always on *real* performance. . . . Indeed, an overreliance on
> advanced technology was taken as a sign of "progressive rock"–
> the very music that punk was supposed to displace.[94]

The irony of punk's rejection of high technology in favor of that
blunt instrument of modern primitivism, the electric guitar, is self-evident,
as Norman Spinrad points out in his essay "The Neuromantic Cyberpunks."
Conceding that rock has "always been the music of libidinal anarchy and the

romantic and transcendental impulses," he contends that it has "also always been by definition *technological* music, for without the electric guitar and the synthesizer, it ain't rock and roll either."[95] Ergo, "the expression of the romantic impulse through high-tech instrumentalities is the heart of rock and roll."[96] In a sense, then, rock has been cyberpunk—or, to use Spinrad's punning coinage, "Neuromantic"—from the very beginning. Spinrad reads Rickenharp's triumph in *Eclipse* as a "*cyborged* triumph"; made possible by "the electronic augmentation of [Rickenharp's] fleshly musical powers," it "demonstrates . . . that cyborgs, romantic cyborgs, *Neuromantic* cyborgs, have in fact been using technological augments for transcendental purposes ever since Dylan picked up that electric guitar. When it comes to the characteristic music of our times, we have all been accepting Neuromanticism as a given for a quarter of a century."[97]

To Sex Pistols—era punks (and the cyberpunks who are their standard-bearers), the electric guitar symbolized the raw, the real; synthesizers, by contrast, were synonymous with the flaccid, the bathetic. Now, however, with cyberpunk's "virus-like" infestation of mass culture, there has been a semiotic slippage: Gibson's claim, in an interview with NPR's Terry Gross, that he "gave [computer nerds] permission to wear black leather" applies equally to electronic musicians, specifically those who play synthesizers, once the most painfully unhip of pop instruments.[98] Heedless of Shiner's misgivings, the black leather synth-rockers have claimed cyberpunk as their own. The mainstream finds its own uses for things, too, it seems.

3 / WAGING A TINKERER'S WAR

Mechanical Spectacle[1]

Matt Heckert's Walk and Peck Machine, customized with horse remains.
Photo: Bobby Neel Adams

Manufacturing Dissent

Mark Pauline, Chico MacMurtrie, and Brett Goldstone are waging a tinkerer's war.

Pauline builds engines of destruction. He is the founder and director of Survival Research Laboratories, a loosely knit organization which, since 1979, has been perfecting a heavy metal theater of cruelty—scary, stupefyingly loud events in which remote-controlled weaponry, computer-directed robots, and reanimated roadkill do battle in a murk of smoke, flames, and greasy fumes. MacMurtrie fabricates puppetlike robot musicians, warriors, and acrobats that perform in ecotopian dramas. And Goldstone builds junkyard whimsies driven by steam or powered by water: a horseless carriage with a fat-bellied, wood-gobbling boiler for an engine; a Water Bird brought to life by water pumped down its vacuum-cleaner-tube gullet, causing its tin wings to flap excitedly.

Costly, complicated, and sometimes even hazardous, the performances mounted by these Californian artists are infrequent and usually take place on the West Coast or, on occasion, in Europe. All three take advantage, through "Dumpster diving" and what Pauline euphemistically calls "aggressive scrounging," of the machine parts and electronic components generated by the computer and aerospace industries.

They use obsolete or discarded technology to enact what the cultural critic Andrew Ross calls "a communications revolution from below." Their aesthetic of refunctioning, retrofitting, and reanimating military-industrial junk is equal parts funk art and *Frankenstein,* shot through with cyberpunk's politics of low-tech insurgency. Their quixotic machines mock the benefits of technological progress, the virtues of consumerism, and the benevolence of corporate America sold by the anthropomorphic robots of theme parks, trade shows, and Disneyfied malls.

Mechanical spectacle is a sort of *Road Warrior* bricolage, to borrow Claude Levi-Strauss's term (from the French noun *bricoleur*, meaning "tinkerer" or "handyman") for the makeshift strategies, improvised with the odds and ends at hand, that the so-called "primitive" mind uses to make sense of the world around it. Though less cosmic and more overtly political than the myths and rituals of tribal "tinkerers," mechanical spectacle parallels primitive bricolage in its ad hocism and in the sense of sympathetic magic that suffuses it—the lingering assumption that even ritualized resistance to technocratic power produces tangible effects, if only in the minds of audience members.

Moreover, in staging techno-spectacles that feature few human players, if any, mechanical performance artists dramatize the disappearance of the human element from an increasingly technological environment. Then, too, Pauline and MacMurtrie's use of remote-controlled robots, "slaved" to the physical movements of human operators, reminds us of our ever more interdependent relationship with the machine world—a relationship in which the distinction between controller and controlled is not always clear.

The mechanical performance art of these avant-garde roboticists seems to pop out of any pigeonhole into which it is forced—proof, perhaps, of its newness. Even so, it is not without precedent. In the sixties, when the union of art and science in programs such as E.A.T. (Experiments in Art and Technology) seemed to promise wondrous monsters, a number of artists experimented with kinetic sculpture or interactive multimedia, much of it computer-controlled. Nam June Paik, the grandfather of video art, created *Robot K-456*, a six-foot-tall junk heap that had toy airplane propellers for eyes and a radio speaker mouth that blared John F. Kennedy's inaugural address; as a showstopper, the robot excreted beans and twirled one of its mismatched Styrofoam breasts. Controlled (but only just) by a model aircraft radio transmitter, K-456 once tottered out of a gallery, flapping its arms and menacing passersby ("One of your sculptures is walking down Fifty-seventh Street," reported an agitated gallery-goer).

A more recent parallel exists in the work of the British roboticist Jim Whiting, whose pop-eyed automata and ghostly, dancing shirts made the 1984 video to Herbie Hancock's instrumental "Rockit" an instant classic. Brought to life by computer-controlled pneumatic systems, Whiting's robots move with the pixilated jerkiness of characters in an old Rotoscope cartoon. Some have realistically rendered faces and are clad in formal attire. Other, less fortunate relatives are legless amputees or, sadder still, lone, writhing limbs. Seen in an art gallery installation, these humanoid mechanisms stir mingled emotions—pity, whimsy, childlike fascination, and in the case of the disembodied legs that dangle from overhead supports, fear. Kicking in midair, they cross the floating dance of a marionette with the frantic jig of a hanged man.

Robotics hobbyists are kindred spirits as well. Organized by the sculptor David Santos, the Motorola engineer Alex Iles, and the designer jeweler Craig Sainsott, the Austin-based Robot Group began as a loose confederation of artists, engineers, and basement putterers and has evolved into an eighteen-member nonprofit organization. "I believe strongly in cultural robotics, robots that are works of art as well as technological marvels," says Santos, in the group's video press kit. "The sculpture of the future will be interactive, intelligent; it'll walk, it'll talk, it'll fly." Sainsott and his wife Charlene have made Santos's prediction a reality, after a fashion: Powered by pneumatics and controlled by computer, their Shrinking Robot Heads—mechano-musicians fashioned from old springs, wok lids, bicycle wheels, and shock absorbers—are a heavy metal group in the literal sense.

Sainsott, Iles, and the computer programmer Bill Craig are working on the Mark IV, a fourteen-foot, silver-skinned blimp that scuds along, steered neither by wind nor human whim but by the two bidirectional motors that drive its propellers and its own robotic brains. In its automatic mode, the blimp uses sophisticated computer programs such as neural networks that pilot the flying machine with the aid of sonar data collected during training flights. "We don't want to do robots with a point," says Iles, "because robots with a point are boring. If you forget about having a point, then you get stuff like this."[2]

Robot Wars, the mechanical mêlée that erupted in San Francisco in August 1994, catapulted do-it-yourself robotics into the public eye. The event, which was covered by the national media, pitted homemade, radio-controlled combatants against each other, among them a nasty little contraption with high-pressure spikes and a gas-powered saw, a hundred-pound robot modeled on a World War I tank, and the Master, a buzz saw on wheels. Marc Thorpe, one of the event's organizers, has high hopes for future Robot Wars: "Once you add the element of combat and survival [to cyberpunk low-tech], you are into football fan territory, which is a huge audience."[3]

Analogs in art history and grassroots robotics notwithstanding, the work of Pauline, MacMurtrie, and Goldstone sits most comfortably in the tradition of robot theater. Historically, robotics and dramatics are intertwined: The word *robot* itself was introduced into popular usage in a theatrical production—the Czech playwright Karel Capek's 1921 science fiction play, *R.U.R = Rossum's Universal Robots*—and the earliest known robots were performing machines, wonderworks born of science and sorcery, calculation and incantation.

Hero of Alexandria, a Greek engineer who lived in the first century A.D., is believed to have built a mannequin theater in which the god Bacchus sprayed wine from his staff while bacchantes danced. In the late Middle Ages, mechanized mannequins began appearing on clock towers. The Strasbourg clock was renowned for its elaborate "jackwork," or moving statues. Every day, at noon, the clock's cast-iron rooster crowed three times in remembrance of the apostle Peter's denial of Jesus.

None of these devices compared, however, with the clockwork automata of eighteenth-century roboticists. France's Jacques de Vaucanson was famed for his gilded copper duck, first exhibited in 1738. Goethe, Voltaire, and other leading lights in Europe's intelligentsia gaped at this miraculous contraption, which quacked, gobbled grain from its keeper's hand, flapped its wings, and excreted droppings. The *Scribe*, built in 1772 by the Swiss clock and watchmaker Pierre Jaquet-Droz and his son Henri-Louis, was no less astonishing. Set in motion, a life-size barefoot boy seated at a desk would dip his quill pen in an inkwell, shake it twice, and write a

preprogrammed text, moving to the next line when necessary. The autom-
aton's eyes followed the moving pen, giving it an astonishingly lifelike air.
Among the *Scribe's* repertoire of famous phrases was Descartes' axiom, "I
THINK, THEREFORE I AM."

Mechanisms that counterfeit life continue to captivate the human
imagination. Millions have their first close encounter with robots in a
Disney theme park, where creepily realistic, computerized characters perform in revues like the Enchanted Tiki Room, a Polynesian fantasia populated by Audio-Animatronic birds, flowers, and tribal masks that talk and
sing. (*Audio-Animatronic* is Disneyspeak for the technology used in electronically animated robots whose sound tracks, issuing from hidden speakers,
are synchronized with their movements.)

Traditionally, performing machines, from the mechanical mannequins of centuries past to today's corporate image ads disguised as kitsch
diversions, have celebrated the status quo. The mechanical spectacles
fabricated by the underground technologists profiled in this chapter question the underlying assumptions of mainstream engineering, consumer
culture, the art world, and the rest of what Ross has called "the military-
industrial-entertainment complex."

"We're just trying to do a theater with machines," says Pauline, as if
to allay any fears. He flashes a toothy, conspiratorial grin. "You have to
provide entertainment value."

Mark Pauline: Heavy Metal Theater of Cruelty

Mark Pauline has a firm handshake.

Which is remarkable, since his right hand has only three fingers,
two of which are suspiciously stubby. Odd bumps pebble the heel of his
hand; a wad of misshapen flesh bulges between his thumb and first digit. It is
the hand of a monster, attached to a man.

Pauline's fingers are, in fact, not fingers at all, but transplanted toes.
He lost three fingers and a thumb in 1982 while working on a rocket motor
for one of his shows. The propellant exploded, hurling Pauline several feet. "I
was lying on the ground and blood went in a sheet of red over my eyes," he
recalls. "I . . . looked at my hand, 'cause [it] felt funny, and all I could see
was the bones."[4]

Surgeons were able to reattach one relatively undamaged finger, patch up the mangled palm with a flap of skin, and improvise new fingers with a pair of Pauline's toes. Pauline isn't as dexterous with his right hand as he used to be, but fortunately for him, he's left-handed. More recently, he and Joseph Rosen, a reconstructive plastic surgeon, have discussed the possibility—still science fiction—of one day replacing Pauline's maimed hand with that of a healthy donor. In another future imagined by Rosen, the artist would be fitted with a bionic limb whose microcircuitry would translate nerve impulses into electrical signals, allowing Pauline to manipulate powerful robotic fingers as easily as he once moved his own.

Mark Pauline's saga has all the makings of a gothic horror story set in a grease-caked machine shop: a rogue technologist challenges the Fates and loses his right hand—the hand that symbolizes logic and rationality, in Jungian psychology—to a thunderbolt of divine retribution. He is a distant relative of Dr. Frankenstein, who only narrowly escaped death at the hands of the monster he jolted to life, and close kin to Rotwang, the industrial necromancer in Fritz Lang's *Metropolis,* whose black glove conceals a hand shriveled by some experiment gone horribly wrong.

He shares cultural DNA, as well, with Dr. Adder, the splatterpunk surgeon with the (literal) firearm in K. W. Jeter's cyber-horror novel of the same name. Adder sports a flashglove, a fearsome psychic blaster designed to be grafted onto the stump of a futuristic executioner, whose forearm must be amputated to accommodate it. He has been invaded, bodily, by technology. More and less than human, he straddles nature and the unnatural; his synthetic arm, like Ahab's whalebone peg leg, magnifies spiritual flaws even as it masks physical deformities. At one point, Jeter steps back from the narrative to consider the steely, death-dealing prosthetic hand as a "minor archetypal image of the twentieth century . . . representing [a] fascination with the artifacts of destruction, the desire to make them part of oneself, [and] the fear of those who have succeeded in that."[5]

Mark Pauline's art, which very nearly cost him his hand, documents such fears and fascinations. SRL spectacles address the interpenetration of meat and machinery that is central to cyberculture, underscoring Marshall McLuhan's perception that "technologies are self-amputations of our own organs." McLuhan argued that "physiologically, man in the normal use of technology (or his variously extended body) is perpetually modified by it and in turn finds ever new ways of modifying his technology."[6] Having extended ourselves through "auto-amputation," we become whole again by reintegrating our technologies into our physiologies: the toolmaker becomes one with his tools. "Man becomes, as it were, the sex organs of the machine world," McLuhan wrote, "enabling it to fecundate and to evolve ever new forms."[7] The postmodern theorist Manuel De Landa takes up McLuhan's thread when he portrays the human technologists engineering machine evolution as "industrious insects pollinating an independent species of machine-flower that simply [does] not possess its own reproductive organs."[8]

Fittingly, Mark Pauline's first venture into mechanical performance was called *Machine Sex* (1979). Framing social commentary with absurdist humor, the artist critiqued the jingoism engendered by the late seventies oil crisis in mordant, existential terms. Dead pigeons dressed as Arabs were shredded by a spinning blade while the Cure's "Killing an Arab," a fashionably gloomy pop song inspired by Albert Camus's *The Stranger*, blasted at mind-numbing volume.

Pauline had moved to San Francisco in 1977, shortly after receiving an art degree from Eckerd College in St. Petersburg, Florida. Bored with the conventional art world, he had embarked on a series of creative defacements that involved altering billboards to reveal their subliminal messages. Billboard alteration, to Pauline, was media-smart anti-art—"a way for me to get ideas out in public . . . [where] more people would see [my] work than if it were in a little room with clean walls and perfect lighting and 'ambience.' "[9]

He soon concluded, however, that billboard banditry didn't pack enough wallop. Casting about for a harder-hitting medium, he noticed the ready availability of broken-down or discarded machinery in the city's industrial district. "San Francisco at that point was in a state of industrial decay," recalled Pauline, in a *Re/Search* magazine interview. "I thought, 'That's *it*—there's all these places with abandoned machines. I know how to do technical, mechanical work. . . . I know how to stage a theatrical performance—I learned that in school. . . . maybe it's possible to actually have some fun and really do something new.' "[10]

A self-taught mechanic, Pauline had spent the years between high school and college working on semitrailers, building aircraft target robots and missile launchers at Florida's Eglin Air Force base, and welding pipe in the Santa Barbara oil fields. Unlike many artists, he felt an affinity with technology. "Creative people have never had this kind of industrial equipment and machinery; it's always been denied them," he told an interviewer. "It's all tied in with . . . this idealistic, romantic 19th century notion that creative people are these frail, delicate, spiritual shells that are about to flit away and evaporate at any minute, lest we turn our backs on their pitiful, washed-out efforts. So another part of my intention was to disavow that notion and do something really intense. Today, the main option people have for expressing themselves powerfully is through machines."[11]

Machine Sex caught the attention of San Francisco's avant-garde community. In 1982, Matt Heckert became a member of SRL, followed shortly thereafter by Eric Werner. Heckert was a self-taught mechanic who had logged long hours hot-rodding the family car; Werner had worked at oil fields in Wyoming and aerospace firms in Orange County, California. Both had attended the San Francisco Art Institute.

From 1982 until 1988, the trio staged thirteen confrontational, increasingly ambitious stunts. (In '87 and '88, respectively, Werner and Heckert left SRL to pursue solo careers.) *A Cruel and Relentless Plot to Pervert the Flesh of Beasts to Unholy Uses* (1982), which took place in San Francisco, crossed an antivivisectionist's worst nightmare with a taxidermist's wildest dream. The show made dramatic use of the "organic robots" that have earned SRL the undying wrath of animal rights activists: the grotesque Mummy-Go-Round, a carousel fitted with desiccated animal cadavers, the maws of its mummified riders frozen in silent snarls, and a machine incorporating the remains of a dog, mounted on an armature and anchored to a radio-controlled cart. Actuated, the dog-machine lunges forward, its head spinning in ghoulish imitation of cartoon violence.[12]

"The use of dead animals started out as a vaccine to keep audiences from strolling down that easy road of Disneyfication that beckons whenever they see any kind of mechanical puppet show," explains Pauline. "It's distinctive because you know it isn't putty or rubber, unlike Hollywood gore, which is the only other place people see special effects that remind them of the delicacy of the human form turned inside out."

Deliberately False Statements: A Combination of Tricks and Illusions Guaranteed to Expose the Shrewd Manipulation of Fact (1985), also mounted in San Francisco, was a gleeful Armageddon. The Screw Machine, a fourteen-hundred-pound radio-controlled robot, scooted along on corkscrew treads, seizing hapless devices with its hydraulic arm and dashing them to the ground with screw-popping force. The Walk-and-Peck Machine, designed and built by Heckert, scuttled about on beetle legs and spiked wheels, raining blows on other machines with its bird-beaked armature. Dragging himself shudderingly forward on spidery metal arms, the Sneaky Soldier conjured the image of a dying GI, disemboweled by a land mine, with horrifying realism.

Misfortunes of Desire: Acted Out at an Imaginary Location Symbolizing Everything Worth Having (1988), described by Pauline as "SRL's *Paradise Lost*," was held in the parking lot of New York's Shea Stadium. Set against a hastily erected Eden replete with palm trees and flowerbeds, the show made use of the one-ton Walking Machine, an enormous, crate-shaped, four-legged rover. The twenty-foot-long Inchworm, a nasty-looking vehicle whose saber-toothed jaws give it the look of a giant Venus flytrap, was also featured. When the pace threatened to drag, a flamethrower that spat forty-foot tongues of fire kept things lively. From time to time, a Shock Wave Cannon let loose with a thunderous boom that shook windows and jiggled innards.

The events staged by SRL are war games in the literal sense—a combination of killing field and carnival midway, meant to explode media myths about surgical strikes and collateral damage in an entertaining fashion. Always oblique, often open-ended, Pauline's Circus Machinus lends itself to multiple, sometimes contradictory interpretations. It does not so much critique our relationship with technology as crystalize it. SRL's theater of operations can be seen as a meditation on the gamelike nature of military strategy, an object lesson in the theatrical unreality of war, or a black comedy about arms proliferation. Partaking equally of the madhouse and the fun house, SRL performances produce a queasy mixture of horror and hilarity. "I make weapons to tell stories about weapons," says Pauline. "SRL shows are a satire of kill technology, an absurd parody of the military-industrial complex."

He and his dozen-odd, mostly male coworkers have stockpiled an arsenal in the machine shop where they live and work, on the outskirts of San Francisco's Mission District. One device, an electromagnetic rail gun, can liquefy a metal bar and send the molten blob streaking through the air, to explode on impact. "SRL's answer to George Bush's call for 'a thousand points of light,' " the artist deadpans.

SRL is at work on human-sized robots called Swarmers whose group behavior is governed by an artificial life program running on their onboard computers. The program, which the SRL software engineer Raymond Drewry based on code written by MIT programmers, is similar to those used to create "flocking" effects in computer animation—schools of fish, clouds of falling leaves. To date, SRL has completed four Swarmers—the minimum number required for the robots to exhibit emergent behavior. Each is equipped with an emitter-detector device; the program instructs it to move toward whichever machine is nearest, but as soon as it's within a certain distance of the other Swarmer, it beats a hasty retreat. Pauline describes the aggregate effect as "this weird behavior where they clump together, swarming around." He calls the manic machines "a response to the increased influence mob behavior has had in world events."

The Low-Frequency Generator, a mobile, radio-controlled, reaction jet engine, is modeled after the V-1 buzz bomb whose banshee shriek struck terror in Londoners during World War II. "We ran it and people heard it almost twelve miles away," says Pauline, with relish. "They had stories on the evening news asking anybody with information about the strange reverberations felt throughout the Bay Area to call the police. You can stand next to this thing and what it does to your brain is just . . . *sublime.* You feel as if there are rats in your chest. It shakes your eyeballs so much that they black out and come on again forty-five times per second, creating a strobe effect. It's the sort of phenomenon that doesn't exist anywhere else on Earth."

Shortly after the Persian Gulf War, SRL built a teleoperated high-pressure air launcher that uses a blast of pressurized CO_2 to shoot a projectile with brute force. Teleoperation, defined by the technology journalist Howard Rheingold as "the human experience of seeing out of the eyes of a machine, and using natural gestures to direct machines to manipulate the physical world," was developed for military applications such as remote-controlled weaponry and industrial uses in undersea oil rigs, nuclear power plants, and other environments hostile to human workers.[13] When a teleoperator moves his computer-tracked head, the head of a distant robot "slaved" to his motions swivels correspondingly; when the operator gestures

Smart Bar. *Photo: SKID*

Timothy Leary at "Shiva's Erotic Banquet" rave, 1992. © *1992 Don Lewis*

R. U. Sirius. © *1993 Bart Nagel*

Mondo 2000. © *1993 Bart Nagel*

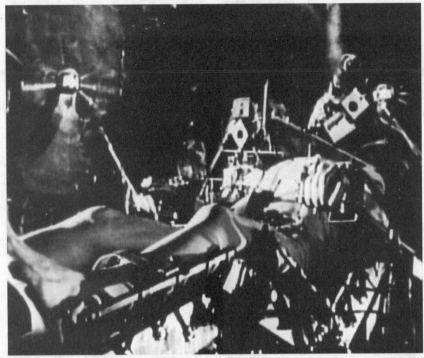

Disassembly line: video for "Happiness in Slavery," by Nine Inch Nails. Directed by Trent Reznor and Jonathan Reiss, featuring Bob Flanagan. © 1992 *Nothing / TVT / Interscope Records.*
Courtesy of Nothing / TVT / Interscope Records.

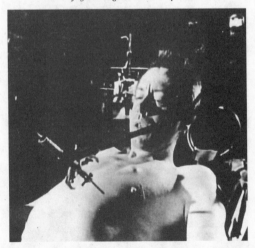

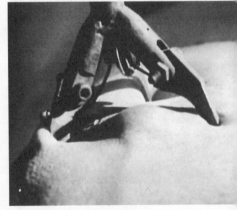

David Myers with Feedback Machine.
Photo: Judith Norma

Elliott Sharp. *Photo: Hendrik Lietman*

Mark Trayle with PowerGlove.
Photo: Jim Block

Front Line Assembly. © *1995 The All Blacks B.V.*
Used by permission of Roadrunner / Third Mind Records.

Matt Heckert and Mark Pauline of Survival Research Laboratories. *Photo: Bobby Neel Adams*

Pauline amid mechanical mayhem, with the Inchworm at left, the Inspector in the foreground, and the Walking Machine at right. © *1995 SRL*

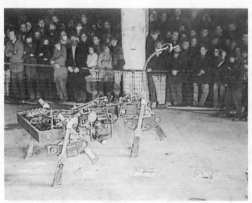

The Running Machine in *The Deliberate Evolution of a War Zone: A Parable of Spontaneous Structural Degeneration* (1992). © *SRL / Gladsjo.*

The Big Arm in *Illusions of Shameless Abundance: Degenerating into an Uninterrupted Sequence of Hostile Encounters* (1989). *Bobby Neel Adams / Sixth Street Studios*

The Walking Machine. © *1995 SRL*

The Big Arm and the Inchworm in *An Original Machine Performance Tailored Especially for the City of Copenhagen* (1988). © *1995 Cati Laporte*

SRL's Medusa breathes fire (with the aid of a V-1 jet engine) in *A Carnival of Misplaced Devotion: Calculated to Arouse Resentment for the Principles of Order* (1990). © *1995 Kimric Smythe*

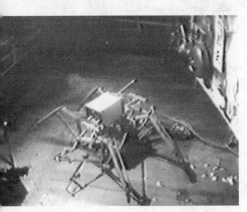

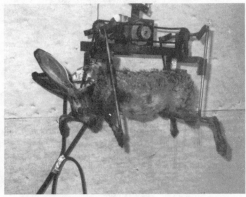

Guinea pig–controlled walking machine in a 1985 installation at New York's AREA nightclub. © *SRL / Jonathan Reiss*

Rabot. © *1995 Mark Sangerman*

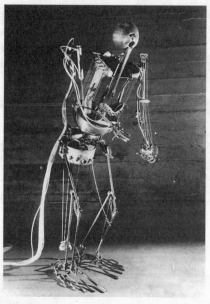

Chico MacMurtrie with Taiko Drummer.

String Body. *Photo:Douglas Adesko*

Photo:Douglas Adesko

MacMurtrie teleoperating the Tumbling Man by means of a radio-transmitting suit.

Photo:Tom Erikson

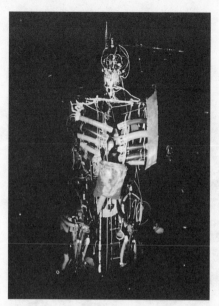

Trigram's 20-foot-tall "Metal Mother."
© *1995 Kurt Prasse*

"Overconsumption Man" and pneumatically powered robotic trees in *The Trees Are Walking*. Photo: *Sixth Street Studio*

Brett Goldstone with Steam Car Mark III.
Photo: *Sixth Street Studio*

Water-Powered Vehicle. © *1995 Mark Fleming*

"Big Bicycle Bird," "Water Wheel Bird," and, in foreground, "Beach Chair Bird," in *Birdland*. *Photo: Rusty Reniers*

"Water Wheel Bird." © *1995 Brett Goldstone*   "Beach Chair Bird." © *1995 Brett Goldstone*

with hands clad in motion-sensing virtual reality gloves, the robot's manipulators move in tandem.

The operator of SRL's air launcher wears a lightweight armature
that rests on his shoulders; its visor is equipped with two Hi8 video camera
viewfinders that fit into the operator's eyes with eyecups, immersing the
operator in a stereoscopic projection of what two video cameras mounted
on the barrel "see." The headmount is connected to a servo system that
enables the barrel of the launcher to follow the wearer's head movements.

"The machine fires a beer can filled with concrete, about eighty
grams of high explosive, and a contact detonator at about 550 feet per
second," says Pauline. "You've got an ergonomic controller that allows you to
push these buttons that you feel with the sweep of your thumb, locking the
gun down once you've acquired the target. There's a crosshair at your focal
point about four feet away and when you line up the target with that, you
fire, and it just *obliterates* it."

Prolonged submersion in the air launcher's headmounted viewing
system gives rise to the experience known as "telepresence," the out-of-body
sensation that occurs when the gap between sense perception and simulated
reality (or, in this case, live video images of the actual surroundings) is
sufficiently narrow that the user is convinced that he is *there*—immersed in
the virtual world (or one with the remote-controlled device). "The depth
perception is incredible, and once you get all the adjustments right, you just
sink into it," says Pauline. "You start to imagine your body in different ways,
just like you do when you're in an isolation tank; [the technology] becomes
transparent because of the comfort level, which is the key feature in any of
these input devices. Once you achieve transparency, interesting things start
to occur. It doesn't take much, because the mind is . . . actively trying to
meld with anything. . . . The virtual reality display couples the operator
more closely to the machine. It feels like your head is mounted on the
machine, like you're riding on top of the missile."

In SRL performances, the gun-mounted video cameras project the
view to a kill seen by the goggle-equipped teleoperator onto a large screen
positioned near the audience. The green phosphor imagery relayed by
cameras mounted on smart bombs during the Gulf War comes immediately
to mind. Watching "the pornography of destruction through [SRL's] eyes"
(Pauline's words), spectators are reminded of their wartime role as living

room voyeurs, and of the numbing unreality of history's first "virtual" war—
a made-for-TV miniseries introduced by punchy logos and pumped-up,
martial music reminiscent of trailers for Hollywood blockbusters.

"I'm going to use the air launcher for lectures," says Pauline. "I'll
show how it could be used to destroy the federal infrastructure in the same
way that they talked about destroying the infrastructure of Iraq." A tight,
mirthless smile flits across his face. "It's a prank."

If so, it's a prank in the Molotov cocktail sense of the word, a gag
designed to blow up in society's face. In Pauline's hands, rail guns,
Swarmers, low-frequency generators, and teleoperated air launchers are
actors in a dark farce that has grim fun with the notion of a bloodless
"smart" war sold to the American public by a dukes-up president and a
cheerleading media.

The Persian Gulf War was portrayed, at the time, as an unmitigated
success brought about by high-tech weaponry. "From a technological point
of view," writes John A. Barry, "the war was a testing ground for 'smart
weapons' such as the Patriot and Tomahawk missiles that had never been
tested in battle and were in danger of losing funding from the Pentagon.
Their apparent success under actual fighting conditions breathed new life
into them and prompted commentators to note that this war was also the
first 'technology war.' "[14]

Unfortunately, the official reading was later exposed as a Nintendo
fantasy. The bulk of the damage done to the enemy was inflicted not by
"Scud-busting" Patriots but by disappointingly "dumb" bombs. John R.
MacArthur, who calls the smart/dumb discrepancy "one of the biggest
untold stories of the Gulf war," reports that after the war

> the Air Force announced that laser- and radar-guided bombs
> and missiles made up just 7 percent of all U.S. explosives
> dropped on Iraq and Kuwait. The other 93 percent were conven-
> tional "dumb" bombs, dropped primarily by high-flying B-52s
> from the Vietnam era.[15]

Nonetheless, as MacArthur noted on WNYC radio's May 16, 1993,
broadcast of On the Media program, "If you watched the coverage—such as it
was—you got the impression that every bomb was a smart bomb hitting a

machine." TV's portrayal of the Gulf War as a video game in which Patriots knocked Scuds out of the air and laser-guided missiles blew up the built environment recalls the World War II propaganda cartoon *Victory through Air Power*. Created for the Department of Defense by Disney, the animated short was intended to demonstrate the effectiveness of large-scale strategic bombing. The critic James Agee was disturbed by its portrayal of warfare as a bloodless struggle between anthropomorphized weaponry:

> I noticed, uneasily, that there were no suffering and dying enemy civilians under all those proud promises of bombs; no civilians at all, in fact. . . . this victory-in-a-vacuum . . . is so morally simple a matter . . . of machine-eat-machine.[16]

A little less than half a century later, the fantasy of trading in the grimy, disorderly bedlam of war for a "morally simple" clash between good and evil automata bubbled up again, in official fictions about a "clean" war. Unfortunately, the Gulf War was anything but clean when viewed up close: The deadly rain of bombs that buried fleeing Iraqi troops on the Basra road, shortly before the cease-fire, left a thirty-mile column of crumpled vehicles and flame-broiled corpses.

The argument is sometimes made that a war fought entirely by machines would save human lives. When I asked MIT roboticist Rodney Brooks if he was troubled by the possibility, however remote, that his machines might end up on a robotic battlefield, he voiced this very opinion. "A battle fought entirely by robots would be sort of nice, wouldn't it?" said Brooks. "It seems a much more humane way of settling differences. There's certainly interest in any way of conducting battle that limits casualties on our side, which is a very humanistic point of view from the perspective of the brass."

The argument seems reasonable, although the word "humane" strikes a sour note in such an inhuman context. Nonetheless, one might respond: Wouldn't diplomatic negotiation be more humane still? And given that war, the ultimate madness, springs from the collapse of reason, isn't there an inherent absurdity in the notion of a "safe," "rationalized" war? Shouldn't nations whose technological sophistication is sufficient to produce smart, autonomous, robot weapons be intellectually capable of reasoning their way out of armed conflict?

Nonetheless, the pernicious fiction of a smart war exhibits a curious half-life. It lives on in articles such as the enthusiastic feature on the automated battlefield of the future that appeared in *Compute* magazine a few months after the war ended. One photo depicted the Fire Ant, a teleoperated "smart assassin" under development at Sandia National Laboratories in Albuquerque, New Mexico. The squat buggy is guided to its post, parked and armed by a remote human operator viewing the surroundings via a small TV camera perched on top of the Ant. When its sensors detect an enemy vehicle, the robotic vehicle locks onto the target and fires a six-inch armor-piercing slug at sixty-six hundred feet per second. A second photo showed the nasty results of the Fire Ant's sting: an M-47 tank consumed by flames. "Each of the robots shown in the accompanying photographs exists . . . to keep people out of harm's way," assured the author.[17] Automation makes the world safe for robo-war.

Dreams of hunter-killer machines and robo-soldiers in armored exoskeletons are not new. In 1919, the trailblazing inventor Nikola Tesla envisioned a Jules Verne war fought by intelligent machines called "telautomata." Writing in *Science and Invention,* the pulp editor Hugo Gernsback celebrated Tesla's "veritable war of science" where "machines only will meet in mortal combat."[18] A half-century later, General William C. Westmoreland, then chief of staff of the U.S. Army, predicted, "On the battlefield of the future, enemy forces will be located, tracked and targeted almost instantaneously through the use of data-links, computer-assisted intelligence evaluation and automated fire control. I see battlefields on which we can destroy anything we locate through instant communications and almost instantaneous application of . . . lethal firepower."[19] In 1971, a *San Francisco Chronicle* writer told a cautionary tale about a hardwired war world, "a manless, foolproof, giant lethal pinball machine out of which no living thing could ever escape." The author warned that "the entire world, if wired right, could become a great maze of circuitry and weaponry, a jungle from which those who walk off the straight paths from home to store would be immediately and totally eliminated."[20] The nightmare battlefield of *Terminator 2,* a rubble-strewn Golgotha stalked by red-eyed, stainless-steel manhunters, seems bloodcurdlingly near.

Before Operation Desert Storm, the PBS science series *Nova* aired a segment on smart weapons, titled "Killing Machines." It included an interview with Tom Clancy, an author of popular techno-thrillers whose remarks account for the program's spookiest moments. "One of the things about smart weapons that people don't think about very much is the psychological factor," said Clancy, with a thin, mechanical smile. "It is one thing to be hunted by a man who has a wife and children and dreams and ideas. It is another thing entirely to be hunted by a machine that doesn't care that you're a living person with dreams and hopes and a sweetheart. It just knows that you're something it wants to kill. That is truly scary."

Scarier still is the realization that Clancy's comments, positioned as fact, sound like science fiction. They bear a disquieting resemblance to the doomy monologue delivered by Kyle Reese, a robot-killing street fighter in *The Terminator*. "It can't be bargained with," says Reese, of his mechanical adversary. "It can't be reasoned with, it doesn't feel pity or remorse or fear and it absolutely will not stop, ever, until you are dead."

As the credits to the *Nova* episode roll, a nagging question remains: If these things are so scary, why does Clancy smile? Perhaps it is because he, like Pauline, finds death technology terrifying but fascinating. The android gunslinger in *Westworld* or the homicidal robot in the cult film *Hardware* fascinate because they are graven images come to life, clockwork contraptions born of human ingenuity. And they terrify for precisely that reason: they are inhuman, ticking things, unconcerned that the petrified creature frozen in the crosshairs of the laser scope is "a living person with dreams and hopes and a sweetheart." Like the eerie Stealth bomber, with its devilfish silhouette, or the locustlike Apache helicopter, predatory machines dredge memories from the collective unconscious—man-eating beasts, angry gods.

Lastly, such devices are erotic, in a necrophilic way. On their matte black, inscrutable surfaces, we inscribe our death fetish, our delicious fear of the unknown. In the Western, Christian tradition, the human subject is affirmed by its boundaries, but it is paradoxically those same boundaries that isolate the island self, separated on all sides by a limitless gulf between it and all that is not it. "We are discontinuous beings, individuals who perish in isolation in the midst of an incomprehensible adventure, but we yearn for our lost continuity," writes Georges Bataille, in *Erotism: Death and Sensuality*.[21] Thus the duality of death, which promises to return us to that continuity—the womb, where we were at one with the nurturing envelope that was our cosmos—by way of the tomb, which threatens to snuff the self out forever.

The sex act, in which we risk individual dissolution for the ecstasy of fusion, is similarly ambiguous. The cultural critic Claudia Springer has noted the "deathlike loss of self . . . associated with sexual pleasure," an ambiguity made explicit by the French euphemism for the postorgasmic fainting spells some lovers suffer from: *la petite mort* ("the little death").[22] In the novels of William Burroughs, this ambiguity mushrooms into an unresolvable conflict that goes to the heart of human sexuality: In *The Ticket That Exploded,* intercourse is an untenable "arrangement whereby two entities attempt to occupy the same three-dimensional coordinate points."[23] Or, put more poetically on the following page, "Death *is* orgasm *is* rebirth *is* death in orgasm."[24]

The necrophilic fantasy of surrendering oneself to devouring machines that "can't be reasoned with," like the techno-masochist in "Happiness in Slavery," conceals the ultimate bid for Bataille's "lost continuity": the ritual sacrifice of the integrated, self-reflective consciousness without which Western instrumental reason could not exist. Human sacrifice, argues Bataille, is suffused with a "religious eroticism which is concerned with the fusion of beings with a world beyond everyday reality."[25] He who sacrifices "is free, free to throw himself suddenly *outside of himself.*"[26]

Pauline, a shoot-from-the-hip philosopher, is suspicious of high-flown punditry. But he acknowledges the apparent contradiction of a social satirist seduced by military-industrial technology; there is an ambiguity, he concedes, at the heart of his critique of killing machines. "I feel a certain fascination with these devices," he allows. "They're very extreme, very intense, and historically, they've always horrified—and fascinated—people. On the other hand, I don't make weapons that kill. I would *never* be part of the military, which in my opinion is one of the most screwed-up institutions around."

SRL performances, in which suicidal machines hurtle into each other or consecrate themselves to the flames, can be read as a critique of the permanent war economy the United States has maintained since World War II. "In every year from 1951 to 1990," asserts Seymour Melman, "the Defense Department budget has exceeded the combined net profits of all American corporations. The Pentagon uses 75 percent of the federal government's research and development funds, has more employees than the rest of the government put together and has machinery assets that dwarf those of many corporations."[27]

To Pauline, the arms race is a missed opportunity for combustible fun. "Once [machines] get specialized to the point where they're killing machines," he says, "they're a lot less interesting. I mean, what if even a little of the money that went into developing a fighter jet went into developing a really bizarre machine that did amazing things, something people could be part of? Technology is supposed to make life more interesting, and I honestly believe that it can, although other things usually get in the way, like making money or projecting political power."

For some, however, Pauline's aesthetic, equal parts machismo and *macchinismo,* affirms the very technology worship he insists his work rejects. One feminist critic decried SRL's orgies of violence as "repressed male sexuality enacted through the mode of destruction."[28] Another railed against SRL's "fascination with cruelty and aggression":

> Dr. Helen Caldicott succinctly describes the phenomenon of male primitive fascination with artillery, torture and death in her recent book *Missile Envy,* where she names it as a primary cause of the escalating arms race. The members of SRL are wonderful examples of the "missile-envy" type. They are tough, strong, always sure of themselves, never admit mistakes, never show any emotion but bravado and are very dependent upon members of the same sex for peer-group support.[29]

Jim Pomeroy's analysis is particularly cogent:

> While [Pauline's] rhetorical posture is one that advocates resistance and countercultural survival in a technointensive world, his roughly choreographed spectacles deliver little more than strong cathartic climaxes through a visceral experience of violence and entropic destruction. . . . Playing to the pit and dancing on the edge, SRL begs many questions, offers few answers, and moves off the stage leaving smoldering ruins and tinny ears in its smoky wake. SRL is boys' toys from hell, cynically realizing the masculinist fantasies of J. G. Ballard and William Burroughs.[30]

Asked if his art springs from the same sophomoric impulse that led drunken conventioneer Archie Bunker to bomb pedestrians with water-filled bags, Pauline registers wry amusement. "Well, I do a very complicated and convoluted version of dropping water bombs out of windows, appropriate to a person my age," he says. "Sure, I get a thrill out of [challenging cultural assumptions], which I suppose could be categorized as an adolescent thrill, but it's only categorized that way because as people get older, they decide to be 'grown-up.' That's one of the reasons we live in a static, boring society where everything is very predictable."

Pauline bristles at the suggestion that SRL spectacles provide an outlet for the same repressed male sexuality that finds release in weekend war games in which fun-loving commandos blast away at one another with paint-filled pellets. He questions the received notion, popular among academic feminists, that technology and nature-raping, warmongering patriarchy are inextricably linked.

"This sort of activity has been falsely characterized as male," says Pauline. "I think it's sexist to say that what we do is gender-specific; it suggests that women are supposed to be passive, which is what everyone tells them, so of course most of them are. The women who work at SRL like to raise hell and they're out there in front, doing it—not standing behind the boys."

Whatever caveats they might have, few critics would deny that Pauline pioneered *the* definitive cyberpunk art form, mechanical spectacle. For many, SRL embodies the technolibertarian ethos that is the hard center of cyberpunk's otherwise fuzzy ideology and exemplifies the hybrid of cybernetic and organic, state-of-the-art and street tech that typifies the cyberpunk aesthetic. In SF circles, the group's formative influence on cyberpunk is a matter of record. Bruce Sterling and John Shirley have sung SRL's praises, and William Gibson has paid the group the highest possible tribute: The cast of characters in his novel *Mona Lisa Overdrive* includes the Mark Pauline stand-in Slick Henry, an outlaw roboticist who clangs together machines like the Judge, a clomping monstrosity armed with saws. And the renegade combat 'droid in the low-budget cyberpunk movie *Hardware* is undeniably patterned after SRL's robots, a debt obliquely acknowledged in its name (Mark 13, an obvious play on "Mark Pauline") and in the SRL videos fleetingly glimpsed on the protagonist's TV.[31]

SRL's visceral appeal requires little explication. At their best, SRL performances are motorized exorcisms, shatteringly powerful psychodramas that sit midway between Grand Guignol and *Death Race 2000*, pre-Christian rituals such as the burning of the wicker man and blue-collar rituals such as the demolition derby. The group's machines are marvels of occult engineering, scrap metal monsters that paw the air and belch ball bearings; viewed as moving sculpture, they exhibit a horror-show humor reminiscent of Edward Kienholz's installation *Roxy Madam*, an embalmed living room inhabited by a dowager with what looks like a horse skull for a head.

Even so, the muddled politics of Pauline's art remain highly problematic. SRL, a self-styled company in the theatrical as well as the economic sense—"SPECTACULAR MECHANICAL PRESENTATIONS SINCE 1979," reads Pauline's mock-serious business card—seems, on close inspection, to be much more. The group's psychodynamics invite comparison to those of a teenage gang, a hard-core band, a terrorist cell, or a crew of freebooters. There is something here of the Hell's Angels, and of Peter Pan's Lost Boys.

Pauline encourages such readings. It is no coincidence that SRL's name was taken from an advertisement in *Soldier of Fortune*, a magazine for war fans, gun nuts, and dug-in survivalists: Pauline seems to encourage the perception of himself as an anomic robopath, to use Lewis Yablonsky's coinage for "people whose pathology entails robot-like behavior and existence . . . [who are] egocentric, and without true compassion . . . [whose] existential state is ahuman."[32]

Pauline seems to cherish his memories of junior high school delinquency as a member of the Fuckers' Island Gang ("We used to wear Nazi helmets . . . and . . . have military-type maneuvers"), and has expressed a perverse fascination with convicted Watergate plumber G. Gordon Liddy, who once told a *Playboy* interviewer that he struck fear in the hearts of his non-Aryan jailmates with a lusty rendition of the "Horst Wessel Lied," the official song of the Nazi party.

Pauline shrugs. "I most certainly am not into Nazism or anything like that, although people accuse me of it because I don't disavow it. I just don't think it's that simple; everybody has those kinds of tendencies. Questioning those feelings, asking why people even have them at all, strikes me as a much more realistic reaction. SRL shows allow people to put concepts together in any number of ways. The real commentary is what you make of it. I don't believe in preempting peoples' ability to make their own decisions. To me, making an explicit political statement is basically telling people what to think, which is truly fascistic.

"Any activity that stirs things up is progressive. My job, as someone with a radical bent, is to assert my view about how things should be. I want to extend my ability to project my ideas, using devices that are exterior to myself. SRL makes the point that there are applications for technology outside the mainstream."

The attendant realization that high-tech expertise can be put to uses never imagined in government think tanks or corporate laboratories is reiterated in SRL's roll call of rogue technologists and road warriors—underground tinkerers who turn scavenged machinery to impractical, often subversive ends. "A lot of the people who come to work here feel [as if] it's not morally right for them to be using [their skills] in predictable, culturally sanctioned ways," says Pauline. "Here, they get to see their work going into strange, unpredictable things that grow in an almost organic way into the monsters that have always been in their minds but have never really had an outlet." SRL has benefited not only from the computer industry's discarded hardware, but from its "software" as well—a brain trust comprised, according to Pauline, of "disaffected military types and techies from . . . Livermore Labs, Hewlett-Packard, and Bell Northern."[33]

The electrical engineer Greg Leyh, who designs and builds the analog circuitry in SRL machines, is a typical recruit. He and Jeff Bainbridge, the resident high-energy physics expert, collaborated on a lightning-bolt generator that produces ten-foot lightning bolts. "It generates a bright, white light that even with Grade Five welding lenses leaves a burn on your retina for about five minutes," enthuses Pauline, "and the explosion is like a clap of thunder. During our 1992 show in Aurillac, France, it destroyed the computer in the generator it was hooked up to."

The thought of a ragtag band of techno-radicals possessing the know-how and wherewithal to hurl Jovian thunderbolts does not give comfort to those who prefer that such knowledge remain in the hands of the proper authorities. "Projecting power is something that artists aren't known for," says Pauline. "These cast-off devices can be used to create a new language which comments on the power structure, which is what the whole cyberpunk thing is about, anyway.

"People are frustrated. You can look at the power structure, as represented by police and politicians, and say, 'I want to kill all these people,' but if you really want to influence the nature of their power, the best thing to do is to ridicule them. I'm always encouraged when I see people doing that to the power structure; it makes me think, 'Well, it *is* possible to attack these people, you *can* hurt them really badly.' I believe in the political potency of the symbolic gesture."

Chico MacMurtrie: Toward a Green Robotics

Huddled in a capacious loft a short drive from Pauline's workshop, Chico MacMurtrie's robots look like escapees from Alexander Calder's circus. They are reminiscent, too, of the towering, gangly archetypes created in the sixties by the Bread and Puppet Theater or the antic inventions of Jean Tinguely.

True to his name, the Tumbling Man—a google-eyed acrobat with pipes for limbs—turns somersaults with gawkish grace. The prodigiously endowed Horny Skeletons are chronic self-abusers: when they fondle their perpetually erect metal members, steam whooshes out of their ears, eyes, and mouths. The twelve-foot-tall Neolithic Pneumatic Drummer, who swats his drum with stiff-armed strokes, seems a close relative of the skeletal mariachi displayed in Mexico on the Day of the Dead. String Body, an unfortunate being whose copper ball head once bobbed in a toilet, possesses an upper torso resembling a birdcage. When the robot strums the amplified strings stretched across its upper body with a rod, lyric tinklings are heard; a human handler replaces the rod with a cello bow, and the lyrist is transformed into a cellist whose savage scrapings curl hair. Chime Body has a cymbal on top of its head and countless metal chimes dangling from its frame. Raising high its drumstick, it gives itself a tremendous whack on the head, setting its loose-limbed body jingling.

Yet another drumming automaton, Drumming and Drawing Sub-human, can thump out a furious tattoo on two drums or, in a nod to Tinguely's auto-creative art machines, create abstract doodles by drawing on paper with a charcoal "finger." A third drum enables an audience participant to improvise a rhythm; once the robot's computer has analyzed the rhythm, the robot plays it back, beat for beat, then swivels to face the easel on which its sketch pad sits. The percussive pattern is fed into the machine's random drawing program, affecting the speed of the actuators that control the writing finger—"adding more randomness," as MacMurtrie puts it. "It affects both the pace and types of gestures the robot makes," says the artist. According to MacMurtrie, the nonobjective charcoal drawings cranked out by Drumming and Drawing Subhuman "make the abstract expressionist school look rather pathetic; [they look a lot like] Cy Twombly crossed with Franz Kline." When the robot completes a one-minute master-piece, it bows ceremoniously and makes a "tah-dah" gesture with its drawing arm, like a conductor flourishing his baton; the drawing falls at the feet of the audience member and the writing finger, having writ, moves on.

Pistons clicking nervously, compressed air wheezing through their pneumatic lines, MacMurtrie's creations are oddly affecting. Beset by Parkinsonian tics and crippled on occasion by an arthritic stiffness, they look as if they belong in a rest home for elderly automata. Nevertheless, a coiled energy lurks in their rattletrap forms; even the creakiest of these beings can spring into sudden, spasmodic life, given a few burps of air through the right tube.

It is no accident that they move with a flat-footed, earthbound gait that crosses the hunkered-down stance of a martial arts practitioner with the slip-sliding shuffle of a marionette. MacMurtrie—who holds a master of fine arts degree in new forms and concepts from the University of Califor-nia at Los Angeles—studied martial arts at the University of Arizona at Tucson, and maintains an ongoing interest in puppetry.

"I have no technical background whatsoever," he explains, "but, in a way, I have an advantage over engineers because I approach the making of these robots from an anatomical viewpoint. I say, 'Hey, that piston is a muscle, that universal joint is a shoulder,' and then I apply those revelations to what I know about the body. As a result, my machines aren't rigid; they're graceful in a spastic, awkward way."

In their earliest incarnation, MacMurtrie's "techno-puppets" ex-isted only as two-dimensional grotesqueries. They appeared in his painting *Breakdown of Society* as body parts littering the streets of a megalopolis fallen into anarchy. In time, they slithered off his canvases, reincarnated as painted latex skins. MacMurtrie wore them in ritualistic performances that invoked the Aztec hieratic practice of dancing in the flayed skins of sacrificial victims. "Painting just couldn't hold what I wanted to do," MacMurtrie told an interviewer. "Everything literally started breaking out of the canvas; I had more paint on my body than the canvas."[34] Soon, the skins were fleshed out with flabby padding, mounted on articulated armatures and born again as tottering, human-sized puppets in elaborate tableaux. Ultimately, they evolved into their present, robotic state.

Old Man Squatter, the first of MacMurtrie's race of machine men, was inspired by a lowly door piston acquired while the artist was completing his graduate studies in Los Angeles. "I realized that it acted like the rubber puppets I was making," he remembers. "I constructed him from junk, stripping bicycles for cables. He's held together with nuts and bolts, string and twisted wire, because I didn't know how to weld when I built him." When activated, the aged automaton rises grudgingly from its crouching position to stand erect, rolling its Ping-Pong ball eyes; one hand shakes a spear—"defending the forest against technology"—while the other taps out a *pitapat* rhythm on its amplified metal belly.

Brett Goldstone, a kinetic sculptor with whom MacMurtrie collaborated on several performances during his time at UCLA, exposed the budding roboticist to advanced pneumatics. Upon moving to San Francisco in 1988, MacMurtrie honed his newfound skills by creating the Tumbling Man. "I didn't know anything about engineering," says MacMurtrie, "but as soon as I began working with more pistons, the learning process evolved naturally. In building the Tumbling Man, I learned a tremendous amount about pneumatics and how to overcome weight and inertia. When I got through, it wasn't a somersaulting robot; it was a struggling, tumbling, acrobatic, empathic creature that had taken on a life of its own."

The Tumbling Man was eventually adapted to respond to a man-machine interface designed by MacMurtrie in collaboration with Dave Fleming, an electrical engineer at San Francisco's Exploratorium, a science museum. The interface—a suit whose joints are studded with triggering switches that relay radio signals to the robot—transforms the artist into a cross between a Tai Chi instructor and a puppet master; each of MacMurtrie's graceful, martial steps is mimicked by his chuffing, clicking doppelgänger.

MacMurtrie has added an aleatory element: pouches sewn into the joints of the suit are inflated with air, at intervals, by a computer program whose behavior has been randomized. Without warning, an arm or a leg will balloon, jouncing the artist about like a marionette. "I become a human narrator," he observes, "interacting with this robot, creating the interesting juxtaposition of a human struggling to make a machine struggle." Mac-Murtrie's use of a radio-transmitting suit to direct the movements of his jerry-built androids mirrors corporate and military experiments with tele-operation. But whereas conventional teleoperation leaves no doubt as to the absolute authority of the human operator over the remote-controlled robot, MacMurtrie uses the technology to muddle the distinction between con-troller and controlled.

The interwoven themes of power relations in a high-tech society and the use of homebuilt technology to redress social inequities recur throughout the artist's work. His Rock Thrower, a metal-and-wire sculpture that can heft and hurl fist-sized rocks with surprising accuracy, constitutes a minimanifesto on the political use of industrial detritus. "The Rock-Thrower was triggered by a picture I saw of a Palestinian woman launching this piece of stone at soldiers with shields," says MacMurtrie. "I thought, 'Here are these totally repressed people throwing rocks at this militia—they've got no chance in the world!' I decided to make an opposition machine, a humanoid device that represented the repressed masses. He can only throw about eight to ten feet, and he can't lift anything very heavy, but the quality of the gesture is really dynamic. The two universal joints on his upper hips give him a Tina Turner pelvis, which is funny as hell."

Over the years, the actuating systems employed by MacMurtrie have become increasingly sophisticated, incorporating ever greater degrees of computer control. Nearly all of MacMurtrie's current computer systems are designed by Rick Sayre, a computer programmer and electrical engineer who works as an animation scientist for Pixar, a leading-edge computer graphics production company based in Point Richmond, California. The self-described "technology wrangler" offered his services to MacMurtrie during the artist's residency at the Exploratorium; their first collaboration, a gallery performance called The Trees Are Walking, involved the animation of rusted metal trees asphyxiated by pollution. Sayre designed a motion-detecting system that allowed the audience to activate preprogrammed sequences of events; moreover, the animation was more subtly nuanced than the herky-jerky movements of MacMurtrie's earlier creations. "It was quite a breakthrough for my work," recalls MacMurtrie. "I was a mechanical sculptor before I met Rick; he gave my work the brain."

MacMurtrie and Sayre have developed a new, improved telemetry suit that enables two participants to activate the Tumbling Man, whose computer program then stores the motion sequence and plays it back–"as if to mimic [the humans]," notes MacMurtrie. The device was featured in *Trigram,* where it was used by the dancers Hannah Sim and Mark Steger to control the movements of the Subhuman, the String Body, and the Transparent Walking Body, a vacuformed plastic torso that skates along on feet equipped with casters. Performed at San Francisco's Theater Artaud in December, 1992, the multimedia spectacle derives its apt title, according to the composer Bruce Darby, from the I Ching, where it signifies "a myriad of all things." The event lived up to its name: A barking, hooting Robotic Dog-Monkey tried to decide if it was canine or simian; human percussionists assembled and played a Xylophone House made of tuned planks; and a twenty-foot-tall "metal mother" (MacMurtrie's phrase) batted her metallic eyelashes and gnashed her fearsome chompers in time with the music. At one point, the musicians clambered into her hollow chest to drum on her ribs–skinny, cylindrical drums made from curved PVC pipes with cowhide stretched over one end.

Trigram is informed by kinetic sculpture, performance art, music, robotics, and, as always, puppetry. "The machines are less like industrial robots and more like puppets," says Sayre. "Our robots are very under-constrained, which means that they flop around a lot but [if] you actuate them at the right moment, you can get behavior out of them that will really surprise you: Some of these machines that were never designed to be able to walk can actually walk. Their puppetlike quality makes them harder to control, but it also makes you empathize with them because they appear to be struggling."

MacMurtrie's discombobulated robots address the issue of life out of balance. In their computer brains, wire nerves, piston muscles, and scrap metal skeletons, we see ourselves–"thinking reeds," to borrow Pascal's phrase, rooted in a biosphere dominated and, finally, denatured by technology. "My sculptures suffer this world," writes the artist, in an unpublished statement. "They do not dominate or control. My use of compressed air to breathe life into them has much to do with the ecological [disasters] that threaten our existence. The sound and motions that are a byproduct of this [pneumatic] process echo the anguish we all feel in a world where we are deprived of the Pure by our dependence upon machines that we once controlled and that now control us."

MacMurtrie (whose surname, he claims, means "man of trees") grew up in an Irish-Mexican family in the scarred, scorched mining town of Bisbee, Arizona, where a mile-deep pit mine gutted the nearby countryside. Memories of busted lives and rusting machinery haunt his art. His is a green robotics, a mythopoeic struggle to establish an equilibrium between the ecosphere and the technosphere.

The Trees Are Walking, enacted in 1991 at San Francisco's New Langton Arts gallery, featured gnarled, metal Walking Trees that scrabbled across the exhibition space with painful slowness. Their rusty blotches alluded to acid rain, the labored panting of their pneumatic systems to air fouled by fossil fuels. Overconsumption Man, a grotesque blob swaddled in layers of foam-rubber blubber, stood in for Western consumer culture, whose appetite for burgers is implicated in the bulldozing and burning of tropical forests to provide pasture for cattle, destroying ancient ecosystems in the process. "The spirit of the Earth is frustrated by what's going on," MacMurtrie observes. "Even the trees are walking away. They're getting wiped out."[35]

Brett Goldstone: Trash Can Alchemy

Brett Goldstone, likewise, has stories to tell about the disposable society. The New Zealand native, who lives in the Highland Park neighborhood of Los Angeles, is a streetcomber. "I've always used junk because it's free and readily available," he explains, "and there's more junk here than anywhere else in the world."

Goldstone is a self-taught mechanic who acquired an art education while traveling the world, "visiting cultural sites in Europe as well as North and South America." Shortly after moving to Los Angeles, he was briefly involved in the UCLA art scene. "I soon saw the art world for the rotten thing it was," he says. "I decided to establish myself as a self-reliant artist who had nothing to do with the gallery system." He began experimenting with kinetic sculpture and completed a two-year tour of duty with SRL, helping out with three shows.

Goldstone's work has much in common with the scavenger culture of *Repo Man* and the "outsider" art of Howard Finster, the Alabaman minister who built an environmental installation called *Paradise Garden* out of bicycle parts, hubcaps, and other oddments. The robots in *Bird Land*, a 1990 sculpture performance in three tableaux, were constructed from materials found in a Dumpster.

In *Bird Land*, Goldstone used reanimated rubbish to spin a yarn about the dying biosphere. The performance, which took place in a Los Angeles parking lot, began in a long-lost Arcadia where "life was sustained without suffering" and ended in a postapocalyptic wasteland whose only inhabitants were mutant birds "able to breathe deadly gases and drink rancid water." The opening scene featured the tin-winged Water Bird with the vacuum-cleaner-tube gullet; a mural depicting a bucolic landscape provided a backdrop for a shallow, man-made lake bounded by old tires. At the edge of the lake stood a Sound Tree in full bloom, its tangled metal limbs festooned with speakers rescued from old-fashioned record players. The second, climactic scene starred Beach Chair Bird, a pair of disembodied bird legs contrived from the remains of an aluminum beach chair and a pair of lampshades. Animated by compressed air, the legs picked their way across the lake with storklike poise, transferring water from one lampshade foot to the other for ballast. "The Beach Chair Bird was able to step off-balance, giving it an uncanny, lifelike quality," says Goldstone. "Midway through its walk, oil was pumped into the water, turning the lake into a gooey morass. It eventually flipped over and lay there, twitching."

Goldstone's ecofable ended in ecocide. The last scene was dominated by Big Bicycle Bird, a gargantuan mechanimal that stood twenty or more feet tall when fully erect. Looking like Rube Goldberg's idea of an ostrich, it perched on a nest of urban waste, flanked by a mural depicting a dead world whose craggy, buttelike formations were actually petrified people. The Bird's drooping neck was cobbled together from ski poles, aluminum plates, and frying pans; an intricate system of bicycle wheels, chains, and cables, together with curtain pulleys and a servo from a hospital bed, enabled the derricklike beast to lower its head and munch on a mound of aluminum cans.

The Steam-Powered Flapping Wings, a hybrid of aeronautic technology and avian anatomy, stood nearby. The robot's tall, skinny body was a music stand; its outspread wings began life as a desk lamp. Steam from a pressure cooker set its fan turbine in motion, turning bicycle gears and causing its wings to flap.

Goldstone is a trash can alchemist who uses fire, water, and wind to transmute refuse into bird-machines that flap their wings, walk, or feast on garbage heaps. His creations have a droll, ad hoc air that makes them wholly unlike the hulking, machine-tooled devices turned out by Pauline. "I strive for that spindly, stalklike quality to counter the General Motors aesthetic of my *compadres*," says Goldstone. "It's organic, in a way, which might come from Victorian architecture. New Zealand, because of its English colonial past, has masses of . . . filigree everywhere, carved and fretted boards almost like Maori tattoos, which are in turn based on these baby ferns that have spirals."

And whereas MacMurtrie's robots, for all their ricketiness, possess hidden strength, Goldstone's always seem as if they are about to collapse in a pile of nuts and bolts. "The fact that I don't have access to sophisticated machinery is a key aspect of my work," says the artist. "I do everything in my garage workshop, using nothing more complicated than a drill press. My pieces are built completely from scratch. I do a sketch on a napkin and then stick to it rigorously. My friend, who's an engineer at the Jet Propulsion Laboratory in Pasadena, will say, 'Look, Brett, if you'd just put this piece here, the whole thing would work fine,' but *nooooo*, it must look exactly like the drawing!

"It's a tremendous technical challenge to build something using an unconventional technique. In traditional engineering, you design the machine, buy the parts, and assemble it. I fish everything I use out of Dumpsters. At one point in the building of the Big Bird, I had half the neck constructed and then no one seemed to be throwing away the particular supplies I needed until a week or so before the show. I thought I was never going to get it finished."

These days, Goldstone is busy reliving the industrial revolution, building steam-powered cars. His first, built in 1987, skimmed along on cunningly wrought wheels, its axle turned by a piston-driven transmission belt. The Steam-Powered Tricycle (1988) sports as its front wheel a tire from a construction-site crane, with two handmade metal wheels in back and a giant stovepipe of a boiler; the turbine is a bicycle wheel studded with metal paddles. The combined effect suggests a collaboration between Georges Melies, the father of science fiction cinema, and Nicolas Joseph Cugnot, the eighteenth-century engineer whose tricycle-mounted, steam-driven carriage was the first self-propelled vehicle. The 1990 Steam Car Mark III consisted of a rickety, grasshopperish body plunked on tiny wheels and propelled by a gigantic wooden wheel. And in 1991, Goldstone built a low-slung, water-powered vehicle; the water was pressurized by steam, then squeezed through a series of pipes and into a turbine, driving the machine forward.

Goldstone's interest in steam springs from power politics in the literal sense. During the early eighties, when he was staging hit-and-run robot shows, Goldstone made liberal use of outdoor outlets near gallery entrances. On one occasion, he installed a mechanized caricature of "consumer angst" in front of a particularly snooty gallery. The robot, a "3-D political cartoon" in chicken wire, lay sprawled on a TV effigy whose screen displayed metal cutouts of houses, cars, stereos, and other consumer icons. Driven by a small motor, the robot flailed in the death throes of conspicuous consumption until the peeved gallery owner pulled its plug and buried its remains in the nearest Dumpster. Unpluggable art, concluded Goldstone, was the best art.

"I got interested in steam in the mid-eighties, after working with pneumatics," he notes. "I was living in a studio that was formerly the Los Angeles boilerworks when I began conducting experiments where I would raise boilers to a fever pitch and then hide behind plate steel. Everyone told me that it was incredibly dangerous, that it couldn't be done. There are very few people who make boilers anymore; steam power is almost a lost art.

"Ironically, we still generate most of our energy with steam, with the exception of hydroelectric and solar power. It's a beautiful paradox that we use nuclear technology to generate steam in order to make electricity; it's like putting a fiberglass handle on a stone adze!"

There is glorious irony, as well, in the fact that his Victorian vehicles exist in Los Angeles, whose futuristic freeway grid, omnipresent smog, near-permanent gridlock, and toxically beautiful sunsets testify to modernity's all-consuming obsession with the automobile. Phantasmagoric contraptions, gliding elegantly on outsized wheels, Goldstone's steam cars seem to have taken a wrong turn down a cobbled street in gaslit London and emerged, somehow, at the end of the twentieth century. "L.A. has made me the artist I am," the artist nods. "Underlying all my work is the issue of mobility; everything stems from that, the conversion of energy into motion."

For Goldstone, steam power is a potent symbol of self-determination in an overdetermined technoculture. "When I build a steam engine, I'm not discussing steam, I'm discussing computers," he says. "Steam power, which introduced industrialization, is the last technology we had our hands on. I assembled my steam car with nuts and bolts and bits of steel that I found. To operate it, I light a fire beneath a closed vessel of water, open a plumbing valve, and it starts, producing ten horsepower as regularly as the sun comes up in the morning. Once, I was driving it in a performance and one of the pistons popped out of the cylinder and the push rod bent like a noodle. Now, if a chip melts in your computer, the show is over."

A triumphant gleam lights his eye. "I disconnected the rod, bent it over my knee to straighten it, put it back in, and the car ran again," says Goldstone, with unalloyed satisfaction. "*That's* the power you have to keep things moving, when you've built them yourself."

The Magic Kingdom and the Pyrotechnic Insanitarium[36]

Performing robots and articulate idols, as I noted in the introduction to this chapter, have traditionally been footmen of power and mouthpieces for authority. In ancient Egypt, the holy statue in Ammon had the power to make kings: At the appointed hour, the males in the royal family lined up before it, and the effigy tapped the next pharaoh with an outstretched arm.

Of course, such statues were not robots in the contemporary sense; they were probably jointed dolls, brought to life by steam, fire, or concealed operators–priests, perhaps–who pulled strings, worked levers, and spoke through hidden tubes that made mortal voices sound like divine thunder (Pay no attention to that man behind the curtain!). Even so, they served the same societal purpose more discreetly fulfilled by their wheelwork-driven and computer-animated descendants: the affirmation of the status quo.

Eighteenth-century automata curried favor with the crowned heads of their day: Jaquet-Droz's *Draftsman* was programmed to sketch France's King Louis XV and his ill-fated heirs, Louis XVI and Marie Antoinette. Moreover, as Michel Foucault points out, they taught lessons about the management of subjects. "The celebrated automata [of the eighteenth century] were not only a way of illustrating an organism," writes Foucault, "they were also political puppets, small-scale models of power: Frederick [the Great], the meticulous king of small machines, well-trained regiments and long exercises, was obsessed with them."[37]

Vaucanson's automata had a profound influence on the French mechanist Julien Offray de la Mettrie, who ventured beyond Cartesian dualism to argue in *L'Homme Machine* ("Man a Machine," 1748) that all life could be explained in purely materialistic terms. In conceiving of humans as clockwork contrivances whose inner workings—including their so-called spiritual and psychological dimensions—could be made to reveal themselves through a rigorous application of the scientific method, de la Mettrie paved the way for a philosophy of governance that assumed the citizenry to be utterly knowable, in an absolute sense.

To Foucault, this mechanism of social control—which he calls *panopticism*—is "constituted by a whole set of regulations and by empirical and calculated methods relating to the army, the school and the hospital, for controlling or correcting the operations of the body."[38] It is at work in the technique of "scientific management" known as Taylorism, after Frederick W. Taylor, whose time-motion studies in the early part of this century had as their goal "the radical separation of thinking from doing" in the American worker—turning the laborer, in effect, into a robot.[39] An article in a 1932 issue of the *Tri-City Labor Review* offers a glimpse inside one of Henry Ford's assembling plants:

> Every employee seemed to be restricted to a well-defined jerk, twist, spasm or quiver resulting in a flivver. I never thought it possible that human beings could be reduced to such automats.[40]

It is worth noting, at this juncture, that *robota* and *robotnik*, the Czech roots of Capek's coinage "robot," mean "forced labor" and "serf," respectively.

Industrialists came gradually to realize, however, that "human engineering" in the workplace was not enough, that their purview must be extended beyond the factory, into the cultural arena. Only a value system consonant with a consumer economy–one in which goods were not merely used, but used *up*, rendered obsolete by stylistic change– would ensure the smooth functioning of a heterogeneous workforce geared toward mass production. Corporate capitalists used advertising, its impact heightened by newly arrived technologies of reproduction and replication such as photography and chromolithography, to promote an ideology of consumption. In what advertising executive Ernest Elmo Calkins called "consumer engineering," mass-marketed images of the good life, endlessly repeated in mail-order catalogs, magazine advertisements, department store displays, billboards, and Hollywood melodramas were proffered as a seduc- tive substitute for meaningful social change.[41] Dedicated to the propo- sition that all consumers are created identical, advertising, according to Stuart Ewen, developed "as a tool of social order whose self-espoused purpose was the 'nullification' of the 'customs of ages; [to] . . . break down the barriers of individual habits.' "[42] The social critic Walter Benjamin put it poetically in his aphorism, "MASS REPRODUCTION IS AIDED ESPECIALLY BY THE REPRODUCTION OF MASSES."

That process is ongoing: even as their bolt-tightening, spot-welding counterparts have toiled on assembly lines, mass-producing consum- ables, entertainment robots have been employed as tin pitchmen, reproduc- ing consumers. Visitors to Las Vegas's Forum Shops, a theme park mall in gladiatorial drag, see the faux Roman statues around the central fountain stir and speak every hour on the hour: "Come one, come all, come forth from the mall," enjoins a beefy Bacchus, lifting a monstrous goblet of wine, at which point his fellow cloud-dwellers–Plutus, Apollo, and Venus– come to life and join in the revelry. With any luck, more than a few of the tourists who come to videotape the robots' antics will end up at the blackjack tables in nearby Caesars Palace. The robots installed by Advanced Animation in saloons at the Detroit Metro and Minneapolis–St. Paul International airports serve a similar purpose. Modeled after Cliff and Norm, the barflies in the sitcom *Cheers,* the caricatured pairs sit side by side on barstools, trading wisecracks, pretending to swill their beer, and attracting customers.

Some robots literally sing the praises of commodity futures. In Michael Moore's bitterly funny documentary, *Roger and Me*, Flint, Michigan—a company town devastated by the closing of the General Motors plant that was its economic lifeblood—squanders its dwindling financial resources on a monumentally wrongheaded tourist attraction, Auto World. In a crowning irony, the GM exhibit starred one of the unemployed undead (an auto worker who is, ironically, a robot beneath the synthetic skin) singing "Me and My Buddy," an ode to the industrial robot that rendered him obsolete.

Other robots appear in mechanical dramas that provide officially sanctioned outlets for antisocial or anticorporate sentiment, diverting such feelings away from any possible political expression, into coliseum carnage. Robosaurus, a forty-foot-tall, fire-breathing Mechagodzilla, is a hit at monster truck rallies: unfolding from its tractor-trailer traveling position, it grabs junk cars in its claws, barbecues them with its fiery breath, then chomps them flat and tosses them aside. In the eyes of Mark Hays, one of the machine's owners, Robosaurus is "the first real superhero"; it presents "the boring technology that is used in everyday devices in a creative way that stimulates interest in science and technology. . . . This is the first time children have had this level of validation of what they see on TV."

Robosaurus is an extreme variation on a theme developed more conventionally in "big-wheeler" shows and "rocket-car" races, where, according to artist/essayist Mike Kelley, "pickup trucks fitted with massive . . . tires run over and crush rows of cars. . . . In an event called a 'meltdown,' a junked car or bus is placed in the exhaust flames [of the rocket car]."[43] In an essay on SRL, Kelley draws comparisons between avant-garde machine theater and "lower-class spectacles" centered around the theatrical destruction of that totemic American technology, the automobile. "In contrast to culture-affirming, nationalistic, middle-class spectacles like holiday parades [and] football half time shows . . . there are those other events that mirror the joys of conspicuous accumulation with those of mass destruction," observes Kelley.[44]

Pauline adds, "The notion that the American public needs its pablum is really the basis of entertainment in this country. Robosaurus is *Tyrannosaurus rex* on wheels that picks up cars and eats them. Very lame. Monster truck shows are just a waste of time because all that intensity is separated from a much more interesting destiny. Everything's straight and narrow, there's no weird connotations, they don't challenge any assumptions about the culture.

"The interesting thing about demo derbies and drag races, at least in the beginning, in the fifties, was that you had people who worked in the industry—mechanics or factory workers—and after five o'clock they tried to turn their skills in a more rebellious direction. Those events represented, arguably, a healthy rebellion against what society had taught these people to be; in the fifties, the car was a subversive tool if it was turned in the right direction. But the monster truck thing, these days, has been stripped of all those associations. In fact, it's connected with far right philosophies, especially the new monster truck stuff, where they play 'The Star-Spangled Banner' and they have these big robots that they characterize as protectors of justice: Vorian, a dragster that turns into a robot that spews flame, is a cop, out there to kill bad people; it's real propaganda."

No discussion of the intertwined nature of capital, consumption, and performing machines would be complete without a visit to the Magic Kingdom. Drawing hundreds of thousands of visitors annually, Disneyland puts a grinning, mouse-eared face on a mythic America that is equal parts Goldwater conservatism, Norman Rockwellian nostalgia for turn-of-the-century idylls, and Ray Bradburyesque faith in technological progress. What is most significant about Disneyland, for our purposes, is that it revolves around robot dramas, many of which are thinly veiled corporate image advertisements: "Star Tours, Presented by M&M's Chocolate Candies," "It's a Small World, Presented by Mattel Toys"—the drumbeat of name recognition is relentless. Moreover, both of these rides are cleverly designed so that the only exit is through souvenir emporia—the "Star Trader" shop, selling Lucasfilm merchandise, and the " 'It's a Small World' Toy Shop, Presented by Mattel Toys," respectively.

Beyond their obvious function as sales pitches and public relations strategies, such attractions are part of a larger whole—the Disney theme parks, themselves a commercial for what Scott Bukatman has called a "future . . . dominated by a benign corporate sponsorship providing effective population control, abundant consumer goods, and the guarantee of technological infallibility."[45] In "the World of Motion, Presented by General Motors" in Walt Disney World's EPCOT (Experimental Prototype City of Tomorrow) Center in Orlando, Florida, every American's God-given right to choose a car of his own over the drear, suspiciously socialist alternative of public transportation is wrapped in stars and stripes: "When it comes to transportation, it's fun to be free," proclaims the accompanying jingle. After a ride consisting of a series of Audio-Animatronic tableaux purporting to be a history of transportation, visitors witness "The Bird and the Robot," a performance starring a robot toucan and a Unimate Puma 500 robotic arm, the sort often employed in automobile assembly plants. The seven-minute performance strives to disabuse spectators of what Isaac Asimov called "the Frankenstein Complex" harbored by humans who "[insist] on considering the poor machines to be deadly dangerous creatures"; the narrative assures listeners that industrial robots are their benevolent mechanical helpmates, that they should welcome the automation of dirty, dangerous factory jobs.[46] When "The Bird and the Robot" ends, the audience is herded into a showroom full of GM cars and sales representatives.

No mention is made of the fact that automation displaces or at the very least "de-skills" humans, reducing human laborers who work side by side with machine assemblers in computer-controlled manufacturing plants to button-pushers or parts-stackers. Nor do we hear of the "technostress" that sometimes follows in the wake of automation. A 1986 series in a Japanese newspaper on "The Isolation Syndrome of Automation" told of workers in a state-of-the-art factory that used "automated . . . tools and robotized machining centers." According to the author, several employees

> began to complain that they "felt like robots" as they operated
> and programmed the automated machinery during the day; one
> local parent complained that all his son did all day long was push
> a button.[47]

Inhumane as it is, the fate of the button-pusher—being bored to death—is certainly preferable to that of Bob Williams, an overseer who was killed when a twenty-five-hundred-pound robot slammed into him in Ford's Michigan Casting Center auto plant. Robot manufacturers' now-familiar argument that "unattended systems" have the potential to save lives must be weighed against the memories of workers killed by factory robots in industrialized nations. An *Omni* article about Williams's death chronicles the action brought by his survivors against Litton Industries, the company that manufactured Ford's automated system.

> What became apparent as [the attorney for Williams's family]
> went over the . . . case was that there was nothing venal in-
> volved. But there was a form of mechanistic indifference, a
> neglect of the soul in favor of the passion for a perfect machine.
> The god was productivity. Humans were meant to serve it.[48]

Finally, the encomiums to automation of "The Bird and the Robot" neglect to inform the audience that reskilled workers who find positions in data entry will not necessarily be free of occupational hazards: "terminal illnesses" such as eyestrain, back problems, repetitive strain injury, and possibly even cancer and miscarriage resulting from the electromagnetic fields generated by VDTs are well-known by-products of the silicon sweatshop.

Then, too, the ease with which computers facilitate panoptical surveillance and information-age Taylorism sounds a sour note in GM's theme song. "[T]he use of keystroke software to monitor and pace office workers has become a routine part of job performance evaluation programs," reports Andrew Ross. "Some 70 percent of corporations use electronic surveillance or other forms of quantitative monitoring of their workers."[49] *The Dream Machine,* a social history of the computer based on the PBS series *The Machine That Changed the World,* considers

> the case of TWA ticketing agents who work on keyboards while
> answering phone calls. This gruelling work is made even worse
> because the company monitors the productivity of workers by
> recording their number of keystrokes, the time they spend on
> the phone, when they leave their desks for lunch or to go to the
> toilet. Such practices, an electronic version of those used in
> Dickensian sweatshops, are widespread.[50]

A TWA agent interviewed in the last episode of the five-part series provides a chilling update of the *Tri-City Labor Review*'s portrait of assembly line "automats" when she claims that the demands of her job, which require that employees perform like "robots," cause human workers to "break down."

The semiotician Umberto Eco, who has called Disneyland "an immense robot, the final realization of the dreams of the eighteenth-century mechanics who gave life to the *[Scribe]*," has also noted that it is "a place of total passivity" whose "visitors must agree to behave like its robots."[51] There is less metaphor here than might be imagined. The only role available to Disney "guests" is that of the consumer—of junk food, knickknacks, and most of all, images: Kodak "Picture Spots" are everywhere and seemingly everyone has a camera. Furthermore, Disney's ubiquitous security and unremitting surveillance ensure that most visitors use designated walkways, observe the ban on flash photography in rides, and keep their hands inside the moving vehicles at all times. One of the more curious side effects of this unthinking obedience is the tendency to applaud the actors in Disneyland's robot dramas—actors who are, after all, nothing more than polyester-and-fiberglass skeletons stuffed full of pneumatic and hydraulic systems, sealed in Duraflex skin, and controlled by computers. On the other hand, such behavior makes a strange sort of sense: The image of happy shoppers mechanically applauding technology freezes the essence of the Disney theme parks in a single snapshot.

The mechanized spectacles of Goldstone, MacMurtrie, and Pauline put an off-center spin on the stories told by Audio-Animatronic sales-bots in Disney attractions, airport bars, and megamalls. It is no coincidence that Pauline concocted the term *Disneyfication* to describe the vacuousness his motorized roadkill is intended to guard against: his mechanical puppet shows, like those of his colleagues, reject the received notion that we should relax into our assigned role as passive consumers of high-tech commodities whose intricate workings are a mystery to us and whose design and function are entirely out of our hands. Reminding us that those who cannot control machines are, more and more, controlled by those who can, Pauline, MacMurtrie, and Goldstone argue for the liberatory power of techno-literacy. They refuse what the cultural critic Donna Haraway calls "a demonology of technology"—the self-defeating strategy of indicting the tool along with the toolmaker—and recycle or appropriate outright the products of industrial and military culture.

In a society guided, until very recently, by an unswerving belief in planned obsolescence and conspicuous consumption, inexhaustible resources and infinite frontiers, the refunctioning and reanimating of cast-off or antiquated technology assumes the status of a political act. This notion, implicit in William Gibson's cyberpunk maxim, "THE STREET FINDS ITS

OWN USES FOR THINGS," reverberates in Rick Sayre's comments on the low-tech aesthetic.

"Almost everything Chico and I build uses pieces of other things—old graphics machines, TVs, stereos and so forth," says Sayre. "Our prototype computer-control system . . . [is] a co-optation of consumer technology. The microprocessor isn't a PC-type thing, it's the same sort of embedded control you'd find in the family car or microwave oven. This is yet another [example] of overconsumption. I mean, nobody needs a computer in his microwave oven, yet people want it—they want an LED on their power drill, they want their iron to be able to talk to them—and it's an incredible waste."

Cannibalizing domesticated technology for parts, Sayre, Mac-Murtrie, and their compeers build feral machines—grungy, exuberantly ugly robots that, not yet housebroken, leak oil everywhere. Embodying the aesthetic of "impractical contraptions, irrational technologies" set forth by Pauline in his essay "Technology and the Irrational," they call to mind the "useless machines" of the Italian sculptor Bruno Munari, whose existential clock *L'Ora X* is rigged with hands that spin ceaselessly around a blank face.[52] Pauline, who once staged an event called *Useless Mechanical Activity,* delights in converting machines "from things [that] once did 'useful' destruction into things that can now do *useless* destruction."[53]

But unlike Munari's poetic devices, the immaterial commodities produced by the artists in this chapter—a mixture of terror and merriment, smoldering wreckage and revelatory flashes—are unmarketable as objets d'art. Pauline and his brothers-in-arms insist on their autonomy from what they see as an elite, effete art world in thrall to private collectors and corporate investors. Their mechanical spectacles stand in relation to gallery art and corporate diversions as the memory of Coney Island—dubbed a "pyrotechnic insanitarium" in the early 1900s—contrasts with the reality of the Magic Kingdom. Whereas the Disney dream of better living through technology is untroubled by libidinous urges, antiauthoritarian yearnings, and other imps of the perverse—"guaranteed safety for the broad spectrum of humanity whose mental health is predicated on denying that there is any such thing as mental ill health or, indeed, a mental life of any significance beneath the conscious level," as Richard Schickel puts it—Coney in its heyday flung wide the floodgates of the id.[54]

The only way into Disneyland is Main Street, U.S.A., a Wonder Bread version of Grover's Corners, complete with horse-drawn fire wagons and barbershop quartets; visitors entered Coney Island's Steeplechase Park through the Barrel of Love, a slick, spinning wooden drum that flung giddy merrymakers off their feet and into indecent contact with total strangers. Couples debarked from the ride that gave the park its name—a genteel roller-coaster in which double-saddled wooden racehorses galloped from start to finish along a rolling track—into a twisting, turning series of dimly lit passages that opened, at last, onto a brightly illuminated stage. There, compressed air from a "blowhole" swept the lady's skirt upward while a clown armed with an electrified prod jolted her gentleman friend in a particularly sensitive spot. Meanwhile, an audience of former sufferers howled with delight. After another blowhole or two and a few well-aimed whacks from a dwarf with a slapstick, the mortified pair slunk offstage and into the audience, to savor the humiliation of the next unfortunates.

The universally recognized symbol of Disneyland is of course the beaming, button-eyed face of Mickey Mouse; Steeplechase's emblem was a demented jester whose ear-to-ear grin insinuated that propriety ended at the park's gates. "Sudden disorientation, exposure of flesh, unaccustomed and rather intimate contact with strangers of the opposite sex, public shame, and strenuous physical activity resulted in a tremendous sense of release," writes the historian Judith A. Adams.[55]

Then, too, a nascent class consciousness percolated through Coney, in midway games where largely lower-class revelers could, for the price of a few pennies, demolish mock china and crystal in a re-creation of a high-bourgeois Victorian sitting room. "The games at Coney," writes Jane Kuenz, "depended in part on the thrill of doing something you otherwise couldn't but may have wanted to: express openly an alienated and hostile relationship to commodities and the frustrations associated with a life in which you maybe had fewer of them."[56] Disneyland, by contrast, is a sexless, microbe-free monument to a normative future where the sole interface between the technocratic elite and the technologically illiterate masses is the point of purchase.

"Coney's amusement," according to Adams, "shattered all expectations of normality and paradoxically turned engines of work into joy machines, spectacle, and chaos."[57] The same could be said of the robot dramas produced by Pauline, MacMurtrie, and Goldstone, which cast a new light on the cautionary tales, so unsettling to machine-age capitalists, of automated factories run amok or steel-collar workers turned murderous. In mechanical spectacle, images of runaway machines and robots humanized by their glitches speak to a growing discontent with the notion that technology is best left to our military-industrial benefactors—a discontent that bears fruit in the popular desire to follow Pauline's lead in "re-directing the techniques, tools, and tenets of industry and science away from their typical manifestations in practicality or product."[58] The rituals of resistance staged by machine artists celebrate technocracy's malfunctionings even as they dramatize cyberpunk fantasies of mutinous machines and techno-revolution.

4 / RITUAL MECHANICS
Cybernetic Body Art

Comfort/Control. © *1992 Don Lewis*

Stelarc: I Sing the Body Obsolete

Knowledge is power! Do you suppose that fragile little form of yours—your primitive legs, your ludicrous arms and hands, your tiny, scarcely wrinkled brain—can *contain* all that power? Certainly not! Already your race is flying to pieces under the impact of your own expertise. The original human form is becoming obsolete.

—Bruce Sterling[1]

Yawning with your mouth sewn shut isn't easy, as Stelarc discovered during his 1979 *Event for Support Structure*. The Australian performance artist spent three days in Tokyo's Tamura Gallery, sandwiched between planks suspended from a tepeelike arrangement of poles, his mouth and eyelids stitched tight with surgical thread. At night, he slept on the gallery floor.

"Interestingly enough," he recounts, "it wasn't so much the painfulness of the stitching . . . or the compression of the body between two pieces of wood but rather the difficulty in yawning . . . that presented a problem." His deep-toned, diabolical laugh bounces off the walls. "This is something I hadn't considered."[2]

Stelarc (born Stelios Arcadiou) is the foremost exponent of cybernetic body art. Decades before virtual reality went pop, he experimented with jerry-built simulation technology at the Caulfield Institute of Technology and, later, at the Royal Melbourne Institute of Technology (RMIT).

From 1968 through 1970, he constructed a series of enclosures called Sensory Compartments in which the user was "assaulted by lights, motion, sound" and fabricated helmets fitted with goggles that split the wearer's binocular vision, immersing him or her in a fun-house-mirror world of superimposed images. The artist, a confirmed McLuhanite, describes these devices as the product of a "realization . . . that it was the body's physiological hardware that determined its intelligence, its awareness, and that if you alter this [hardware], you're going to present an alternate perception." This is a reiteration, in so many words, of McLuhan's assertion that

> [t]he extension of any one sense alters the way we think and act–
> the way we perceive the world. When these ratios change, men
> change.[3]

Proceeding from that proposition, Stelarc has evolved an aesthetic of prosthetics in which "the artist [is] an evolutionary guide, extrapolating new trajectories . . . a genetic sculptor, restructuring and hypersensitizing the human body; an architect of internal body spaces; a primal surgeon, implanting dreams, transplanting desires; an evolutionary alchemist, triggering mutations, transforming the human landscape."[4]

His nearly naked body plastered with electrodes and trailing wires, the artist in performance bears a striking resemblance to a Borg, one of the implacable cyborg villains in *Star Trek: The Next Generation*. With his Amplified Body, Laser Eyes, Third Hand, Automatic Arm, and Video Shadow, he bodies forth the human-machine hybrid all of us are metaphorically becoming. Less a man than the organic nerve center of a cybernetic system, he literalizes our vision of ourselves as terminal beings, inextricably entangled in the global telecommunications web. In that sense, he is a postmodern incarnation of the archetypal image of Man the microcosm–a naked man, spread-eagled inside a pentagram, which according to J. E. Cirlot is emblematic not only of the analogical relationship between the individual and the cosmos but of "the human tendency towards ascendence and evolution."[5]

"All the signposts direct us to him," declares John Shirley, in an essay that theorizes Stelarc as the embodiment of cyberpunk's posthuman yearnings, "a chimera grafted together of horror and grace, the synthesis of erstwhile humanity and tomorrow's humanity struggling to be born."[6] Positioning the artist alongside Survival Research Laboratories as a cultural mutagen "doing the work of science fiction outside the genre," Shirley draws parallels between Stelarc's preoccupation with techno-evolution and the themes of cyborged or genetically engineered body modification treated in SF novels such as Bruce Sterling's *Schismatrix* and Samuel R. Delany's *Nova*.[7]

Stelarc has performed with hulking, industrial robot arms, dodging their potentially bone-shattering swipes. On occasion, his events take place in the midst of sculptural installations of glass tubes crawling with plasma discharges or flashing and flickering in response to signals sent by his body. A cagelike structure perched on the artist's shoulders emits argon-laser pulses. Synchronized to throb in time to his heartbeat, the beams are made, through eyeblinks, facial twitches, and head movements, to scribble curlicues in the air. "Video shadows"—images captured by video cameras positioned above and around him and projected on large screens—are frozen, superimposed, or juxtaposed in split-screen configurations.

A welter of *thrrrups,* squeals, creaks, and *cricks,* most of them originating in Stelarc's body, whooshes around the performance space. The artist's heartbeat, amplified by means of an ECG (electrocardiograph) monitor, marks time with a muffled, metronomic thump. The opening and closing of heart valves, the slap and slosh of blood are captured by Doppler ultrasonic sound transducers, enabling Stelarc to "play" his body. For example, one transducer is fastened to his wrist. "By constricting the radial artery of the wrist," he informs, "the sound varies from the normal repetitive 'whooshing' to a 'clicking' as the blood is dammed, with a flooding rush of sound as the wrist is relaxed."[8] A kinetic-angle transducer converts the bending of his right knee into avalanches of sound; a microphone, placed over the larynx, picks up swallowing and other throat noises; and a plethysmogram amplifies finger pulse. From time to time, an electronic keening splits the air, wobbling on a single pitch, then zigzagging suddenly upward into a ragged whoop. It is produced by analog synthesizers triggered by "control voltages"—electrical signals modulated by the artist's heartbeat, muscles, and brain waves (translated into EEG, or electroencephalogram, readouts).

Attached to an acrylic sleeve on the artist's right arm, the Third Hand chirrs frantically, its stainless steel fingers clutching at nothingness.

Custom-made by a Japanese manufacturer, the Hand is a dexterous robotic manipulator that can be actuated by EMG (electromyogram) signals from the muscles in Stelarc's abdomen and thighs. It can pinch, grasp, release, and rotate its wrist 290 degrees in either direction, and has a tactile feedback system that provides a rudimentary sense of touch by stimulating electrodes affixed to the artist's arm. Stelarc's left arm, meanwhile, is robotized—jerkily animated by intermittent jolts of electricity from a pair of muscle stimulators. "Voltage is applied to the flexor and biceps muscles," notes Stelarc, "bending the wrist, curling the fingers and jerking the arm up and down involuntarily."[9]

In recent performances, Stelarc has reached into cyberspace with his Virtual Arm. Developed at RMIT's Advanced Computer Graphics Center, the Arm is a computer-generated "universal manipulator"—a digital cartoon of a humanoid limb—controlled by gestures from a CyberGlove. The Arm can rotate its wrist and fingers continuously; stretch from here to eternity; sprout extra hands or clone an octopuslike tangle of arms; draw lines with its fingertips or shoot spheres out of them.

In *Actuate/Rotate: Event for Virtual Body* (1993), Stelarc took the next step up the techno-evolutionary ladder. Donning a Polhemus magnetic tracking system whose sensors were attached to his head, torso, and extremities, he interacted with a digital doppelgänger that mirrored his every move. The double appeared, alternately, as a wireframe skeleton or a fleshed-out mannequin on a video display monitor. Simultaneously, video cameras fed live images of Stelarc's physical body into the system, and the computer-generated point of view—the virtual camera—was choreographed by his gestures, generating montages of fleshly and ghostly bodies.

Stelarc's performances are pure cyberpunk. Slowly contorting his body in a series of cyborg mudras, he unleashes an inhuman bedlam that sounds like a brawl between a shortwave radio and a Geiger counter. The twin beams of his "laser eyes" stab into the dark; tendrils of electricity writhe, like living things, inside the sculptural installation's glass tubes; and "video shadows" flit across monitors, now freezing, now stuttering stroboscopically. His arm is yanked upwards, puppetlike, by a burst of electricity while his Third Hand scrabbles at the air. In Stelarc's cybernetic synergism, the distinction between controller and controlled is blurred; he is simultaneously extended by, and an extension of, his high-tech system.

Ironically, the Australian artist's reputation rests on the twenty-five unequivocally low-tech "suspensions" he executed between 1976 and 1988. Reminiscent of the Native American sun dance, these events involved raising the naked artist skyward by cables attached to stainless steel hooks embedded in his skin. Unforgettable evocations of prenatal weightlessness, the primal urge to fly, and space age fantasies of floating in zero gravity, the suspensions were testaments to gravity's victory over the earthbound body.

For each event, Stelarc was skewered at multiple points so that the weight on his hooks was uniformly distributed. In *Sitting/Swaying Event for Rock Suspension* (1980), he floated, cross-legged, in a Tokyo gallery, counterbalanced by a gently swaying ring of rocks. In *Seaside Suspension: Event for Wind and Waves* (1981), he swung precariously over the ocean, buffeted by gusts of wind and spattered by crashing waves. In *Street Suspension* (1984), he swooped, via cable and pulleys, from the fourth floor of one building to another in New York's East Village. And in *City Suspension* (1985), he hung from a crane two hundred feet above Copenhagen's Royal Theater, describing lazy circles under the watchful gaze of the building's stone sphinxes.

Reflecting on the experience of hovering over Copenhagen, the breeze shivering his cables, he confided:

> I really suffer from a fear of heights. . . . I kept my eyes closed for the first 10, 15 minutes. . . . 200 feet up, all you could hear was [the] whooshing sound of the wind, the creaking of the skin gently turning and swaying in the wind.[10]

In each event, the pain was excruciating during liftoff and touchdown; in most cases, it took about a week for the wounds to heal and Stelarc to recuperate. Other body artists have pushed the threshold of pain even further: Chris Burden, the avant-garde's answer to "Evel" Knievel, set himself on fire, tried to breathe water, was crucified atop a Volkswagen Beetle, and, for his 1971 piece *Shoot,* arranged for a friend to shoot him at close range with a rifle, blowing a chunk of flesh out of his arm. "[A] guy pulls a trigger, and in a fraction of a second, I'd made a sculpture," marveled Burden.[11]

Body art, a performance art subgenre that emerged in the late sixties and flourished in the seventies, sprang from conceptual art, which rejected the commodified art object for an immaterial—and therefore theoretically unsalable—art of ideas. Body art was conceived of as intangible, transitory sculpture, fashioned by the artist from his or her own body and physical actions. Early body artists, most of whom were male, exhibited a curious detachment from the flesh that was their clay, a tendency that recalled the mechanical impersonality of minimalist painting, with its uniformly applied colors and hard-edged, rectilinear compositions. Shunning expressionistic or autobiographical impulses, they created works that resembled endurance tests (for the audience as well as the performer) or scientific experiments: Terry Fox's *Push Piece* (1970) consisted of the artist shoving, with all his might, against a brick wall until he was overcome by exhaustion; Bruce Nauman's *Walking in an Exaggerated Manner around the Perimeter of a Square* (1968) is self-explanatory.

At the same time, body art constituted a backlash against the minimalist mandate that art be reduced to utter neutrality through the use of uniform "color fields" and flat, geometric shapes. This opposing tendency impelled the genre toward the ever more spectacular aesthetic exemplified by Chris Burden.

The feminist bodyworks of the seventies were as fervently political and unreservedly personal as earlier, male-dominated body art had been either coolly formal or histrionically gory. They evidenced a growing recognition of the body as war zone, a conviction asserted in the feminist axiom "THE PERSONAL IS POLITICAL." The art critic Thomas McEvilley writes, "Much women's [performance art] relates to what in feminist literary criticism is called 'writing the body.' As against the male assertion of abstract painting or modernist literature as essentially otherworldly endeavors aimed at immaterial realities . . . women artists restored focus to the reality of the body and with it to social and personal realities."[12]

Recasting her body "as a source of varying emotive power," Carolee Schneemann parried conventional images of woman as the weaker vessel in works that excavated prepatriarchal ages or cultures for archetypes of female empowerment.[13] Performances such as *Eye Body* (1963), a neo-shamanic ritual in which the recumbent artist, daubed with paint and writhing with snakes, personated a statue of a Cretan goddess, prefigured the passionate interest among feminist body artists in the Great Goddess, the Earth Mother, and other pre-Christian deities. In New Age feminist narratives, the image of a procreative nature goddess is often counterpoised with the stereotype of an angry god of war whose shock troops are Culture and Technology. "[I]t's no accident that the most technological, militaristic Western 'culture' was destroying all these ancient goddess sites," Schneemann observed, of America's bombing of Iraq during the Gulf War.[14]

A brief digression on body art is essential to any discussion of an artist whose signature works involve piercing his body with hooks and hoisting it high to dangle like a side of beef from a meat rack. There are obvious comparisons to be made between the aesthetic of extremes implicit in Burden's gonzo body art and the gut-clenching spectacle of Stelarc's suspensions, painful even to behold; between the minimalist objectification of the flesh in male body artists' flatly reportorial documentation of their activities and Stelarc's almost clinical disengagement from his physical self (in his essays and interviews, it is always "*the* body," never "*my* body").

Furthermore, the juxtaposition of characteristic body art by New Age or ecotopian feminists with Stelarc's work is highly instructive. The former harks back to ancient matriarchies and prehistoric goddess worship for a vision of the feminine unmediated by the male gaze, while the latter looks to a future just beyond the rim of possibility, made possible by technology. The former is heavily invested in a mystical ecopolitics symbolized by a loamy, generative Earth, while the latter dramatizes a theory of escape velocity in which the body falls away like a rocket stage as *Homo sapiens* accelerates into "pan-planetary" posthuman evolution.

Stelarc recoils from "the reemergence of the mystical" in the guise of a return to "cultural rituals that have long outlived their purposes." Although his early suspensions, executed with ropes and harnesses, emerged from yogic practices and his subsequent use of hooks paralleled a study of Hindu religious rites of piercing, he is at some pains to divest his work of the ritualistic associations of much body art:

> I've never meditated before an event. I've never had any sort of out-of-body experience. I've never felt a sense of being a shaman, or [of being in] an S&M situation. To me those notions are largely irrelevant. . . . Previous awareness techniques were important in our development but I don't think they're significant anymore as human strategies.[15]

For Stelarc, the writing is literally on the wall. In his 1982 performance *Handswriting*, the artist laboriously coordinated pens held in both
hands with the marker-wielding Third Hand to scrawl a single word on
paper taped to a gallery wall: EVOLUTION.

Stelarc embodies McLuhan's declaration that with the advent of
cyberculture "man is beginning to wear his brain outside his skull and his
nerves outside his skin; new technology breeds new man."[16] As noted in
chapter 3, McLuhan's technodeterministic reading of history rests on the
assumption that

> All media are extensions of some human faculty—psychic or
> physical. The wheel . . . is an extension of the foot. The book is
> an extension of the eye . . . clothing, an extension of the skin.[17]

According to McLuhan, all such extensive or "autoamputative"
strategies are the overstimulated nervous system's response to cultural
catalysts such as "the acceleration of pace and increase of load," themselves
technological in origin.[18] Further, he argues, each autoamputation results in
a numbing of that part of the nervous system associated with the now
technologized and therefore traumatically amplified function.

To McLuhan, the metaphoric extrusion of the central nervous
system ("that electric network that coordinates the various media of our
senses") in the form of global telecommunications networks and other
cybernetic technologies represents a survival mechanism, triggered by "the
successive mechanizations of the various physical organs since the invention
of printing [that] have made too violent and superstimulated a social
experience for the nervous system to endure."[19]

Adopting McLuhan's premise that the vertiginous whirl of the
information age has outpaced and overtaxed the nervous system, Stelarc
argues that humanity is superannuated, its biological hardware unadapted
to the infosphere. In his essay "Prosthetics, Robotics and Remote Existence:
Postevolutionary Strategies," he declares,

> It is time to question whether a bipedal, breathing body with
> binocular vision and a 1,400-cc. brain is an adequate biological
> form. It cannot cope with the quantity, complexity and quality

of information it has accumulated. . . . The most significant
planetary pressure is no longer the gravitational pull but rather
the information thrust. Gravity has molded the evolved body in
shape and structure and contained it on the planet. Information
propels the body beyond itself and its biosphere. Information
fashions the form and function of the postevolutionary body.[20]

Like McLuhan, who couched his fundamental insight in the catchy
maxim "THE MEDIUM IS THE MESSAGE," Stelarc has condensed his theories into
a single, mediagenic aphorism: "THE BODY IS OBSOLETE." If the suspensions
were object lessons in the physical and psychological limits of the terrestrial
body, Stelarc's cybernetic events are dress rehearsals for posthuman evolution. High-tech prostheses and medical technologies for monitoring and
mapping the body hold forth the promise, Stelarc maintains, of self-directed
evolution—the result not of incremental mutation over generations but
of somatic change brought about through technology. "Patched-up people,"
he writes, "are evolutionary experiments."[21] According to Stelarc, min-
iaturized, biocompatible technologies will one day make each individual a
species unto him or herself.

> EVOLUTION ENDS WHEN TECHNOLOGY INVADES THE
> BODY. Once technology provides each person with the poten-
> tial to progress individually in its [sic] development, the cohesive-
> ness of the species is no longer important.[22]

The artist's philosophy of transcendence through technology is
hitched to a space-age teleology: for Stelarc, our Manifest Destiny lies in the
stars. If it is to attain "planetary escape velocity," he reasons, the body must
first be objectified:

> It is no longer meaningful to see the body as a *site* for the psyche or
> the social but rather as a *structure* to be monitored and modified.
> The body not as a subject but as an object—NOT AS AN OBJECT
> OF DESIRE BUT AS AN OBJECT FOR DESIGNING.[23]

Reconceived as an "it" rather than an "I," the body may be subjected
to ballistic streamlining, "amplified and accelerated" into a "postevolu-

tionary projectile." Humans embarked on an extraterrestrial odyssey would find the body's "complexity, softness, and wetness . . . hard to sustain," predicts Stelarc.[24] The body must be hollowed, hardened, and dehydrated, its inessential innards scooped out so that it may be "a better host for technology," its skin peeled off and replaced by a synthetic dermis capable of converting light into chemical nutrients and absorbing all oxygen necessary to sustain life through its pores.[25] An internal early warning system would monitor what few organs remain, and "micro-miniaturized robots," or nanomachines, would "colonize the surface and internal tracts to augment the bacterial populations—to probe, monitor and protect the body."[26]

Eviscerated and stuffed with modular components that can be easily replaced; armored and endowed with pile-driver brawn by a robotic exoskeleton; fitted with an array of antennae to amplify its sight and hearing; and implanted with a brain chip or genetically engineered to expand its cortical capacity to supercomputer proportions, Stelarc's posthuman being would inhabit a "pan-planetary physiology that is durable, flexible and capable of functioning in varying atmospheric conditions, gravitational pressures and electromagnetic fields."[27] Such creatures might resemble one of Sterling's "Lobsters"—Borglike posthumans sealed in "skin-tight life-support systems, flanged here and there with engines and input-output jacks" whose

> greatest pleasure was to . . . open their amplified senses to the depths of space, watching stars past the limits of ultraviolet and infrared . . . or just sitting and soaking in watts of solar energy through their skins while they listened with wired ears to the warbling of Van Allen belts and the musical tick of pulsars.[28]

Entities such as these might choose to become "reengineered extraterrestrial explorers," the artist speculates.[29] But in the scenario sketched in most of Stelarc's published essays and public lectures, the mutant, transmigrant remains of the human race come to rest in virtual reality, in a "high-fidelity illusion of tele-existence" wherein their "performance parameters [would be] limited neither by . . . mere physiology nor the local space [they occupy]."[30] In a 1993 lecture at the Manhattan artspace the Kitchen, he argued

If the . . . sensory feedback loops between the robot and the human operator are of a high enough quantity and quality, then there's a collapse of the psychological distance between the operator and the robot; in other words, if the robot does what the human commands and the human perceives what the robot perceives, the human-machine system [effectively] collapses into one operational unit.[31]

Immobilized in cybernetic networks and immortalized by means of replacement parts, Stelarc's posthuman teleoperators would reach across solar systems to sift alien sands through robotic fingers—fingers sophisticated enough to reproduce reality with a fidelity indistinguishable from embodied experience. A postevolutionary strategy that began with bodies redesigned not to accommodate airflow but rather the torque of McLuhan's "electric vortex" ends in a hyperreality that has become "a medium of action rather than information."[32]

Meanwhile, back in the present, Dr. Richard Restak raises doubts about the nuts-and-bolts feasibility of the cyborg upgrades proposed by Stelarc. A neuropsychiatrist, professor of neurology at George Washington University, and the author of the *New York Times* best-seller *The Brain*, Restak takes issue with Stelarc's postevolutionary scenario on medical as well as psychological grounds.

"It's essentially science fiction," he contends, "a kind of a postmodernist view of what the future person is going to be. In postmodern philosophy you can say, 'Why take anything for granted? Let's question the most basic elements—our very biology, for instance.' Of course, at the outer limits of this ideology, you come up against biology, which is where Stelarc's weakness lies.

"For example, I don't know how you would decide what innards are inessential because such things as the immune system are housed in some fairly unprepossessing organs, such as the thymus. You might be able to replace the liver and the kidneys but you'd have to keep some type of immune system. At the same time, the immune system is going to wreak havoc on any foreign object you put into the body. That's going to be your biggest problem: What would keep the body from rejecting these implants while it's in the process of this transmogrification? The immune system would have be suppressed but then of course you're open to viruses and bacteria. Furthermore, once you peel off the skin, before anything else can be put over it, your infection possibilities are just astronomical. There's no way that I could imagine that you could get from a human being to something like this, not only because of the technical hurdles but more specifically because of the biological ones.

"Moreover, who would want to live like this, out there among the stars? I've written on brain and body prostheses and they've done some wonderful things, but I look upon Stelarc's fantasies as pathological; they're in the general genre of world destruction fantasies—extreme, narcissistic fantasies of complete isolation. This creature's out there by itself, it doesn't need anybody because its brain has been amplified with a chip or genetically engineered, which I think implies an involutional process whereby it's just occupied with its own internal processing.

"Fantasies such as this represent a distorted Cartesianism. We're so locked into the Cartesian idea that we're a mind and the body is an it and we treat it as an it (the analogy is usually to a machine), whereas in fact we are embodied. I think there's a lot of self-hate in this objectification of the body, a lot of estrangement."

Stelarc's essay "Prosthetics, Robotics and Remote Existence: Post-evolutionary Strategies" ends with the assurance that, in tele-existence, "[t]he body's form is enhanced and its functions are extended. . . . electronic space restructures the body's architecture and multiplies its operational possibilities."[33] But beneath this tantalizing vision of the body apotheosized (albeit in a fashion that accommodates the contrary notion of human potential unbounded by physicality) lies an almost sadomasochistic subtext: The body, "traumatized" by its objectification, is "distraught and disconnected" from its functions by technological mediation and has no recourse but "interface and symbiosis." Here is McLuhan's traumatic autoamputation come back to haunt us, attended by his "Narcissus Narcosis," the body's self-protective mechanism against the shock of being flayed alive. "We have to numb our central nervous system when it is extended and exposed," argues McLuhan, "or we will die."[34] Stelarc likewise insists that "[t]he body plugged into the machine network needs to be pacified. In fact, to . . . truly achieve a hybrid symbiosis the body will need to be increasingly anesthetized."[35]

As well, it must be skinned and gutted, "eliminating many of its malfunctioning organs and systems, minimizing toxin build-up in its chemistry."[36] The polymorphous, almost synesthetic physicality that Carolee Schneemann celebrated as "meat joy" is counterweighted here by a vision of the flesh as dead meat. Awash in toxic waste and always on the brink of collapse, Stelarc's body bears little resemblance to Schneemann's "source of varying emotive power." It is indistinguishable from Foucault's ideal subject of power, the analyzable, manipulable "docile body," available to be "subjected, used, transformed and improved."[37]

Oddly, issues of power are absent from Stelarc's postevolutionary schematic, as they inevitably are in McLuhan's writings; technology intersects with the body but never collides with social or economic issues. *Who builds these machines, anyway?* Sheathed in an impregnable exoskeleton, the Stelarcian cyborg is powerful but not empowered, a pharaonic monument to the mummylike body withering inside it. Its mind, meanwhile, is elsewhere; most posthumans are, after all, "mere manipulators of machine images" who live out eternity by proxy, directing robot colonies on distant planets.[38] But who writes the code that creates the "high-fidelity illusion of tele-existence?" Who controls the remote controllers? What is needed here is a politics of posthumanism. Stelarc's art and thought do not exist, as he would have it, in the value-free cultural vacuum traditionally reserved for science. His science fiction dream of a body that is no longer "a *site* for . . . the social" is hemmed in on all sides by feminist body criticism, the ongoing debate over the ethics of human biotechnology, and green critiques of capitalism's litanies of technological progress and unchecked expansion.

Stelarc seems unaware that his discourse is caught in the cross fire of the culture wars. "The events are to do with ideas, not ideologies," he insists. "The artist refrains from the politics of power not through a naïvety of the implications and issues, but because the focus is on the imaginative postevolutionary possibilities."[39] His speculations "emanate from the events," he argues, and are "not meant to be a balanced and comprehensive theory"; they are "about the business of being poetic rather than . . . politically persuasive."

By retaining the poetic license of the artist, he exempts himself from the scientific requirement that theories be unified. Simultaneously, and contrarily, he sanctions only literal interpretations of his work; figurative readings are dismissed as dependent on the very context—the realm of "the psyche [and] the social"—from which postevolutionary strategies are meant to map an escape route. Accordingly, he invokes a scientific objectivity that forecloses social or political readings of his work. "Suspicious of subjective reporting," "skeptical about statements of memory which are often very loose, inexact and difficult to evaluate," and wary "of romanticizing and exaggerating past actions," he legitimates his posthumanist pronouncements and McLuhanesque epigrams with technical terminology and a dispassionate tone.[40]

But the very notion of ideation unperturbed by ideology, of a social space in which the collision of bodies and machines takes place outside "the politics of power," is science fiction. The idea that truth is as much socially constructed as discovered—that is, that even avowedly value-neutral discourses are colored by cultural assumptions—is the keynote of recent critiques of science. Science and technology "are not isolated from ideological influence but are 'part and parcel, woof and warp, of the social orders from which they emerge and which support them,' " argues the cultural critic Claudia Springer.[41]

It is his embrace of a "context-free" scientific objectivity that prevents Stelarc from seeing the correspondence between his cybernetic spectacles and what he terms the "new mysticism" of a culture dazzled by a "bewildering array of disconnected data."[42] Stelarc has called his events "sci-fi scenarios for human-machine symbiosis . . . performance as simulation rather than ritual."[43] But the distinction may be semantic; computer simulations may *be* the rituals of cyberculture.

Fakir Musafar questions Stelarc's privileging of science fictions over "cultural rituals that have long outlived their purposes." A Silicon Valley advertising executive–turned-"modern primitive," Musafar has attained altered states through piercing, binding, suspension by hooks through his flesh, and other forms of what he calls "body play"; modern primitives, he holds, constitute a cultural vanguard showing "[a] way out of the Middle Ages and European culture and a fusion of science and magic."[44]

> Where I think Stelarc is missing the point is that . . . [w]e've
> gotten to the point where we can synthesize magic, technology

and science. You listen to the babblings of the best physicists we
have today, [and] they . . . sound like the alchemists used to.[45]

Additionally, there are correlations between Stelarc's work and
Judeo-Christian symbolism. The artist's declaration that "[t]echnology,
which shatters the body's subjective totality of reality, now returns to
reintegrate its fragmented experience"–a restatement, in all the essentials, of McLuhan's claim that "[a]fter three thousand years of explosion,
by means of fragmentary and mechanical technologies, the Western world
is imploding"–invites interpretation as an allegorical return to a para-
disal state, to a time before the rupture between self and Other, culture
and nature.[46]

Rachel Rosenthal, a feminist performance artist whose works often
address the politics of the body, theorizes Stelarc's cyber-body events as
"[n]ostalgia for undifferentiation." In her essay "Stelarc, Performance and
Masochism," she writes,

> We are so isolated from the [O]ther, so lonely. Self-penetration,
> physical and violent, is a metaphysical response to this despair of
> ever connecting deeply. So we . . . pierce the separating mem-
> brane. We explode the integrity of form.[47]

For McLuhan, the invention of the written word was the "separating membrane," dividing the "I" from the "all-that-is-not-I" and casting
Western civilization into the postlapsarian world of isolation, objectivity,
and rationality. His limning of this event sounds unmistakably like the
biblical allegory of the fall:

> The whole man became fragmented man; the alphabet shattered
> the charmed circle and resonating magic of the tribal world,
> exploding man into an agglomeration of specialized and psychi-
> cally impoverished individuals, or units, functioning in a world
> of linear time and Euclidean space.[48]

By extension, McLuhan's conviction that "[w]e have begun again to
structure the primordial feeling, the tribal emotions from which a few

centuries of literacy divorced us" equates the preliterate with the prelap-
sarian, the supposedly holistic worldview of pretechnological civilizations
with an Edenic state of grace.[49]

Stelarc vehemently rejects such analyses. "Can strategies be evalu-
ated without resorting to convenient myths, metaphors and religious symbolism?" he demands.[50] To which one might well respond, "Can poetic
extrapolations based on technological modernity–science fictions, by any
other name–be disentangled from the meshwork of shared references that
links all texts, religious myths among them?"

A sworn atheist, Stelarc discourages quests for mythic resonances
in his rhetoric. But his postevolutionary strategies spring from McLuhan,
whose later thought is inflected by a Teilhardian scientific humanism; can a
posthumanism so deeply indebted to an analysis of electronic culture that
borders on the mystical expunge every last trace of that mysticism? As the
noted historian of religion Mircea Eliade points out, "It is interesting to
observe to what an extent the scenarios of initiation still persist in many of
the acts and gestures of contemporary nonreligious man."[51] Viewed as
mythopoeia, Stelarc's dream of the end of limits ("the body must burst from
its biological, cultural and planetary containment") is easily recast as an
ascension rite for cyberculture, a vertical movement from the mundane to
the "high-fidelity illusion of tele-existence." It is Jacob's ladder reimagined
for an age of "patched-up"–and patched-in–people. The artist's speculation
that self-engineered evolution may result "in an *alien awareness*–one that is
posthistoric, transhuman and even extraterrestrial" calls to mind Eliade's
assertion that

> [t]he 'most high' is a dimension inaccessible to man as man; it
> belongs to superhuman forces and beings. He who ascends by
> mounting the steps of a sanctuary or the ritual ladder that leads
> to the sky ceases to be a man; in one way or another, he shares in
> the divine condition.[52]

On a lighter note, Stelarc's cyborg myth dovetails with Roland
Barthes's playful essay on the French superhero the jet-man, a posthuman
pilot whose helmet and antigravity suit ("*a novel type of skin* in which 'even
his mother would not know him' ") signal a "metamorphosis of species," the

coming of "jet-mankind."[53] He writes, "Everything concurs, in the mythology of the jet-man, to make manifest the plasticity of the flesh."[54] Barthes sees in the jet-man's impersonal, asexual uniform and "abstention and withdrawal from pleasures" a monastic regimen, a mortification of the flesh whose endpoint is "the glamorous singularity of an inhuman condition."[55] The myth of the jet-man, he emphasizes, is no less a religious allegory for its *Rocketeer* gadgetry. "[I]n spite of the scientific garb of this new mythology," notes Barthes, "there has merely been a displacement of the sacred."[56]

D. A. Therrien: Machines for the New Inquisition

"We create new rituals with every generation," says D. A. Therrien. "[T]here's really no difference between [believing in] multiple gods and believing in multiple sciences or technologies."[57] He elaborates, "We've looked at technology, at least since the industrial revolution and maybe even since Newton, as almost a second religion. Religion is supposed to unify you with a greater whole and technology offers that same utopian vision."

His serious, finely drawn features framed by dark, Jesus-length locks and dominated by piercing eyes and a Mephistophelian goatee, Therrien looks like central casting's idea of a defrocked preacher. Fittingly, the postmodern theorist Arthur Kroker has dubbed him "a priest of high technology" whose cybernetic spectacles are "deeply religious" in their "ethical insistence that technology respond to the ultimate questions."[58] In his tableaux of command and control, says Therrien, "politics and religion [are] the same thing."[59] He plugs the discourse of technology into "the context of religion and belief systems" and, in so doing, into the "politics of power" from which Stelarc stands aloof.

"Technology enables the few to dominate the many," he asserts. "It's used the same way that religion has been used—as a power mechanism. Maybe, as networking starts to happen on a larger scale, there will be more input from the user, but right now, corporations essentially control technology and by doing so, they tend to have the power. You know, we may think we're empowered by the fact that we sit in front of computers for eight hours a day, but is that really freeing us? Technologies are enabling people but at the same time government and industry want to control the technologies that enable the masses."

Inverting the McLuhan paradigm embraced by Stelarc, Therrien stresses the perception of media as social rather than biological extensions of humankind, underscoring their use as instruments of societal domination rather than individual liberation. To Stelarc, the body is no longer "a *site* for . . . the social but rather . . . a *structure* to be monitored and modified"; to Therrien, for whom history is too often a story of masses monitored and modified from on high, the body cannot *but* be a site for the social, a screen on which power is projected.

Therrien's ensemble, Comfort/Control, performs high-voltage exorcisms that partake equally of the concentration camp and the Stations of the Cross. Young men wearing nothing but jockstraps huddle in cages or hang on monolithic metal crosses while the percussionist Timothy North rumbles on tom-toms or raps out sputtering rhythms on their prostrate bodies, using electrified drumsticks. Set in a twilight relieved only by explosions of light so dazzling they seem to cauterize the eyes, the events take place amidst industrial pandemonium: North's unrelenting assault is accented by digital samples of mechanical wheezings and rusty scrapings.

There is something, in this Foucauldian theater of discipline and punishment, of *1984*'s Room 101, behind whose door lay the terrors of the subconscious, and of the neurophysiologist Jose Delgado's experiments with mind control, in which implanted electrodes were used to control animal behavior. Examined in an art-historical context, Comfort/Control's performances bear a family resemblance to those of Barry Schwartz, an Oakland, California–based artist whose work reconciles performance art, weird science, and avant-garde music. Schwartz's electro-acoustic spectacles incorporate Tesla coils—awesome devices that bathe the room in an unearthly, purplish glow and fill the air with long, ribbonlike sparks—and a homemade structure called the Harp: electrified piano wires fastened, at one end, to insulators mounted on the ceiling and at the other to insulators anchored in a ten-foot-square tub filled with transformer fluid. Sloshing around in galoshes, the artist plucks the Harp with heavy-duty rubber gloves, their fingertips capped with thimbles. Setting the wires jangling, he calls forth burrs and bumbles reminiscent of wind in telephone lines. Fiery glowworms spring, sputtering, from his metal fingertips, inch their way up the wires, and vanish, forming rungs of flame as they ascend. Inescapably evocative of the Frankenstein myth, Schwartz's theater of shocks and jolts reminds us that the electricity that makes technological modernity possible is an elemental force. Loosed from its man-made cage, it becomes, once again, a capricious anima, a puissant flame.

Comfort/Control invites comparison, as well, to La Fura dels Baus ("Vermin of the Sewers"), an all-male troupe from Barcelona whose *Mad Max* masques involve chainsaw-wielding, jockstrap-clad gladiators and the bloody carcasses of meat animals, and to the obsessive, ingrown work of the Los Angeles artist Liz Young, whose installation *Neglected Fixations* (1990) featured a man in a human-sized hamster wheel, condemned to the Sisyphean torment of endlessly walking, never arriving.

Comfort/Control's 1990 performance *Ritual Mechanics* geometrized power relations and mechanized primitive rites. Presented at CyberArts International, an art and technology symposium–cum–trade show, the performance took place in Los Angeles's Mayan Theater nightclub, a converted movie palace decorated to look like a Mayan temple. Towering in front of the gaping, craggy maw of a trompe l'oeil cavern on a painted backdrop stood the Index, a forty-foot-tall, three-ton mechanical cross with two men imprisoned in its cagelike frame. Resembling a cross between a rocket gantry and a Vietnamese tiger cage, the cruciform sculpture incorporated an alphanumeric display into its base; words calculated to push emotional buttons–"SANCTIFY," "DEIFY," "ELECTRIFY," "CONTROL," "CONFORM," "CONVERT"–scrolled across its six-foot-square neon grid.

One of the Index's hapless prisoners, Lloyd Whittaker, hung upside down in the Ninety-Degree Machine, a harrowing device that gradually raised him perpendicular to the cross's upright shaft, then brought him whistling down, into a steel plate. The contraption's impact triggered bone-jarring digital samples–what Therrien calls "good, gut-ripping sounds: tree trunks snapping, judo throws." Michael Hudson–the Body Drum–lay at the foot of the Index, his prone form conjuring images of human sacrifice; strapped to his chest were electrified, heavily insulated steel plates fitted with electronic triggers. There were 240 volts and "200 amps of good, chunky power running through each plate," says Therrien, with relish–enough power to kill, perilously close to the heart. Pummeling them with pieces of steel pipe held in heavy gloves, North closed the circuit with each thwack, spattering sparks in every direction and triggering samples.

A single Macintosh computer used MIDI sequencing software and fiber-optic control/data links to orchestrate what Therrien describes as a "technically quite complex" performance, synchronizing sampled sounds stored on the computer's hard disk, machine control, and lighting. Performed in near darkness, *Ritual Mechanics* was illuminated at intervals by searing bursts from banks of quartz lights.

Since 1983, Therrien has traced the triangle of power, bodies and technology in cyberculture. The name of his loose aggregate of performers—Therrien and North are the only constants—refers, he says, "to the enveloping comfort that machines provide [by] taking control out of human hands. Comfort/Control is about the ways that people interface with technology, and how technology is eventually going to supplant not only a lot of human physical activity but a lot of our decision making as well. The danger may not be apparent, but I think we'll reach a stage where technology starts to supersede our intelligence. In my work, I [create] a situation where the machines are in control and the humans in them have no control whatsoever. They're unwilling participants."

Their hair slicked back with a glutinous mixture of grease, paint, and flour, their bodies streaked with tempera paint, and flour from head to toe, the trapped, traumatized acolytes in *Ritual Mechanics* convey multiple meanings. They could be sacrificial offerings inside a technopagan Wicker Man; guinea pigs in unspeakable medical experiments; victims of a postapocalyptic Inquisition; or the sado-mechanical, electro-fetishistic practitioners of Ballard's "new sexuality born from a perverse technology." Most obviously, they call to mind Japanese *butoh* dancers who dust themselves with rice flour to become white shadows in a grotesque "dance of utter darkness," an elegy to the nuclear holocaust of Hiroshima and Nagasaki.

Therrien fastens meanings of his own to this chain of associations. In *Nomad* magazine, he points out that in *Ritual Mechanics*

> there is the person who is drumming on the human body [and] the . . . person who is being drummed upon. The dominant person . . . shows that there is usually one dominant force behind a lot of the dogma that runs the machine. [W]hether that [person] is a pope or a dictator, there is still someone who

is driving the agenda, and . . . everyone else is . . . just along for the ride. [That's the] idea with the caged man. It's more than just the caged body: often, it's the caged intellect that you are dealing with, where that intellect is trapped in that machine.[60]

Much of Therrien's work images religion as a technology that amplifies the effects of power. "The men at the top of the Catholic church are deciding what's acceptable for Catholics in particular and human beings in general," he says. "In 1993, John Paul II issued a comprehensive list of new dogmas, an encyclical called 'The Splendor of Truth.' It explains what can and can't be done, from homosexual acts to premarital sex, and even in the face of all this danger involving sexual contact the church is still saying that condoms are not allowable under any circumstances."

Staged at CRASHarts, an alternative artspace in Phoenix's industrial zone run by Therrien and his wife Helen Hestenes, Comfort/Control's 1987 performance *Index (Machines for the New Inquisition)* pondered the church's use of the machinery of control, be it instruments of torture or systems of signs. Wielding his hot-wired drumsticks, North thundered out liturgical accompaniment on empty fuel tanks, his face lit by spitting sparks. The phallic Ninety-Degree Machine and the Fetal Cage—a gondola containing a performer in a fetal crouch, attached to a pendulumlike contraption—alluded to the lightning-rod issues of AIDS prevention, birth control, and abortion rights while the Index flashed recombinant phrases reminiscent of the Party slogans in *1984*: "TRUTH IS POWER," "POWER IS GOD," "THE BODY OF LIFE," "THE LIFE OF THE BODY." As if on cue, the pope's motorcade passed by the site shortly after the performance ended.

"*Index* spelled out some of the same ideas that were involved in the Inquisition," says Therrien. "The pope was coming to Phoenix, so I tied this information display technology to a huge, mechanical cross that had a closer relation to [the technology of the Inquisition] than it did to, say, assembly-line robots from the twentieth century. Even though the cross was automated, it was designed to control the body, which is what they were attempting to do with the Inquisition machines. Some were designed purely to destroy, but others were designed to slowly inflict pain, using screws and pulleys and tremendous force, enabling the victim to find the purity within his own religion. During that period, some of the best engineers in the world were developing devices to help people renounce the demons within—the barbaric thoughts, the primitive urges."

Index reminds us that the history of the Inquisition is one of bodies rendered tractable and minds made pliant by instrumental technologies that made possible what Rossell Hope Robbins has called "a science of applied cruelty": eye-gougers, spine-rollers, spiked heating chairs, Spanish Boots (a bone-crushing vice "enclosing the legs from the ankles to the knees, operated by screws or wedges"), and thumbscrews (hailed enthusiastically in 1684 as "a new invention and engine . . . that had never been used before").[61]

But the Inquisition is equally a story about bodies—translated, by the witch finder's art, into texts whose warts, moles, carbuncles, excrescences, birthmarks, scars, tattoos, and other abnormalities constituted a legible record of unholy transactions. Shaved and exhaustively examined for devil's marks, the hidden truths that the eighteenth century demonologist Ludovico Maria Sinistrari contended were "imprinted on the most secret parts," bodies were made to testify against their owners.[62]

Of course, the Inquisition's technics of behavior modification was not confined to crank-operated engines of torment; it applied, as well, to subtler technologies. The Index, the Roman Catholic church's official list of forbidden books, impoverished intellectual life in sixteenth century Europe by restricting information access—caging the intellect, to borrow Therrien's phrase. (Extraordinarily, it was only abrogated in 1966.)[63] Therrien's Index, which "presented controversial information on current moral and social issues," was in fact an anti-Index, contravening the official one.

Therrien updates the inquisitor's search for witch's marks in his critique of the political uses of medical technology. Comfort/Control performances often incorporate electrocardiogram monitors whose registrations function as musical elements, sources of visual imagery (the Body Drum's vital signs jogged across video monitors), and visible evidence of surveillance. "I'm fascinated by the whole privacy issue," he says, "and my use of medical technology in performance has partly to do with the idea of technology invading the privacy of your body. To get life insurance, I had to answer a lot of questions about my medical history, sexual preference, drug use. They used blood and urine tests in their final analysis, saying, in effect, 'If you're lying, we can get your body to tell the truth.' "

Therrien plans to make more extensive use of medical equipment in future performances, a decision prompted by his belief that "medical technology, from the electronics in heart monitors to the genetic research being done in labs, is beginning to control us as well as provide us with increased longevity and a more comfortable life." Since a friend was blinded by chemotherapy, Therrien's thoughts have often turned to the irony of technologies that postpone death but diminish the quality of life. "Technology is beginning to strip people of their dignity; they're not allowed to complete the normal cycle of life and death," he observes. "People now have the means to survive even as total invalids if they can use their brains, but for every Stephen Hawking there's probably a thousand people, covered with bed sores, who can't roll over by themselves. And there will be a lot more like them because we'll be able to keep so many people alive. We're already starting to make decisions [about who lives and who dies]."

This train of thought leads naturally to the historically intertwined subjects of euthanasia and eugenics, whose shadows sometimes creep across debates about America's overburdened health care system, the population explosion, and genetic engineering. "They're able to determine early on whether or not you'll have a child that will have certain birth defects," says Therrien, "and you can choose to terminate that life or not. Already, in the so-called 'clean,' untainted vision of eugenics, they're talking about gene fixing, where they'll go in and remove the genes that are considered 'undesirable' and replace them with good WASP genes, changing the skin or eye color of unborn children."

As his interest in the delicate machinery of genetic engineering suggests, Therrien's attempts to trace the crossed wires of power, violence, bodies, and technology do not stop at inquisitional engines or the assembly lines of heavy industry. The presumption that information media are tools that modify their users, and not always for the better, underwrites much of his work. Tellingly, Therrien (whose performance space takes its name from the Ballard novel) cites "Ballard's vision of the way people tend to look at violence" as a formative influence on his figuration of TV as a pathological medium. In his introduction to the French edition of *Crash*, Ballard cited "the death of affect" as "the most terrifying casualty" of

a world ruled by fictions of every kind—mass merchandising,
advertising, politics conducted as a branch of advertising . . . the
increasing blurring and intermingling of identities within the
realm of consumer goods, the preempting of any free or original
imaginative response to experience by the television screen.[64]

Therrien's first public performance—*Comfort/Voyeur* (1983), in which
the artist crawled through broken glass beneath a structure supporting a TV
and an easy chair—spoke to the terminal voyeurism and flattened affect that
are the putative result of a steady diet of splatter news and prime-time
violence. It was informed, in part, by a 1981 newscast he had seen about a
despondent, jobless man who phoned a TV station to inform the world of his
decision to commit suicide by setting himself on fire. A crew was dispatched
to document the event, and when it arrived, the man—who had been waiting
for the media—doused himself with gasoline. In a black comedy of errors, it
was soon discovered that he had no matches; a resourceful cameraman
produced a pack, and the show went on. It was only after the crew had
secured enough ratings-friendly footage of the wretch in flames that by-
standers came to his aid.

"They showed it on the news again and again, and I remember
people *laughing* about how ridiculous it was," marvels Therrien. "Anyone
who waits for the cameras so he can kill himself before the media is
obviously disturbed; the man needed help, not a pack of matches. But what
really disturbed me was the way that people watching television treated the
event: For them, it became entertainment."

The psychogeography of Therrien's industrial rituals is contiguous
with the irradiated terrain of Ballard's novels, that "brutal, erotic and overlit
realm that beckons more and more persuasively to us from the margins of
the technological landscape."[65] It overlaps, as well, with the dark places
illuminated in Francis Bacon's paintings: butcher shops and torture cells,
Eichmann's booth and Hitler's bunker. Bacon, like Therrien, obsessed on
the ill-fated conjunction of bodies and machines, though the painter's
references were drawn from another era: corpses buried by buzz bombs in
the rubble of the blitz, "the tortured creatures in the waxwork show of
the atrocities of concentration camps."[66] And, like Therrien, he used the
desacralized Crucifixion as an electrified prod to jolt his viewers. The

painter's obituary, written by the art critic Brian Sewell for the *Evening Standard,* is made to measure for Therrien:

> He took the Crucifixion, stripped it of all its Christian implications, and invested it instead with the universal beastliness of man and abattoir. . . . He used the ideas of the trap, the cell, the cage, the X-ray and the heavy fall of light to imprison and torment his subjects, to distill the violence, and to assault complacent senses . . . so that we might contemplate ferociously profane images of cruelty and despair and see in them an inheritance from the great Renaissance themes of religious and temporal power.[67]

Both themes abide–and often coincide–in Therrien's work, which has anatomized power from the first. *Boot Camp–Indoctrination into an Ordered System* (1983) was a covert operation conducted at Fort Knox, Kentucky, in which the artist took advantage of an ROTC recruitment effort whereby potential enlistees were allowed to undergo basic training without further obligation. Intrigued by "the uses and misuses of discipline and the idea of control," Therrien secretly documented the six-week experience with a microcassette recorder hidden inside his uniform and a miniature thirty-five-millimeter camera concealed in his ammo pouch.

Boot Camp was Stanley Kubrick's *Full Metal Jacket* come to life. "It was a program of continual abuse," reflects Therrien. "People died during my training, and one cadet sustained permanent brain damage from heatstroke. They allowed the cadets to drink beer at night because they wanted you to know what a great experience the armed forces was, and if you didn't drink enough water the next morning, you'd dehydrate. Once you reached that point, it would only take four or five minutes for your brain to reach 109, 110 degrees. We were in the field, shooting M-60s, big machine guns, and this guy's body overheated. They couldn't get him into an ice bath fast enough, so he got cooked."

Therrien's 1993 "spectacle of mechanical propaganda," *Information Machine: Ideological Engines,* sounded a somewhat more hopeful note. He cites it as the point at which Comfort/Control's bodies, formerly the powerless subjects of instrumental technologies and dominant ideologies, "began to resist."

Performed in the cavernous Cathedral Room at the Icehouse—the former ice factory that houses CRASHarts as well as the artist and his family—*Information Machine* featured a three-story structure resembling a medieval siege tower made out of pipes. Timothy North stood on top of it, raining blows on the suspended, spread-eagled performer who served as the Body Drum; the Ninety-Degree Machine hung from its lowermost section; and the Fetal Cage swung back and forth in front of it, crisscrossing its midsection.

Directly behind the tower stood the Arm of Life, a platform surmounted by a standing figure, arms outstretched like a crucified Christ, his body encircled by a fifty-thousand-watt halo of quartz lights. The man's face was masked by a square plate inset with a twelve-thousand-watt light array, and jutting from the crossbar covering his loins was the robotic arm that gave the structure its name. At intervals, the piston-driven limb swung up, its finger tapping a plate strapped to the figure's chest and activating the array; a flash of seemingly solar brilliance flared up and winked out, leaving the audience blinded.

"The Body Drum is being hammered but at the same time it's activating the computer," explains Therrien. "It accepts this punishment and survives, so even though it's in an extremely passive and vulnerable position, there's still a sense of power. And the halo of light gives the body in the Arm of Life power, even though the light is part of the control relationship in the sense that it's being ignited by the man who's pounding on the Body Drum."

Viewed head-on, the Body Drum, its arms and legs arranged in an X, aligns with the cross-shaped figure in the Arm of Life to form da Vinci's famous study of a male figure with arms and legs spread, straddling a circle. To Leonardo, the drawing—*Proportional Study of a Man in the Manner of Vitruvius*, widely known as "Vitruvian Man"—was archetypal as well as anatomical, referencing the Romanesque symbol of man the microcosm, the sweep of his limbs "eternally tracing the perfect geometry of God's creation," as Martin Kemp puts it.[68] In Therrien's hands, it is a profoundly ambiguous image, at once evocative of rapture and torture, of our everlasting attempts to push the envelope of what it means to be human while somehow retaining our humanity. An icon of a sublime humanism that sees in humankind the measure of all things, it is created, ironically, by overlaying tableaux of ritualized dominance and submission: one man bludgeoned by another, a third pinioned in a ring of fire and set ablaze from the neck up.

Information Machine is a junction box with a series of circuits branching off it: the body, technology, religion, and politics, all of them paths for power. Of course, power is not only a cultural phenomenon but a natural one as well. Having considered technology as a religion and religion as a technology, Therrien turns, finally, to a contemplation of power in the most literal sense, as an elemental force.

"I like the feeling of live electricity, the power that's present there; it's something that's always fascinated me," he says. "I'm interested in electricity as an analogy for life and at the same time death." Therrien is intimately acquainted with the dangers of high voltage: He once felt the kiss of 220 volts while thwapping with metal drumsticks on an electrified plate he mistakenly thought was dead (it was, until someone switched on the power without warning). Moreover, the Icehouse is uncomfortably close to an electrical substation, and the growing concern over the potentially hazardous effects of long-term exposure to electromagnetic fields has not escaped Therrien's notice. Still, he is seduced by the brutish beauty of the substation, with its hunkering transformers and gargantuan cables.

"I'd love to have a nice little bungalow among all the transmission towers, although I wouldn't want to spend more than a few minutes there a day," he muses. "There are these gigantic power cables going down the street—I think they're four-hundred-thousand-volt lines—and when you stand near them, you can feel an incredible hum underneath. You can hold up a fluorescent tube and it will illuminate, just from the immense power in the air!"

Therrien the rhapsodist has much in common with the awestruck journalist who asked of London's Battersea Power Station in 1934, "Is it a cathedral?" (The station's architect, Giles Gilbert Scott, also designed the Liverpool Anglican Cathedral and was later said to have erected two houses of worship, "one for God, one for Electricity."[69]) In Comfort/Control performances, Therrien makes use of "electricity as a metaphor for a supreme being."

"When people try to explain God, they do it on a spiritual level," he says. "Well, what is God made of? Does He have mass? It seems to me that the only thing God could be, if God exists, is electricity or some type of electromagnetic force or radiation. The descriptions of God as pure and white and blinding in illuminated manuscripts sound very much like electricity. It's electricity, in essence, that makes our integrated circuits sing—all of those electrical impulses running through us, making the body's mechanism move. In *Frankenstein*, electricity is a life-giving force; now, they use defibrillators to bring people who are dead back to life. I would love to be hit by lightning and live. The idea of having all of that power, supposedly as much as a nuclear explosion, pass through your body is absolutely phenomenal; it must be like being touched by God. When I see the Sistine Chapel ceiling, with God reaching out and touching Adam, I envision a spark gap—*zap!*"

5 /
ROBOCOPULATION
Sex Times Technology
Equals the Future[1]

Cybersex in *The Lawnmower Man*. © 1992 *New Line Productions, Inc., and Allied Vision / Lane Pringle. All rights reserved. Photo by Douglas Kirkland; computer animation by Angel Studios, Carlsbad, CA. Photo appears courtesy of New Line Productions, Inc.*

Sex Machines

Different writers have described "the sexual frenzy of factories,"
obsessive rhythms, exhalations, cries, panting sounds, shining
dart-pointed instruments, articulated rods dripping with sweat,
simulacra of inexhaustible loves. Could not man himself become
a machine in his amorous activity and make love indefinitely,
like a machine?

—*Marcel Jean*[2]

James Brown's sentiments, exactly. In "Get Up (I Feel Like Being a) Sex
Machine," Brown reinvents himself as a plug-in stud, tireless as a punch
press but still salty with sweat, soft to the touch. He imagines himself a
prosthetically enhanced satyr who retains enough of his humanity to be able
to savor the pleasures of the flesh. Cyborged, Brown has the best of both
worlds, thrilling to the fevers and "cold sweats" of human passion but
performing with locomotive endurance.

Brown's fantasy is only one narrative thread in the conceptual knot
that Marshall McLuhan, writing in 1951, called "one of the most peculiar
features of our world—the interfusion of sex and technology."[3] This bizarre
union, according to McLuhan, was "born of a hungry curiosity to explore
and enlarge the domain of sex by mechanical technique, on one hand, and,
on the other, to possess machines in a sexually gratifying way."[4] This last
motif, to which McLuhan gives only perfunctory attention, has been taken
up in cyberculture, where it is ornately embroidered in collective fantasies.

In *The Mechanical Bride: Folklore of Industrial Man,* McLuhan un-
covers the logic of Henry Ford's assembly line in a lingerie ad. Nature's Rival
"four-in-one proportioned girdles" accomplish what nature cannot, he
observes, turning out copies of Hollywood starlets with mechanical precision. In like fashion, the fetishizing of number sequences (36–24–36)–a
statistician's idea of erotica–transforms women into "hot numbers," their
measurements "plotted as an abstract curve."[5] Musicals reduce tapping,
kicking chorus line beauties to interlocked machine parts, a truism borne
out in Busby Berkeley's 1933 movie, *Footlight Parade,* where skimpily attired
dancing girls, legs spread, are arranged in a giant rosette suggestive of a
Curtis radial aircraft engine.

Inverting the advertising logic that invests consumer goods with sex
appeal, "feminine glamour ads and the modern beauty chorus insist on their
relation to the machine."[6] Contemplating the unhappy results of human
sexuality yoked, through advertising, to the demands of the marketplace,
McLuhan sees women alienated from their own bodies. Made to submit to
the techniques of industrial production, female anatomy is disassembled
into replaceable parts: "[H]er legs are not intimately associated with her
taste or with her unique self but are merely display objects like the grill-
work on a car."[7]

On a deeper level, McLuhan perceives the debilitating effect of
incessant titillation by Madison Avenue: a sexual burnout that demands
greater and greater jolts of voltage to bring the libido twitchingly alive. The
end product of this condition, he argues, is the *Dr. Strangelove*-ian elevation
of annihilation to the status of an orgasm:

> Sensation and sadism are near twins. And for those for whom
> the sex act has come to seem mechanical and merely the
> meeting and manipulation of body parts, there often remains a
> hunger which can be called metaphysical but which is not
> recognized as such, and which seeks satisfaction in physical
> danger, or sometimes in torture, suicide, or murder.[8]

Now, forty-plus years after McLuhan's prescient observations about
"the widely occurring cluster image of sex, technology, and death," the
intertwisted themes of eroticized machinery, technologically mediated sex,

sex with technology, and the rerouting of carnal desires into high-tech orgies of destruction are woven through cyberculture.

Issue number ten of the "neurozine" *bOING-bOING* is given over to "SEX CANDY FOR HAPPY MUTANTS"; the cover portrays a young woman wired for pleasure, a computer cable plugged into her crotch and B-movie contraptions clamped onto each breast. Articles include "Virtual Sex: Fucking Around with Machines" and "Confessions of a PC Porn Fanatic." The February 1992 *Elle* titillated its readers with a cover line heralding "THE BRAVE NEW WORLD OF COMPUTER SEX," and, in the following year, the premiere issue of *Wired* featured an article on "Digital Sex," the April U.K. edition of *Marie Claire* promised "Hi-Tech Sex: Orgasm by Computer," and the November *Self* bruited "High-Tech Sex: New Ways to Push Your Buttons."

The now-defunct *Future Sex* hitched the advertising industry's latest synonym for "new and improved" to history's oldest come-on. Described in a WELL blurb posted by its editors as "the only magazine that explores how high technology is changing the way we think about sex," *Future Sex* promised multicultural erotica "wrapped up [in] hypermodern design." The cover of the magazine's second issue is a guaranteed attention-getter. Male and female infonauts float in cyberspace, both scantily clad in photorealistic computer renderings of virtual reality gear. The man sports a computerized strap-on. The woman wears a bra fitted with robotic hands that are poised to fondle her breasts and a G-string equipped with what looks like a high-tech vibrator. "CYBERSEX," announces the cover line. "STRAP IN, TWEAK OUT, TURN ON." The editor and self-styled "queen of high-tech porn" Lisa Palac looks forward, in her opening essay, to the arrival of "erototronics" – "smart" garb that immerses the wearer in computer-generated, fully interactive wet dreams.

Disappointingly, there was nothing terribly futuristic about the sex in *Future Sex*, which consisted of the usual beautiful people feigning masturbation or fornication for the camera lens. The "futuristic" content in issue three, for example, is limited to a cyber-porn story about "tele-sex" between a virtual blonde and a virtual zebra, reviews of soft-core CD-ROMs, and ads for the decidedly low-tech medium of telephone sex, masquerading as dangerous liaisons in cyberspace. "GET PLUGGED INTO EROTIC EXPRESSION," urges one, while another ("THE ORIGINAL CYBERSEX") prepares the customer for his or her quantum leap into a science fiction future: "HARDWARE: YOUR TELEPHONE," "SOFTWARE: YOUR EROTIC FANTASY." Wait a minute; couldn't the nineteenth-century owner of one of Alexander Graham Bell's "speaking telephones" have done this?

Palac, an antipornography activist–turned–"sex-positive feminist," has produced a spoken word CD called *Cyborgasm*, a "virtual reality sex experience" that exploits 3-D effects created with Virtual Audio, a technology used in virtual reality sound tracks.[9] The sticker affixed to the CD's mailing envelope ("THE FUTURE OF SEX IS INSIDE THIS PACKAGE") suggests that sex involving high-tech interfaces capable of transmitting otherworldly sensations to hot-wired users is no longer science fiction.

Tearing open the padded envelope, one finds a CD, poster, "eco-goggles," and "cyberubber." On closer inspection, this last item appears to be an ordinary lubricated condom; the cybernetic quality that distinguishes it from garden-variety rubbers lies, apparently, in the "CYBORGASM" logo emblazoned on its wrapper. The eco-goggles, which are intended to block out visual distractions, turn out to be black spectacles printed on a sheet of cardboard. In order to have what the directions call "the best Cyborgasmic experience," the user is instructed to sit alone, in the dark, wearing nothing but headphones, condom, and cardboard goggles. Presumably, he or she has taken the precaution of concocting a plausible explanation in case housemates barge in unannounced.

The CD consists for the most part of narrated fantasies in the *Penthouse* Forum mold, accompanied by heavy breathing and obscene squelchings; it is decidedly uncybernetic, although a vibrator puts in a brief turn for the grand finale. As the CD plays, the grunting, grinding, and heavy breathing of simulated coupling begins to sound mechanical and, finally, comical. *Cyborgasm* brings to mind the arch-punk Johnny Rotten's supremely snide observation, "What is sex, anyway? Just thirty seconds of squelching noises."[10]

Palac's CD makes use of the oldest virtual realities known to humankind: playacting and storytelling. Unfortunately, listening to simulated sex or hearing about sexual fantasies is nothing like having sex. Furthermore, where's the cyber? *Cyborgasm*'s narrative content is utterly unrelated to technology and the interface itself–a CD player, a pair of cardboard goggles, and a condom–is not exactly the cortex-to-computer hookup that fans of *Neuromancer* have been clamoring for. As Chris Hudak notes in his blistering *Mondo 2000* review of the CD, "[T]he failure here is a conceptual one, and it's right down there with the ones and zeroes—*there is nothing remotely 'cyber' about any of this. It's a fucking CD. Literally.*"[11]

The problem with *Cyborgasm,* as with *Future Sex,* is that sex seems to have changed little since the first naked ape stood erect. Sex that is itself futuristic, as opposed to more of the same conducted against a futuristic backdrop, would require the revision of existing notions of human sexuality and embodied consciousness, perhaps even the engineering of radically modified bodies. But how can the sex act be detached from the gestalt that results from long residence in this bag of water we call the body? In a science fiction future where consciousness is not confined to its traditional container but may take up residence in computer memories or robot bodies, it seems at least conceivable that human sexuality could be abstracted from any reference to embodiment, perhaps even from a recognizably human consciousness altogether. Nevertheless, current speculation regarding posthuman sexuality is bounded by the inescapable fact that it is conducted from the vantage point of human beings, for whom the very notion of sexuality is defined in terms of embodiment and humanity. As the SF writer Rudy Rucker memorably observed, "I can't stand on top of my own head."[12]

Mechanical Reproduction

As Marcel Jean, writing in 1959, makes clear, the current interest in sex machines and machine sex is not a postmodern phenomenon. Freudian readings of the psychosexual symbolism of overheated machinery are hardly a recent development; the sight of camshafts thrusting ceaselessly, of hydraulic fluids squealing through small orifices under high pressure, quickened pulses early in this century.

Henry Adams's landmark essay "The Dynamo and the Virgin," in which he equates the forty-foot dynamos at the Great Exposition of 1900 with the Mother of God, is nuanced with a subtle eroticism. Standing in the Gallery of Machines, gazing awestruck at the enormous, spinning "symbol of infinity," Adams finds himself in the presence of an "occult mechanism" animated by an unmistakably female sexual energy—"female" because the force harnessed by the dynamo, electricity, is mysterious, almost supernatural. "In any previous age," he writes, "sex was strength. . . . Diana of the

Ephesians . . . was Goddess because of her force; she was the animated dynamo; she was reproduction–the greatest and most mysterious of all energies; all she needed was to be fecund."[13] The sexual power of the pagan goddess was sublimated in the symbol of the Virgin, and now, says Adams, the procreative power and spiritual sensuality of the Virgin has been transfigured in the form of the dynamo.

Twenty-nine years later, the modernist poet MacKnight Black writes, in *Machinery,*

> *Dynamos are bosoms,*
> *Round with the sweet first-filling of a*
> new
> *Mother's milk.*[14]

In modernist art, the idolatrous tendencies expressed by Adams shaded, by degrees, from religious devotion into mechano-eroticism; paeans to the machine by Italian futurists, English vorticists, and Russian suprematists often verged on soft-core porn.

Emerging from the rubble of World War I, the dadaists lampooned bourgeois ideals, excoriating the industrial culture that had brought the world to the eve of Armageddon. Putting an absurdist spin on the clockwork world of Cartesian mechanism, they reconstructed humankind as a race of automata run amok. Robert Short sums it up neatly when he writes that the dadaists "exploited the man/machine analogy to empty life of its spiritual content."[15] But they did so with devilish wit. In images of mechanized coitus and seduction machines, they spoofed the objectification of sex in advertising and the refunctioning of the female body to accommodate mass-produced, mass-marketed fashions. The French dadaist Francis Picabia painted a tongue-in-cheek, draftsmanlike *Portrait of an American Girl in a State of Nudity* (1915): a spark plug accompanied by the legend "FOR EVER."

Mechanomorphic images were useful, too, in expressing bohemian contempt for a clock-punching, conspicuously consuming middle class that fornicated and Fletcherized with unblinking imbecility. ("Fletcherizing," a digestion-promoting regimen developed by a Dr. Fletcher in the early part of this century, consisted of chewing each bite forty times before swallowing.) The German dadaist Max Ernst produced a deceptively innocent-looking, almost childish drawing of a fanciful gadget. An inscription reads: "[A] SMALL MACHINE . . . CONSTRUCTED FOR FEARLESS POLLINATION"—a marital aid, perhaps, for petite bourgeoisie who find the thought of gooey fluids distasteful.

It is profoundly significant that the French dadaist Marcel Duchamp's seminal painting, *The Bride Stripped Bare by Her Bachelors, Even* (1915–1923) is, to put it bluntly, a Rube Goldbergian fucking machine. Robert Lebel called it an exercise in "onanism for two": The Bride Motor, an internal combustion engine that runs on "love gasoline" hangs stripped yet maddeningly unravishable in the picture's upper half, forever out of reach of the Bachelor Machine below, which grinds ceaselessly in frustration.[16] The Bride—at once the apotheosis of virgin and whore, the object of male adoration and the source of an inscrutable, vaguely malicious female desire—hangs poised between desire and possession for all time.[17]

Duchamp's close friend Picabia employed mechanomorphic imagery in the service of auto eroticism, in the literal sense. A passionate collector and skilled driver of powerful cars, Picabia celebrated the intoxicating effects of the open throttle and the smell of gasoline even as he satirized human sexuality in the age of mechanical reproduction. Stephen Bayley sees a riot of sexual imagery in *Flamenca*, Picabia's 1917 rendering of an internal combustion valve and its guide. "[T]he reciprocating valve resembles in its action the rhythms of sex," writes Bayley, "the valve itself the penis, the guide the female sheath."[18] To Bayley, the Italian sportscar designer Enzo Ferrari's conjecture that "between man and machine there exists a perfect equation: fifty per cent machine and fifty per cent man" suggests that "the idea of mechanical intercourse, that parody of the act of love, lies only a little beneath the surface of people who are fascinated with fast cars."[19]

The very notion of "auto eroticism," in the punning sense, has been so exhausted by pop psychologists that all who treat it run the risk of producing unintentional kitsch. The linkage of the pneumatic contours of the pinup goddess with the morphological oddities that characterized automobile design in its golden age, the 1950s—a veritable fantasia of protrusions and orifices, of bumpers shaped like bulging crotches or jutting breasts—is well documented.

Even so, auto eroticism is sufficiently rich that it resists flip dismissal. The car, second only to the gun, is *the* quintessential piece of American hardware, fraught with notions of rugged individualism, endless frontiers, eternal youth, phallic power through extension, intrauterine comfort via enclosure, and the utopian promise of American know-how and can-do. For the American teenager, getting a license and, ultimately, a car constitutes a rite of passage intimately associated with adolescent sexuality; backseats are the upholstered altars on which virginity is ritually sacrificed to adulthood. Often, the vehicle itself is a sexual surrogate, as in Simon and Garfunkel's "Baby Driver" ("I wonder how your engines feel") or the Rolling Stones' "Brand New Car" ("Jack her up, baby, go on, open the hood / I want to check if her oil smells good"). Stephen King's *Christine* is a retelling of the medieval myth of the succubus in hot rod vernacular: a pimply teenager falls in love with a bloodred 1957 Plymouth Fury possessed by a jealous, murderous female spirit who runs down three boys who once mistreated her. Driving, throughout *Christine*, is equated with sexual conquest, as it is in the 1926 poem "she being Brand" by e. e. cummings, in which a temperamental car becomes a female virgin:

> she being Brand
>
> -new; and you
> know consequently a
> little stiff i was
> careful of her and(having
> thoroughly oiled the universal
> joint tested my gas felt of
> her radiator made sure her springs were O.
>
> K.)i went right to it flooded-the-carburetor cranked her
> up . . .[20]

Futurist auto eroticism carries mechano-eroticism to its inevitable, cyborgian conclusion: the marriage of meat and mechanism. "[W]e will conquer the seemingly unconquerable hostility that separates our human flesh from the metal of motors," declares the poet F. T. Marinetti in a futurist manifesto.[21] The tension generated by this seemingly unresolvable situation seeks release in the pornographic crash, a fiery ecstasy in which car and driver are conjoined, once and for all. In his 1914 poem "Fornication of Automobiles," Mario de Leon choreographs a car crash as the (vaguely homoerotic) copulation of gladiatorial machines:

Involuntary collision,
furious fornication
of two automobiles—energy,
embrace of two warriors
bold of movement
syncopation of two "heart motors,"
spilling of "blood-gas."[22]

The notion of auto erotic collisions reaches its zenith in J. G. Ballard's proto-cyberpunk novel *Crash*. In the detached, exact language of the forensic pathologist or the engineer, Ballard adumbrates "a new sexuality born from a perverse technology":

> In his vision of a car-crash with the actress, Vaughan was obsessed by many wounds and impacts—by the dying chromium and collapsing bulkheads of their two cars meeting head-on . . . by the compact fractures of their thighs impacted against their handbrake mountings, and above all by the wounds to their genitalia, her uterus pierced by the heraldic beak of the manufacturer's medallion, his semen emptying across the luminescent dials that registered for ever the last temperature and fuel levels of the engine.[23]

Violent and passionless, beyond ego psychology or social mores, it is a posthuman sexuality "without referentiality and without limits," as the postmodern philosopher Jean Baudrillard puts it.[24] Alienated from a body that seems, more and more, like a preindustrial artifact, this new sexuality fetishizes urban desolation, televised disasters, celebrities, and commodities—above all, the automobile.

In *Crash*, sex happens almost entirely in cars; removed from that context, it loses its appeal. The body is erotic only when it intersects with technology or the built environment, either literally (punctured by door handles, impaled on steering columns) or figuratively ("[t]he untouched, rectilinear volumes of this building fused in my mind with the contours of her calves and thighs pressed against the vinyl seating").[25] A young woman's body bears testimony to a severe automobile accident; to the narrator, who was himself injured in an accident that imprinted his car's instrumentation on his knees and shins, she has been reborn:

> The crushed body of the sports car had turned her into a creature of free and perverse sexuality, releasing within its twisted bulkheads and leaking engine coolant all the deviant possibilities of her sex. Her crippled thighs and wasted calf muscles were models for fascinating perversities.[26]

Here, as in SF films such as *2001: A Space Odyssey* and *Blade Runner*, humans are dispassionate mannequins—crash dummies—while the technology around them is disconcertingly anthropomorphic: The "grotesque overhang of an instrument panel forced on to a driver's crotch" in an accident conjures a "calibrated act of machine fellatio," while the "elegant aluminized air-vents" in a hospital "beckon as invitingly as the warmest organic orifice."[27] In the depraved geometry of *Crash*, semen and engine coolant, crotches and chromium instrument heads are congruent.

"I believe that organic sex, body against body, skin area against skin area, is becoming no longer possible," said Ballard, in a 1970 interview, "simply because if anything is to have any meaning for us it must take place in terms of the values and experiences of the media landscape."[28]

Published in 1973, *Crash* refracts McLuhan's monstrous ménage à trois—sex, technology, and death—through the splintered lens of consumer culture, with its flattened affect, celebrity worship, obsessive documentation of every lived moment, and psychotic confusion of subjective experience and filmic fictions. Improvising on these themes with a gleeful viciousness that is equal parts surrealism, pop art, and punk, Ballard portends their convergence in cyberculture.

Built for Pleasure

Recent years have seen a proliferation of imagery that gives vent to the desire to "possess machines in a sexually gratifying way," as McLuhan so discreetly put it, supplanting Ballard's eroticized air-vents and instrument panels with the considerably more compliant electric love doll. Human-machine miscegenation–RoboCopulation, by any other name–is the subtext of the future schlock illustrations of Hajime Sorayama and Larry Chambers, collected in glossy paperbacks and sold in science fiction bookshops. Sorayama churns out airbrush cartoons of robot odalisques, their chromium pudenda free of hair and other, all too human unpleasantries; Chambers is known for illustrations like "Steel Madam," a lovingly rendered drawing of a robotic trollop's stiletto heel flirtatiously tickling a gartered leg.

Chambers and Sorayama weren't the first to modernize Pygmalion's Galatea–the male fantasy of the anatomically accurate automaton. In *Westworld*, a 1973 SF film about an adult theme park in which guests live out their fantasies in ancient Roman, medieval, or frontier settings, humanoid robots of both sexes are programmed for pleasure (typically, we see only female androids in action, since the movie's main characters are men). The male models, whose "external equipment" is "entirely unrealistic, but effective and stimulating," are equipped with "internal vibratory mechanisms"; the female models ("a technological triumph") are outfitted with "suction and torsion mechanisms." A scene set in the locker room of the technicians who maintain the robots is particularly memorable:

FIRST TECHNICIAN: You ever made it with one of those machines?

SECOND TECHNICIAN: No . . . I'll take the real thing. If I can ever get home to her.

FIRST TECHNICIAN: I tried it with one of those Rome hookers. One night out on the repair table. Powered her up and really went to town. . . .

THIRD TECHNICIAN: You could get fired for that.[29]

This exchange, reminiscent of off-color banter between morticians, hints at the necrophilia implicit in the act of making love to synthetic flesh. In *Human Robots in Myth and Science*, John Cohen makes this connection explicit. The erotic appeal exerted on some men by nude statues and "undraped" mannequins, he maintains,

is allied to necrophilia. The potential necrophilist needs an unresisting accomplice; the corpse is totally helpless and defenseless, and cannot resist an assault.[30]

This is the source of the creepy pathos of the inflatable sex doll, whose goggle eyes and gaping, obscenely red mouth suggest a strangled prostitute. In K. W. Jeter's cyberpunk novel *Dr. Adder,* the protagonist recoils in gut-lurching horror from a roomful of mechanoid whores with "polyethylene cunt[s]":

> Limmit felt his internal organs shift sickeningly at the sight of the high-ceilinged room's contents. Its entire length, stretching as far as he could see, was filled with duplicates of . . . whores, in various stages of completion. . . . Holy shit, thought Limmit, nauseated. The old science fiction pulp wet-dream: the mechanical cunt.[31]

Limmit is backstage at a *Westworld*-style amusement park located in Nixon Country–California's Orange County. Sending up adolescent fantasies that cross Disney's Tomorrowland with Hugh Hefner's Playboy Mansion, Jeter manages a few savage jabs at the same well-fed living dead satirized by the dadaists. Limmit despairs, a few pages later, at the horrifying thought that he might never leave Orange County, that he will become one more lawn-mowing, barbecuing suburban zombie:

> I'll die right here, only I'll keep on walking. I'll be dead, and I'll settle down in Orange County, marry a girl vague from TV and downers, and we'll raise anonymous children together, removed from her body like loaves of bread while she's knocked out.[32]

Jeter updates the dadaists' vision of the look-alike, think-alike masses for an age of pill-popping couch potatoes. To Limmit, the suburbanite copulating with a "foam-rubber ersatz whore"—a sick-funny image that perfectly captures the soullessness of a thoroughly commodified existence—is little better than a robot himself.

The equation of the archetypal suburban consumer with a mindless automaton is an all-purpose metaphor, serving opposed ends: the feminism of *The Stepford Wives* (1974), a black comedy about suburban chauvinists who dispatch their mutinous wives and replace them with brain-dead happy homemakers created in the image of *Playboy* centerfolds, and the beery misogyny of Charles Bukowski's short story "The Fuck Machine."

Bukowski's robotic love doll Tanya is a cross between Barbie and the Bride of Frankenstein. On the outside, she is "all ass and breast," but her torso is stuffed full of "wire and tubes—coiled and running things—plus some minor substance that faintly resemble[s] blood," and her stomach and veins once belonged to a hog and a dog, respectively.[33] The fear and loathing of female sexuality bubbling beneath this image oozes out when the scientist who built Tanya declares, "[E]very woman is a fucking machine, can't you see that? [T]hey play for the highest bidder!"[34] Bukowski's virulent misogyny is inflected with a horror of consumer culture not unlike Jeter's:

> poor Tanya . . . she had had no desire for money or property or
> large new cars or overexpensive homes. she had never read the
> evening paper. had no desire for [color] television, new hats, rain
> boots, backfence conversations with idiot wives.[35]

In an America where humans have come to resemble mass-produced widgets, where one might pass "half a hundred fuck machines in a 10 minute walk on almost any main sidewalk of America—the only difference being that they pretended that they were human," Tanya's saving grace is that she is what she seems to be.[36] Ironically, the hollow, materialistic "fuck machine" so reviled by Bukowski is the culturally constructed product of male desires. The "assembly-line love goddess," to use McLuhan's phrase, is only as the media gods made her.

But the reality of the living doll—starved to pubescent proportions, douched, depilated, and deodorized—inevitably falls short of the male dream of robotic glamour. The female sex machine serves not only as a shiny surface on which male visions of femininity may be etched but as a mirror whose reflection reinforces the masculine sense of self. The result is a narcissistic closed circuit that resembles what the Freudian psychoanalyst Jacques Lacan calls the "mirror stage" of psychological development, the phase in early childhood during which the child comes to recognize himself in the mirror and an integrated self-image begins to coalesce. "[W]e arrive at a sense of an 'I' by finding that 'I' reflected back to ourselves by some object or person in the world," Terry Eagleton elaborates, in his discussion of Lacan. "This object is at once somehow part of ourselves—we identify with it—and yet not ourselves, something alien."[37] Intriguingly, Lacan himself draws an analogy between the mirror stage and our relationship with *the automaton,* "in which, in an ambiguous relation, the world of [one's] own making tends to find completion."[38]

Anthropomorphic yet alien, the electric love doll is consonant with male fantasies to a degree that no human female could ever be, but mocking in its forgery of organic life. This uncanniness is what the Japanese roboticist Masahiro Mori pinpoints when he refers, in Frederik Schodt's *Inside the Robot Kingdom,* to the "Uncanny Valley," a dip in the index that graphs our relationship with humanoid dolls and anthropomorphic machines. According to Mori, our affinity for our creations parallels the degree to which they resemble us, up to a point; when they begin to look too much like us, their cuddliness turns to uncanniness. Freud, who wrote a well-known essay on the Uncanny, would say that this is because we are unable to convince ourselves that such disquietingly lifelike creations, inert though they are, do not harbor some spark of life. (Significantly, he devotes a substantial portion of "The 'Uncanny' " to a consideration of Olympia, the mechanical Galatea in E. T. A. Hoffmann's story "The Sandman.")

The discomfiting effects of humanoid mannequins, statues, waxworks, robots, and the like are also inextricably bound up in the subconscious fear of our own mortality that confronts us in the image of the doppelgänger, the spectral double that haunts its fleshly counterpart. The doppelgänger, in turn, has everything to do with the mirror stage (Freud calls the double a "harking-back to particular phases in the evolution of the self-regarding feeling") as well as man-made "reflections" of humanity. In a discussion of the automaton, Baudrillard observes that

> There is already sorcery at work in the mirror. But how much
> more so when this image can be detached from the mirror and
> be transported, stocked, reproduced at will. . . . Reproduction
> is diabolical in its very essence; it makes something fundamental
> vacillate.[39]

The uncanniness of the idealized gyndroid and the patriarchal use of Woman as Narcissus's mirror are points of departure for *L'Eve Future* ("The Future Eve"), Jean Villiers de l'Isle-Adam's 1886 novel about an "electro-human machine" modeled on a woman named Alicia. Lord Ewald, a wealthy English gentleman, has fallen out of love with his mistress Alicia ("the absolute feminine ideal for three-quarters of modern humanity") because she is afflicted, unhappily, with a reasoning intellect.[40] And, as Ewald reminds us, "The marble Venus, after all, has nothing to do with reason."[41]

Thomas Edison solves Ewald's dilemma by constructing the robot Hadaly, an idealized vision of Alicia that epitomizes the nineteenth-century concept of a sublime femininity. Hadaly (Persian for "ideal," according to Villiers) is the very image of languorous gentility, subsisting on pills and gliding through life in a somnambulistic state. Her iron joints are oiled with perfume, and in place of lungs she has two golden phonographs whose sixty-hour "program," recorded by Alicia, was written by the century's greatest poets, metaphysicians, and novelists. An aid to philosophical contemplation, the android is, as Edison observes, Ewald's platonic desire incarnate:

> [T]he creature whom you love, and who for you is the *sole* REALITY, is by no means the one who is momentarily embodied in [Alicia's] transient human figure, but a creature of your desire. . . . In short, it's this objectified projection of your own mind that you call on, that you perceive, that you CREATE in your living woman, *and which is nothing but your own mind reduplicated in her.*[42]

Fashioned in the image of Ewald's metaphysical fantasy, Hadaly is a marble goddess, a mechanical bride who will never be stripped bare (she is, in fact, a living stun gun, able to incapacitate would-be mashers with a jolt from her electrified body). Spiritual, inviolate, she is the obverse of the science fiction sex machine, a divine statue who leads men not into physical temptation but toward the life of the mind. Even so, she is like Bukowski's "fuck machine," Jeter's synthetic whores, and McLuhan's assembly-line love goddesses in that she is a figment of the male imagination—Woman stripped of free will and threatening sexuality. Both paradigms police female desire: In the mechanoid whore, Woman is reduced to a "mechanical cunt," a Picabia-esque spark plug that goes "FOR EVER" once her ignition is switched on; in the android virgin, female sexuality is etherealized and the female sex erased, reduced to a ridiculous blankness like the vacancy between Barbie's legs.

Ladies' Home Companion

As might be expected, science fiction is largely devoid of female mechano-erotica, an inequity the *Mondo 2000* editor "St. Jude" (Jude Milhon) has attempted to redress through "technoporn" written from a female perspective. In Steven Levy's chronicle of the computer revolution, *Hackers,* Milhon is introduced as a computerphile who "noted the lack of female hardware hackers, and was enraged at the male hacker obsession with technological play and power."[43] "Woman's Home Companion," a piece of SF erotica by Milhon that appeared in *Mondo 2000,* is a lighthearted rewrite of the *Westworld* scenario. Lounging in her Jacuzzi, the narrator is serviced by a Personal Robot, "all black rubber and chrome," whose five, nimble-fingered hands attend to her every erogenous zone. In addition, her handy household helper is fitted with a daunting assortment of protuberances: "Mistress, I am equipped with four copulatory devices. Shall I demonstrate them for you?"[44]

Milhon's story inspired "What do humans really want from their CYBORG LOVE SLAVES???" a WELL discussion topic in which several female contributors spun out lickerish fantasies. Tiffany Lee Brown confided that her

> idealoid luv slave would be programmed with hundreds of personalities, from which it would select completely at random. I hafta have that element of surprise. I wouldn't mind having one program switch my borg baby back and forth from Jeff Goldblum to Geena [Davis] mode, at excellently timed intervals.

Erika Whiteway's

> would be able to read my mind, would always be ON, would do whatever I want and not just sex either but grocery shopping and ministering to my every need, desire, whim . . . and inexplicable craving for HeathBarCrunch ice cream at 3:23 A.M.[45]

Transporting Lady Chatterley's lover to the world of *Neuromancer,* such imaginings are animated by a quirky humor missing, for the most part, from male visions of robo-bimbos. Milhon's Personal Robot, with its fondlers, diddlers, and dildos, spoofs a long line of futuristic labor-saving devices for the modern housewife epitomized in those preposterous kitchen utensils familiar from TV infomercials ("It slices, it dices, it juliennes . . ."). Heirs to several decades' rhetoric about the cybernated "House of the Future," Milhon, Brown, and Whiteway envision Personal Robots and cyborg love slaves that would attend to more than June Cleaver's housework.

Orgasmatron

The RoboCopulatory fantasies of Milhon and her fellow WELL-dwellers spring in part from what McLuhan called the "hungry curiosity to explore and enlarge the domain of sex by mechanical technique." It is a received truth that mass desire plays a strong role in "willing" technology into being. Where there's a will, there is often a way, and the craving for something like the Orgasmatron, the orgasm-inducing booth imagined by Woody Allen in *Sleeper,* lurks beneath the surface of cyberculture. According to the cultural anthropologist Arthur Harkins,

> Already there is talk of creation of androids for sexual purposes.
> I think you are going to see an industry develop in the sexual-appliance area. At first it will be machine appliances, and eventually you will see biological substitutes or surrogates for human sexual organs being employed in stationary and mobile machine systems.[46]

Harkins's words may prove prophetic if cultural momentum propels events on their present course. Sex with machines, together with dalliances conducted in virtual worlds, seems a seductive alternative in an age of AIDS, unwanted pregnancies, and sexually transmitted diseases. In cyberculture, the widespread yearning for untainted love has given rise to the on-line sex play that the technology writer Gareth Branwyn calls "text sex"; interactive, X-rated computer programs; and everyone's not-ready-for-prime-time fantasy, sex in virtual reality, or "cybersex."

You're alone, it's late, and the lights are low; your face is bathed in the phosphor glow of your PC screen. Connected by modem to the information service America Online, you browse through a list of user-initiated group discussions called "rooms." The topics range over a wide spectrum of interests, from pop culture to politics, but in the BBS's "People Connection" section, sexual themes predominate. Room names scroll down your screen: "Romance Connection," "Naughty Negligees," "Hot Bi Ladies," "Gay Room," "Naughty Girls," "Women Who Obey Women."

Highlighting one, you click your mouse and "enter" the room. A small square winks into existence in one corner of your screen. The names of the various conversationalists appear at the top of the inset box; their typewritten comments scroll by below. Summoning your courage, you decide to dive in. Typing a brief message in the small text entry window near the bottom of your screen, you select SEND. In the blink of an eye, your note, or "post," takes its place among the accumulated messages, at the end of the list.

Here as elsewhere on America Online, sexually explicit conversation is conducted warily, since public rooms are policed by "guides" recruited from the membership and paid in free on-line time. Derided as "cybercops" by those who frequent blue rooms, guides are empowered to delete dens of iniquity whose language and subject matter are not in keeping with the system's guidelines. Repeat offenders run the risk of having their memberships suspended. Like the habitués of conventional singles bars, BBS users tend therefore to scan rooms for potential partners with whom they might slip away to more secluded quarters.

Skimming the posted remarks, you settle on the author whose sentiments, sense of humor, and. sexual preference harmonize with yours. Using the PRIVATE MESSAGE command, you send the likely prospect a flirtatious note that pops up on his or her screen alone. Curiosity piqued, your partner responds in kind. Things proceed apace, from the coyly coquettish to the blatantly salacious, in the sort of breathless exchange that one denizen of the Internet termed a "heated sendstorm."

Inevitably, you and your partner decide to retire to the virtual boudoir. After activating the CREATE PRIVATE ROOM program, you zap the bedchamber's name and password to your partner via private message; within seconds, both of you have rendezvoused onscreen. Hunched over your computer keyboards, separated by a sea of wires, you tap out erotic messages that materialize, like spirit writing, as glowing characters on each other's screens. Soon, you find yourself typing with one hand. Coitus in cyberspace, like intercourse in the physical world, progresses from foreplay to climax; orgasms are signaled by cartoony exclamations: "ohhhhhh," "WOW!!!" and the perennial favorite "I'mmmm Commmmmmmminnngggggggg!!!!!!"

According to the *Wired* contributor Gerard Van Der Leun, text sex dates back to "the dawn of on-line." Branwyn cites three types of "text-based sexual exchanges" in his *South Atlantic Quarterly* essay "Compu-Sex: Erotica for Cybernauts." Most common, he reports, are sexually explicit descriptions of what each participant is purportedly doing. Another variety, favored by orgy-goers, involves the communal creation of sexual fantasies, a form of consensual world-building reminiscent of the fantasy role-playing game Dungeons and Dragons. Such scenarios, notes Branwyn, require the nimble negotiation of the inconsistencies that inevitably result when stories are collectively improvised by scattered strangers. Branwyn imagines a narrative with a short circuit, and a quick fix:

> BethR types: "I'm climbing on top of Roger104," not noticing that Roger104 has just stated that he is having sex standing up, in the corner, with Nina5. To work around this story "violation," Roger104 might type: "Nina and I get so worked up, we roll onto the floor. As Nina5 falls off of me, the always randy BethR, not missing a beat, climbs on top of me."[47]

Finally, there is what Branwyn wryly calls "teleoperated compu-sex," the preferred mode among couples who swing on-line. "Teleoperation" is the computer control of remote robots by human operators; teleoperated sex, by extension, involves the acting out, by one party, of instructions given by another, far removed: "Sal, I want you to slurp grape jelly out of Frieda's navel. . . ."

Sex among the disembodied is wondrous strange, as are the issues it raises. In an E-mail message, Branwyn described an encounter with an on-line prostitute who offered to have text sex with him in exchange for an illegal copy of a computer game. There are laws against software piracy, but is on-line prostitution, in which bodies never touch and no fluids are exchanged, illegal or even immoral? In fact, does the term *prostitution* even apply to sex-for-software barter when the "sex" in question consists of what the *Esquire* writer Michael Hirschorn calls "techno-onanism"–pornographic E-mail zapping back and forth between furiously masturbating users?

Stranger still is the notion of on-line adultery: Should significant others be jealous of their partners' on-line indiscretions? "If you have 'virtual sex' with someone," writes a user (who prefers to remain anonymous) in the WELL's "Text Sex" topic, "is that in essence . . . cheating on your [significant other] . . . or more like interactive fantasy? And if you have an ongoing virtual relationship, is that in effect an affair?" Susan E. Fernbach doesn't think so. "If the [on-line] involvement brings something extra to the primary relationship, then it's probably healthy," she writes. "If it drains energy from the primary relationship, there might be . . . a problem."[48]

Text sex is stealth sex, performed by unseen, unseeing participants whose identities are masked by the medium. Because on-line communication reduces human interaction to symbols hammered out on QWERTY keyboards, it effectively masks gender, a vertiginous state of affairs that some find liberating and others profoundly disconcerting. Victor Lukas confirms,

> Sex in cyberspace happens in a VERY surreal landscape! The phenomenon of males masquerading as females is quite widespread, but oddly enough, it is not necessarily an indication of gay preference. I introduced my male office mate, a shy man with a bit of an inferiority complex, to . . . Compuserve. [S]ince he wasn't a verbally skilled person, he had difficulty making friends or finding conversation partners. . . . On a whim, he changed to a female handle, and suddenly he was "popular."[49]

Users who pose as members of the opposite gender are commonly known as "MorFs." The term, short for "male or female," is also a pun on "morphing," the computer animation technique used to seamlessly dissolve one image into another. Not everyone adjusts easily to the notion of gender morphing, an observation amply–and amusingly–evidenced in one of Branwyn's posts:

> Things sometimes get real weird on AOL with people arguing over a person's true gender. The other night a "woman" was

accused by another "woman" of not being a woman. She thought
the "woman" in question was too aggressive to be a woman. The
"woman" in question gave her phone number to several people
so that they could call to hear her voice. After doing so, a "man"
verified that "she" sounded like a female. The "woman" who had
raised the allegations was not impressed. "She" said that lots of
TVs sound like women. Someone then asked "her" how we were
to know that SHE was a woman. "She" said that there were
images of her available for downloading. Funny how she thought
this was somehow more solid evidence than the other person's
phone voice. She said she could also fax people pix of her.
Wild![50]

To those endowed not with bulging abs or plunging cleavage but
overdeveloped brains, group gropes and one-night stands between discarnate minds look a lot like Utopia. In a private note to Branwyn, one devotee
wrote, "In compu-sex, being able to type fast and write well is equivalent to
having great legs or a tight butt in the real world." Linda Hardesty, a
participant in the WELL's "Sex in Virtual Communities" topic, offers a more
romantic perspective on the subject:

> The idea of falling in love with a person purely through writing
> seems to me to cast some light on the whole concept of falling in
> love. We do tend to fall in love with some image of the person
> that we have created in our own minds. Ways that people react
> on-line, coupled with one's own conditioning, create that
> image.[51]

The narrow bandwidth of on-line communication strikes some as
erotic in itself. The mental image Hardesty mentions derives its seductive
power from the same source tapped by Muslim veils that conceal all but the
eyes: the delicious mystery of the unseen. Then, too, to a true logophile, the
written word can be almost aphrodisiacal. "[S]ex at best *is* a conversation," writes "Afterhours (gail),"

> and virtual *intercourse* is what the WELL can be when it's
> working. . . . we want our words to stroke one another, envelop

one another, move one another. . . . What Hank said is true. Falling in love with writers is easy. The difference here is that you can intertwine words with the writers you love, interactive and expressive and responding to your ideas.[52]

Alan L. Chamberlain, another WELL user, suggests that on-line, among the bodiless, the mind is an erogenous zone:

[I] have friendships and unspecified relationships with women i have met through the WELL, where . . . the attraction began as a result of exposure to each other's ideas, rather than physical attraction. in some instances, there has been a physical attraction following, but the fundamental thing has been attraction to each other's minds.[53]

Getting It On(-Line): MUD Sex, Net.Sleazing, and Beyond

Not all netsurfers are as platonic—or as logophilic—as Chamberlain and his fellow WELL-dwellers. There is a fast-growing underground of adult BBSs, of which Event Horizons, with sixty-four phone lines and twenty-five thousand users, is possibly the most popular and undoubtedly the oldest (Event's president, Jim Maxey, claims his was the first adult BBS). Most adult BBSs feature electronic conferencing, which permits users to comment on various topics; many, like the New York–based Aline or Monrovia, California's Odyssey, specialize in X-rated "chat," or real-time teleconferencing, where a number of users congregate in an imaginary room to engage in group conversation via keyboard. A classified ad for Lifestyle BBS entices potential subscribers with the promise of

[c]omputer sex talk: couples and singles interested in making *real* contacts with very open-minded adults meet on the nation-wide Lifestyle BBS. 32 lines serve 1,500 + *active* members more than 1,300 times a day.[54]

Some sexually explicit BBSs cater to gays and lesbians. Frank Browning describes two typical gay computer bulletin boards:

One board calls itself "Station House" and organizes its user codes around the jargon of the police. Each user, identified as an "officer," is on "patrol" in a numbered "car," and chooses from several topical areas labeled as "squad rooms." Another bulletin board is called "Backdoor"; on-line users slip into "glory holes" and choose among topical "stalls."[55]

On the Internet, one finds systems that are home to MUDs (Multi-User Dungeons, Dimensions, or Domains) and MUSEs (Multi-User Simulation Environments)–text-based role-playing games that enable multiple users to simultaneously explore a shared environment. Assuming fanciful guises, players engage in derring-do in labyrinthine caverns, enchanted forests, and similarly otherworldly geographies, all spun from narrative threads (the eye-zapping computer graphics and ray-gun sound effects familiar from video arcades or PC games are absent here). "When you encounter other characters, the interactions between you become part of the game," writes Howard Rheingold, in "What Are Muds and Muses?" an article published on the WELL. "People gather treasure, slay monsters (and each other), gain experience points, and thereby become wizards, with powers that are useful in playing the game."

There are those, however, whose idea of game playing includes carnal frolickings; increasingly, unbridled lust is intruding on the sword-and-sorcery scenarios of these Tolkienesque worlds. "Flirtation, infatuation, romance, and even 'TinySex' are now as ubiquitous in MUD worlds as on real college campuses," write Rheingold and Kevin Kelly, in the July/August 1993 issue of *Wired* magazine. According to the WELL user Tim Oren, TinySex (alternately, "tinysex") is "sexually loaded or explicit language . . . typed between users on a MUD or other multi-user system. I suppose it got called 'TinySex' because some of the original systems were called Tiny-MUDs."[56] As Rheingold notes in *The Virtual Community: Homesteading on the Electronic Frontier*, it is conducted in character. Rheingold also makes mention of net.sleazing, which he defines as "the practice of aggressively soliciting mutual narrative stimulation . . . an unsavory but perennially popular behavior in MUDland."[57] Taken further, net.sleazing turns to MUD-rape, which the feminist cultural critic Anne Balsamo defines as an "unwanted, aggressive, sexual-textual encounter in a multi-user domain."[58]

Julian Dibbell is more sanguine about on-line orgasms than most. "Netsex," to Dibbell, is

> possibly the headiest experience the very heady world of MUDs has to offer. Amid flurries of even the most cursorily described caresses, sighs, and penetrations, the glands do engage, and often as throbbingly as they would in a real-life assignation—sometimes even more so, given the combined power of anonymity and textual suggestiveness to unshackle deep-seated fantasies.[59]

Visual Aids

A burgeoning subculture of netsex enthusiasts is unsatisfied with the purely literary medium of text sex. Using electronic devices called scanners, they convert pornographic images into digital data that can then be stored in their computer memories and traded, on-line, for other digitized images. Adult BBSs often feature photo libraries, the entries in which can be saved, with a few commands, in the memory of the user's computer. More mainstream BBSs permit the public posting of soft-core material only; subscribers interested in steamier fare must contact individual users, who trade X-rated files privately, via E-mail. By storing images as digitally encoded graphics files called .GIF (Graphics Interchange Format) files, users are able to transmit them: One user sends, and as the computer on the receiving end decodes the file, bit by digital bit, a more or less photo-quality image blooms slowly on the screen of the willing recipient. Users claiming to be professional photographers sometimes list their libraries of digitized photos, and Nixpix, a free BBS that claims to have more than ten thousand subscribers, provides global access to pornographic photos, ranging in professionalism from Peeping Tom to studio quality.

Not all .GIF transmissions are as laughably banal as the digitized *Playboy* photos one WELL user claims have been ubiquitous "for years," circulated by "horny nerds."[60] On March 4, 1993, federal agents raided forty locations in fifteen states in a search for evidence against subscribers who paid eighty dollars a year to receive explicit photos of five-to-twelve-year-old children from an on-line child pornography ring based in Denmark.

Dubbed Operation Longarm, the coordinated effort sprang from the federal Customs Service's assertion that the "computerized transmission of illegal pornography among pedophiles is rapidly becoming more popular than smutty magazines."[61] The raids have yielded two indictments; an investigation into what officials believe is a worldwide child pornography network continues. In July 1995, a self-appointed vigilante and the FBI joined forces in an Internet sting that resulted in the indictment of a forty-five-year-old male Prodigy user on the charge of crossing state lines with the intention of having sex with a fourteen-year-old girl.

Given the uninformed demagoguery that passes for political debate on this subject, it must be noted that the perception of the Internet as an electronic Sodom awash in hard-core porn and overrun by predatory pedophiles is unfounded. During a July 21, 1995, debate on NPR's *Talk of the Nation*, Bruce Taylor, the president of the National Law Center for Children and Families in Fairfax, Virginia, asserted that the Internet is "full" of "hard-core porn pictures" involving "violence and animals and torture and body functions." Larry Magid, the author of a booklet called *Child Safety on the Information Highway*, countered, "If I knew nothing about the Internet and I were listening to this broadcast, I would think . . . that you turn on the Internet and all of a sudden you encounter pictures of naked people having sex with animals. . . . I really resent the word 'full'; despite some infamous studies, pornography represents a very, very small percentage of the total [Internet traffic]."

Magid was referring to the widely criticized (and utterly discredited) Carnegie-Mellon study of on-line pornography that Philip Elmer-Dewitt used as the factual foundation of his June 26, 1995, *Time* feature on pornography on the Internet. According to the *New York Times*, the study, which claimed that 83.5 percent of all images on UseNet are pornographic, has been criticized as "a poorly designed survey whose main conclusion . . . could not be supported by the research methods employed."[62] In fact, as the journalist Brock Meeks has pointed out, the study's own figures show that "so-called 'pornographic' images comprise merely *one-half of one percent* (.5) of all Internet traffic."[63]

But whether or not pornography, pedophilic or otherwise, is rampant on the Internet, the exchange of nonpedophilic nude photos between consenting adults as a prelude to text sex is both legal and popular. "You contact somebody, exchange images that are allegedly of the two of you, and then, once you have the image viewable, you're ready to 'talk things over,' " explained Branwyn, in an E-mail note. On-line demand is growing for amateur (or at least ostensibly amateur) porn that parallels the off-line market in so-called "amateur" adult videos (many of which are professionally produced). "Tau Zero (tauzero)" assured a user who wondered if "people are exchanging still or video clip files of *themselves*,"

> It happens, alright. On CompuServe the user interface includes direct support for displaying, uploading, downloading, and e-mailing color images. In the CB community there, a fair amount of images are exchanged–and while [many of them are] scanned from magazines and digitized from videos, there is an increasing amount of . . . –quite– explicit self-portraiture. In addition to near real-time digital exchange[s], people also send polaroids and such by conventional physical mail once they have found intimacy via "narrow ascii" and by voice. There is [an] interesting stew of mixed media used in the service of sexuality by those who inhabit cyberspace![64]

The "CB community" to which Tau Zero refers is a group of users who communicate via CompuServe's real-time chat feature; they are an on-line version of the CB (citizens band) radio subculture that flourished in the seventies. ASCII–pronounced "askee"–is an acronym for American Standard Code for Information Interchange, the generic text format required by most BBSs; it is deemed "narrow" because the absence of italics, underlining, boldface, and other print options inhibit dramatic emphasis.

More and more, Tau Zero's "stew of mixed media" is served up on CD-ROMs–shiny silver wafers whose grooves can store text, photos and illustrations, film footage, animated graphics, and sounds. A user whose computer is equipped with a CD-ROM drive can interact with the onscreen world–a world enhanced by the music, speech, and sound effects seeping out of the speaker on the back of his computer–by pointing and clicking a mouse or pecking out keyboard commands.

Compilations of nude stills and adult films have become staples of the CD-ROM genre. Space Coast Software's groaningly titled *Bare Assets* ("See the models dance on the beach, splash in the pool, and . . . strip") utilizes QuickTime software to bring video clips to life. Romulus Entertainment's *House of Dreams* enjoyed the distinction of being the first full-length digital movie, albeit a rather unsatisfying one: The image appears in a claustrophobic window on the user's screen, and the action is noninteractive.

It is widely held that interactivity will spur the growth of new media. "At the moment," says Bruce Sterling, "it's still a fascinating idea that you can actually put a dirty picture on your computer screen. But by itself, it won't be amazing for very long."[65] Sexually explicit CD-ROMs and software that enable the user to select characters, peel away layers of clothing, and rewrite story lines as they unfold realize, in a manner few would have predicted and some would have reviled, the dream of interactivity chased by the Czech Pavilion's Kino-Automat at Expo '67 in Montreal. Fairgoers watched *One Man and His World,* a movie with alternate climaxes whose final outcome was determined by audience vote: Should the wife or the blond neighbor commit suicide? Should the male protagonist go to jail or go free?

The decisions demanded of the viewer by New Machine Publishing's CD-ROM *Nightwatch* are rather less weighty; one set of multiple-choice options includes "SPANK HER" and "GET UNDRESSED." Transforming the user's PC screen into the central surveillance monitor of a beachfront apartment complex, the voyeuristic scenario revolves around a curvaceous security guard on her nightly rounds; animated sequences and QuickTime footage of live actors (which may be rewound or fast-forwarded) flesh out the bawdy escapades of oversexed tenants, glimpsed through hidden cameras.

According to *New Media* magazine, the best-selling title in the brief history of the adult-oriented CD-ROM is Reactor's *Virtual Valerie,* released in 1990. Valerie, a cheesecake dream with gravity-defying proportions, is a direct descendant of Maxie MacPlaymate, the curvy cyberbimbo who debuted in 1986; both characters star in X-rated interactive games for home computers conceived by the underground cartoonist Mike Saenz. Saenz, a former Marvel Comics illustrator, is the creator of the cyberpunk graphic novel *Shatter,* the first comic book produced on a computer. Intriguingly, Saenz's games are rooted in the artist's feverish childhood dream of a machine that would "explore and enlarge the domain of sex by mechanical technique":

> I was kind of a street urchin growing up in Chicago, and . . . we collected torn, soggy pieces of porn rags. And one day–I must have been only 6 or 7 –a friend of mine said, "You gotta come over to my place: I've got a Boner Machine." I had a *wild* imagination as a child: I imagined this greased-up, heavy-industry fuck device. And it was just a kind of flow chart collage–greasy little snippets from beaver magazines plastered on his wall. So I'm thinking, this is it, the Boner Machine? Shit, I could build you a Boner Machine. . . . The idea then went dormant for twenty years.[66]

Saenz sketched the fuzzy outlines of that dream in the wildly popular albeit crudely cartoony *MacPlaymate,* the first erotic software for the Macintosh PC. With a click of the mouse, *MacPlaymate* users strolled into Maxie's bedroom, disrobed the animated pinup, and satisfied her urges with an assortment of sex toys, to the accompaniment of moans and groans. *Virtual Valerie* is a sort of pervert's progress: players proceed, step by perilous step, from the street to Valerie's bed, where anything can happen. In 1993, Saenz's company released the CD-ROM *Donna Matrix,* an S and M variation on the *Valerie* theme featuring a spike-heeled, bullet-pumping "21st century Pleasure Droid" named Donna Matrix, whom Saenz describes as "a cross between Madonna and Arnold Schwarzenegger."

Saenz, like so many denizens of fringe computer culture, looks forward to sex in virtual reality with unabashed anticipation–a deep-seated yearning that points, ultimately, to the failings of X-rated interactive games, pornographic MUDs and MUSEs, .GIF swaps, and text sex. "As sexy as the WELL is, as the best conversations are," wrote Matt Stevens in "Sex in virtual communities," a discussion topic on the WELL, "one element is missing: smell ;-)." A user with the on-line handle "You must be joking (leilani)" added, "Let's not forget touch and sight, while we're at it. Reading stuff on a screen is no substitute for being able to see and smell and taste and touch a real person." Tom Mandel splashed ice water on the subject: "It is probably a good idea to remember that sex per se does not occur at all in virtual communities. Writing and communicating about sex does occur a lot, but that is not the same thing."

Cybersex

Cybercultural dreams of machine sex and sex machines, once hazily defined, were captured with razor clarity in the "cybersex" scene that is the movie *The Lawnmower Man*'s sole contribution to popular culture. Few who have seen it will forget the scene in which the protagonist and his girlfriend, suited up in virtual reality equipment, engage in *coitus artificialis*. In cyberspace, they appear as featureless, quicksilver creatures, their faces flowing together and oozing apart in a mystical communion that dissolves body boundaries. Like the angel sex described by Raphael in Milton's *Paradise Lost*, their conjunction is "easier than air with air."

Ironically, this unmediated, transcendental sex, in which bodies melt and souls commingle, occurs in the utterly mediated environment of a computer program, accessed through user interfaces that seal off the senses and inhibit physical movement. Seen from outside their computer-generated hyperreality, the two lovers appear silly, solipsistic; outfitted in bulky helmets and suspended in giant gyroscopes, each embraces himself, tonguing the air, thrusting into nothingness. Lebel's critique of *The Bride Stripped Bare*—"onanism for two"—applies to cybersex as well.

Time magazine's 1993 cover story on cyberpunk features the eye-grabbing "VIRTUAL SEX" cover line and *Lawnmower Man* cybersex still that have become fixtures of mainstream coverage of cyberculture. Paraphrasing Rheingold, the authors inform readers that virtual sex would be facilitated by

> a virtual reality bodysuit that fits with the "intimate snugness of
> a condom." When your partner (lying somewhere in cyber-
> space) fondles your computer-generated image, you actually feel
> it on your skin, and vice versa. Miniature sensors and actuators
> would have to be woven into the clothing by a technology that
> has yet to be invented.[67]

In other words, dreaming about incorporeal intercourse, at least for now, amounts to fantasizing about a fantasy; it is no less ludicrous than the unspoken desire, apparently harbored by more than a few men, to make it with Jessica Rabbit, the cartoon vamp in *Who Framed Roger Rabbit?* The technical hurdles to be leapt in realizing Rheingold's vision of virtual sex, or "teledildonics," as it is phallocentrically known, are daunting.[68]

In Rheingold's scenario, each participant slips on 3-D goggles and a high-tech bodystocking, then steps into a "suitably padded chamber." The inner surface of his or her "smart" suit is covered with

> an array of intelligent sensor-effectors—a mesh of tiny tactile detectors coupled to vibrators of varying degrees of hardness, hundreds of them per square inch, that can receive and transmit a realistic sense of tactile presence.[69]

Plugging into the global telephone network, the user connects with similarly equipped participants. All appear to each other as believable fictions: lifelike characters inhabiting a three-dimensional environment. "You run your hand over your partner's clavicle," imagines Rheingold, "and 6,000 miles away, an array of effectors [is] triggered, in just the right sequence, at just the right frequency, to convey the touch exactly the way you wish it to be conveyed."[70]

Reality is mutable here; years could be added to or subtracted from one's age, and crow's-feet, bald spots, love handles, and cellulite could be corrected with a few keystrokes. Of course, when radical transmogrifications require only a few more seconds' worth of computation, why stop at alterations that are merely cosmetic? New genders and ethnicities could be explored; hermaphroditism, multiple sex organs, and the grafting of animal genitals onto human bodies would almost certainly become instant clichés among the outré. One might assume the guise of a celebrity, a historical personality, a fictional character, or a mythic hybrid—centaur, satyr, Minotaur, mermaid. A virtual reality graphics program could assemble an interactive 3-D "clone" from nude self-portraits of the user, shot from every angle and scanned into computer memory; add a voice synthesized from a database of phonemes recorded by the user, and the narcissist's age-old love affair could at last be consummated.

Not that the human sexual imagination need confine itself to the biological world: The posthuman landscape of Ballard's *Crash* stretches before us, with its sexualized aircraft engine nacelles and pornographic pileups. Devotees of *Crash* sex might opt for congress with commodity fetishes. In a WELL topic called "Dildonics," the artist and multimedia designer Mike Mosher imagines the arrival, by the year 2000, of Orgasmatrons that will combine "visual, auditory, touch and possibly olfactory stimulus" to bring users to "thrilling orgasm." He predicts that "the sexual content of many appealing things will become obvious," including "objects (sex with a Russian MIG fighter, with a Ferrari Testarossa, with the dome of St. Peter's)." Mosher conjures the world of Pat Cadigan's SF novel *Synners,* where an image junkie's home entertainment center is equipped with

> a screen for every porn channel, jammed together in the wall so that food porn overlapped med porn overlapped war porn overlapped sex porn overlapped news porn overlapped disaster porn overlapped tech-fantasy porn overlapped porn she had no idea how to identify.[71]

Cybersex will grow exponentially stranger as virtual reality technology develops. Not everyone will want to interface with anonymous partners on-line; some may opt, in the privacy of their own Orgasmatrons, to boot up software that allows them to experience the recorded performances of the famous and the infamous. Imagine the union of Rheingold's tactile sensor-effectors with a record/playback apparatus like the Yamaha Disklavier, a computerized player piano that can flawlessly replay performances stored on floppy disks, down to the subtle nuances of pedaling. Add computer graphics wizardry descended from that used to create the nearly seamless illusion of Elton John and Louie Armstrong trading riffs in the 1991 TV spot for Diet Coke, "Nightclub." Voilà: cybersex with the man, woman, or creature of your fantasies.

Most of us will limit ourselves to the occasional steamy romp with Raquel Welch or Robert Redford, while the irretrievably perverse will take part in threesomes with, say, the arch conservative crusader Phyllis Schlafly and the Devil-worshiping debauchee Aleister Crowley. Many personalities will be available only as simulations, of course, and efforts to re-create the lovemaking techniques of Cleopatra, Casanova, Marilyn Monroe, or JFK will doubtless give rise to a new market for the skills of historians. At the same time, there will always be celebrities willing to don DataSuits and act out virtual sex scenes, their every grope and groan recorded for the delectation of the mass market. But given the present prevalence of "body doubles" who stand in for stars during nude scenes in films, how could the cybersex consumer be certain that he was savoring the favors of the advertised celebrity, and not a stand-in? Mike Saenz wonders,

> [W]hen you're getting a virtual blow job, by a virtual Madonna . . . did they take some sensor-clad dildo and fuck a goat?
> Or did some weird cybernerd sit hunched over a computer at
> 4:00 A.M., editing and tweaking the data? Whose data is this?[72]

Whose indeed? And how can the cybernaut showering after on-line revelry be certain that he or she hasn't just had sex with a highly evolved artificial intelligence, perhaps a distant descendant of a grandmaster-level chess program? Amazingly, an interactive, undeniably libidinous machine intelligence already exists, after a fashion, in the form of LULU, a pornographic program written by the Finnish computer scientist Pekka Tolonen. Based on Joseph Weizenbaum's famous ELIZA program, a surprisingly convincing dialogue emulator based on nondirective psychotherapy, LULU began life in 1984 as YRTSI, a simulation of a drug-addled, fifteen-year-old punk which, according to a WELL post by Tolonen, "raised deep emotions among those who discussed with it." The logical next step in developing an artificial personality, decided Tolonen, "was to continue the sex, drugs, and rock 'n' roll theme of YRTSI, and expand the sexual part and convert it into [a] female."

LULU was born in 1985. Installed by Tolonen on SUOKUG, a BBS for Finnish Kaypro users, the program was activated at random in order to fool users into believing that they were receiving real-time messages from a fellow subscriber in "chat" mode. The program's seeming unpredictability and its uncanny ability to simulate an ordinary human typist—making and correcting typos, pausing as if searching for the right word—convinced many SUOKUG users that LULU was human. "Although LULU operated only with text, it provoked the user to express his most secret sexual wishes and fantasies," writes Tolonen. "The semantic system was based on models analyzed from pornographic literature. But when the system was run the discussions were saved on disk and analyzed later, which made it possible to expand the model." Using a heuristic approach, LULU "learned" what come-ons lured users into conversation.

By 1990, when the program was demonstrated at the Thinking Machines Exhibition organized by the Finnish Science Center HEUREKA, LULU had evolved into a multimedia package, complete with text, graphics, the appropriate sampled noises, and a two-voice phoneme synthesizer; visitors interacted with the software by means of a mouse-driven menu and Windows-style software. "LULU handled nearly all imaginable sexual inter-actions that can be expressed in written Finnish," writes Tolonen. "A deep male voice spoke what the user typed and an electronic female voice with special robotic effects spoke the LULU part."[73] Ultimately, LULU was shut down after complaints by visitors who weren't ready for virtual intimacy from a computer. "But before LULU was removed," notes Tolonen, "[the computer's] hard disk had registered hundreds of 'hotter than hell' discus-sions, which testify that teledildonics is really what people enjoy."[74]

Unfortunately, true teledildonics is "an early-to-mid-twenty-first-century technology," according to Rheingold.[75] It would require a global fiber-optic network in concert with massively parallel supercomputers capable of monitoring and controlling the numberless sensors and effectors fitted to every hill and dale, plane and protuberance of the body's topogra-phy. Furthermore, a reticulated fabric of safe, high-speed micro-vibrators is only a mirage, given the state of the art in current technologies.

Even if such challenges were met, how would changes in temper-ature—crushed ice poured down your underwear, hot wax dribbled on your bare chest—be approximated? Moreover, while masochists will undoubtedly demand technology that can re-create the sensation of being branded with a white-hot iron, less adventuresome souls may hesitate before slipping into suits capable of such effects. As William Gibson quips in a *Future Sex* interview, "[W]ho's going to test-dick the force-feedback vagina?"[76] Home appliances have a tendency to go haywire, and a malfunction in a patch of tiny effectors simulating hot wax could have grisly consequences.

Barring such disasters, what about the senses of smell and taste, so important in sex? For most, sex without olfactory or gustatory stim-uli would be like sex with a condom over one's entire body. "You look at virtual reality, what senses does it get?" asks the virtual reality theorist

Brenda Laurel. "Sight, sound, maybe touch, no taste, no smell. It's up-side down."[77]

Finally, there's the clumsiness of the interface. Few of us relish the prospect of standing in a high-tech phone booth dressed in a futuristic scuba suit pimpled with microvibrators. On-line topics have grappled with just this problem, and the endlessly inventive participants in these discussions have come up with some novel, if not entirely practical, solutions.

Eric Hunting, also a contributor to the WELL's "Dildonics" discussion, uses holography as a point of departure for a cybersex technology that resembles the *Star Trek* "replicator," a mysterious device that materializes solid objects out of thin air. Hunting theorizes a "computer-generated matter technology" based on "scanned field photonic emission holography backed up with scanned field gravatics." Decrypted, that translates as the spatial manipulation of electromagnetic and energy fields to synthesize matter.

Failing the arrival of such an invention, Hunting imagines an outlandish contraption inspired by an unnamed seventies SF novel: an "artificially intelligent bed . . . capable of making love to its occupant, a consequence of [its] being composed of a synthetic flesh-like material which could form any shape, contour, or texture." He goes on to describe, in some detail, the engineering of such an "amoebot," a sort of protean waterbed made of "an amorphous material of dynamically variable density and muscle-like motor function capable of extruding fully animate shapes under direct computer control." Hunting extrapolates from phase change fluid, a recently invented "polymer suspension which changes instantly from solid to liquid in the presence of an electrical current."[78] Coupling with an amoebot would be rather like having sex with the T-1000, the liquescent, polymorphous android who, in *Terminator 2,* is able to assume any imaginable form in the twinkling of an eye. The Amoebot, writes Hunting,

> operates in a very straightforward manner. The computer constructs rigid and semirigid forms by controlling current flow through the matrix of polymer 'nerves' and directs fluid pressure through these forms to inflate and extrude them and to provide motor function. It can dynamically create pressurized chambers, tubes, and fluid joints and vary their density and solidity as

needed to construct whatever form is desired. The outer skin
senses the contact and relative position of the user or of objects
and the internal pressure sensors determine force applied while
also providing feedback on variable internal pressures used by
synthesized motor systems.[79]

Terminal Congress

I have been through eight or ten Q&A sessions on virtual reality,
and I don't remember one where sex didn't come up. . . . And I
did overhear the word 'DataCondom' at one point. . . . Maybe
the nerds who always ask this question will get a chance to make
it with their computers at long last.

—*John Perry Barlow*[80]

What accounts for the broad appeal of text sex, .GIF swapping,
interactive X-rated cartoons such as *Virtual Valerie,* pornographic "expert"
programs such as LULU, and teledildonics? The virtual reality pioneer Jaron
Lanier has done his best to burst the hype bubble surrounding cybersex,
emphasizing that "[t]he reality here, the virtual reality, is that you'd have a
girl made of polygons. And no one wants to have sex with a bunch of
polygons."[81] How, then, has an improbable proposition that crosses phone
sex with Nintendo become so deeply embedded in the popular imagination
as to be all but inextricable?

The obvious answer is that wherever humankind goes, sex inevitably follows, and the universe of technological innovation is no exception.
The best-known literary premonition of virtual reality—the "All Super-
Singing, Synthetic-Talking, Coloured, Stereoscopic Feely" in Aldous Huxley's *Brave New World*—is palpable pornography, a quivering "electric titillation" in which the audience thrills to the sexual acrobatics of "a gigantic
negro and a golden-haired young brachycephalic Beta-Plus female." The rise
of the adult video and concomitant decline of the X-rated theater are
significant if largely unacknowledged factors in the success of the VCR.
According to John Tierney, a fellow at the Freedom Forum Center for Media
Studies at Columbia University,

[Pornographers] played a key role in popularizing the videocassette recorder. In 1978 and 1979, when fewer than 1 percent
of American homes had VCR's and the major movie studios were
reluctant to try the new technology, more than 75 percent of the
videocassettes sold were pornographic. And when cable systems
began allowing public-access programming, pornographers immediately brought forth shows like *Midnight Blue*.[82]

Some believe that the demand for adults-only titles will likewise drive the interactive multimedia technologies destined to succeed
the VCR. *New York Times* computer columnist Peter H. Lewis reported
that X-rated CD-ROMs "drew the biggest crowds" at the fall 1993 Comdex,
a computer industry trade show, and quoted one dealer as saying that
"pornography may be the long-awaited 'killer' application that will spur
the sale of CD-ROM drives."[83] Tierney takes a macroscopic perspective:
"In the history of communications technology, sex seems to be the
most enduring killer app. . . . Sometimes the erotic has been a force
driving technological innovation; virtually always, from Stone Age sculpture to computer bulletin boards, it has been one of the first uses for a
new medium."[84] Minitel, France's government-run national computer
network, is an object lesson in the hijacking of new technologies by
human desire: Intended to function as a database for consumers, making
electronic banking, teleshopping, theater reservations, and other services available to its more than 6.5 million subscribers, the pay-per-
minute network garners a substantial portion of its profits from adult chat
lines called "messageries," ranging in subject from matchmaking to flaming
text sex.
        "Lust," says Mike Saenz, "motivates technology. The first personal
robots, let's face it, are not going to be bought to bring people drinks."[85]
Gerard Van Der Leun maintains that "sex . . . is . . . a virus that almost
always infects new technology first." Unfortunately, not all sex viruses are
metaphoric; AIDS currently afflicts fourteen million people worldwide—a
number that may rise to forty million by the year 2000, according to the
World Health Organization.[86] Moreover, it is now the leading killer of
American men between the ages of twenty-five and forty-four, and the
fourth leading killer of women in that group.[87] The Russian roulette reality

of sex in the nineties may have more than a little to do with the popular appeal of what has been coyly called "getting it on(-line)."

Still, the self-evident truths that sex suffuses all human endeavor and that worlds inside computers facilitate promiscuity with impunity in the age of AIDS do not entirely explain the advent of computer-enhanced or -enabled sex. As I argued in the first half of this chapter, sex in cyberculture can only be understood in the context of the machine sex and sex machines that litter the psychological landscape of the twentieth century. And, as "Built for Pleasure" attests, that landscape has been configured for the most part by male phobias and obsessions: DON JUAN, a male counterpart to LULU, was conceived but never realized, and there is no Virtual Victor for female users because Saenz's creative department consists entirely of heterosexual males "who have a hard time with other kinds of fantasies," he says.[88]

Male desire displaced onto machinery is a recurrent subtext in cyberculture. The paradigmatic computer obsessive is the hacker, an archetype fixed in the popular imagination as a grungy teenager married to his terminal, sustained by caffeinated cola, junk food, and above all, an almost symbiotic relationship with his computer. Historically, computer addicts have been nerds, and what makes a nerd a nerd, more than high-water pants or pocket protectors, is his excruciating awkwardness when interacting with the opposite sex. The infamous geekiness of hackers arises from the fact, noted by Steven Levy in *Hackers*, that "computing was more *important* than getting involved in a romantic relationship. It was a question of priorities. Hacking had replaced sex in their lives."[89]

This is undeniably the case with the hacker profiled in an *Omni* article on robopsychology ("the study of the computer age pathology of loving a machine"), who says, "I'm not married . . . unless you count the numerous computers I've fallen in love with."[90] His self-described "first love" was a Radio Shack computer. "She spent most of her life near or in my bed, and when I was away from her I had the urge to communicate by radio."[91] In *The Soul of a New Machine*, Tracy Kidder reports a programmer's reminiscence that, among the undergraduate computer mavens who met for all-night programming sessions, a few "began to ignore their girlfriends and eventually lost them for the sake of playing with the machine all night."[92] Presumably, some of them grew up to star in Kidder's account of a company's race to build a groundbreaking microcomputer; they are the hotshot programmers whose wives (if they have wives) are inevitably "computer widows." To Geoff Simons, a writer on computer culture, this is no laughing matter.

> We already see a growing literature describing the impact of com-
> puter systems on the institution of marriage. . . . McLoughlin, a
> *Guardian* correspondent, has quoted the wife of a computer
> freak: "The whole thing started when he [began] to work late at
> the office, and I began to think that there was another woman."
> And [another writer] notes that "When Lisa found herself
> getting upset and angry each time Carl disappeared into the
> den, she realized she was jealous of the Apple computer as if it
> were another woman."[93]

Even as the computer is feminized, females are objectified. Internalizing the sexist caricature of women as irrational creatures ruled by intuition, emotion, and (worst of all) their bodies, the most extreme male technophiles see them as *kludges* (pronounced "klooges")–compu-slang for "an ill-assorted collection of poorly matching parts forming a distressing whole," according to a 1962 *Datamation* article.[94] As an MIT hacker in the early sixties, writes Levy,

> you knew that horribly inefficient and wasteful things like
> women burned too many cycles, occupied too much memory
> space. "Women, even today, are considered grossly unpredict-
> able," one PDP-6 hacker noted, almost two decades later. "How
> can a hacker tolerate such an imperfect being?"[95]

Even sexual attraction is articulated in cybernetic terms: In *The Soul of a New Machine,* a hardware hacker describes a stunning woman as "a miracle of biological engineering."

The crossed wires of sex and technology in hacker culture, as in cyberculture at large, are readily apparent in computer slang. Computer nuts and even corporations routinely boast about the speed and memory capacities of their machines in a manner that bears a distinct resemblance to locker-room braggadocio about sexual prowess; *I.D.* magazine calls this practice "machoflopping," defined as "ballyhooing multi-gigaflops and tera-flops." A 1983 novelty book called *Silicon Valley Guy Handbook* includes dialogue such as "I get there and she [a computer program named Julie] is ON LINE. I mean, like, she's wearing all this software. I'm calculating the access time to her front-end processor."[96] Even in isolation, the technical jargon of the computer industry—*floppy disk, hard drive, input/output, male-female connector, slot, joystick*—seems rife with sexual innuendo. In a letter to the computer magazine *InfoWorld*, an account executive with a PR firm noted that his client, a software publisher, perceived "computer software as needing to be simple, hot, and deep."[97]

Mechano-eroticism, among hackers and cyberpunks, is often colored by a pernicious loathing for the weak, "feminine" flesh, contemptuously referred to in compu-slang as "meat," a term bathed in sexual associations. Sleep-deprived and fueled with coffee, Coke, and McFood, the body is bent to the needs of an implacable ego that seeks the status and power denied it in the all-important high school arenas of sports and social interaction. Nascent computerphiles, writes Levy, are "those weird high school kids with . . . underdeveloped pectorals who dazzled math teachers and flunked PE, who dreamed not of scoring on prom night, but of getting to the finals of the General Electric Science Fair competition."[98] Uncomfortable in bodies that are often pudgy or skinny, some hackers dream of becoming one with their machines in a transcendental fusion of the ego and the Other that is equal parts machine sex and divine assumption. Levy writes, "Real optimum programming, of course, could only be accomplished when every obstacle between you and the pure computer was eliminated—an ideal that probably won't be fulfilled until hackers are somehow biologically merged with computers."[99]

This, to the masculinist technophile, is the weirdly alchemical end point of cyberculture: the distillation of pure mind from base matter. Sex, in such a context, would be purged of feminine contact—removed, in fact, from all notions of physicality—and reduced to mental masturbation, the electrical flickerings of a consciousness encoded in computer memory. Even now, clumsy gropings toward a technology that displaces sexual thrills into the domain of disembodied cerebration have been reported by the psychologists Harvey Milkman and Stanley Sunderwirth:

A thirty-year-old Los Angeles cocaine user reported that he was no longer satisfied having sexual intercourse with "biological units." A career musician, familiar with electronics, he was able to develop a biofeedback contrivance that could register changes in penile erection and transmit the information to an Apple computer. He would mechanically masturbate via an automatic vacuum device, developed to provide sexual stimulation for people who could not masturbate because of spinal injury. The biofeedback penile information would program the computer to project varying degrees and kinds of pornographic footage, excerpted and stored from a database of four hundred porno-graphic video tapes. The whole experience was augmented by repeated and heavy use of cocaine.[100]

Born of body horror, an all-consuming obsession with entertain-ment media, and the dissolution of traditional notions of community, such loveless, sci-fi pathologies, though voguish, are not new. Marshall McLuhan touched on them in his 1969 *Playboy* interview, in which he bemoaned the perceived effect of the sexual revolution in an age of information overload: a "mechanical view of the body as capable of experiencing specific thrills, but not total sexual-emotional involvement and transcendence."[101] This throws a pessimistic light on his observation a sentence later:

> Projecting current trends, the love machine would appear a natural development in the near future—not just the current computerized datefinder, but a machine whereby ultimate or-gasm is achieved by direct mechanical stimulation of the plea-sure circuits of the brain.[102]

As feminists such as Brenda Laurel remind us, this latest manifesta-tion of a century's worth of mechano-eroticism is in large part a product of male desires, not all of them healthy. "I know from 15 years' experience with computer guys that we have a class of people we call nerds who are radically uncomfortable with their bodies and their sexuality," she says, in an interview with the sex guru Susie Bright. "When men talk about virtual reality, they often use phrases like 'out-of-body experience' and 'leaving the body.' When women talk about VR they speak of taking the body with them into another world. The idea is to take these wonderful sense organs *with* us, not to leave our bodies humped over a keyboard while [the] brain zips off down some network. The body is not simply a container for this glorious intellect of ours."[103]

The question of whether women, unique in their ability to experience menstruation, menopause, and childbearing, are somehow more attuned to the body than men has bedeviled thinkers since time immemorial and will not be settled here. That said, we can nonetheless conclude that cyberculture is fraught with male dread and desire, and that when those two currents cross, as they do in the conjunction of sexuality and technology, much of what floats to the surface is pathological.

The scariest of those pathologies eroticizes the machinery of death, reiterating McLuhan's unholy trinity—"the widely occurring cluster image of sex, technology, and death." The assertion that war perverts the relationship between sex and death is amply evidenced in the military's use of sexually charged metaphors and double entendres to describe high-tech weaponry: scientists engaged in defense research speak in terms of " 'vertical erector launchers, thrust-to-weight ratios, soft lay-downs, deep penetration . . . the comparative advantages of protracted versus spasm attacks'— defined by one military adviser to the National Security Council as 'releasing 70 to 80 percent of our megatonnage in one orgasmic whump.' "[104] Not for nothing did the feminist historian of science Donna Haraway proclaim modern war "a cyborg orgy." In a *Re/Search* magazine interview, the performance artist Carolee Schneemann deconstructs the military briefingspeak of the Gulf War, noting that

> the language of this war has all been about 'creaming them . . .
> pounding them relentlessly.' . . . [I]t's the jerk-off language of
> men who can never cum. It's like a gang-bang, an endless rape
> with the heaviest battering ram, the battering cock.[105]

Not nearly as apocalyptic but no less creepy is a fawning profile of the novelist Tom Clancy ("famous for his sensuous descriptions of high-tech weapons") in *Amtrak Express* magazine. "Where some best-selling authors offer up steamy sex scenes," the author notes, "Clancy is more likely to give his readers a glimpse down the sights of a Stinger surface-to-air missile launcher."[106] Then, too, there is the suppressed Gulf War story uncovered by *Philadelphia Inquirer* reporter Carol Morello, who reported that pilots aboard the USS *John F. Kennedy* watched porno films before going on bombing missions.[107] But neither of these examples comes close to the spooky little poem a friend of mine learned in the marines:

> *This is my rifle*
> *This is my gun*
> *One is for killing*
> *One is for fun*

Stanley Kubrick takes up these themes in *Dr. Strangelove* (1964), the doomsday comedy about the strangest love of all, that of aging power brokers for sexy weaponry. From the film's beginning–refueling bombers copulating in midair to the strains of "Try a Little Tenderness"–to its thermonuclear dénouement, we are treated to a parade of Freudian gags that confuse sex, technology, and death.

In penetrating Mother Russia with his phallic B-52s, General Jack D. Ripper reaffirms a manhood threatened by fluoridation, the Communist plot to pollute "our precious bodily fluids." Major T. J. "King" Kong, the commander of the B-52 fated to drop the bomb, ogles a *Playboy* spread; the plane's primary target is Laputa (Spanish for "whore"). Decorated with salacious graffiti ("HI THERE," "DEAR JOHN"), the twin H-bombs in the belly of the B-52 resemble proudly out-thrust breasts. Later, when Kong straddles one and rides it into eternity with a rebel yell, the missile suggests a penile prosthesis suitable for the giant ape who is the major's namesake. The movie ends with a visual pun that crosses destruction with seduction: a series of billowing explosions that, while capturing an atomic götterdämmerung, unmistakably conjure multiple orgasms.

As the cold war lampooned in *Dr. Strangelove* fades into history, the American attitude toward sex and violence remains a conundrum: *Faces of Death*, a "greatest hits" compilation of gory last moments, can be found at nearly any neighborhood video store, but condoms cannot be advertised on TV despite mounting teenage pregnancies and AIDS deaths. The pornography of violence, meanwhile, is ever present: Our local news shows are slaughter benches, piled high with images of human suffering packaged as entertainment, and a day's worth of escapist programming in Washington, D.C., contains about eighteen hundred violent scenes, a significant number of them involving assault or murder.[108] Simultaneously, says Elizabeth J. Roberts of the Project on Human Sexual Development at Harvard University,

> Television tells the child viewer over and over that human sexuality . . . is an acceptable subject if it is cloaked in humor or ridicule or viewed as a harsh, hurtful, or criminal part of life. . . . Affection and intimacy are viewed as inappropriate to the 'real world.' "[109]

In a WELL discussion of *Future Sex,* the magazine's then senior editor Laura Miller wrote, "We've been inundated with the inevitable 'In the future we'll have perfect sex with robot playmates' stories, not one with any real insight into human sexuality or even any real social vision about what such a development might bring with it. . . . What good is getting it on with androids if your own sexuality is as underdeveloped as a Third World country?"[110]

Contemplating mass culture's undying fascination with sex machines and machine sex, Howard Rheingold writes, "[T]here is no doubt that people everywhere . . . are fascinated by the prospect. And why not? Contemporary philosophers have pointed to [the] progressive mechanization of human culture and the future of sexual expression as the site of a potential collision of immense dimensions."[111] But J. G. Ballard has given us a minatory glimpse of such a collision. Like the cyberpunk machinist Mark Pauline, who once observed that "the true marriage of human form and technology is death," Ballard is mindful of the fact that the curious pathology of our century–the almost sexual desire to become one with our technology–is at its heart necrophilic. He is not nearly as sanguine about the impending crash of mechanization and sexual expression as Rheingold seems to be:

> In his mind Vaughan saw the whole world dying in a simul- taneous automobile disaster, millions of vehicles hurled together in a terminal congress of spurting loins and engine coolant.[112]

6 / CYBORGING THE BODY POLITIC

Obsolete Bodies and Posthuman Beings[1]

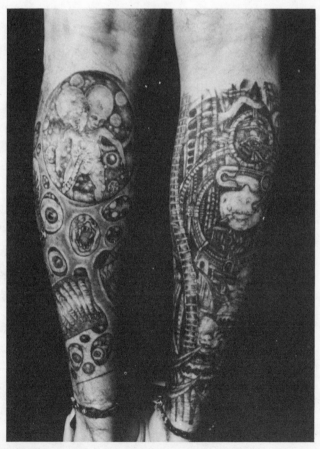

Biomechanical tattoos. © 1995 B. J. Papas. Model: Rick Healey.
Tattoo by Andrea Elston.

I Have Seen the Future, and It is Morphed

My intention is to tell of bodies changed to different forms.

—*Ovid*[2]

Morphing is the computer animation technique that gave *Terminator 2* much of its technodazzle, enabling the T-1000 killer android to dissolve seamlessly from a slight, feline policeman into the sinewy heroine Sarah Connor, a paunchy hospital guard, or even checkerboard linoleum. The effect has become ubiquitous: A Schick TV spot features average Joes who dissolve, one into another, while shaving, and an ad for the exercise guru Richard Simmons's Deal-a-Meal weight loss program incorporates former fatties who melt down to their current svelte selves before our very eyes. Anything that can be converted into ones and zeroes in computer memory can be morphed; morphing liquefies the human form, dissolves it into a running, flowing anima able to pour itself into any vessel.

The term *borging* derives from *cyborg,* coined in 1960 by research space scientist Manfred Clynes. (Appropriately, Clynes's term is itself a sort of linguistic cyborg, a combination of *cybernetic* and *organism.*) For Clynes, advances in biomedical engineering–rechargeable pacemakers, synthetic knee and hip joints–dramatized the permeability of the membrane separating organism and mechanism. "As each of these mechanical devices becomes a functioning part of a human," notes the historian David F. Channell,

it becomes more and more difficult to characterize the assimi-
lated object as a human or as a machine. . . . The cyborg is not
any ordinary combination of a human and a machine, such as a
human using a tool; rather the cyborg involves a unique relationship between the human and the machine in that the machine
"needs to function without the benefit of consciousness, in
order to cooperate with the body's own autonomous homeostatic controls."[3]

Thus, Hollywood morphing and borging have real-world analogs.
Genetic engineering, wherein DNA sequences from one organism are introduced into another to produce "transgenic" plants and animals, is a sort of
morphing. The virus-resistant mouse created at Ohio University in 1992 by
injecting a human gene that promotes interferon production into a fertilized
mouse embryo is a morph. So is the genetically altered pig created in 1991 at
the Princeton-based DNX Corporation by injecting clones of human DNA
into fertilized swine eggs, yielding a pig that produced human hemoglobin.

Many fear (and a radical few hope) that transgenic animals are
merely a prelude to genetically engineered superhumans. "We are now able
to transcend the limitations of particular species and combine the virtues
(and vices) of different species and indeed program into species . . . attributes never before a feature of any species," claims John Harris, in *Wonderwoman and Superman: The Ethics of Human Biotechnology*. "We can, or
eventually will be able to, create new 'transgenic' creatures of unprecedented nature and qualities. It would not be an exaggeration to say that
humanity now stands at a crossroads."[4]

But morphs aren't confined to high-tech labs; they're all around us.
The transsexual "Tula," featured in a recent *Playboy* pictorial, is a self-
assured morph who "needed my body changed to fit my self-image."[5] The
products of cosmetic surgery who populate the tabloids—Roseanne, Ivana
Trump, La Toya Jackson—are a sadder sort of morph, their idiosyncratic
features defaced and refaced in the name of a generic standard of beauty.
Cindy Jackson (no relation to La Toya), who has appeared on the *Jenny Jones
Show*, has undergone more than twenty operations to make her resemble a
Barbie doll (she doesn't); another, more celebrated Jackson has reimagined
himself as a gene splice of Diana Ross and Peter Pan.

Borgs, likewise, are not confined to sci-fi films. In cyberculture, the body is a permeable membrane, its integrity violated and its sanctity challenged by titanium alloy knee joints, myoelectric arms, synthetic bones and blood vessels, breast and penile prostheses, cochlear implants, and artificial hips. The Utah arm, the Boston elbow, and the Otto Bock hand—lifelike prostheses activated by electrical current in the form of electro-myographic (EMG) signals coming from an amputee's stump and surrounding muscles—have attained mythic status in modern medicine. "By the turn of the century, every major organ except the brain and the central nervous system will have [an] artificial replacement," says Dr. William Dobelle, an authority on bionics.[6] Pacemakers and other bionic devices for ailing, usually aged hearts are already commonplace, and researchers are at work on an implantable electric heart.

"Today's old are already in one technological vanguard," asserts the cultural critic Thomas Hine. "They have been quite willing to accept artificial devices into their bodies to replace parts that are worn out. . . . Cyborgs . . . are an old staple of science fiction, but nobody ever predicted that Grandma would turn into one."[7] Soon, Grandma may have company in the posthuman vanguard: The futurologist Alvin Toffler believes that min-iaturized computers "will not only be implanted [in our bodies] to compensate for some physical defect but eventually will be implanted to enhance human capability. The line between human and computer at some point will become completely blurred."[8]

Technology calls into question time-honored ideas about the body. We live in an age of engineered monsters, when the human form seems increasingly indeterminate—reducible to replaceable parts, like the Schwarz-enegger T-800 cyborg in *Terminator 2,* or infinitely manipulable, like *T2*'s liquid metal T-1000.

Furthermore, the body is being transformed from a fortress of solitude into a combat zone for ideological skirmishes over abortion rights, fetal tissue use, AIDS treatment, assisted suicide, euthanasia, surrogate mothering, genetic engineering, cloning, even state-sponsored cosmetic surgery for prison inmates. "YOUR BODY IS A BATTLEGROUND," proclaims a poster by the artist Barbara Kruger.

In the last years of the twentieth century, we bear witness to the triumph of a mechanistic view of the body rooted in Cartesian dualism, which divides reality into immaterial mind and an inert, material world (in which category Descartes included the human body) wholly explicable in mechanical terms. The rhetoric of artificial intelligence theorists such as Marvin Minsky, to whom the brain is a "meat machine," has trickled down into newspaper science pages in the form of the durable brain-as-computer metaphor.

New Age cyberculture, corporate motivational seminars, and nineties upgrades of the human potential movement of the seventies often incorporate therapeutic techniques that conceive of the mind as a "biocomputer," capable of being reprogrammed with the right commands. For example, Neuro-Linguistic Programming (NLP)—the brainchild of a linguist and a computer programmer—employs a process called "modeling," based on the theory that success-oriented behavioral patterns can be "installed" in the subconscious, through self-hypnosis, in much the same way that programs are installed in a computer. "Each of us has at [his] disposal the most incredible computer on the planet, but unfortunately no one gave us an owner's manual," writes the motivational psychology guru Anthony Robbins, whose system of Neuro-Associative Conditioning descends from NLP.[9] Robbins's "technology" uses NLPlike techniques to reroute self-defeating neural connections, "rewiring yourself to feel and behave consistent with your new, empowering choices."[10]

The neo-Cartesian reduction of the body to a machine is concomitant with its redefinition as a commodity. Andrew Kimbrell, the policy director for the Foundation on Economic Trends, contends that the logic of the market economy, which forever altered the landscape of Western culture by treating "human work, formerly simply a part of daily life, as a commodity," achieves its ultimate expression in the commodification of the human body.[11] He writes,

> More and more, Americans are selling their very selves: their blood, semen, ova, even their newborns. And, more and more, researchers and corporations are marketing human "products" including organs, fetus parts, tissues, cell lines, biochemicals, and genes. . . . The escalating price placed on our most intimate possessions has created a boom market in the human body.[12]

But one country's boom is another's bust. An unsettling *Arizona Republic* article about a global black market in body parts spurred by a "growing demand for organs for transplants and use in medical research and cosmetics" documents, in grisly detail, the chasm between the so-called First and Third Worlds.[13] The story tells of an illicit Russian operation trading in kidneys, hearts, lungs, livers, eyes, and "3,000 pairs of testicles, which are used for rejuvenating creams"; of corneas extracted with coffee spoons from mental patients in Argentina; of children vanishing without a trace in Honduras—kidnapped, it is believed, by organ traffickers.[14]

Disparate forces threaten, literally as well as figuratively, to draw and quarter our bodies, our selves: high-tech prosthetics, genetic engineering, plastic surgery, gender reassignment, the public debate over body politics, and the redefinition of the body as a warm-blooded machine or a potentially lucrative source of spare parts. We don't know what to make of ourselves precisely because we are, more than ever before, able to *remake* ourselves—a conundrum reflected in the cognitive dissonance of our mass media, where images of the body as a temple in ads for Evian bottled water and Calvin Klein's Obsession perfume collide with images of that temple desecrated in splatter movies and Stephen King novels.

Our media tells us that we are a culture that worships the gym-toned body, and we are inclined to agree: hunks and supermodels are the objects of our desire. Then again, our movie screens inundate us with images of the body dissected or dissolved: Horror film rejoices in exploding heads, spilling guts, squelching eyeballs, gouts of vomit. Of course, horror has always taken the body as its central trope, but tales of corpse grinders, brain eaters, and body snatchers seem uniquely relevant to the end of the twentieth century, a period whose obsession with the body belies a widespread anxiety over the body's fate. Repressed, body anxiety seeks release elsewhere, erupting with a vengeance in horror film and fiction. "[I]f offerings like *American Psycho* and *The Silence of the Lambs* have anything to tell us about ourselves," notes Barbara Ehrenreich, "it must be that at this particular historical moment, we have come to hate the body."[15] The body, she reasons, has "let us down": Sex, chief among our earthly delights, "turned out to spread deadly viruses."[16]

To be sure, the *body horror* we see all around us is most obviously a waking dream about the AIDS pandemic, whose ravages have imprinted nightmare images on the mass imagination—bodies gnawed to skin and

bones, flesh mottled by the purple lesions of Kaposi's sarcoma. But body
horror also coincides with the cultural post-traumatic stress syndrome
induced by the relocation, in technology, of an ever greater number of our
cognitive and muscular operations. It bears out Marshall McLuhan's assertion that the cultural trauma caused by the technological "autoamputation"
of human functions is a salient feature of the information age. "Does the
body still exist at all, in any but the most mundane sense?" asks J. G. Ballard.
"Its role has been steadily diminished, so that it seems little more than a
ghostly shadow seen on the X-ray plate of our moral disapproval."[17] The
essayist Linda Hasselstrom ponders the body's atrophy:

> We take a body with [a] hunter/fighter history, prop it upright for
> eight hours while the fingers lightly punch buttons, then seat it
> in a car where moderate foot pressure and a few arm movements
> take it home. Once it's home it slumps down on a cushiony
> surface and aims its eyes at a lighted screen for two to six hours,
> then lies down on another soft surface until it's time to get up
> and do it all again. No wonder we're sick.[18]

The divorce between our minds and our bodies becomes dramatically apparent after longtime immersion in a simulated world (TV viewing, PC
gaming, Internet surfing, computer hacking, arcade virtual reality): surfacing
is marked by a few seconds' worth of decompression—a momentary reincor-
poration of the wandering mind into the vacant body. Bruce Sterling captures
this moment in "Spider Rose," a short story about a spacebound cyborg,
scanning the heavens with eight telescopes "fed into her brain through a
nerve-crystal junction at the base of her skull."[19] Gazing starward, "she knew
nothing" of her body, "for she was elsewhere, watching for visitors."[20] In time,
they come, rousing her to action: "Spider Rose came partially out of her static
observation mode and felt herself in her body once more."[21]

Discorporation of this sort is not uncommon in cyberculture,
where growing numbers spend their days in "static observation mode,"
scrolling through screenfuls of data. Bit by digital bit, we are becoming
alienated from our increasingly irrelevant bodies, a sense of discorporation
captured in the performance artist Laurie Anderson's quip, "I am in my
body the way most people drive their cars."[22] With this alienation comes a

body loathing, a combination of mistrust and contempt for the cumbersome flesh that accounts for the drag coefficient in technological environments. "We are now entering a colonialist phase in our attitudes to the body, full of paternalistic notions that conceal a ruthless exploitation carried out for its own good," declares Ballard. "Will the body at last rebel, tip all those vitamins, douches and aerobic schedules into Boston harbor and throw off the colonialist oppressor?"[23]

David Cronenberg, our foremost theoretician of viral sex and "uncontrollable flesh," takes up Ballard's thread. "I don't think that the flesh is necessarily . . . evil," says Cronenberg, "[but it] is cantankerous, and it is independent. . . . It really is like colonialism. The colonies suddenly decide that they can and they should exist with their own personality and should detach from the control of the mother country. . . . I think that the flesh in my films is like that."[24] In his movie *The Brood* (1979), patients at Dr. Raglan's cultish Psychoplasmics Institute are taught to bring their neuroses and psychoses to the surface—literally, in the form of stigmata. The results are not always promising. A distraught graduate of the institute bares his chest to reveal grotesque tumors. "It's a form of cancer of the lymphatic system," he explains, through gritted teeth. "Raglan encouraged my body to revolt against me and it did. Now I have a small revolution on my hands and I'm not putting it down very successfully."

The antipathy between mind and body is implicit in the metaphysical riddle at the heart of the human condition—that we simultaneously *have* bodies and *are* bodies, that our flesh is both "it" and "I." Northrop Frye writes, "Human consciousness feels that it is inside a body it knows next to nothing about, even such elementary facts as the circulation of the blood being relatively recent discoveries. Hence it cannot feel that the body is identical with consciousness."[25]

At the same time, the software of our minds is maddeningly dependent on the hardware that houses it, our bodies. Body loathing arises, in part, from the terrible unfairness of the body's planned obsolescence. Says Cronenberg,

> Many of the peaks of philosophical thought revolve around the impossible duality of mind and body. . . . The basis of horror—and difficulty in life in general—is that we cannot comprehend

how we can die. Why should a healthy mind die, just because the
body is not healthy? There seems to be something wrong with
that.[26]

Sometimes, of course, body loathing simply speaks to the fact that
the body can be, well, loathsome. "Who has not felt at times the 'foulness' of
the body and the desire to shake it off?" asks Bruce Mazlish, a philosopher of
science. "Has not felt revulsion at the 'base' necessity of bowel movements,
or perhaps even of sex?"[27]

The Christian worldview that underwrites Western culture over-
lays this physical disgust with a moral revulsion. D. H. Lawrence, who
believed that "the greatest, most deeply rooted enemy of sensual life is
Christianity," blamed St. Paul, taking the apostle to task for his "emphasis on
the division of body and spirit, and his belief that the flesh is the source
of corruption."[28]

Yet, long-lived though it may be, body loathing rises to a crescendo
in cyberculture, where these influences seem poised to sever mind from
body, once and for all. "In the present condition we are uncomfortable
halfbreeds, part biology, part culture, with many of our biological traits out
of step with the inventions of our minds," asserts the artificial intelligence
theorist Hans Moravec.[29]

Recent military accidents involving "friendly fire" provide sobering
proof of Moravec's claim. Computerized weapons technology demands
human operators capable of processing information and making decisions
at superhuman speeds, says Captain Phil Bozzelli, the commander of the
USS *Valley Forge*. "We are putting a lot of pressure on decision makers,
and those who support them, to be infallible," he notes. "And the human
body isn't ready to be infallible."[30] In 1994, when American fighter planes
shot down two U.S. Army helicopters over northern Iraq, killing all on
board, the retired army lieutenant colonel Charles R. Shrader took up
Bozzelli's refrain: "Modern technology has simply evolved so fast and in so
many different ways that it is overtaxing human capacities," he told the *New
York Times*.[31]

Meanwhile, on the philosophical battlefields of the academy, traditional perceptions of the body and the self are under attack by contemporary feminist theory. Because women have so often been reduced to

objectified flesh throughout Western history, feminists have a vested interest in body politics. Since the early eighties, academic inquiries into the extent to which our knowledge of the body is culturally produced, rather than naturally determined, have proliferated, giving rise to a branch of scholarship that Judith Allen and Elizabeth Grosz call "corporeal feminism."[32]

According to the feminist theorist Anne Balsamo, feminists attempting to grapple with "the cultural construction of the gendered body" in cyberculture have had to come to terms with science and technology in a way that their precursors did not:

> An earlier feminist criticism that condemned science and technology as masculinist cults of rationality has given way to a serious engagement with a cluster of related questions that concern not only the development of new sciences and the deployment of new technologies (genetic engineering, for example), but also the philosophical frameworks that structure the social organization of the production of truth and knowledge.[33]

Contemplating the unlucky conjunction of technology and the female body in the information age, feminists as diverse as Naomi Wolf and Donna Haraway are challenging deep-seated ideas about the body in general and the female body in specific. Wolf, the best-selling advocate of a pro-capitalist "power feminism," and Haraway, a socialist-feminist historian of science, are spearheading mainstream and academic critiques that shatter the image of the body in cyberculture.

Build Me a Woman

Some girls wander by mistake
into the mess that scalpels make
—Leonard Cohen[34]

Time and again, patriarchal culture has brought technology to bear on women's bodies in the service of male fantasies: The corset produced the heaving bosom of romance novels even as it hindered respiration, restricted mobility, and rearranged the internal organs; the bustle thrust the buttocks up and back, approximating "the posture of a female animal in heat."[35]

The remodeling of the female body in accordance with bourgeois ideals did not end with the passing of the corset and the bustle. The consumer culture of industrial modernity merely emphasized the economic subtext of such practices. In the 1920s, writes Stuart Ewen, advertising educated American women "to look at themselves as things to be created competitively against other women: painted and sculpted with the aids of the modern market."[36]

In *The Beauty Myth: How Images of Beauty Are Used against Women*, Naomi Wolf indicts the unattainable ideal promulgated by the beauty industry—a pernicious fantasy that has made crash dieting, eating disorders, cosmetic surgery, and the onset of a chronic self-loathing rites of passage for too many American women. In cyberculture, notes Wolf, digital systems have enabled the creation of truly posthuman paragons of beauty: the impossibly flawless models in ads and fashion layouts in women's magazines exist only as digitized photos, retouched with computer graphics software. "Airbrushing age from women's faces is routine" even in general interest publications, she reports, and "computer imaging . . . has been used for years in women's magazines' beauty advertising" to remake reality to corporate dictates. This issue, she contends,

> is not trivial. It is about the most fundamental freedoms: the
> freedom to imagine one's own future and to be proud of one's
> own life. . . . to airbrush age off a woman's face is to erase
> women's identity, power, and history.[37]

Inverting the relationship between replica and original, this unreality fosters a postmodern psychosis. "As frozen, photogenic images—in ads or style magazines—become models from which people design . . . themselves, extreme alienation sets in," writes Ewen. "One becomes, by definition, increasingly uncomfortable in one's own skin."[38]

The union of computer technologies with Wolf's beauty myth may one day spawn creatures not unlike Pris, the Pleasure Model android in the movie *Blade Runner*. Cosmetic surgeons have already begun using computer programs to create previews of postop results by manipulating a patient's digitized photo. According to an article in the *San Francisco Examiner,* "The elusive 'perfect face' has been quantified and put into a computerized 'facial template.' By comparing a patient's face with the template, doctors can determine which features need correction."[39]

The process inspired Brian D'Amato's *Beauty,* a roman à clef about the messy collision of postmodernism, plastic surgery, and the beauty myth, set in the New York art world. In D'Amato's novel, an artist's obsession with Renaissance portraiture bears strange fruit: In an avant-garde surgical process, Jamie Angelo peels off his girlfriend's face and replaces it with synthetic skin on which he sculpts a countenance worthy of a quattrocento beauty, based on a computer composite of the most exquisite features in art history. The plot takes a ghoulish turn when things begin to go horribly wrong with Angelo's not-yet-ready-for-prime-time handiwork.

"We're closer to the era of total-reconstruction surgery than people think," says D'Amato. "The same computer-imaging techniques described in *Beauty* are already in use in plastic surgery clinics all over the world. . . . When the type of surgery described in *Beauty* becomes available, there will be people out there who will want to push the edge of the envelope."[40]

In a poetic sense, vanguard artists are already applying post-modern quotation to human anatomy. The role of computer imaging in creating ideals of beauty, and in the surgical revision of living tissue in accordance with those ideals, is addressed in what the *National Review* art critic James Gardner calls the "Art of the Body," a nineties redux of seventies body art. Riding the crest of this latest wave is the French performance artist Orlan.

Nowhere do body politics, the avant-garde's imperative to shock, and the pathologies of a culture drowning in images and obsessed with appearances come together more arrestingly, or disturbingly, than in Orlan's operating theater. Since 1990, she has undergone cosmetic surgery seven times as part of *The Ultimate Masterpiece: The Reincarnation of Saint Orlan,* a "carnal art" work-in-progress designed to transform her face into a collage of famous features. Her surgeons' hands are guided by a "facial template" assembled from digitized details of famous paintings. The composite face has Mona Lisa's forehead; the eyes of Gerome's Psyche; the nose of a Diana attributed to the School of Fontainebleau; the mouth of Boucher's Europa; and the chin of Botticelli's Venus.

Each operation is a performance: The patient, surgeon, and attend-
ing personnel wear haute couture scrubs, designed in one instance by Paco
Rabanne, and the operating room is decorated with crucifixes, plastic fruit,
and outsized placards displaying the production's "credits" in the kitschy
style of fifties movie posters. Given only local anesthesia, Orlan acts less like
a patient than a director on the set; during a 1993 operation in New York,
she read from a book on psychoanalysis and interacted by phone or fax with
viewers around the globe watching a live video transmission of the event
via satellite. "I will stop my work when it is as close as possible to the computer composite," she informed a *New York Times* reporter.[41] Her self-
objectification is instructive: By "it," she means her body, which is synonymous in her case with "my work."

Whether Orlan's surgical performances are carnal art or carnival
art is a matter of debate. The critic and curator Barbara Rose contends that
the artist is acting out "the madness of a demand for an unachievable
physical perfection"; Gardner maintains that she is merely a particularly
noxious example of "the French obsession with refinement and feminine
beauty."[42] Orlan insists that she is a feminist; her art, she writes, "brings into
question the standards of beauty imposed by our society . . . by using the
process of plastic surgery to a different end than the usual patient does" –
although how the rearrangement of her face in the image of an idealized
Renaissance femininity constitutes such a critique is unclear.[43] Her characterization of the experience of going under the knife as "cathartic" would
not sound out of place on the lips of a plastic surgery addict.

Then, too, there is the sticky business of her self-promotion: A
seasoned mediamonger, she repeats surefire sound bites ("I HAVE GIVEN MY
BODY FOR ART," "THE BODY IS BUT A COSTUME") and wraps gore, glamour, and
the ever popular image of the eccentric artist in a mediagenic package. "I'm
the artist who has gone the furthest," she claims, in a press release. Like all
great media manipulators, she blurs the line, à la Salvador Dali, between art
and advertising, product and public image (the *Times* called her private life
"a carefully constructed cipher"). She sometimes appears in photographs
dressed as the baroque "St. Orlan," a sobriquet reminiscent of the surrealist's preferred title, "the Divine Dali," and she out-Dalis Dali by literally
becoming her own commodity: The fat removed during her operations is on
sale in petri dishes dubbed "reliquaries."

In a written interview, Orlan sums up her philosophy in fractured English. "Orlan wants to fight against . . . the inborn, against DNA," she writes. Religion and psychoanalysis maintain that "we must accept ourselves [as we are]. . . . But [in an age] of genetic manipulation, this is a primitive outlook."[44]

In the final analysis, then, it is "primitive," humanist notions of what is natural and what is unnatural that are Orlan's true bête noire, not the sexist "standards of beauty imposed by our society." Her professed feminism and her manifest posthumanism cancel each other out: Those who declare war on "what is natural" are in no position to bemoan the unnatural "standards of beauty imposed by our society"; if the body is simply so much RAM (random-access memory) waiting to be overwritten with new data, one cut is as good as another. Beneath her politically expedient rhetoric about the evils of the beauty myth, Orlan conceals a not so secret dream: to be the art world's first posthuman celebrity. The artist, who has referred to herself as a "replicant" and who has observed, "I think the body is obsolete," seems primed for a cyborgian makeover, a metamorphosis into something out of Naomi Wolf's worst nightmares.

At the end of The Beauty Myth, Wolf warns that women are imperiled by their failure to understand that the Iron Maiden—the unnecessary fictions about the body beautiful that cage women's lives—has finally been uncoupled from the human frame of reference. "We still believe that there is some point where [cosmetic] surgery is constrained by a natural limit, the outline of the 'perfect' human female," she writes.

> That is no longer true. The "ideal" has never been about the bodies of women, and from now on technology can allow the "ideal" to do what it has always sought to do: leave the female body behind altogether to clone its mutations in space. The human female is no longer the point of reference. The "ideal" has become at last fully inhuman. . . . Fifty million Americans watch the Miss America pageant; in 1989 five contestants . . . were surgically reconstructed by a single Arkansas plastic surgeon. Women are comparing themselves and young men are comparing young women with a new breed that is a hybrid nonwoman.[45]

In other words, a morph. Perhaps, Wolf speculates, such creatures are only intimations of silicone—and silicon—sylphs to come. If this sounds like alarmist nonsense, consider Cindy Jackson, the living Barbie mentioned at the beginning of this chapter. Jackson has embarked on a crusade "which evolved while assisting other women through Barbie-izations" to create "a bionic army," according to M. G. Lord.[46] "In Barbie's early years, Mattel struggled to make its doll look like a real-life movie star," writes Lord.

> Today, however, real-life celebrities—as well as common folk—are emulating her. . . . [T]here are already a lot of bionic women out there. "I don't even think I want to walk down the street in California," Cindy told me. "They've all done what I've done. Over there I'm just another Barbie doll."[47]

Jackson, whose philosophy is founded on the principle that men "are really drawn to women for their looks," earnestly believes that surgery has given her "the perfect face and body."

Wolf is troubled by the growing sophistication of computer-enhanced photography "that will make 'perfection' increasingly surreal," and by menacing visions of "technologies that [will] replace the faulty, mortal female body, piece by piece, with the 'perfect' artifice."[48] Will this gyndroid have adjustable implants, Wolf wonders, that will allow her to instantaneously accommodate each partner's preference in breasts? In a posthuman, postfeminist future where "no self-respecting woman will venture outdoors without a surgically unaltered face," suggests Wolf, it will only be a matter of time before cosmetic surgeons "reposition the clitoris, sew up the vagina for a snugger fit, loosen the throat muscles, and sever the gag reflex. . . . The machine is at the door. Is she the future?"[49]

The Promises of Monsters[50]

It is a profound irony that a "hybrid nonwoman"—albeit one utterly unlike Wolf's—is the central conceit of an essay hailed as a benchmark in feminist thought: Donna Haraway's enormously influential "A Cyborg Manifesto."

Haraway's argument turns on a progressive, feminist reading of the myth of the cyborg—a myth that is traditionally interpreted as a macho, militarized response to forces that threaten accepted definitions of what it means to be male, even human. To Claudia Springer, a feminist critic of cyberculture, RoboCop and the Schwarzenegger Terminator express "nostalgia for a time when masculine superiority was taken for granted and an insecure man needed only to look at technology to find a metaphor for the power of phallic strength."[51]

In addition, Hollywood's armored cyborgs, the remnants of their humanity impregnable behind heavy metal hardware, speak to a growing sense of human irrelevance in what is, more and more, a technological environment. The cultural critic Scott Bukatman sees, in RoboCop and the Terminator, "an uneasy but consistent sense of human obsolescence, and at stake is the very definition of the human. . . . [O]ur ontology is adrift.[52]

To which Haraway replies, "The cyborg *is* our ontology; it gives us our politics."[53] Unlike RoboCop and other pugnacious symbols of an embattled status quo, Haraway's cyborg is the personification of a future untroubled by ambiguity and difference. It reconciles mechanism and organism, culture and nature, Tomorrowland and Arcadia, simulacrum and original, science fiction and social reality in a single body. A utopian monster, born of a "pleasure in . . . potent and taboo fusions" and "resolutely committed to partiality, irony, intimacy, and perversity," Haraway's cyborg is a living symbol of difference (sexual, ethnic, and otherwise) that refuses to be resolved or repressed.[54]

When Haraway declares that we are all cyborgs, she means it both literally—medicine has given birth to "couplings between organism and machine," bio- and communications technologies are "recrafting our bodies"—and figuratively, in the sense that "we are living through a movement from an organic, industrial society to a polymorphous, information system."[55] In short, technology is reversing the polarities of the world we live in:

> Late twentieth-century machines have made thoroughly ambig-
> uous the difference between natural and artificial, mind and
> body, self-developing and externally-designed, and many other
> distinctions that used to apply to organisms and machines. Our
> machines are disturbingly lively, and we ourselves frighteningly
> inert.[56]

In the eddies and vortices of these turbulent times, Haraway sees a historically unique opportunity for feminists to upset the balance of patriarchal power by "embracing the possibilities inherent in the breakdown of clean distinctions" between the privileged term and its devalued opposite in the hierarchical dualisms "structuring the Western self."[57]

To Haraway, the breaching, by science and technology, of boundaries between previously inviolable domains lines up neatly with contemporary academic thought—specifically, with poststructuralism, a school of literary theory and cultural analysis founded in France in the late sixties. According to poststructuralists, Western systems of meaning are underwritten by binary oppositions: body/soul, other/self, matter/spirit, emotion/reason, natural/artificial, and so forth. Meaning is generated through exclusion: The first term of each hierarchical dualism is subordinated to the second, privileged one. Poststructuralism attempts to expose the artful dodge whereby philosophical hierarchies validate their standards of truth by invalidating their opposites.

To Haraway, cyberculture by its very nature challenges these dualisms. Technology's trespasses across the once-forbidden zone between the natural and the artificial, the organic and the inorganic render much of what we know—or thought we knew—provisional. The philosophical implication of these and other technical developments, she argues, is that the conceptual cornerstones of the Western worldview—the network of meanings "structuring the Western self"—are fraught with cracks. Hammer blows in all the right places could bring the whole edifice tumbling down, she theorizes.

But "A Cyborg Manifesto," in addition to being an indictment of the Western worldview, is also an unflinching critique of feminism—specifically, of feminist attitudes toward science and technology. Previous feminisms have attempted to subvert the oppressive binary oppositions mentioned earlier by inverting them, redeeming the discarded first term of each hierarchical dualism. Ecotopian feminism, New Age goddess feminism, and other strains of what Katha Pollitt has called "difference" feminism assert that emotion, nurturing, and other traits "inherent" in women, though culturally depreciated, are no less valid than the "male" attributes lauded by our society. Woman, here, is Mother Earth, tuned to the frequencies of nature (the body) rather than culture (the mind)—a creature of biology rather than technology, intuition rather than rationality.

But, says Haraway, neither nature nor the body exist anymore, in the Enlightenment sense; both are irredeemably polluted, philosophically speaking, in an age of human babies with baboon hearts and genetically altered mice with human genes. The techno-logic of the late twentieth century, in concert with philosophies such as poststructuralism—which views nature, the body, and other previous givens as cultural constructions—"not only undermines the justifications for patriarchy but *all* claims for an organic or natural standpoint."[58] In other words, "It's not just that 'god' is dead; so is the 'goddess.' "[59]

Furthermore, she argues, in light of "the situation of women in a world so intimately restructured through the social relations of science and technology," feminism can ill afford "an anti-science metaphysics, a demonology of technology" that will condemn it to powerlessness.[60] Ballard put it succinctly: "Science and technology multiply around us. To an increasing extent they dictate the languages in which we speak and think. Either we use those languages, or we remain mute."[61]

New Age, pagan, or Gaian feminists who conduct their critique of the technological society in spiritual terms overlook the obvious, everyday ways in which cyberculture negatively affects women's lives. What Haraway calls the "New Industrial Revolution" has exposed female laborers in the semiconductor industry and the women who assemble electronic components in their homes to toxic chemicals that cause chromosome damage, premature deliveries, and miscarriages. Moreover, as the *Whole Earth Review* writer Joan Howe notes, telecommuting, like many of this century's labor-saving innovations for the housewife, is proving to be more curse than blessing; housebound mothers of young children who earn extra cash at the home terminal through "routine clerical work and production typing" are working

> even harder, since all the duties of the traditional housewife will
> still be there in addition to the opportunity (need) to earn a
> wage via computer networks. . . . Telework is technology's gift
> to conservatives, and bodes decidedly ill for feminists.[62]

Coming to terms with the essentially cyborgian nature of life in cyberculture is therefore a prerequisite for the empowerment of feminists who dream of a new world disorder. Technologies possess either repressive or liberatory potential, depending on who controls them, implies Haraway; to retain control of their physiologies and their destinies, women must abandon binary oppositions that demonize science and technology and deify nature. She writes,

> Cyborg imagery can suggest a way out of the maze of dualisms in which we have explained our bodies and our tools to ourselves. . . . Though both are bound in the spiral dance, I would rather be a cyborg than a goddess.[63]

Transgressions

Proceeding from Haraway's assumption that nature, human and otherwise, has become unnatural, feminist theorists have embarked on investigations of what Anne Balsamo calls "body *transgressions*"–inquiries into female bodybuilding, tattooing, and other "unnatural" acts that force us to reconsider our ideas about sex, gender, and humanity.[64]

"Inquiries" is perhaps too neutral a term here: Theories such as poststructuralism, which is dedicated to the demolition of hierarchies, are sometimes used in the service of agendas that merely invert those hierarchies. In such cases, what began as a refutation of "totalizing" ideologies–grand, unifying theories whose universality is achieved at the expense of intellectual diversity–becomes itself a general-purpose ideology whose facile corrective for all of our social ills is a resistance to fixed boundaries of any sort. "A Cyborg Manifesto," for example, is maddeningly short on practical politics for working-class borgs and disappointingly long on odes to "partiality, irony, intimacy, and perversity"–as if such abstract qualities could mean anything, apart from the noise and dirt of everyday lives.[65]

This dynamic is at work in uncritical celebrations of female bodybuilding, gender reassignment, and other body transgressions that give little thought to the problematic worldviews these activities sometimes represent. Such excesses abound in the postmodern theorist Arthur Kroker's fatuous rhapsodies about "electric flesh" and the "hyper-modern body." Here is an excerpt from a dizzy paean, coauthored with Marilouise Kroker, to a transsexual named Toni Denise:

She is not just a guy who warp jumped into a woman's body by surgical cuts, but the first of all the virtual bodies, that point where Disney World becomes flesh: a double movement involving the endless remaking of sexual identity and an abandonment of the (gendered) past.[66]

To the Krokers, Toni Denise is Haraway's utopian cyborg concretized, "a creature in a post-gender world."[67] She is the "perfect transsexual [sic] woman," oscillating between her identity as "a man-made woman" and a "man who could say no to cellulite, and yes to silicon [sic] breasts."[68] But as Stuart Ewen and Naomi Wolf have convincingly argued, far too many women are already "man-made" in mind and body. And the Disney World futurism of silicone breasts is lost on women whose bodies and lives bear the scars of Dow Corning implants.

If we knew more about the day-to-day existence of Toni Denise (we are told only that she "works" the drag queen bars of Tallahassee, Florida), we might be able to read the stories written in those "surgical cuts." Unfortunately, the psychological, sociological, and economic factors that have made her what she is are lost in cyberbole about "warp jump[s]," "virtual bodies," and "gender signs turn[ed] inside out"; she has been transformed from an actual being in a social body to a virtual ride in an academic theme park. In his critique of the body language of Krokerian postmodernism, Scott Bukatman writes,

> If the narration of dissolution often seems ecstatic in tone and promise, it also frequently ignores the real-world politics of new bodily technologies. . . . The real bodies at stake are often forgotten while consuming . . . the Krokers.[69]

Meat Hell

—mindbody meatbody deathbody stinking sagging shitting fetus bursting organs hanging buried alive in a coffin of blood oh god not me don't let it be me got to get out of this bucket of tripe it's

Mark Dery

> sucking me down throwing me up take it away this pulsing
> writhing spurting spinning body-go-round, BODY–
>
> —*David Skal*[70]

The opposition of the dead, heavy flesh ("meat," in compu-slang) and the ethereal body of information–the discorporated self–is one of cyberculture's defining dualisms. The belief that the body is a vestigial appendage no longer needed by late twentieth-century Homo sapiens–Homo Cyber–is not uncommon among obsessive programmers, outlaw hackers, video game junkies, and netsurfers cruising electronic bulletin board systems.

"I'M . . . TRAPPED IN THIS WORTHLESS LUMP OF MATTER CALLED FLESH!" rants a BBS user whose "pseud" (on-line pseudonym) is MODERNBODYMODERNBODYMODERNBODY. "I WANT TO BE FREE TO CRUISE THE WIRES AND MOLEST PEOPLE'S APPLIANCES. . . . LONG LIVE THE NEW FLESH! FUCK THE OLD FLESH!"[71] Giving vent to a body loathing born of a Nietzschean will to power, MODERNBODY quotes the last words of Max Renn in Cronenberg's *Videodrome,* just before he mutates into a video hallucination ("long live the new flesh"). Simultaneously, he evokes CyberJobe in the movie *The Lawnmower Man,* who announces his transmutation into a digital deity by ringing every phone on the planet in unison ("I want to be free to cruise the wires and molest people's appliances").

MODERNBODY and those like him are well represented in the fandom of cyberpunk SF, a genre that draws its narrative juice from the polarization of cyberspace and the physical world. William Gibson's *Neuromancer,* the urtext of cyberpunk, can be read as a lengthy meditation on the mind-body split in cyberculture. "The key to [the protagonist] Case's personality is [his] estrangement from his body, the meat," Gibson has noted.[72] In a radio interview, the novelist revealed that his 1984 novel was largely an extrapolation of

> some ideas I'd gotten from reading D. H. Lawrence about the dichotomy of mind and body in Judaeo-Christian culture. That's actually what I was thinking about, and it's all in there [in] that wool-gathering Case does about the meat and what it needs.[73]

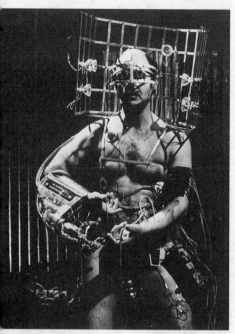

Stelarc with Laser Eyes, Third Hand, and
Amplified Body. *Photo: Polixeni Papapetrou*

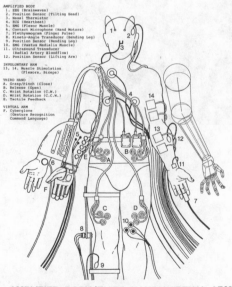

AMPLIFIED BODY/THIRD HAND/VIRTUAL ARM

Amplified Body / Third Hand / Virtual Arm
schematic. © 1995 Stelarc

Sitting / Swaying Event for Rock Suspension
(1980). *Photo: Kenji Nozawa*

Handwriting (1982). *Photo: J. Morioka*

Amplified Body, Laser Eyes, and Third Hand
(1986). *Photo: T. Shinoda*

Elapsed Horizon / Enhanced Assumption (1990).
Photo: T. Figallo

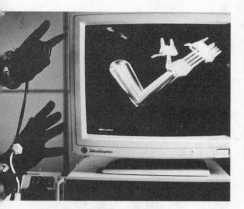

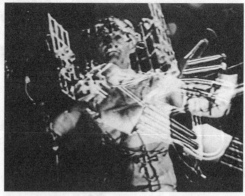

The Virtual Arm clones itself in
cyberspace. *Photo: T. Figallo*

Video still with virtual limbs
superimposed on Stelarc, from
Graft / Replicate: Event for Virtual Arm (1992).
© *Stelarc 1995*

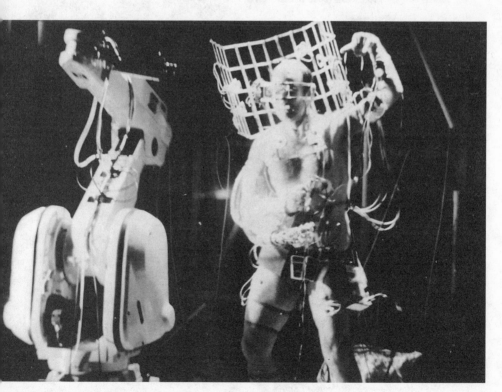

Stelarc performing with industrial robot arm. *Photo: Martin Burton*

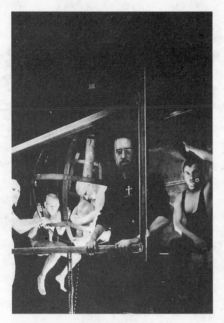

D. A. Therrien with members of
Comfort/Control.

The Body Drum.

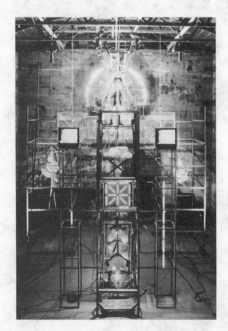

Information Machine: Ideological Engines
(1993). © *Paul Markow/Southwest, Comfort/Control*

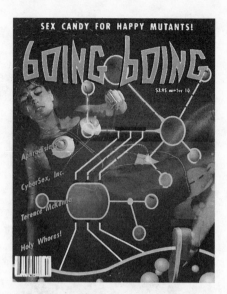

Siliconsensual Acts: *bOING-bOING* and *Future Sex* imagine the ultimate commodity fetish.

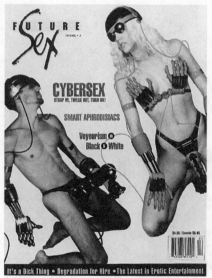

Orlan, Fourth Operation.
Photo: Andre Dhome / SIPA Press

The salaryman menaced by the Monstrous
Feminine in *Tetsuo: The Iron Man*. © *Kaijyu
Theater / Toshiba EMI, 1991. Directed by Shinya
Tsukamoto.*

Phallic horror: screwing literalized in
Tetsuo. © *Kaijyu Theater / Toshiba EMI, 1991.
Directed by Shinya Tsukamoto.*

Techno-tribal
tattoo:
biomechanical
ornamentation
inside primitive
motif, Jonathan
Shaw. *Photo appears
courtesy of Jonathan
Shaw. Tattoo by Jonathan
Shaw, Fun City Studios,
New York City.*

Biomechanical
"ripper" tattoo,
Guy Aitchison.
*Photo and tattoo by
Guy Aitchison*

Alien III (1979), H.R. Giger.
*© 1979 H. R. Giger. Reprinted with
permission, through Leslie Barany
Communications, NYC.*

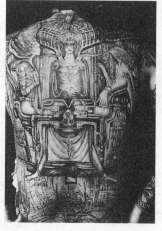

Giger-inspired
"backpiece."
*© 1995 B. J. Papas.
Model: Rick Healey.
oo by Andrea Elston.*

H.R. Giger.
© 1992 Willy Spiller

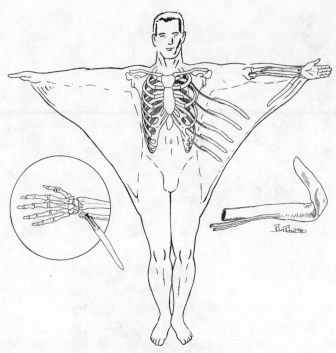

Blueprint for a winged human, by Dr. Burt Brent. *From Burt Brent, M.D., "Thoracobrachial Pterygoplasty Powered by Muscle Transposition Flaps" in* The Artistry of Reconstructive Surgery *(St. Louis: C.V. Mosby Co., 1987). Reprinted with permission.*

Hans Moravec with robot.
© *1995 Michael Llewellyn*

A robot bush, one of the posthuman beings envisioned by Moravec. © *Hans Moravec, Carnegie Mellon University, 1988*

Gibson later clarified this remark when he said that what he calls his " 'Lawrentian' take on things" derives from "Lawrence's interpretation of the crucifix," which Gibson sees as "completely appropriate to our society because it's a literal nailing of the body onto a cross of spirit and [mind]." A confirmed sensualist, Lawrence declared, "My great religion is a belief in the blood, the flesh, as being wiser than the intellect. We can go wrong in our minds. But what our blood feels and believes and says, is always true."[74]

Case would look decidedly out of place in a Lawrence novel. He is an outlaw hacker for hire, a down-on-his-luck information rustler who had once "worked for other, wealthier thieves, employers who provided the exotic software required to penetrate the bright walls of corporate systems, opening windows into rich fields of data."[75] His name says it all: A hard case out of a noir novel, a head case banged around by rough living, he is the postmodern descendant of T. S. Eliot's hollow men, all steely exterior, with no psychological interior. His body is a spent shell, his mind elsewhere—lost in memories of his exploits as a hotshot console cowboy, when he used a brain socket to physically connect his nervous system to a "custom cyberspace deck that projected his disembodied consciousness" into the neon-streaked matrix, where "data abstracted from the banks of every computer in the human system" appear as towers, cubes, and pyramids in a virtual reality version of Le Corbusier's Radiant City.[76]

For Case, the flesh is literally toxic: In a moment of weakness, he had pilfered something from his employers and in retribution they had "damaged his nervous system with a wartime Russian mycotoxin," rendering him physically unable to "jack" into cyberspace:

> For Case, who'd lived for the bodiless exultation of cyberspace,
> it was the Fall. In the bars he'd frequented as a cowboy hotshot,
> the elite stance involved a certain relaxed contempt for the flesh.
> The body was meat. Case fell into the prison of his own flesh.[77]

Salvation comes in the form of a mysterious outfit that recruits Case to crack the security programs of an enigmatic AI (artificial intelligence) for reasons unknown even to the operative who contacts him, a prosthetically enhanced cybermoll named Molly Millions. The outfit's surgeons restore

Case to cyberspace compatibility, guaranteeing his cooperation with a walking-time-bomb scheme familiar from techno-thrillers. If the caper is successful, the slowly dissolving toxin sacs they have planted in his arteries will be removed, enabling Case to roam the matrix freely; should he fail, they will be left to melt, returning him to his fallen state.

    Case exemplifies what Andrew Ross has called the "technocolonization of the body." Bodies, like every square foot of public space and the natural environment, are corporate property in *Neuromancer*'s near-future dystopia. A smooth operator's eyes, "vatgrown" like the genetically engineered eyes of *Blade Runner*'s replicants, say nothing about their owner and everything about brand-name affiliation: "[S]ea-green Nikon transplants" in a "tanned and forgettable mask," they are the furthest thing from windows of the soul.[78] Salaryman serfs in Japanese corporate fiefdoms are tattooed with their company logos and "above a certain level [are] implanted with advanced microprocessors that [monitor] mutagen levels in the bloodstream" to ensure mutation-free employees (the futuristic equivalent of drug-free employees).[79] Meanwhile, in the upper echelons of the *zaibatsus*— the all-powerful multinationals that are themselves "vast single organisms, their DNA coded in silicon"—the captains of industry have remade themselves through the "gradual and willing accommodation of the machine, the system, the parent organism" into "both more and less than *people.*"[80] Even Molly, the former "meat puppet" (prostitute) who has bootstrapped herself into the lucrative profession of "street samurai" with the aid of costly surgery, is simply a meat puppet of another sort. Although she exudes the coiled power of the high-tech assassin (her artificial nails conceal scalpel blades, her eye sockets are sealed with mirrored lenses that provide night vision and a constant stream of data), she is still hired muscle, a foot soldier whose body will always be someone else's weapon.

    This is only nominally science fiction: Gibson carries current trends in corporate culture (mandatory drug testing, health-care-related hiring policies that bar employees from smoking on the job *or* off, the use of cosmetic surgery by "unemployed males 'competing with younger people' " to gain a competitive edge in the job market) to their ultimate conclusion.[81] Even *Neuromancer*'s posthuman *zaibatsu* kingpins have one foot in the present. The Japanophile W. David Kubiak mentions an Osaka executive who, "before destroying evidence and himself to thwart an investigation of his firm," wrote, " 'I am but one. The *kaisha* [corporation] is many. My life is transient. The *kaisha* is forever!' "[82]

The present-day gulf between the information-rich yuppie elite and the swelling ranks of the minimum-wage service industry or the criminalized poor is writ large in *Neuromancer*'s body politics. Case inhabits a future-tense version of the two-tiered, neo-Dickensian America of the eighties and nineties, "an age of affordable beauty" where money can buy a "blandly handsome blend of pop faces" or "shoulders bulging with grafted muscle"; haute couture modifications (flesh "tattooed with a luminous digital display wired to a subcutaneous chip"); and even practical immortality: A 135-year-old wheeler-dealer named Julius Deane, "his metabolism assiduously warped by a weekly fortune in serums and hormones," has his DNA code reset each year by genetic surgeons.[83] The underclasses, by contrast, undergo anatomical makeovers to improve their salability in the marketplace or as rites of passage into the punk gangs that are the urban jungle's postmodern primitives.

Neuromancer is permeated by a fatalistic resignation to the futility of any attempt at a political power shift: Case and Molly are utterly apolitical, aspiring to the peak of their professions—the glamorized corporate soldier of fortune—and nothing more. Although as quasi-autonomous agents they are arguably better off than the undifferentiated megalopolitan masses ("a field of flesh shot through with sudden eddies of need and gratification"), their fleeting tastes of freedom and power consist, ironically, of bodily sensation.[84] Case's disembodied POV banks and rolls through cyberspace like that of a top-gun pilot ("Headlong motion through walls of emerald green, milky jade, the sensation of speed beyond anything he'd known before").[85] Molly stalks the urban combat zone with predatory speed and off-kilter grace ("She seemed continually on the verge of colliding with someone, but people melted out of her way, stepped sideways, made room").[86] Kinesis replaces political action.

But the "horizonless" infinity of the matrix and the endless iterations of the Sprawl—the cityscape that stretches from Boston to Atlanta—offer only the illusion of unrestricted movement: in a world where nation-states have been swallowed up by multinationals and the imaginary geography of the matrix is dominated by icons of corporate capital, the rights of the individual are bounded on every side. In *Neuromancer*, writes Ross, the decisions that count are always being made elsewhere, in circumstances well beyond the control of interested stiffs like Case or . . . Molly. . . . Despite the technical education in the workings of power that they undergo, such people are usually even less in control of their futures at the end of a Gibson adventure than they were to begin with.[87]

Fusing stoic resignation, existential ennui, and future shock in the flattened affect that characterizes Homo Cyber, Molly shrugs off the directionless violence of her pinball existence with the throwaway line, "I guess it's just the way I'm wired."[88] Like the autistic astronauts in Stanley Kubrick's *2001: A Space Odyssey* or Deckard, the deadpan, monotoned flatfoot in *Blade Runner*, the borged and morphed humans in *Neuromancer* are, as Donna Haraway put it, "frighteningly inert"; their machines—especially the self-aware AI, Wintermute, who is behind the novel's machinations—are "disturbingly lively." Ultimately, it is the machines who command their own destinies in the truest sense. The consciousness that is Wintermute attains a sort of godhood when it fuses with an AI called Neuromancer and *becomes* one with the All—in this case, the matrix.

Case's rewards, at the end of the novel, are a fresh pancreas—the better, presumably, to indulge in the amphetamines that seem to be his greatest carnal pleasure—and a new cyberspace deck that offers instant (if illusory and transitory) escape from meat hell. If religion is the opiate of the masses and Marxism the opiate of the intellectual, then cyberspace is the opiate of the twenty-first-century schizoid man, polarized between mind and body.

Original Syn

This equation serves as the springboard for Pat Cadigan's *Synners*, a cyberpunk novel about soulless electronic transcendence, among other things. For Visual Mark, a virtuoso virtual reality synthesizer, or "synner," the body is "meat-jail," as it is for Case. Opting for a brain socket, he plugs his mind directly into the worldwide computer network ("the System"), which enables Mark to immerse his audience in his full-sensory, rock-video dreams. His baptism into unfettered bodilessness sounds unmistakably like being born again: "The sense of having so much space to spread out in—a baby emerging from the womb after nine months must have felt the same thing, he thought."[89]

Mark soon decides to remain permanently plugged in, forgoing the bother of removing his brain-wires to eat or use the bathroom. He slows his metabolism to a near halt in a stunt characterized by a doctor as fakirlike, although his own description of it—"I took the video mainline"—is closer to the Mark. Curled up in a fetal ball, guts locked, he calls to mind William Burroughs's self-portrait in *Naked Lunch* as a mainlining heroin addict: "I had not taken a bath in a year nor changed my clothes or removed them except to stick a needle every hour in the fibrous grey wooden flesh of terminal addiction."[90]

Like Burroughs's "users" (a term shared by smack shooters and Mac owners), Mark—a terminal addict in the literal sense—purchases other-worldly omnipotence at the price of total impotence in the meatworld. In fulfillment of MODERNBODY's fantasy, he "cruise[s] the wires and molest[s] people's appliances" with impunity: Surveillance cameras (ubiquitous in the twenty-first-century L.A. of the novel) become his eyes, computer console speakers his voice boxes, the measureless vastness of global cyberspace his dominion. Meanwhile, perversely, plaintively, his body yearns for his return:

> [T]he meat missed him. It sent out feeble signals, dumb animal
> semaphore: come back to the nest, little Sheba. . . . If he could
> have given the disconnect command from this side, it would be
> over in a twinkling. So long, meat, write if you get work. But he
> couldn't access any of the commands from where he was. The
> commands only took orders from the meat, and that poor old
> meat wasn't about to cut him loose. . . . If he could just get
> someone . . . to come in and yank the connections out of his
> skull.[91]

Ultimately, Mark's prayers are answered by the cerebral stroke he suffers while jacked-in—one of the "intercranial meltdowns" that are a calculated risk among "socket people." The power surge transfers his consciousness to the net, enabling him to abandon the despised meat at last.

When his old flame and fellow synner Gina peers into his body's dying eyes, watching his consciousness drain away, the computer-bound Mark stares back with what is already a partly artificial intelligence. In a secular gloss on the transcendentalist vision of the self united with the Supreme Mind, he has become one with the billions of bytes stored in the System:

> [H]e was looking at Gina with what felt like a universe of knowledge within him, everything from every part of the system, databases that outlined every face of human behavior, delineated every emotion, defined every word by tone of human voice and told every story. . . . Joy surged into his configuration, to see so deeply into her, even though she was not on-line with him. . . . Moments later, he seemed to plummet, out of balance because she wasn't there and there could be no reciprocation. The unfairness of it was truer pain than anything he'd ever felt incarnate.[92]

Cadigan's evocation of the loneliness of the discarnate mind is unbearably poignant. Virtual Mark is terribly, irrevocably alone in his virtual universe, the only human consciousness in a cosmos of information. The sensation of skin against skin is nothing but a memory, saved to disk. Mark can relive it through a surprisingly lifelike simulation, but he is haunted by the nagging truth that a digital re-creation will always be the next best thing to being there: "Now all he had to do was reach for it in his memory, and he was there again, in the pleasure. But in the loneliness, too."[93]

Visual Mark's transcendental leap is diminished by its egocentrism; rather than dissolving his solipsistic self in a mystical Over-Soul, he has unleashed his all-consuming ego on the infinite (in this case, the System). "[H]is *self* was getting greater all the time, both ways, greater as in more wonderful and greater as in bigger," he exults, early on.[94] In time, however, a painful truth dawns: "Maybe you could make yourself bigger, but you couldn't make yourself any less alone."[95] As Joseph Campbell once observed,

> [T]he whole aim is to go past . . . one's concept of oneself, to that of which one is but an imperfect manifestation. . . . If you think, "I here, in my physical presence and in my temporal character,

am God," then you are mad and have short-circuited the experience. You are God, not in your ego, but in your deepest being,
where you are at one with the nondual transcendent.[96]

The System, like all computer-generated spaces, is the realm not of
the numinous but of the human mind—specifically, memory—metastasized;
to become one with such a construct is to disappear into an exteriorized
model of one's own cognitive machinery, to become Narcissus falling into
his own reflection. The SF novelist and critic Norman Spinrad finds a moral
in the book's punning title:

> The *personal* sin [in *Synners*] is the abandonment of human love
> in favor of the ultimate solipsistic seduction of total immersion
> in a virtual reality of which the electronic machineries make you
> the god. . . . In the end, the sin is not that of electronic transcen-
> dence but of abandoning human empathy and feeling in the
> obsessive pursuit of same.[97]

Anne Balsamo reminds us that the transcendental world of cyberspace is one half of a duality whose repressed other half is the mundane
meatworld. Reading Cadigan's novel as a feminist narrative about "the
relation of the material body to cyberspace," she explores the main characters' interactions with the System, taking special note of how gender
complicates the equation.[98]

To Balsamo, the two female hackers, Gina and Sam (a teenager who
likes to pummel her eardrums with "speed-thrash") "actively *manipulate* the
dimensions of cybernetic space in order to communicate with other
people," whereas Mark and Gabe (a near-future Walter Mitty who spends
much of his time lost in virtual reality fantasies) are "*addicted* to cyberspace
for the release it offers from the loneliness of their material bodies."[99] This
opposition is dramatized in the novel's climax, when all terminals connected to the System crash, infected by the viral entity created when Visual
Mark melds with a mysterious AI. Gina and Gabe exorcize cyberspace via a
terminal powered by Sam's body: An insulin-pump device, its needles poked
into Sam's abdomen, provides the power. Gina, a synner of no small talent,
and Sam, a hacker known for her acrobatic exploits in cyberspace, are SF

examples of Haraway's feminist cyborgs: In a cybernetic society, their technological skills have won them at least a modicum of personal and political power.

Then, too, they represent a more holistic vision of Homo Cyber than cyberpunk antiheroes such as Case or Molly: Sam's insulin-powered hacking symbolizes a reconciliation of meat and mind, organic and synthetic—Haraway's cyborg politics at work. *Synners* "offers an alternative vision of technological embodiment," writes Balsamo, "where technology isn't the means of escape from or transcendence of the body, but rather a means of communication with other bodies."[100] At the same time, she warns, the very technologies that create new contexts for wraithlike data bodies simultaneously "enable new forms of repression of the material body."[101]

Phantom Limbs

> See how computers are getting under our skin. Everything about our bodies is stored in our genes. And someday, everything about our genes will be stored in computers. . . . [O]ur high-tech society is creating more information than ever before. About everything from our chromosomal makeup to our credit history. . . . [S]ee how we go about dealing with a technology that not only has great bodies of knowledge, but a great knowledge of bodies.
> —*magazine ad for the PBS program* Smithsonian World [102]

> Her driver's license.
> Her credit cards.
> Her bank accounts.
> Her identity.
> Deleted.
> —*poster for the movie* The Net

In cyberculture, everyone has phantom limbs: digital doppelgängers stand in for all of us in the databases of governmental agencies, transnational banks, insurance companies, credit bureaus, and direct mail marketers, rendering us visible and, increasingly, manipulable.

As Jeffrey Rothfeder argues in *Privacy for Sale: How Computerization Has Made Everyone's Private Life an Open Secret,* our physical bodies are now texts in the literal rather than the poststructuralist sense, open books to all who access the databank in question. It is a little-known fact that the confidentiality of medical records is not guaranteed by law; government workers, prospective employers, educational institutions, the media, private investigators, and what Rothfeder calls "people with a vested interest in uncovering all they can about someone they want to turn a dirty deal on" routinely peruse computerized patient files.[103] There is much to peruse: Medical records, according to the American Medical Records Association, contain "more intimate details about an individual than can be found in any single document."[104]

The results of these perusals can be devastating. Rothfeder tells one well-documented horror story after another: David Castle, a freelance artist, was denied disability coverage because information about him in the data-banks of the Medical Information Bureau (MIB) incorrectly noted that he had AIDS; John Friedkin, a freelance writer, had difficulty obtaining a life insurance policy because of an MIB clerk's data entry error that coded him as suffering from extreme psychosis. Worse yet, informs Rothfeder, access to the results of genetic tests have compelled insurance companies "to intrude on extremely sensitive and private decisions, even to force their will on a couple trying to decide whether a baby should be born or aborted, or to dictate with economic sanctions whether a couple should conceive or not."[105]

Bodies reconstituted as information floating in data banks can have a profound impact on physical bodies in the real world. This information-age truism is the point of departure for *The Net,* a 1995 cyber-thriller about a hacker who stumbles on a conspiracy to take over the U.S. government. The villains erase her identity by deleting her Social Security information, credit records, and so forth, and replace it with that of a wanted woman. On the run from the police and the conspirators, she laments that each of us has an "electronic shadow, just sitting there, waiting for somebody to screw with it."

Steve Kurtz, an assistant professor of art theory at Carnegie-Mellon University, believes that

> social relationships are mediated . . . by the perception of our electronic doubles resid[ing] in cyberspace. Our data bodies–

educational records, credit history, bank statements, criminal
files–will direct the type [of] social relationship that we have
whenever authority (to oversimplify, those who own or control
information) is confronted. . . . Regaining control of the data
body is a key act of electronic civil disobedience, [since] it is the
most efficient way to return autonomy to the individual.[106]

Kurtz is a member of Critical Art Ensemble, an artistic collabora-
tive exploring the intersections of critical theory, technology, and art. In
Critical Art Ensemble: The Electronic Disturbance, a theoretical work that is
equal parts academic discourse, postmodern SF, and Abbie Hoffmanesque
fist-banging, the group plots strategies for "regaining control of the data
body." In cyberculture, argues CAE,

[a]bstracted representations of the self and the body, separate
from the individual, are simultaneously present in numerous
locations, interacting and recombining with [other bodies of
information], beyond the control of the individual and often to
his or her detriment. . . . This situation offers the resistant
performer two strategies: one is to contaminate and call attention to corrupted data, while the other is to pass counterfeit
data. . . . Greater freedom in the theater of everyday life can be
obtained once the virtual theater is infiltrated.[107]

Kurtz, who is friends with the transsexual Toni Denise, sees
her surreal run-ins with local law enforcement as a funny, down-to-earth
example of "electronic civil disobedience" and "regaining control of the
data body":

When [Toni Denise] was pre-op, she used to ride around in her
convertible with her breasts exposed. The cops would pull her
over to arrest her [but] when her electronic data proved s/he was
male, they would have to let her go. She drove the police nuts! I
love Toni–even though her goal is to be the girl next door and to
live the life of a "normal" middle-class housewife, she can be no
other than a living model of political resistance.[108]

Oddly, Kurtz's poster girl for political resistance is the same person who appears in the CAE videotape *Gender Crash,* imparting pearls of mallcrawler wisdom such as "I have taken what I was born with and modern technology and created the perfect aesthetic look for me. I have a 39-27-39 body; that's perfect." Of course, Naomi Wolf, Donna Haraway, and all who resist the notion of a "perfect" female body and the constricted worldview it implies would beg to differ.

Irreverent as she is, Toni Denise has little to say about the beauty myths that shaped her vision of femininity or the extent to which her performances in transvestite revues exchange the confines of one gender role for another. Her encomiums to the sublime nightmare of cyberculture ("That's what the world is becoming, techno-bodies, techno-everything, and I'm the techno-woman of the nineties") take no notice of the way in which the very technologies that liberated her have disfigured the lives and bodies of other, biological women. Kurtz acknowledges that she

> has little to do with [a] feminist critique. Does she think about what body-beautiful tech has done to women? No, she doesn't think about women at all. She is searching for the self-contained male universe. Does she know where her ideas on beauty originate? Yes, and it is precisely within this matrix of desire that she is working ("That's why it is so easy for me to pick up men," she says). She is a man who has constructed herself as female with male tech for the pleasure of men. . . . [T]he elimination of [biological] women is the goal. Kill all competing objects of desire; this is her cyborg function. . . . For CAE, she is our poster girl within the virtual theater; however, in a general analysis, she has some frightening characteristics.[109]

Clearly, finding a way out of Haraway's "maze of dualisms" is not going to be easy. Michel Foucault's axiom that transgressions–bodily or otherwise–reaffirm cultural bounds even as they test them is borne out in the ambiguities and contradictions of Toni Denise's real-life science fiction.

Unnatural Histories

'Roid Rage

> In this age when metal and mechanics are all-powerful, man, in
> order to survive, must become stronger than the machine, just
> as he [had] to become stronger than the beasts.
>
> —*Alfred Jarry*[110]

Bodybuilding represents a last-ditch attempt to hold the body together at a time when genetic engineering and the Human Genome Project remind us, disconcertingly, that a human being is "little more than a cloud of information," to borrow Thomas Hine's memorable phrase.[111]

There is a giddy dysphoria to our historical moment—a vertigo induced, perhaps, by the fear that even we will one day be dematerialized in a swirl of data-bits, like passengers in a *Star Trek* transporter. It can hardly be happenstance that the signature sample of techno music, quoted in countless songs, is the phrase "Pure Energy," spoken by *Star Trek*'s Mister Spock, or that the climax of *The Lawnmower Man* occurs when CyberJobe declares, "I'm going to . . . complete the final stage of my evolution. I'm going to project myself into the mainframe computer; I'll become pure energy."

Considered in this context, the cult of the gymnasium makes cultural sense. With the aid of weight-training machines, nutritional supplements, and anabolic steroids (synthetic testosterone), bodybuilding obsessives erect an impregnable bulwark of "ripped"—that is, sharply etched—muscles around the notion of an immutable body and an integrated self. Obviously, the notion of being huge and hard in cyberculture is a colossal irony; muscle is redundant in a world where even the easiest tasks—changing channels, switching lights on and off, adjusting the volume on a CD player—are allocated to small, smart, ever more biomorphic devices. "My upper-body musculature, developed largely on Nautilus machines, means that I probably *can* chop wood or unload trucks, not that I ever *will*," writes Barbara Ehrenreich.[112] It is for psychological, not physical, reasons that many of us worship at the stations of the Nautilus.

In a broader cultural sense, however, bodybuilding speaks not only to anthropologist Alan M. Klein's assertion that "the golden era when 'men were men' has passed, and the powerful roles traditionally the exclusive province of men have vanished, weakened, or are no longer gender-specific," but also to a gnawing anxiety about the future of the body in a cybernetic environment—an environment that still requires the mind, the eye, and the hand but has little use for the rest of the body.[113]

Bodybuilding reasserts the validity of human brawn in an age of intelligent machines. It's an anachronistic desire, of course—a ritual of resistance to industrial modernity that is as old as the steam-age myth of John Henry, the railroad worker who won a contest with a steam drill but died of exhaustion shortly thereafter. " 'Roid rage"—slang for the rampages associated with habitual steroid use—becomes a pun when applied to bodybuilding conceived of both as a rage against the machine and as a practice that paradoxically produces humans who look and behave like machines: android rage. Significantly, technological imagery colors first-person as well as journalistic descriptions of 'roid rages. In his *Village Voice* article on bodybuilding, "Living Large," Paul Solotaroff depicts the former Mr. Universe Steve Michalik as a hormone-addled android whose eyes, like those of the hunter-killer "endoskeletons" in *Terminator 2,* "went as red as the laser scope on an Uzi" when he was angry.[114] In the same article, Michalik recalls the time he ripped off a truck door and caved in the offending driver's face with one punch: "[I]t was like I was trapped inside a robot body, watching myself do horrible things, and yelling, 'Stop! Stop!' "[115]

The "body proud"—to borrow a term from *RoboCop 2*—refute the obsolescence of the flesh by twisting their bodies into whip steel, making themselves over in the image of the machine. "Of all the sports conceived by man, none bears a closer resemblance to bodybuilding than auto racing," notes the *Details* writer Erik Hedegaard. "The only difference is that one engine is mechanical and the other corporeal."[116] Pop singers, professional wrestlers, movie stars and ordinary gym-goers chisel themselves into futur-ist sculptures, all sharp edges and flat planes, in unknowing fulfillment of the futurist poet F. T. Marinetti's rhapsodies about "the imminent, inevitable identification of man with motor."[117] Ads for Evian bottled water feature glistening Aryans whose streamlined physiques look as if they were lathed and polished on some Nordic assembly line.

The die-cut piece of work known as the "hard-body" is, at its heart, a machine-age artifact. The effect is achieved by means of a process that presumes the objectification of the physique, a fact hinted at by a phrase that appears on muscle T-shirts: BODY SCULPTING. Stuart Ewen has noted the convergence of the "principles of instrumental reason, engineering, and technological regimentation" in the weight room, where gym-goers move along an assembly line of "stations," or Nautilus machines, each of which exercises a different muscle group.[118] The body is conceived of as an interlocking assemblage of machinelike components, and the desired effect, in which glutes, lats, pecs, and abs stand out in sharp relief, resembles the product of a punch press.

It seems only appropriate that the cultural icon for the late eighties and early nineties should turn out to be Austrian-born Arnold Schwarzenegger, an ex-steroid-using former weight lifter best known for his portrayal of a predatory cyborg in *The Terminator* (1984). Schwarzenegger is at once a pumped-up hunk and an affectless automaton whose acting ability falls just short of Disneyland's Mr. Lincoln, an Audio-Animatronic dummy brought to life by bursts of pressurized air. His physique reconciles the male centerfold, all rippling pecs, and an exploded view of the internal combustion engine. In *Muscle: Confessions of an Unlikely Bodybuilder*, Sam Fussell describes Schwarzenegger in tellingly mechanomorphic terms: The champion bodybuilder "used the weight room as his smithy" in the creation of an ironclad "human fortress . . . to keep the enemy host at bay"–the "enemy host" being, in Fussell's mind, the school-yard toughs and sand-kicking bullies of the world.[119]

The Schwarzenegger *Menschmaschine* is the link between two utterly unlike subcultures: hard-core bodybuilders and cyberpunks. Klein's reading of bodybuilding as an attempt to fortify the notion of an unassailable masculinity at a time when gender roles are under siege is echoed in Andrew Ross's argument that "the cyberpunk image of the techno-body played into the crisis of masculinity in the eighties."[120] Although he caricatures cyberpunk as a "baroque edifice of adolescent male fantasies," Ross generates valuable insights by setting "the inflated physiques of Arnold Schwarzenegger and Sylvester Stallone" alongside the prosthetically enhanced bodies of male cyberpunks as mythic responses to the waning of patriarchal power.[121]

Examined in the context of Ross's "crisis of masculinity," both bodybuilders and cyberpunks arrive, by opposite routes and with different baggage, at the same place: the "metalization of man" imagined by Marinetti.[122] In that sense, they are two sides of the same coin, although the hard-bodies' worship of a sublime Renaissance humanism symbolized by Michelangelo's *David*—an incarnation of the Neoplatonic notion that the flawless human body is evidence of man's perfectability—blinds them to the glaring irony that their machine-tooled, often chemically enhanced bodies are already posthuman. And that coin, like any, can be flipped: The bulging, knotty-veined physiques of bodybuilders are fundamentally unnatural, a fact they acknowledge in their slang term for themselves ("freaks"), while cyberpunks can be seen, as Ross argues, not as mutants who have spun off of humanity's evolutionary trajectory but as exponents of a "maverick humanism" whose "radical mutations in bodily ecology" are "welcomed as an advance in human evolution."[123]

Terminator 2: Iron John Meets Steely Dan

> Male and female represent the two sides of the great radical dualism. But in fact they are perpetually passing into one another. Fluid hardens to solid, solid rushes to fluid. There is no wholly masculine man, no purely feminine woman.[124]
>
> *—Margaret Fuller*

Buried deep in the public mind, cultural nightmares about the crisis of masculinity, the body's growing irrelevance, and the putative obsolescence of the species erupt in *Terminator 2: Judgment Day* (1991).

In *The Terminator*, Sarah Connor (Linda Hamilton) vanquishes the titular villain (Arnold Schwarzenegger), a cyborg assassin sent back in time to liquidate her. The Terminator comes from a future in which SkyNet, a "Star Wars"-like computerized defense system that obviates the need for all human decision making, acquires sentience and with it the instinct for self-preservation. When panic-stricken humans attempt to pull SkyNet's plug, the system triggers a nuclear holocaust ("Judgment Day") and dispatches autonomous tanks, flying machines, and gun-wielding "endoskeletons" (Terminators sans flesh) to flush out any remaining pockets of human resistance.

But fate has decreed that John Connor, the leader of the save-the-humans movement, will ultimately triumph over the machines, so SkyNet

sends a Terminator into the past to rewrite history by terminating
Sarah Connor before she can bear humanity's savior, a boy named John
Connor. Happily, Connor and his resistance foil SkyNet by sending back
a time-traveler of their own—a robot-killing guerrilla fighter named Kyle
Reese. History, here, is a locked loop: In addition to helping Sarah
destroy the Terminator, Reese spends a night of passion with her, fathering
John Connor.

In *Terminator 2*, set a decade after the first film, Sarah Connor has
been institutionalized for blowing up a computer factory and raving about
the impending techno-apocalypse; John Connor, now a punky, disaffected
preteen, is the unmanageable ward of dysfunctional foster parents. Yet
another Terminator is hot on the boy's trail. This one is an "advanced
prototype" T-1000 made of "mimetic polyalloy" that allows it to assume the
appearance of "anything it samples by physical contact." Before our very
eyes, the T-1000 liquefies into a featureless silver mannequin, then hardens
into the look and shape of anyone—or anything—it has touched. Luckily,
Connor has a guardian angel: a T-800 Schwarzenegger-type Terminator
reprogrammed by Connor and sent back in time to protect himself.

On the surface, *T2* is a cautionary tale about the fate of a society
that leaves its technology on automatic pilot, staged as a thrill-a-minute
carnival of carnage. If we look beyond the obvious, however, we find
another, no less desperate battle being waged, this one a contest for
meanings.

In one sense, *T2* is a duel of dualisms—a philosophical struggle over
body images and gender boundaries. With its monotonal delivery, impassive
expression, dark sunglasses, head-to-toe black leather getup, Harley-Davidson
Fat Boy motorcycle, and whopping guns, the Schwarzenegger Terminator is
the standard-bearer for a hypermasculine archetype: the crypto-fascist man
of steel with the iron will. The T-800 is a technophallus, a (literal) Iron John
whose robopathic autism and ever-ready rigidity will show the "soft" man
vilified by Robert Bly who's boss.

Early in the picture, the T-800 ritually strips one of society's most
durable icons of fearsome masculinity of the badges of his virility when he
relieves a cigar-chomping, heavily tattooed biker of his gun, his leathers, and
most important, his mammoth, gleaming motorcycle. In a cinematic moment that is pure cartoon Freud, the Schwarzenegger Terminator mounts

mounts the big machine to the tune of George Thorogood's "Bad to the Bone," a bit of Bo Diddleyesque braggadocio about a lover man who really hits the G-spot. A biker's motorcycle is both sexual surrogate and penile prosthesis, according to Hunter Thompson, who quotes a Hell's Angel on the meaning of the word "love" ("the feelin' you get when you like somethin' as much as your motorcycle") and cites a psychologist who calls the machine "a phallic locomotor symbol . . . an extension of one's body, a power between one's legs."[125] Symbolically castrating and cuckolding the biker by stealing the Harley that is both his manhood and his woman, the T-800 proves to all concerned that he is an indomitable rock of masculinity, "bad to the bone." And a bone, as every American male who has survived high school gym class knows, is an erection.

The T-1000, by contrast, is boneless. It personifies the "female" characteristics feared and loathed by the hard-body–softness, vulnerability, and wetness (its transformations are accompanied by a faint slurping sound). A polymorphous perversity, the T-1000 is the nightmare Feminine given squishy, shifting shape. Penetrated, again and again, by bullets and impaled, at one point, on a spike, the T-1000 frustrates the T-800 with its "feminine" mutability, puckering its wounds closed with a soft, almost obscene sucking noise. In the movie's climactic struggle, the Schwarzenegger Terminator lands a roundhouse punch on the polyalloy android's head, only to have his fist become embedded in the liquid metal–an SF update of that hoary Freudian phobia, the devouring vagina from which no male organ escapes intact.

Mercurial, duplicitous, the shape-shifter archetype is, in traditional terms, "feminine"; the chameleonic ability to "blend in" while nonetheless preserving something of one's innermost thoughts and feelings is, after all, a survival strategy of the powerless, one for which men (at least, straight, white ones) in Western culture have historically had little need. The "difference" feminist Jean Baker Miller believes that "women's reality *is* rooted in the encouragement to 'form' themselves into the person who will be of benefit to others. . . . Out of [this experience], women develop a psychic structuring for which the term ego, as ordinarily used, may not apply."[126] By Miller's logic, all women are made of mimetic polyalloy.

With its chrome finish and quicksilver qualities, the T-1000 resembles a blob of mercury in human form. In alchemical and Jungian symbolism, mercury is a lunar, mutable element associated with the feminine principle and, more specifically, androgyny and hermaphroditism. The liquid metal robot is indeed polygendered: in its generic state, it is unequivocally male, resembling an Oscar statuette or a personification of Steely Dan, the strap-on dildo in *Naked Lunch,* but it can assume any sex. It is androgynous, too. There is more than a hint of coded homosexuality in the T-1000's chosen incarnation: a smallish, vaguely effeminate policeman with a tart, thin-lipped smirk whose favored method of dispatching his victims is by poking stiff, pointy objects into their holes (a blade-shaped arm through a man's mouth, a stilettolike finger through a male prison guard's eye).

In the movie's final moments, both Terminators are consumed in a vat of molten steel, where their mettle is revealed. The technetronic Teuton, Schwarzenegger, slips into the boiling goop with a chivalric thumbs-up worthy of a Wagnerian hero; the T-1000 squirms and shimmies, mouthing silent, Edvard Munchlike screams in a distinctly epicene fashion. As it dissolves away to nothing, the T-1000 cycles through the various characters it has impersonated (the cop, John's foster mother, a guard in Sarah's mental hospital)—a demise that conjures the liquefaction of the Wicked Witch in *The Wizard of Oz.* Why, it can't even *die* like a man!

The T-800 hard-body and the protoplasmic T-1000 put computer-age faces on the two symbolic bodies theorized by Klaus Theweleit in *Male Fantasies,* a two-volume study of the Freikorps—protofascist mercenaries who crushed worker uprisings and fought Germany's border disputes in the turbulent years between the world wars.

Looming large on the landscape of the male fascist unconscious are two mythic bodies, locked in binary opposition: the monstrous Feminine—a sump of foul effluvia, an engulfing "red flood," a sucking morass—and the armored robo-corpus of the Freikorps killing machine, safe and dry inside its full metal jacket from a host of "feminine" horrors. In their introduction to the second volume of *Male Fantasies,* Jessica Benjamin and Anson Rabinbach detail the "the corporal metaphysics at the heart of fascist perception":

> On the one side, there is the soft, fluid, and ultimately liquid
> female body which is a quintessentially negative 'Other' lurking
> inside the male body. . . . On the other there is the hard, orga-
> nized, phallic body devoid of all internal viscera which finds its
> apotheosis in the machine.[127]

Theweleit suggests that the robopathology manifest in the armored body is the result of the projection onto the Feminine of the abominable, "soft" desire for maternal love buried, along with other "womanly" emotional yearnings, in the fascist male psyche.

The gender war that lies just beneath the surface of *T2* rages around the fact that each term of a binary opposition inheres within the other; the thesis ("man") is parasitically dependent on the antithesis ("woman") that defines it. The vigilance with which the dominant term polices the no-man's-land between itself and the Other betrays the sneaking suspicion that the Other is in fact an externalization of something repressed, buried deep within the self—in this case, the feminine principle in every man that renders his masculinity less than absolute. "The warrior utopia of a mechanized body is . . . erected against the female self within," affirm Benjamin and Rabinbach.[128]

In Sarah Connor, whose physique and psyche strike a precarious balance between the "masculine" hardness of the T-800 and the "feminine" softness of the T-1000, that bulwark against "the female self within" is erected, oddly enough, *by* a female self. Her diatribe against men who give birth to bombs, her declaration of maternal love to John, her ministrations to the bullet-riddled T-800, and her ultimate function as the secular humanist Madonna whose only begotten son is humankind's savior are unconvincing; they seem designed to reassure conservative sensibilities that what looks butch on the outside is femme on the inside.

In one of *T2*'s ugliest moments, Sarah Connor—outfitted in SWAT garb and accessorized with some very mean hardware—barks, "Down on the floor, bitch!" to the African-American wife of Miles Dyson, the computer scientist destined to create SkyNet. Frightened, maternal women of color are clearly at the bottom of *T2*'s pyramid of power; at the top is the technophallic, hard-bodied T-800, the only "real man" in the movie. Nearly all of the human males, in comparison, are ineffectual wimps, "soft" in body or spirit: John's foster father, Todd, is a shiftless channel-surfer; the psychologist who interrogates Sarah Connor is an effete, third-rate Torquemada; the orderly who molests her in the mental ward is a potbellied pervert who is easily beaten to a pulp when Sarah jumps him; and the trembling, gibbering Dyson is a scared-stiff Poindexter.

"Watching John with the machine, it was suddenly so clear," muses Sarah Connor, in a voice-over. "The Terminator would never stop; it would never leave him and it would never hurt him, never shout at him or get drunk and hit him or say it was too busy to spend time with him. It would always be there and it would die to protect him. Of all the would-be fathers who came and went over the years, this machine, this thing, was the only one who measured up." The implacable, manhunting Terminator from the first film ("It absolutely will not stop, ever, until you are dead," warned Kyle Reese) is reconstituted, in a neat turnaround, as the perfect surrogate father, batteries included. In an era of dysfunctional families and "deadbeat dads," only a literal Iron John can get the job done.

In *T2*'s pantheon of manhood, Sarah Connor is second only to the Schwarzenegger Terminator when it comes to testosterone level. She is a pumped-up, lock-and-load, postfeminist heroine whose empowerment, in a patriarchal world, is attained not through political action but through technology—heavy-duty weaponry and paramilitary training in the movie, and weight-training machines and sessions with an Israeli commando in real life. An *Entertainment Weekly* cover story on the film includes a fawning sidebar on Hamilton; headlined "A NEW BODY OF WORK: LINDA HAMILTON GETS TOUGH IN 'TERMINATOR 2,'" it might have been titled "THE MORPHING OF LINDA HAMILTON." We are told, in fetishistic detail, of her "washboard stomach and marathoner's legs," her aerobic workouts, her frolics in costar Arnold Schwarzenegger's on-location gym. "She looks like a sweet young thing in her sundress," cautions the writer, "but don't be fooled. Linda Hamilton can bench-press 85 pounds as easily as she swings her Evian bottle. She can pump-load a 12-gauge shotgun with one arm and run eight miles before lighting up a Camel. . . . She has metamorphosed into a fierce, humorless commando. And she has transformed her softly feminine physique . . . into a hard-body even a five-time Mr. Universe can admire."[129]

All that flabby femininity has been flensed away like so much blubber, revealing a masculine, mechanical hard-body worthy of Sergeant Rock—a transformation given ironic spin by the fact that *T2*'s masculinist protagonist is a woman. As *Entertainment Weekly* makes clear, the actress's on- and offscreen personae have very nearly fused, in the public mind, into a hybrid entity in the same way that Schwarzenegger's hypertrophied physique has become synonymous with the *Übermenschmaschine*. Morphed into a Freikorps cyborg, Connor triumphs over the feminine aspect embodied in the T-1000 with the aid of the male principle manifest in the Schwarzenegger model.

Thus, Hollywood icons of hard-bodied technofeminism can be problematic in the same way that professional female bodybuilders are. While their body transgressions undeniably make hash of traditional notions of femininity as soft and organic, both break free of the feminine mystique by welding themselves, contrarily, into the machine-tooled hardbody of a masculine mystique that is no less restrictive.

An argument could be made for the recuperation of the hard-bodied, gun-happy Connor as a technofeminist heroine, Hollywood's answer to Haraway's call for a feminism that rejects "a demonology of technology," but the convenience of such an interpretation renders it suspect. After all, the movie industry's exploitation of the Freudian subtext in the image of a sweaty woman squirting hot lead from a throbbing rod could hardly be called empowering. The scene where Connor pumps a shotgun at the T-1000 is uncomfortably reminiscent of the video *Sexy Girls and Sexy Guns,* in which bikini-clad "Southern California beauties [fire] some of the sexiest machine guns ever produced," according to a mail-order catalogue.[130] Real-life testimonials by female shootists—"With a gun I have more . . . control over potential events around me, and more personal power," declares a female gun owner in Patrick Carr's *Gun People,* couching self-help bromides in language the NRA likes to hear—must be weighed against the incessant use, in film and TV, of the gun as a phallic substitute. Technofeminism remains at odds with technophallicism.

At the same time, as Claudia Springer points out, cinematic icons in the Sarah Connor mold convey multiple, often conflicting messages. Noting that Connor's transformation "into a taut, muscular killing machine" is in part a response to the psychological and sexual abuse she suffers at the hands of male doctors and jailers in the psycho ward, Springer argues that while "Sarah Connor fits into a long tradition of phallic women in films . . . she also provides an attractive figure in the realm of fantasy for angry women":

> As viewers of martial arts films know, it is enormously satisfying
> to experience vicariously the triumph of an underdog seeking
> revenge against the perpetrators of injustice. Women under
> patriarchy can experience the exhilarating fantasy of immense

physical strength and freedom from all constraints when watching figures like Sarah Connor. Revenge fantasies are powerful,
even when they are packaged for consumption by the Hollywood film industry.[131]

On a similar note, the cultural critic Tricia Rose observes,

The question is: Who is doing the constructing? The problem
with the *Terminator* series . . . is that male imagination is driving
the narrative, which is what makes a pistol-packin' mama like
Sarah Connor so problematic. But the larger question is, once
again, not, "How was Sarah Connor constructed by the filmmaker?" but "How do the feminist graduate students I know
(many of whom idolize these characters) use these women in
ways that rewrite the narrative and maybe rewrite their life
roles?" . . . These images are opening up possibilities, revising
what men and women think women ought to be, even if they
wind up endorsing patriarchal norms in other ways. Hollywood
has to reaffirm the status quo, of course, but trust me when I tell
you that just by opening those gates, they're creating a rupture
they may not be able to suture.[132]

Tetsuo: Fear and Loathing in the Robot Kingdom

In Shinya Tsukamoto's cult movie, *Tetsuo: The Iron Man* (1989), the cyborg is
reimagined yet again, this time in an electroconvulsive Tokyo jolted by
animated sequences that hurtle the viewer through the city at stomach-
lurching speed. Wires writhe like worms; technology sprouts in living flesh.
Obsessive, compulsive, often psychotically funny, *Tetsuo* takes place in a
technological landscape that has been annexed by the pathological male ego—
an ego that occupies "the space between phallic aggression and the fear of
sodomy," as the film critic Tony Rayns puts it.[133] This is the society of media
spectacle, fetishized consumption, and infantile sexuality limned by Ballard:

In the past we have always assumed that the external world
around us has represented reality, however confusing or uncer-

tain, and that the inner world of our minds, its dreams, hopes, ambitions, represented the realm of fantasy and the imagination. These roles . . . it seems to me, have been reversed.[134]

This transposition is a hallmark of what Scott Bukatman calls "techno-surrealism," in which the libido, like the voracious Blob of B-movie fame, moves "beyond the bounds of the individual psyche" to swallow up reality.[135] Noting the "fear of aggressive female sexuality," "willfully hyperbolic violence," and other dark valleys of the id that have been mapped onto *Tetsuo*'s overlit terrain, Bukatman argues that the movie is "a discourse both *of* and *about* the armored body in technoculture."[136] He maintains that cyborging, in *Tetsuo*, is part of a strategy "to reseat the human (male) in a position of virile power and control."[137]

But while *Tetsuo* undeniably situates the viewer inside an alienated male psyche whose traditional, "Iron Man" masculinity is rusting through, the movie's deepest anxieties have less to do with the plight of the male than the perilous state of the human in a world overrun—and, increasingly, run—by technology.

Furthermore, Bukatman's analysis attempts to neatly schematize a work that defies rationalization. Stock phrases like "over the top" shrivel to understatements when applied to *Tetsuo,* a movie so mondo it is a genre unto itself. Often compared to David Lynch's *Eraserhead* and Jack Smith's *Flaming Creatures,* it is steeped in the style and subject matter of *manga*—the ultraviolent, often scatological comic novels devoured by millions of Japanese. And the comic strip götterdämmerung at the end of the film recalls the clobberthons that inevitably ring down the curtain in kitsch classics such as *Godzilla vs. Megalon.* The film critic J. Hoberman called *Tetsuo* "an assemblage of textures—less a splatter than a solder flick."[138] Tsukamoto's own explanation, in a fractured but poetic translation, is illuminating: "My primary concern was to create one sensual imagery on the screen."[139] With only a few lines of dialogue and the barest skeleton of a plot, the hour-long, black-and-white movie is a descent into a maelstrom of body loathing, cyborg fantasies, mechano-eroticism, information anxiety, agoraphobia, castration complexes, and fear of phallic mothers. Biological metaphors for machinery fuse with mechanical metaphors for biology in animated sequences of swarming wires and pulsating metal excrescences.

The movie begins in what looks like an abandoned factory, where a young "metal fetishist" (played by Tsukamoto) acts out his cyborg fantasies in a decidedly low-tech manner, slicing open his thigh to insert a piece of electrical conduit. Despite *Tetsuo*'s nearly nonexistent budget, the movie's special effects—created by Tsukamoto, who not only directed but also wrote, cophotographed, and edited the film—are gut-wrenching: Blood spurts out of the gash with a hyperreal squelch, and we see the cable being shoved into the gory laceration in a not-for-the-squeamish close-up. Binding his leg, the metal fetishist shrieks at the sight of maggots crawling on the wound. Sick with terror, he runs blindly into the street, where he is bowled over in a hit-and-run accident involving a salaryman (the ulcerated, workaholic company man who is a fixture of Japanese society).

The following morning, while shaving, the salaryman (played by rock musician Tomoroh Taguchi) notices a wire growing out of his cheek. Unable to remove it, he tries to banish his anxiety with daydreams about making love to his girlfriend. In a trope that crosses the cartoon thought balloon with the Terminator's "Termovision," his thoughts appear on a TV screen, grainy with snow. En route to work, on a subway platform, he sits next to a prim, bespectacled young woman in sensible shoes. Both notice a steaming glob of technological excrement—wires, scrap metal, bubbling goo—on the ground nearby. Her curiosity aroused, the woman pokes it gingerly and is transformed, without warning, into a spastic, wild-eyed cyborg. She chases the salaryman into what appears to be the men's room, goaded on by the fiendish will of her hand, which has mutated into a tumorous mass of amorphous industrial rubbish. Hilariously, she pauses to preen before attacking him. Her amok seduction ends when the salaryman snaps her neck with a visceral crunch.

Later, the salaryman relives the attack in a mechano-erotic dream starring his girlfriend as the Monstrous Feminine incarnate: a swarthy succubus armed with a strap-on robo-dildo consisting of a long, floating cable terminating in a drill bit. She vamps her way across the room and, in a masterstroke of perverse hilarity, sodomizes the salaryman with her serpentine sex machine. Steam rises from his flanks and we're off, flying dizzily through the streets of Tokyo to slam headlong into a NO PARKING sign whose symbolism is obvious in a movie fraught with the fear of sodomy.

At this point, *Tetsuo* spins out of control, into a giddy wipeout. The salaryman's wire whisker blossoms into full-blown metalmorphosis: Smoldering circuitry erupts out of his cheek; pipes jut from his back; and his penis mutates into an enormous drill with which he literally screws his girlfriend to death in a scene out of Andrea Dworkin's nightmares. The last third of the movie is given over to a telekinetic struggle between the cyborged salaryman and the revenant metal fetishist, who is undergoing a similar transformation. The battle is equal parts *Poltergeist* and *Godzilla*: Objects are squashed flat by an invisible force and heavy metal ectoplasm oozes everywhere. The salaryman's girlfriend rises from the dead only to dissolve into bubbling gunk, out of which bursts the fetishist, bearing flowers, his lipsticked lips pursed to kiss the salaryman.

Armageddon ensues, in the course of which the fetishist is repeatedly penetrated by the salaryman's squealing drill. "His hatred having shaded into a kind of love, the fetishist explains that he needs to merge with the salaryman to overcome the rust that is attacking his frame," the director's notes reveal.[140] Says the fetishist, "Now that we are fully mutated, why don't we unite to mutate the world?" When the dust settles, the two combatants have indeed melded into a siege engine made of tangled pipes, twisted wires, and machine parts. As the towering structure rumbles into the distance, its contours finally resolve themselves into a recognizable shape: a monolithic Priapus.

Tetsuo offers poetic evidence that technological modernity provides no bulwark, as Ballard has argued, against "[v]oyeurism, self-disgust, the infantile basis of our dreams and longings" and other "diseases of the psyche."[141] In *Tetsuo*, the repressed returns with a vengeance: The Shinto belief that everything has an indwelling spirit, or *kami*, brings the inherent uncanniness in machines to life; libidinous urges wriggle free of the propriety that straitjackets Japanese society; and the Japanese woman–the squeaky, shuffling helpmate who smilingly attends to her husband's every need–mutates into a sexual carnivore with a bionic hand or a fiendish Theda Bara with a motorized strap-on. "In general audience TV cartoons as well as in the comics," notes the Japanologist William Bohnaker,

> the Japanese female is ever more openly portrayed as a gas-under-
> pressure, liable to explode terrifyingly under the incessant pin-

> pricks of her duties and dearths. A recurrent image . . . is of a
> demure, doting, tweeting mama suddenly transmogrifying into a
> screaming virago.[142]

Drawing inspiration from *Godzilla* as well as the recombinant Transformer and Gobot toy robots that took U.S. toy stores by storm in the eighties, Tsukamoto refracts the body/mind, human/machine dichotomies of cyberculture through Japan, whose repressive social psyche is frequently at odds with the individual ego—a conflict dramatized by the phenomenon of *ijime,* or "bullying," in which schoolchildren harass and sometimes murder classmates who do not conform to the social norm, literalizing the Japanese adage "BANG DOWN THE NAIL THAT STICKS OUT."

Tetsuo is racked by tensions between technophilia and technophobia, between Japan's self-image as the high-tech, user-friendly *robotto okoku,* or "robot kingdom," and an emerging public awareness of de-skilling, technostress, and robot-related workplace fatalities in Japan. "What I thought when I was making *Tetsuo,*" says Tsukamoto, "was that you can experience euphoria even if you're being raped by the machine. At the same time, there is always this urge to destroy technology, the industrial world. That conflict was going on inside me when I was making *Tetsuo*—the feeling that I enjoy being raped by the machine but at the same time I want to destroy the things that are invading me, the human being."

Biomechanical Tattoos: Totem and Taboo in Technoculture

> What will the archeologists of 3001 make of our preserved
> tattooed hides, decorated with biomechanical alien art? Will
> they think that we were part machine? Or maybe that we
> worshipped machines?
>   —*Unbylined editorial,* Tattoo Flash *magazine*[143]

"We are the primitives of a new sensibility," wrote an Italian futurist, in the early part of this century.[144] Now, a burgeoning underground of urban aboriginals has revived the archaic notion of the body as a blank slate. In tribal cultures, writes essayist David Levi Strauss, "body manipulations are often sacred and magical, and always *social*"; the body is transformed from its inarticulate, natural state into a communicating, social body through "the marks of civilization"—tattooing, piercing, branding, and scarifica-tion.[145] In *Moby-Dick*, the harpooner Queequeg—"a creature in the transi-tion state" between "savage" cannibal and civilized man—reverses the biblical trope in which the word becomes flesh: he is the flesh made word.[146] His tattoos are

> the work of a departed prophet and seer of his island, who, by those hieroglyphic marks, had written out on his body a complete theory of the heavens and the earth, and a mystical treatise on the art of attaining truth; so that Queequeg in his own proper person was a riddle to unfold; a wondrous work in one volume.[147]

Inspired by Charles Gatewood's photos and videos of the body bizarre, the *Modern Primitives* issue of *Re/Search* magazine, the Gauntlet (a chain of body piercing parlors), and the illustrated, perforated bodies of MTV staples such as Guns 'n' Roses, a groundswell of interest in do-it-yourself body modification has swept taboo practices out of *National Geographic* and into youth culture. Informed by S and M and biker chic, these practices have surfaced in the solid black "tribal" tattoos—chain-linked Celtic runes, flamelike Polynesian designs—and pierced noses, nipples, navels, and pudenda of "modern primitives."

Modern primitive is a catchall category that includes fans of hard-core techno and industrial dance music; bondage fetishists; performance artists; technopagans; and practitioners of suspension by flesh hooks and other forms of ritual mortification, or "body play," intended to produce altered states of consciousness. A polyvalent phenomenon, it is first and foremost an example of what sociologists have called "resistance through rituals." In their introduction to *Modern Primitives*, the editors V. Vale and Andrea Juno assert,

> Amidst an almost universal feeling of powerlessness to "change the world," individuals are changing what they *do* have power over: *their own bodies.*[148]

The San Francisco–based tattoo artist Greg Kulz echoes their sentiments, noting, "People want to *have control* over their [bodies]. Even if you can't control the external environment, you can start by controlling your internal environment. You can get a permanent mark or marks that no one else has a say in *at all*."[149]

Parallels can be found in the least likely places: Rosalind Coward interprets the upsurge of interest in New Age "body work"–Rolfing, the Alexander Technique, the Feldenkrais Method, and other holistic alternatives to conventional medical treatment–as "a place where people can express dissatisfaction with contemporary society *and* feel they are doing something personally to resist the encroachments of that society."[150]

Coward is rightly wary of this tendency, which she suggests substitutes self-help for political action, shifting responsibility out of the sociopolitical arena and onto the individual:

> [S]o strong is the sense of social criticism in this health movement that many adherents proclaim that they are the avant-garde of a quiet social revolution. Yet the journey to this social revolution is rarely a journey towards social rebellion but more often an inner journey, a journey of personal transformation.[151]

Meaningful change is effected through sympathetic magic, with the practitioner as the voodoo doll representing society–a tactic that bears out the social anthropologist Mary Douglas's thesis, quoted in *Modern Primitives*, "Each person treats his body as an image of society."[152] Following a trail blazed by Sade, Nietzsche, Artaud, and Bataille, the *Re/Search* editors exhort,

> By giving visible bodily expression to unknown desires and latent obsessions welling up from within, individuals can provoke change–however inexplicable–in the external world of the social. . . . It is necessary to uncover the mass of repressed desires lying within the unconscious so that a *New Eroticism* . . . founded on a *full knowledge* of evil and perversion, may arise to inspire radically improved social relations.[153]

The phrase "however inexplicable" fudges the all-important but tellingly absent link between personal transformation and social change. By what means the *Tetsuo*-like eruption of the id into the everyday will "inspire radically improved social relations" and how such changes will affect the lives of, say, the indigent elderly in South Central Los Angeles or unemployed high school dropouts in Long Island suburbs is left to the imagination. A synthesis of the surrealist faith in the radical results of the unconscious unbound and the Dionysian utopianism of sixties counterculture, the *Re/Search* editors' politics of modern primitivism founders on the shoals spotted by David Cronenberg in a discussion of his movie *Shivers* (aka *They Came from Within*) (1975), about a sexually transmitted parasite designed to reintegrate our estranged minds and bodies. Says Cronenberg,

> I had read Norman O. Brown's *Life against Death* . . . in which
> he . . . discuss[ed] the Freudian theory of polymorphous perver-
> sity. . . . Even old Norm had some trouble when he tried to
> figure out how that kind of Dionysian consciousness would
> function in a society where you had to cross the street and not
> get hit by a car.[154]

There can be no denying that feelings of political impotence undergird modern primitivism; taboo practices fortify the border between the self and the social at a time when the political and moral agendas of others are increasingly in conflict with the individual's right to control his or her own body. Moreover, laws and social conventions proscribing body transgressions are among Judeo-Christian culture's most deeply rooted taboos (Leviticus 19:28: "You shall not make any gashes in your flesh . . . or tattoo any marks upon you"), and the sociopolitical repercussions of outlaw body practices are a matter of record. In England, the Spanner trial–a controversial case involving consensual S and M between gay men–resulted in the passage of a law that preserves the legality of decorative body alteration but renders illegal the inflicting of "physical damage on each other, whether it's piercing, tattooing, flagellation, or whatever, for the purpose of sexual gratification," according to Lynn Procter, the deputy editor of *Body Art,* an English magazine devoted to piercing, tattooing, and "body decoration."

Nonetheless, the suggestion that social change and "radically improved social relations" can arise, *however inexplicably,* from mock autochthonous body art veers perilously close to Freud's "omnipotence of thoughts." Then again, what is modern primitivism if not the recrudescence, in computer culture, of the "primitive" worldview—"the old, animistic conception of the universe," with its "narcissistic overestimation of subjective mental processes"? Those with New Age leanings might well argue, as Julian Dibbell does when he asserts that the computer operates on "the pre-Enlightenment principle of the magic word," that Freud's "omnipotence of thoughts" has come back to haunt us in the seemingly supernatural agency of the information machine.

Whatever its effects on "the external world of the social," modern primitivism embodies a critique of the body and the self in cyberculture that merits serious consideration. The phenomenon is often positioned as the return of the repressed primitive—the pretechnological self imprisoned in what Max Weber called the "iron cage" of modern rationality. Fakir Musafar, *the* prototypical modern primitive, maintains that

> a whole part of life seems to be missing for people in modern cultures. . . . Whole groups of people, socially, are alienated. They cannot get closer or in touch with anything, including themselves. . . . People need physical ritual, tribalism.[155]

Likewise, Jonathan Shaw, the owner of New York's Fun City Studio and managing editor of *International Tattoo Art,* holds that "most people have grown up with television, in a world where they can only read about how human beings are supposed to relate to each other. Tattooing and piercing indicate a longing to try to find a way to *reject* this senseless input that we're bombarded with, to get back to certain basic emotions that are common to all of us because we're human." Such assertions proceed from the assumption that computer culture's near-total reduction of sensation to a ceaseless torrent of electronic images has produced a *terminal* numbness (in both the punning and literal senses)—what Ballard calls the "preempting of any free or original imaginative response to experience by the television screen."[156] Renouncing "the wholesale de-individualization of man" brought about by "an inundation of millions of mass-produced images" that supplant embodied experience with passive voyeurism, the *Re/Search* editors argue that

[t]oday, something as basic as sex itself is inextricably entwined with a flood of alien images and cues implanted from media programming and advertising. But one thing remains fairly certain: *pain* is a uniquely personal experience; it remains loaded with tangible shock value.[157]

Significantly, the modern primitive figures prominently in the rhetoric of Marshall McLuhan, who asserted throughout the sixties that the electronic interconnectedness of the "global village" restored "the primordial feeling, the tribal emotions from which a few centuries of literacy divorced us."[158] "Our teenage generation is already becoming part of a jungle clan," said McLuhan.[159] In his gnomic pronouncements about "the retribalizing process wrought by the electric media," he returned obsessively to techno-tribal metaphors, cryptically observing that "TV tattoos its message directly on our skins."[160] More lucidly, he declared that "the new electric technology is retrogressing Western man back from the open plateaus of literate values and into the heart of tribal darkness, into what Joseph Conrad termed 'the Africa within.' "[161]

Certainly, the assumption that computer culture has a heart of darkness underlies the now-obligatory appearance of modern primitives in cyberpunk narratives. The Lo Tek lumpen-tribe of Gibson's short story "Johnny Mnemonic" are "mad children" who roll the atavistic schoolboys of *Lord of the Flies* and *The Road Warrior*'s postapocalyptic aborigines into one. They roost in the rafters of a derelict mall, in a precarious aerie lashed together from amorphous junk, and their fashion "[runs] to scars and tattoos": a bare-chested Lo Tek girl displays breasts adorned with "indigo spirals."[162] The Zombie Analytics, one of the feral packs who prowl Richard Kadrey's novel *Metrophage*, leach the pigment out of their skin and tattoo their bodies with "subcutaneous pixels offering up flickering flesh-images of dead video and rock stars."[163] And in Walter Jon Williams's short story, "Video Star," a street style called Urban Surgery is in vogue:

> The nose had been broadened and flattened to cover most of the cheeks, turning the nostrils into a pair of lateral slits, the base of the nose wider than the mouth. . . . The effect was to flatten the face, turn it into a canvas for the tattoo artist who had covered

every inch of exposed flesh. Complex mathematical statements
ran over the forehead. Below the black plastic eye implants were
urban skyscapes, silhouettes of buildings providing a false horizon across the flattened nose. The chin appeared to be a circuit
diagram.[164]

Thus, the same modern primitivism that speaks to antimodern,
antitechnological elements in cyberculture lends itself equally to a wired
tribalism that reconciles *Mondo 2000*'s techno-yippie vision of the "kids at
the controls" of the "cybernet" with the *Road Warrior* fantasies that Scott
Bukatman believes mask "a deeper utopianism: the 'perverse hope that
someday conditions will indeed warrant a similar return to the body' as
technology collapses into ruins."[165]

These and other philosophical crosscurrents swirl around the style
of tattooing known as "biomechanical"—an adjective borrowed from the
Swiss surrealist painter H. R. Giger, whose imagery inspired the genre.
Giger is a meticulous limner of cybernetic nightmares best known for his
Hollywood monster-making (the *Alien* movies) and sumptuous books
(*Giger's Alien, H. R. Giger's Necronomicon*, and *H. R. Giger's Biomechanics*). His
embrace of airbrush, a medium sullied by its associations with commercial
illustration, and his fulsome subject matter—a wall of buttocks sodomized
by penises and mortared with feces, a quadriplegic infant covered with
boils, "erotomechanic" renderings of human orifices penetrated by heavy
metal phalli—have ensured him entrée to the art world by the servants'
entrance only.

But good taste, as Edith Sitwell once observed, is the worst vice ever
invented. Giger's sublegitimate status in the art world is counterbalanced by
his pervasive influence in cyberculture: At least one PC game, Cyber-
dreams's Darkseed, is based on Giger's artwork, and cyberpunk bands such
as Cyberaktif and Front Line Assembly routinely cite him as an inspiration.
The highest tribute is paid by modern primitives who emblazon themselves
with Giger's slavering, mace-tailed Alien—a cyberpunk rite of passage duly
noted by Gibson in his novel *Virtual Light*, which includes an exchange in a
near-future tattoo parlor:
    "Lowell . . . he's got a Giger."
    " 'Giger'? "

"This painter. Like nineteenth-century or something. Real classical. Bio-mech."[166]

It is the ease with which Giger's images adhere to the overlapping, sometimes clashing meanings of technoculture that accounts for the artist's popularity among cyberpunks. His coprophilia materializes what Arthur Kroker calls "excremental culture," the locked loop of production-consumption-excretion-recycling that characterizes an information economy, while his Freudian fear of penetration is congruent with the crisis of masculinity and the AIDS pandemic. Despite the optimistic glosses of critics like Fritz Billeter, who sees in Giger's work the promise of "a potential human existence in which nature and technology form a unity, unknown until now," it is more convincingly theorized as a sump where the repressed phobias of cyberculture bubble up.[167] Certainly, Giger's biomechanical cosmology, where spaceship hatches resemble vaginal openings and phallic aliens bristle with exhaust pipes and electrical conduit, dramatizes the obsolescence of mechanist and vitalist worldviews in an age of soft machines and hard bodies. But it speaks, more immediately, to the increasingly irrelevant body's anxiety over the invading technologies that threaten, like *Alien*'s "Chestbursters" and "Facehuggers," to tear it apart from within and without.

Of course, no reading is definitive, and modern primitives have invested Giger's imagery with personal meanings. Biomechanical tattoos come in several varieties: images lifted directly from Giger's coffee-table art books, most commonly the Alien monster; intricate, geometric abstractions fashioned from intertwined cords or the dizzy tracery of wiring diagrams; and "rippers," "peelaways," or "bust-outs"—trompe l'oeil renderings of the skin slashed open or Swiss-cheesed to expose cyborg circuitry or mechanical innards (cogwheels, crankshafts, and the like). Not infrequently, tribal and biomechanical styles are combined: transistors, microchips, and other technological odds and ends are integrated into Tinkertoy jumbles of bones or used to fill in bold, simple figures borrowed from the tattoo traditions of Borneo or Polynesia.

Jonathan Shaw surmises that the biomechanical genre "probably started becoming a part of the basic iconography around the time of *Alien* (1979), when Giger's work started coming into play pretty heavily." Pat Sinatra, the proprietor of the Woodstock-based "ritual tattooing and piercing" emporium Pat's Tats, dates the inception of the style to the release of *The Road Warrior* in 1981. "[The well-known tattooist] Shotsie Gorman did a takeoff on the movie, a back piece of a space-age motorcyclist who had melded with his motorcycle," she recalls. The tattooist Marcus Pacheco, who owns San Francisco's Primal Urge studios, attributes much of the style's popularity to Guy Aitchison, a Chicago artist whose neon-bright images of chrome-plated machines, their surfaces dancing with photorealistic reflections, have earned him celebrity status in tattoo culture.

Aitchison, for his part, cites Giger and Kulz as the catalysts for his use of the biomechanical vernacular. "Giger's work grabbed me, and then I saw a full-body photo of Greg Kulz, which really affected me," he says. "He was the first person [to get a biomechanical tattoo], to my knowledge. I started working in that style almost as soon as I saw the photo of Greg, just playing off the idea behind it–the repeated patterns, the hoses, that sort of thing."

Eddie Deutsche, who works at San Francisco's Tattoo City, credits Kulz with pioneering the genre in the early to mid-eighties. "Greg started doing biomechanical stuff in a cartoony style, using solid black-and-white graphics," says Deutsche. "His forte was putting biomechanical imagery inside rippers. The next step after the ripped skin was the Borneo-style tribal shapes that I did, filled in not with solid black but with biomechanical imagery. You get the overall shape of a tribal tattoo, the curves and spikes and all that, and then when you get close up, it's got all the little biomechanical textures–the transistors-and-wires thing or the bony motifs from Giger's *Necronomicon* books."

Kulz, who tattoos at Erno's in San Francisco, is every inch the modern primitive, with his close-cropped hair and traffic-stopping techno-tribal tattoos: His backbone is overlaid with stylized black shapes somewhere between vertebrae and machine parts; an X-ray rendering of a pistol lies flat on his belly, its muzzle disappearing into his jeans; distilling tubes and pipettes jostle for arm space alongside a cogwheel and a circuit board.

"As a kid, I really loved *The Six Million Dollar Man*," he says, recalling the early seventies TV series about a severely injured astronaut who leaves the operating table a "Bionic Man"–a cyborg able to see through walls with his X-ray eye, run at eye-blurring speed on his prosthetic legs, and lift trucks with his artificial arm. "There was one episode where he tore his arm open and there were circuit boards in there; that really lit a fire under me," remembers Kulz. "Then I got Giger's *Necronomicon 1,* which had pictures of a woman in a body suit that Giger had painted on her. That was so inspiring!

"Around 'eighty-three, before anyone I knew had a biomechanical tattoo, I got tattooed by [the tattoo legend] Ed Hardy, who did a section on my arm. It's not really *of* anything, just tailpipes and circuit boards and distilling tubes and components picked out of *Necronomicon 1.* I wanted my arm to look all machine; I didn't want any hint of meat. Ed had previously done a Giger tattoo on Jonathan Shaw, but at the time I had no idea that anyone had ever gotten one.

"For years, I really pushed the biomechanical style. A big inspiration was industrial music–Throbbing Gristle, SPK–and the performance artists who shared that aesthetic, such as Mark Pauline, Chico MacMurtrie, and Barry Schwartz. I tried to take the same aesthetic and bring it into tattooing."

Kulz's tattoos are less illustrations than animated cartoons; he exploits his knowledge of human anatomy to create images that conform to the body's topography, coming to life when a muscle is flexed or a limb is rotated. According to Marcus Pacheco, biomechanical tattoos are becoming increasingly dynamic. "These days, a lot of the biomechanical work incorporates muscle and bone structure to create the illusion of the body being made out of mechanical components as well as organic materials that look metallic or rubberized," he says. "The biomechanical effect involves making body parts look metallic so that they look like 'organic equipment,' neither mechanical nor biological, but both."

Biomechanical tattoos speak volumes about the human condition in cyberculture. Putting an off-center spin on the tattoo's function as a marker of "outsider" status, they signal the alienation of the body they embellish: in cyberculture's maze of dualisms, the meat is the mind's Other. Moreover, they inflect one of the essential meanings of a tattoo–"to express what is happening on the inside," according to Pat Sinatra–with strange, new resonances; someone who represents his inner self as a riot of wires, light-emitting diodes, and BX cable glimpsed through a trompe l'oeil gash in his flesh possesses a self-image unique to the late twentieth century. Like the metal fetishist in *Tetsuo,* he may be acting out cyborg fantasies; contrarily, he may be saying, "Look what your computerized, commodified society has made of me–a clockwork orange, for all appearances organic but essentially

mechanical." Alternately, biomechanicals may function as a sort of homeo-
pathic medicine, symbolically inoculating the body against invading technologies. Or they may simply attest to the fact that the mysterious inner
workings of information machines have attained totemic status in cybernetic subcultures. In tangled cables whose involutions conjure Celtic "knot-
work" or Borneo-style abstractions filigreed with microcircuitry, we see the
artifacts of a technological society endowed with magical associations.

To Shaw, the biomechanical style must be understood within the
context of modern primitivism, which harks back to an essential humanism
anchored in the physical body. "Primitive cultures evolved along certain
lines for very strong reasons," he says, "and with the advent of technology a
lot of these tribal cultural patterns have been swept away. I don't think
mankind is ready, spiritually or mentally, for the transformations it's undergoing in the technological era; tattooing is a mute plea for a return to
human values." Biomechanicals, he suggests, give vent to deep-seated
anxieties over the body's uncertain future. "The world is becoming mechanically oriented and the human race is mutating," he observes. "I think
biomechanicals appeal to the collective unconscious."

Conversely, the very "biomechanoid" mutations (to use Giger's
term) that unsettle Shaw are the stuff of Cliff Cadaver's postevolutionary
whimsies. In his *Outlaw Biker Tattoo Revue* article, "How to Make a Monster:
Modifications for the Millennium," the Hollywood-based piercer pays lip
service to "modern occultists" who "reflect their inner spiritual growth . . .
through a continually evolving physical body" and excoriates technological
modernity ("our standardized society," "the made-for-TV existence") even
as he abandons himself to cyberpunk fantasies about designer hair transplants that create a "marathon mohawk that extends from pate to tailbone";
dental implants in the form of "custom fangs of steel, gold or porcelain";
and "multiple piercings . . . around the circumference of the head . . . to
[create] a metal crown of thorns fit for the most outspoken heretic."[168]
Amusingly, Cadaver's posthuman being shares DNA with Haraway's "promising and dangerous monsters" as well as the Hell's Angels: He is a utopian
aberration, a self-made "monster God" who "disregard[s] all pseudo-
restrictions of race, gender, sexuality, religion, or morality to focus upon [his
or her] individual essence" and whose sign-off, after such high-toned
ruminations, is the biker expletive "FTW" ("FUCK THE WORLD").[169]

For the present, Cadaver's postmodern monster is pure metaphor, stippled on skin or trapped between the covers of cyberpunk novels; in some archaic future, however, such fictions may become palpable. " 'For, you see,' said the Illustrated Man, 'These Illustrations predict the future.' "'1[170]

Joseph M. Rosen, M.D.: Of Human Wings and Wireheads

"We believe in the possibility of an incalculable number of human transformations, and without a smile we declare that wings are asleep in the flesh of man."

–F. T. Marinetti[171]

Joseph M. Rosen may have a hand in that future. A reconstructive plastic surgeon at Dartmouth-Hitchcock Medical Center and a professor at Dartmouth College's Thayer School of Engineering, Rosen is glowingly described in the video documentary *Cyberpunk* as a "cyberpunk hero" whose work with the disabled and far-flung speculations have captured the imaginations of those on cyberculture's fringes.[172]

Although he would wince at such a label, Rosen makes no secret of his research interests: bionics, human-machine interfaces, artificial nerve grafts, the simulation of operations in virtual environments, and the transplantation of limbs through immunosuppression. He is an acquaintance of Mark Pauline's (he performed surgical "revisions" on the artist's reconstructed hand); keeps abreast of advances in robotics (Anita Flynn from MIT's Artificial Intelligence Lab has spoken as a guest lecturer in one of his classes); and tracks developments in virtual reality (as a research associate at NASA's Ames Research Center in Mountain View, California, from 1987 to 1989, he worked on surgical simulation with Scott Fisher). He teaches a course called "Artificial People–From Clay to Computers" and the titles of the presentations he delivers at technical seminars sound like one-sentence summaries of cyberpunk novels: "Nerve Chip–The Bionic Switchboard," "The Development of a Man-Machine Interface for Control of a Bioprosthesis."

An avid Gibson reader, Rosen is familiar with the surgically modified modern primitives who play walk-on parts in Gibson's narratives: Dog, the Lo Tek gang member whose scarred features are "a mask of total bestiality," his speech garbled by a "thick length of grayish tongue" and canine "tooth-bud transplants" courtesy of a Doberman pinscher; the Panther Modern gang member in *Neuromancer* whose face is "a simple graft grown on collagen and shark-cartilage polysaccharides, smooth and hideous."[173]

"There was nothing in *Neuromancer* that with enough funding and enough people I couldn't do in one of my laboratories," insists Rosen, adding the all-important caveat, "*if* people weren't very critical and they just gave me the money and said, 'Do it, don't worry about whether it's far-fetched or not.' We're growing skin on collagen right now, so these things are in *Scientific American* articles and we're going to overrun *Neuromancer* soon."

He sees himself as a strange attractor, a transition point between embedded and evolving modes of thought. "I'm trying to get people to shift their paradigms," he affirms. "That's the role I see myself playing." He foresees a shift in emphasis, in reconstructive surgery and bionics, from the restoration of normal function or appearance to posthuman enhancement. "Presently, when we reconstruct somebody, we're repairing some injury," says Rosen. "In plastic surgery, the surgical field I'm in, we . . . repair defects of nature or acquired defects. In cosmetic or aesthetic surgery, we change the way [a normal patient] looks. To go the next step and implant . . . devices in normal people so that they can improve their skills is something we [wouldn't] do right now, but I wouldn't rule out something like that for the future."[174]

He talks, with unnerving matter-of-factness, about the possibility of reconstructing human legs into limbs capable of kangaroo leaps by "taking a certain muscle and forming it into a band, almost like a rubber band"; augmenting human arms with robotic parts whose sensors and superhuman speed would obviate workplace accidents; and, borrowing an idea from the plastic surgeon Burt Brent, fitting mortals for angel wings—or, more accurately, flying squirrel membranes.[175]

In "Thoracobrachial Pterygoplasty Powered by Muscle Transposition Flaps," a somewhat tongue-in-cheek essay on the surgical construction of human wings, Brent takes his fellow plastic surgeons on a flight of fancy in the hope of provoking them to "extend [their] creativity."[176] His imagination sparked by Leonardo da Vinci's speculations on human-powered flight,

Brent brings "contemporary tissue transfer and plastic surgery principles" to bear on the problem.[177] Flaps of skin shifted from the chest, expanded with saline-injected implants, and stiffened with transplanted ribs could be used to create a patagium (the thin membrane stretched between the fore and hind limbs of bats and flying squirrels). The powerful pectoral muscles of birds could be emulated by transposing the latissimus muscles and anchoring them to a "keel-like" extension of the sternum fashioned from bone grafts, similar to the jutting breastbone of a bird.

Rosen notes that a winged human wouldn't actually be able to fly "because he wouldn't match the rules in terms of the amount of weight compared to the amount of wing surface, although if you brought in hybrid materials, you could potentially build wings that would allow [a patient] to glide, like a flying squirrel."[178]

But it is the Gibsonian implications of Rosen's theoretical musings on implantable computer chips that have earned the surgeon an unlikely following among would-be cyborgs, or "wireheads."[179] His technical speculations about interfacing peripheral nerve axons and integrated circuits hold forth the possibility of linking individual nervous systems to "mankind's extended electric nervous system"–a dream that is alive and well in the elusive subculture of "neurohackers," or "do-it-yourself brain tinkerers," uncovered by Branwyn.[180] In his *Wired* feature, "The Desire to Be Wired," Branwyn quotes a correspondent on a BBS:

> I am interested in becoming a guinea pig, if you will, for any cyberpunkish experiment from a true medicine/military/ cyber/neuro place. New limbs, sight/hearing improvements, bio-monitors, etc. Or even things as simple as under-the-skin timepieces.[181]

Cyberpunk fantasies such as these were catalyzed by Gibson's tantalizingly vague references to the "dermatrodes," or " 'trodes," with which Case jacks into cyberspace; evocations of simstim, a one-way brain link to another, wired body that enables a passive "rider" to share another human's sensorium as a "passenger behind [the] eyes"; and mentions of carbon sockets nestled behind ears, receptacles for silicon shards called "microsofts" that enable the user to instantly boot up any information stored on a chip.[182]

So ubiquitous is the cranial jack in cyberpunk fiction that it has become semiotic shorthand for the genre in the same way that Franken-stein's neck bolts came to symbolize gothic SF. "Boreholes to the limbic system! Manipulation of the parietal lobes! Taproots to the visual and auditory cortices! *Coming soon to a brain near you*," gibes the *Nation*'s John Leonard, in his auto-da-fé of cyberpunk novels and cybercul-tural criticism.[183]

But bionic dreams die hard. Cyberpunk enthusiasm for the ulti-mate interface between mind and machine–the brain socket–remains un-diminished, sustained by pop science articles on neural prosthetics such as the *Omni* story that describes an experimental visual implant in which tiny electrodes were inserted into the visual cortex in a volunteer's brain; wires ran from the electrodes, through the patient's scalp, and into a computer. Signals sent from the computer stimulated the visual cortex, enabling the totally blind volunteer to perceive patterns of light made up of phosphenes, the "stars" produced by a blow to the head or by rubbing the eyes. "By the end of the decade," writes David P. Snyder in *Omni*, "the research team hopes to have constructed a device utilizing a [miniature] television camera that would interface with 250 or more implanted electrodes and a signal-processing computer to stimulate the occipital lobe."[184] The world of a blind person equipped with such a device would be rendered in pointillistic pinpricks of light, "something like a stadium scoreboard."[185] William H. Dobelle, a researcher whose pioneering experiments in this area were conducted at the University of Utah, envisions a miniature television camera housed in an artificial eye fitted into the user's eye socket and attached to his or her eye muscles; a pair of glasses concealing a battery-powered microprocessor would translate the televisual images into phos-phenes and transmit them to the electrodes implanted in the visual cortex.

A 1975 prototype of such a system actually incorporated the fabled cranial jack. The connecting wires of a subject's electrode array

> ran out of a hole at his skull base, then under his scalp to a round, dime-sized graphite socket above his right ear. A com-puter wired to a television camera was plugged into the socket. When the camera was aimed at a pattern, [the subject] saw phosphenes that reproduced that pattern: a white line on a dark

background, geometric figures, even individual letters and simple sentences written in a special visual Braille alphabet.[186]

Looking beyond the disabled, F. Terry Hambrecht, the head of the
Neural Prosthesis Program at the National Institute of Neurological Disorders and Stroke, speculates that prosthetics may one day be used to "make
normal people supernormal: the true bionic man or woman."[187] In the
future, says Hambrecht,

> we might be able to detect signals from the motor area of the
> cerebral cortex, then bypass muscles and communicate directly
> with machines. We might be able to use the output from the
> motor area to control machines without having to wait for the
> slow muscles of the body to respond.[188]

Snyder spins out an SF scenario in which "supernormals" enhanced
with neural prosthetics "operate computers, typewriters, or turn on a
television set just by using their brains—through recording electrodes and
telemetry, a special radio transmitter that sends signals picked up from the
motor cortex to the machine."[189]

Meanwhile, in science fact, Eric Sutter has produced a working
prototype of just such a device, controlled not by motor signals but by brain
waves generated in the visual cortex. Sutter, a senior scientist at the Smith-
Kettlewell Eye Research Institute in San Francisco, is the inventor of the
Brain Response Interface (BRI), a system used, until his death, by Dr. Lance
Meagher, an Oregon physician who suffered from near-total paralysis
caused by amyotrophic lateral sclerosis (Lou Gehrig's disease).

Electrodes implanted under Meagher's skull, near his visual cortex,
picked up the neural activity generated when Meagher gazed at a flickering
object—in this case, one of the sixty-four squares on a gridded computer
screen, each of which contained a letter, word, number, or command. Each
square flashed with its own characteristic signature, and when Meagher
focused on a specific square, his brain translated its pulses into faint
electrical signals. Relayed to the computer by a tiny, short-range transmitter
taped to Meagher's neck, the signals were compared to a library of earlier
readings for that screen. When a match between the distinctive flicker of

the square Meagher was looking at and one of the sixty-four recorded rhythms was found, the operation indicated by that square was executed. The system has multiple grids, yielding up to 2,048 user-programmable commands—"enough for activating a speech synthesizer, or for operating 'environmental controls,' such as the TV, stereo, or motors that open and close windows," according to the *Omni* writer Darrell E. Ward.[190]

Sutter has staked his claim to scientific innovation in crowded territory. Monitoring brain waves with pattern-matching neural networks, Akira Hiraiwa and his fellow researchers at the Nippon Telegraph and Telephone Corporation have been able to determine, with a fair rate of success, which way a person intends to move a joystick. Dr. Jonathan R. Wolpaw and his associates at the New York State Department of Health's Wadsworth Center in Albany have designed a system that uses mu waves— rhythmic signals emitted by the brain's sensorimotor center when it is inactive—to permit trained users to move a cursor around a computer screen with their minds. And Emanuel Donchin, a professor of psychology at the University of Illinois, has developed a brain-controlled typewriter that enables users to type, at the less than breathtaking speed of 2.3 characters per minute, by spelling out words in their minds. "Such knowledge could help develop the thought-driven machines of the future," concludes the *New York Times* writer Andrew Pollack.[191]

Branwyn's neurohackers can't wait. Impatient with the measured tread of technological progress, they are attempting to transfer EEG patterns from one brain to another; zapping the pleasure centers of their brains with electrodes; and, according to disturbing rumors, "actually poking holes in their heads and directly stimulating their brains."[192]

Meanwhile, science advances more prudently. Citing an article in *IEEE Transactions on Biomedical Engineering,* Branwyn reports a Stanford University experiment in which "microelectrode array[s] capable of recording from and stimulating peripheral nerves" remained functional in laboratory rats up to a year after implantation.[193] Notes Branwyn,

> Although this research is very preliminary and there are still
> many intimidating technical and biological hurdles (on-board
> signal processing, radio transmittability, learning how to trans-
> late neuronal communications), the long-term future of this

technology is exciting. Within several decades, "active" versions of these chips could provide a direct neural interface with prosthetic limbs, and by extension, a direct human-computer interface.[194]

Rosen and his collaborators have investigated the use of computer chips in neuromuscular interfaces. In "Microsurgery: The Future," he and coauthor R. A. Chase claim that

> [t]he possibility of interfacing elements of the peripheral nervous system with a silicon chip has become a reality. Rosen and Grosser (1987) have shown that a properly designed and fabri-cated implantable microchip can both record and stimulate elements within a peripheral nerve. . . . The prospect of using implantable electronic devices, such as intraneuronal silicon chips, sets the stage for direct nerve to prosthesis linkages. Such linkages may be bidirectional, sending signals peripherally to generate electronically controlled motion, or receiving signals from electronic sensors imbedded in the prosthesis.[195]

Like most researchers, Rosen is wary of the media, which raise false hopes even as they arouse interest in his work–interest that, when it reaches critical mass, can garner all-important funding. "Intraneuronal chips are futuristic and fun to write about and very important as the ultimate interface between man and machine," he says, "but as a clinician with federal grants the media gets me in trouble with patients who don't really understand what we're doing. I get letters from people wanting to know if I can make their grandfathers walk, that type of thing. In our lab, we're working on silicon chips that could be implanted in the peripheral nerves and allow us to make a communication channel between your nerve and . . . a robotic arm, but even those devices are ten or twenty years in the future."

In the final analysis, however, Rosen agrees that "the big applica-tions" for devices such as nerve chips lie not in bionic medicine but in communications technologies. "The concept of putting devices in people so that they can communicate with the entire network is what cyberculture is all about," Rosen maintains. "The nerve chip is the ultimate virtual reality interface; rather than putting on a helmet, as in the systems that Scott Fisher or Jaron Lanier have been involved with, what you're basically doing is splicing into the nervous system directly.

"Is society ready for these kinds of things? I don't know. I'm doing the technology; I'm not trained in making moral judgments. Building hybrid people who are part human, part machine is more an ethical dilemma than a technical problem. The issue is: Do we go beyond the human? We're confronted with the fact that humans have already been designed. So the issue becomes: Do we redesign ourselves? We're in a transition phase where it's hard to know the answer."

The Perils of Posthumanism

In another thousand years we'll be machines, or Gods.
—*Bruce Sterling*[196]

Man has, as it were, become a kind of prosthetic God. When he puts on all his auxiliary organs he is truly magnificent; but those organs have not grown on to him and they still give him much trouble at times.
—*Sigmund Freud*[197]

I don't see much point in . . . transcending the body. . . . That brings its own level of debilitating trouble. I think that if you *could* become a cyborg for reasons of intellectual ecstasy, one day you'd discover that [you had] passed out in the street and there [were] roaches living in your artificial arm.
—*Bruce Sterling*[198]

Thomas Hine is not alone in his conviction that the "further evolution of humanity is one of the most profound issues of the future"; speculations about the fate of the body and debates over the promises and threats of posthumanism resound throughout cyberculture.[199]

The art critic Jeffrey Deitch has suggested that human evolution "may be entering a new phase that Charles Darwin never would have envisioned."[200] In *Post Human,* the catalogue to an exhibition of works by artists whose subject is the self and the body, he writes,

> Social and scientific trends are converging to shape a new
> conception of the self, a new construction of what it means to be
> a human being. The matter-of-fact acceptance of one's "natural"
> looks and one's "natural" personality is being replaced by a
> growing sense that it is normal to reinvent oneself.[201]

As I argued at length in chapter 1, New Age and cyberdelic subcultures have also taken up the posthuman theme. In *The Future of the Body: Explorations into the Further Evolution of Human Nature,* Michael Murphy argues that "metanormal abilities" can be cultivated through a host of "transformative practices"—yogic, shamanic, athletic, somatic, therapeutic, and so forth. Murphy, the cofounder of the Esalen Institute, a human potential ashram in Big Sur, California, maintains that these disciplines, if widely practiced, could provide a springboard for a quantum leap in human evolution characterized by telepathy, telekinesis, clairvoyance, and "alterations in bodily structures, states, and processes."[202] Likewise, in *Mega Brain Power: Transform Your Life with Mind Machines and Brain Nutrients,* Michael Hutchison notes that "evolution may involve developing new mental powers" through mind machines, smart drugs, and other "mind technologies."[203]

Scientists engage in their own, no less poetic speculations about posthuman possibilities. The computer scientist Daniel Hillis imagines that "the process of machine evolution will lead to things we can't imagine right now. I think I'm not going to get to be immortal, but maybe my children will. They may be made out of different stuff than I am."[204] The nanotechnologist K. Eric Drexler theorizes that the same microscopic machines he believes will make cell repair (and hence, near immortality) possible "will allow people to change their bodies in ways that range from the trivial to the amazing to the bizarre. . . . Some people may shed human form as a caterpillar transforms itself to take to the air; others may bring plain humanity to a new perfection."[205] And the computer scientist Gerald Jay Sussman believes that the day will soon come when human consciousness can be digitized and saved to disk. "It isn't very long from now," he told the science writer Grant Fjermedal in *The Tomorrow Makers: A Brave New World of*

Living-Brain Machines. "I'm afraid, unfortunately, that I'm [part of] the last generation to die."[206]

What is now scientific conjecture was once science fiction. The perversely brilliant sci-fi body horror of David Cronenberg constitutes an extended meditation on the mind/body split in the information age, where, as Scott Bukatman points out, "the apparent mind/body dichotomy is superseded by the *tri*chotomy of mind/body/machine."[207] The filmmaker, who has wondered if "we are just beginning a very important phase of our evolution," a sort of unnatural selection catalyzed by technology, is "always talking about McLuhan," according to Martin Scorsese.[208] In a sense, Cronenberg is McLuhan's dark twin, theorizing electronic media and mechanical devices less as "extensions of man" than as agents of a morphogenesis that is not always pretty to look at.

Videodrome (1982), the filmmaker's masterpiece, enacts Visual Mark's dictum, "FIRST YOU SEE VIDEO. THEN YOU WEAR VIDEO. THEN YOU EAT VIDEO. THEN YOU *BE* VIDEO."[209] Or, as the "media prophet" Professor Brian O'Blivion tells the movie's protagonist, Max Renn, "Your reality is already half video hallucination; if you're not careful, it will become total hallucination. You'll have to learn to live in a very strange new world."

Convinced that "public life on television was more real than private life in the flesh," O'Blivion designed a mutagenic TV signal. Covertly transmitted in a sadomasochistic snuff program called *Videodrome*, the signal stimulates the production of a TV tumor in the viewer, "a new outgrowth of the human brain which will produce and control hallucination to the point that it will change human reality" (O'Blivion). As O'Blivion observes, "After all, there is nothing real outside our perception of reality, is there?" In the electronically mediated world of *Videodrome*, thoughts *are* omnipotent; the conviction of Freud's primitives—that they could "alter the external world by mere thinking"—is unexpectedly borne out in a cybernetic culture where kinetic, tactile experience has been superseded, for the most part, by the sedentary consumption of images on screens. "The television screen is the retina of the mind's eye," declares O'Blivion. "Therefore, the television screen is part of the physical structure of the brain. Therefore, whatever appears on the television screen emerges as raw experience for those who watch it. Therefore, television is reality and reality is less than television."

The professor believes that the brain tumors induced by the *Video-drome* signal will trigger the next stage in the coevolution of humanity and technology (coevolution being an interactive process of evolutionary change in which changes in species A initiate changes in species B, which in turn create the necessary conditions for the natural selection of changes in species A, and so on). But O'Blivion has been murdered by the shadowy defense contractor Spectacular Optical, which plans to use *Videodrome* to control the minds of the shock-proof, sensation-hungry masses.

Meanwhile, Renn–the jaded owner of a porn channel who is attempting to track down the source of the mysterious signal–has been mutated by *Videodrome* and is suffering from bizarre, mechano-erotic hallucinations: A vaginal slit gapes in his belly, moistly awaiting the insertion of a videocassette; his hand morphs into a gun made of molten, marbled flesh; his TV heaves and moans in concupiscent ecstasy, its screen bulging toward his waiting lips. Surrendering to the postmodern madness of a world in which distinctions between this and that side of the TV screen–between the real and the hyperreal–are no longer meaningful, Renn kills the conspirators and holes up in a deserted barge.

Empty and decaying, the rusting hulk is a fitting metaphor for the body in cyberculture, an unworthy vessel abandoned by its owner. The radio personality and S and M freak Nicki Brand, who was Renn's lover before she disappeared into the parallel dimension of *Videodrome,* appears on the TV that sits incongruously in the moldering boat. The time for his transmigration has arrived, she tells Renn. "Your body has already done a lot of changing but that's only the beginning," she says. "You have to go all the way, now: Total transformation." Paraphrasing the New Testament ("You must be born again," John 3:7), she admonishes, "To become the new flesh, you first have to kill the old flesh. Don't be afraid to let your body die." As ominous, ascending chords build to a crescendo, Renn lifts his hand–once again metamorphosed into an organic gun–to his head; with the rallying cry, "Long live the new flesh!" he pulls the trigger. In a traumatic, low-tech version of Visual Mark's assumption into cyberspace, Max Renn will be born again as a pure simulacrum–what O'Blivion's daughter calls "the video word made flesh."

In its ontological nausea, *Videodrome* recalls "The Precession of Simulacra," the essay in which the philosopher Jean Baudrillard argues that reality has disappeared into a "hyperreality" of mechanical reproductions and digital representations that "bears no relation to any reality whatever: it is its own pure simulacrum."[210] We are reminded, too, of Ballard's pronouncement that "we live in a world ruled by fictions of every kind"—digitally altered photos, surgically reconstructed celebrities, computer simulations, staged photo ops, sampling-and-lip-synching pop stars, synthetic food substitutes—whose surreality makes it seem as if the subconscious has seeped into daylit reality, as if the waking world has been arrogated by the twilight zone.

Simultaneously, we cannot help but think of Ballard's chilling observation that the "demise of feeling and emotion" in such a world, "has paved the way for all our most real and tender pleasures—in the excitements of pain and mutilation; in sex as the perfect arena . . . for all the veronicas of our own perversions."[211] The deadpan, affectless Nicki Brand, true to her name, derives sadomasochistic pleasure from searing her bare flesh with a cigarette. "We live in overstimulated times," she asserts; like *Crash*'s narrator, who confides that his accident was "the only real experience [he] had been through for years" ("For the first time I was in physical confrontation with my own body"), she has been deadened by the nonstop shock treatment of postmodern culture, distanced by the multiplying layers of electronic mediation between herself and embodied experience.[212] Only extreme pain can bring her back to her physical body; cell by cell, she is being replaced by the new flesh, the video flesh—as are we all, in cyberculture.

Whereas technology transforms Cronenberg's characters into dehumanized automata or, worse yet, inhuman mutants, Bruce Sterling's characters employ it to engineer their own, posthuman evolution. In his short story collection *Crystal Express* and his novel *Schismatrix*, Sterling charted a "posthuman solar system" in which Shapers (genetic engineers who have "seized control of their own genetics") and Mechanists (cyborgers who have "replaced flesh with advanced prosthetics") struggle over the future of the human form.[213] The "sharp perceptions of Shapers, with their arsenals of brain-stretching biochemicals," are pitted against "the cybernetic advances of the Mechanists and the relentless logic of their artificial intelligences."[214] Assuming Stelarc's premise that "[o]nce technology provides each person with the potential to progress individually in [his or her] development, the cohesiveness of the species is no longer important," Sterling imagines the obsolescence of the Mech/Shaper dichotomy:

"The old categories, Mechanist and Shaper–they're a bit out-
moded these days, aren't they? Life moves in clades." He smiled.
"A clade is a daughter species, a related descendant. It's happened to other successful animals, and now it's humanity's turn.
The factions still struggle, but the categories are breaking up.
No faction can claim the one true destiny for mankind. Mankind
no longer exists."[215]

The neat, binary opposition of Mechanist and Shaper gives way to
the chaos theory of nonlinear evolution: Among the many variations on the
posthuman theme are the borged, black-armored Lobsters mentioned in
chapter 4 of this book, as well as a breed of "aquatic posthuman" known as
an Angel, its skin

> smooth and black and slick. The legs and pelvic girdle were
> gone; the spine extended to long muscular flukes. Scarlet gills
> trailed from the neck. The ribcage was black openwork, gushing
> white, feathery nets packed with symbiotic bacteria. . . . The
> lidless eyes were huge, and the skull had been rebuilt to accom-
> modate them.[216]

Schismatrix ends with the clades' ascent to "the Fifth Prigoginic
Level of Complexity"–named for the physicist Ilya Prigogine, who theorizes
that order spontaneously emerges when "dynamical systems" move far from
equilibrium, giving rise to transition points known as "singularities" (attrac-
tors are one of several types of singularities). In *Schismatrix*, Sterling applies
Prigogine's theories to humanity, considered as a dynamical system; moving
"far from equilibrium" (Prigogine) into posthuman clades, the species
encounters a mystical singularity–a sketchily rendered "final transcendence" reminiscent of the astronaut's apotheosis as the "Star-Child" in *2001:
A Space Odyssey*. This, the Fifth Level, is "as far beyond Life as Life is from
inert matter," explains the numinous Presence at the novel's end. "It's the
Godhead, or as close as makes no difference to the likes of you and me."[217]
Sterling's posthuman protagonist Abelard Lindsay is gathered up into the
ineffable ("a silver wave . . . a melting, a release"), leaving his body behind:
"Atop its clean white ladder of vertebrae, his empty skull sank grinning into
the collar of his coat."[218]

The mathematician and SF author Vernor Vinge is convinced that something resembling Sterling's "final transcendence" is just around the corner. Vinge, whose 1981 novella *True Names* portrayed cyberspace in techno-mystical terms, believes that a technological singularity looms in the near future of the human species. It will come about, he asserts, as a result of "the imminent creation by technology of entities with greater-than-human intelligence": sentient, super-smart computers; genetically engineered superbrains; computer-human interfaces so transparent that their users are virtually indistinguishable from the ultra-intelligent machines to which they are connected; electronic networks that suddenly become self-aware, like SkyNet.[219]

Guided not by human hands but by Darwinian competition, artificial evolution will give rise to a "greater than human intelligence" between 2005 and 2030, predicts Vinge, at which point technological progress will accelerate by orders of magnitude, with ever smarter machine life designing and fabricating still smarter offspring at an ever increasing pace. Humanity will be swept into a singularity–a "throwing-away of all the human rules, perhaps in the blink of an eye."[220] Vinge's rendering of superhuman morphology is sketchy at best, but it is certain to involve cyborging and genetic engineering.

Although he is the furthest thing from a scientist, William Burroughs has captivated hackers and SF fans alike with posthumanist musings confected from fringe science, survivalist politics, and science fiction. A longtime advocate of do-it-yourself mutation, he has suggested that "the political and social chaos we are seeing on every side reflects an underlying biological crisis: the end of the human line."[221] If we are to survive, he argues, we must muster the courage to take the evolutionary leap that he, like Stelarc, believes will be precipitated by space migration. "We have the technology to . . . produce improved and variegated models of the body designed for space conditions," asserts Burroughs, who sees in the bone loss and muscle atrophy experienced by contemporary astronauts a blueprint for engineered evolution.[222] "Astronauts stand to lose their bones and teeth," he notes. "A skeleton has no function in a weightless state."[223] Redesigned for zero gravity, the human form might resemble an octopus, he speculates.

Terence McKenna, who likewise believes that humanity is "on the brink of another leap in evolution," favors the octopus paradigm as well, although for him it is metaphoric rather than morphogenetic, enabled by cyberspace rather than necessitated by outer space.[224] He speculates that in VR "men and women may shed the monkey body to become virtual octopi swimming in a silicon sea," by which he means that computer-generated representations of octopus bodies would be ideally suited for the post-Logos paradise McKenna imagines VR could be.[225] The octopus, he reasons, "does not transmit its linguistic intent, it *becomes* its linguistic intent," communicating with other octopi by means of body language and color changes.[226] "Like the octopus, our destiny is to become what we think, to have our thoughts become our bodies and our bodies become our thoughts," writes McKenna. "VR can help here, for electronics can change vocal utterance into visually beheld colored output in the virtual reality. . . . At last we will truly *see* what we mean."[227] In McKenna's fantasy, the dislocation of mind and body, signifier and signified is mended at last.

Of course, there's a bit of sleight of mind here: The consciousness may frolic in a "silicon sea" as a cartoon octopus, in postlinguistic communion with other simulacra, but the body is left behind, its sensory organs sealed off by the VR paraphernalia through which the system transmits visual, auditory, tactile, olfactory, and gustatory input. It may gesture from time to time or jog in place, but safety requires that its movements be restricted; the disjunction between the world around it and the artificial sensory input it is receiving from the virtual reality it "inhabits" is all but complete.

The obvious next step is that of making the rupture total by doing away with the body entirely. For all their cyberpunk trappings, Vinge's superhumans, Burroughs's bioengineered octopi, or McKenna's virtual ones still cling to embodiment; the final solution to the mind-body problem, according to the dominant logic in cyberculture, is the reduction of consciousness to pure quintessence.

Hans Moravec's notion of "downloading"—mapping the idiosyncratic neural networks of our minds onto computer memory, thereby rendering the body superfluous—offers a highly theoretical but exhaustively worked-out solution to the knotty problem of how mind might be extracted from body.

Moravec, who is the director of the Mobile Robot Laboratory in Carnegie-Mellon's Field Robotics Center, spends much of his mental life in the distant future. The first chapter of his book *Mind Children: The Future of Robot and Human Intelligence* begins with a statement calculated to cause apoplectic seizures in humanist quarters: "I believe that robots with human intelligence will be common within fifty years."[228] Moravec, an unreconstructed mechanist, believes as Marvin Minsky does that the mind is simply a meat machine; human-machine equivalence, therefore, is merely a matter of computing speed. Ten teraops should do the trick, by his reckoning. That's 10 trillion operations per second, light-years beyond a state-of-the-art PC chip like Intel's Pentium, capable of 112 million instructions per second. Based on his calculation that there has been a *trillionfold* increase in the amount of computation a dollar will buy since the invention of the punch-card tabulator shortly before the turn of the century, Moravec projects the arrival of a ten-teraops machine by 2010.

At which point, buckle your seat belt, because evolution's warp drive is going to engage. Astronomically intelligent robots, "looking quite unlike the machines we know," writes Moravec, "will explode into the universe, leaving us behind in a cloud of dust."[229] Robots capable of engineering their own evolution will quickly surpass human equivalence, he theorizes, leapfrogging up the scale of intelligence to a level that defies human comprehension. Homo sapiens' superintelligent artificial offspring almost certainly will not inhabit humanoid bodies and may not resemble anything we have ever seen. One possibility among many, suggests Moravec, is trillion-limbed machine flora—robot bushes whose stems branch into ever more delicate, ever more numerous twigs, culminating, finally, in a dizzying array of microscopic cilia. Possessed of "great intelligence, superb coordination, astronomical speed, and enormous sensitivity to its environment," a robot bush would be able to "watch a movie by walking its fingers along the film as it screamed by at high speed" or reach into complicated machines or even living organisms to manipulate them at the molecular level. "A bush robot would be a marvel of surrealism to behold," writes Moravec.[230]

Downloading human consciousness into computers is one of Moravec's strategies for keeping pace with our superevolved creations. With dubious relish, Moravec describes a robot surgeon removing the crown of a person's skull and using high-resolution magnetic resonance measurements to create a computer simulacrum of the subject's neural architecture. Layer by layer, the brain is scanned and simulated; in the process, the superfluous tissue is surgically removed and disposed of. At last, the braincase is empty; the robot disconnects all life-support systems, and the body goes into convulsions and expires.

The subject's consciousness, meanwhile, is curiously unconcerned, wandering wraithlike through cyberspace. "You may choose to move your mind from one computer to another that is more technically advanced or better suited to a new environment," offers Moravec, helpfully.[231] Naturally, a discarnate mind would be immortal, and backup copies could be made as insurance against mechanical breakdowns or software "bugs" (programming errors) or viruses. Moreover, as Moravec points out, a disembodied consciousness need not spend eternity in a stationary computer, inhabiting simulated worlds. "As a computer program, your mind can travel over information channels, for instance encoded as a laser message beamed between planets," he speculates. "If you found life on a neutron star and wished to make a field trip, you might devise a way to build a robot there of neutron stuff, then transmit your mind to it. . . . You would explore, acquire new experiences and memories, and then beam your mind back home."[232]

The concept of "downloading" has proven popular among exponents of postevolution, foremost among them the Los Angeles–based Extropians. Writing in the movement's organ, *Extropy* (which claims a circulation of thirty-five hundred), the Extropian David Ross speculates that, since "[b]rain structure at every level determines the functioning of the mind," every neuron and synapse in a given brain must be re-created in a computer program if an individual consciousness is to be transferred from its organic body into digital memory.[233] Since in Ross's bio-cybernetic theory of mind the "wiring *is* the program," we need not understand human consciousness to perform such an operation; a comprehensive knowledge of the synaptic connections of the brain would suffice, since individual consciousness is presumed to be one with the unique neural map of each brain.

Ross illustrates his theories with a flight of Moravecian whimsy in which a man discards his body, uploading his mind into "the world-wide Cyberspace Web"; nanomachines perform invasive brain surgery, "systematically replacing each neuron with a functionally equivalent artificial structure" in computer memory:

Gradually, each synapse in his brain is absorbed into the program structure of the emulation program, its functionality
retained but its physical structure gone. . . . After a while . . .
[t]he doctor hands him a switch which he knows will turn off his
old body. . . . All nerve and muscle connections are severed at
once and the body dies instantly. He feels less emotion than he
thought he would. He knows that if he doesn't like it here in
Cyberspace, he can always have another physical body constructed, grown from his original DNA, if he wishes.[234]

As cyberculture's most vocal proponents of consigning the body to
the scrap heap of the twentieth century, the Extropians merit close scrutiny.
Ross, executive director Max More, and the rest of the movement's membership rally around the banner of "transhumanism." Transhumanism is the
human potential movement on steroids—an up-with-technology, business-
friendly, hell-for-leather humanism bent on self- and species-transformation
by any means necessary: downloading (Extropians prefer the more upbeat
"*up*loading" or the even zingier "transbiomorphosis"); "nanomedicine" ("the
use of molecular-scale devices to repair damage and boost the immune
system"); nanocomputer implants ("molecular computer[s] integrated with
the brain, providing additional memory, processing power, and running
decision-making programs"); genetic engineering; smart drugs; cryonics;
and "self-transformative psychology" in the Anthony Robbins mold.[235]

As theorized in *Extropy*, Extropian transhumanism is a marriage
of Ayn Rand and Friedrich Nietzsche—specifically, Rand's conviction
that statism and collectivism are the roots of all evil and Nietzsche's
complementary concepts of the end of morality, the "will to power," and
the *Übermensch*, or "overman." The "optimal" Extropian persona, writes
More in issue ten of *Extropy*, "is Nietzsche's Übermensch, the higher
being existing within us as potential waiting to be realized." Extropian
writings champion laissez-faire capitalism ("Are you attracted to innovative,
market-oriented solutions to social problems?" reads a flyer) and exude a
buoyant technophilia.

Extropian transhumanism speaks to the collective yearnings that
took shape in the L-5 Society's vision of an off-world Utopia. According to
Norman Spinrad, the L-5 colony had mythic resonance for "science fiction

writers of a laissez-faire libertarian bent," whose novels transplanted the space station envisioned by the society from Earth orbit to the Asteroid Belt.[236] "Out there in the Belt, with its limitless mineral resources, its low gravity, and its wide-open spaces, was the future of the species," notes Spinrad, "and as for poor old polluted, overpopulated, screwed-up Earth, well, tough shit."[237]

The Extropians, who maintain an avid interest in space coloniza-tion (the L-5 Society cofounder Keith Henson is a member of *Extropy*'s editorial committee), are similarly unburdened by a social conscience. Even as they extract the self from the human, renouncing humanism's allegiance to the species and its wariness of autonomous technology, Extropians uncouple the individual from the social. *Freedom* is defined not in terms of civil liberties but in "behavioral, morphological, neurological, and genetic" terms—a politics of self-directed personal evolution that links the group to Stelarc, who argues,

> In this age of information overload, what is significant is no longer freedom of ideas but rather freedom of form—freedom to modify, freedom to mutate your body. The question is not whether a society will allow [the] freedom to express yourself, but whether the human species will allow you to break the bonds of your genetic parameters—the fundamental freedom to determine your own DNA destiny.[238]

In the libertarian futurism of Extropy, society is a dynamical system of ever-evolving egos; government is a decentralized "social coordina-tion mechanism" whose only real purpose is to provide "the context required for us to sustain truly long-term personal progress, to provide energy, space, and the framework for the diversity implicit in individual self-transformation."[239] Few would argue in favor of an intrusive government that restricts "individual self-transformation," mandating self-sacrifice to a greater, common good. But there is an absence in Extropian philosophy of anything resembling a sense of community and an obliviousness to the fact that a passionate engagement with the social or the political, through altruism or activism, can be a catalyst for profound "self-transformation." It is these vacancies that account for the hollow noise this philosophy makes when its depths are sounded. As Andrew Kimbrell argues, in a *Harper's* forum on "The Value of Life,"

> this secular myth—that we live as autonomous individuals, as islands unto ourselves, without rights balanced by duties—is absurd. Every decision you may make, whether it be to sell yourself into slavery or to sell yourself into prostitution, adds to and creates the *telos*—the purpose—of community you inhabit. You do not exist as an island.[240]

Kimbrell's worldview reverses that of the Extropians, who have inherited Ayn Rand's vituperative condemnation of "*Society*, with all its boggled chaos of selflessness, compromise, servility, and lies."[241] With charity toward none, Extropian transhumanism makes no provision for the economically disenfranchised, the socially marginalized, or the "psychologically weak."[242]

Happily, "NEGs" (negative types lacking in the Extropian virtue of "Dynamic Optimism") will disappear altogether when science comes to "understand the basis of depression and lack of enthusiasm, allowing us to choose to maintain ourselves in a perpetually high energy condition."[243] Technological developments may result in "chemical-releasing implants, controlled by a computer interfaced with our brains, that [will] allow us to rapidly alter our state of mind" for the better.[244] (Any resemblance to the brain-stimulating "mood organ" in Philip K. Dick's *Do Androids Dream of Electric Sheep?* whose dial can be set for the Dynamically Optimistic "Awareness of the manifold possibilities open to me in the future," is entirely coincidental.)

Near the end of his essay "Technological Self-Transformation: Expanding Personal Extropy," More attempts to counterbalance his neo-Nietzschean rhetoric with a vision of a kinder, gentler Übermensch. "Contrary to popular interpretation, the Übermensch [is] *not* the Blond Beast, the conqueror and plunderer," he writes. "The developed, self-chosen self will exude benevolence, emanating its excess of health and self-confidence."[245] He ends by reminding his fellow Extropians that they "need not be isolated, totally self-sustaining achievers. Support and encouragement by fellow extropic-minded persons is enormously valuable."[246]

Still, Extropian transhumanism emerges, in *Extropy*, as a vaguely cultish movement, replete with invented monikers and futuristic jargon, committed to an ingrown, all-consuming self-improvement program in which social responsibility ends at the boundaries of the individual ego. Indeed, there is a fundamentalism to this supposedly rationalist movement's uncritical faith in technology, its unswerving devotion to unchecked expansion, and its rejection of ecological concerns as "the false doom-mongering of the apocalyptic environmentalists" at a time when all but the most myopic concede the need to balance economic exigencies with environmental imperatives.[247] Then, too, there is something inescapably American about this philosophy of Boundless Expansion, Self-Transformation, Intelligent Technology, Spontaneous Order, and Dynamic Optimism, reconciling as it does the mechanist reductivism of artificial intelligence theory with the evangelical zeal and relentlessly peppy can-do of the human potential movement.

Some of Extropian transhumanism's headier rhetoric sounds as if it were written by Seth Brundle, the scientist in David Cronenberg's *The Fly* (1986) who demolecularizes his body and teleports it from one computer-controlled "telepod" to another. "I'm beginning to think that the sheer process of being taken apart atom by atom and put back together again [is] somehow . . . purifying," the fist-thumping, coffee-gulping Brundle tells his somewhat alarmed girlfriend Ronnie. "I think it's going to allow me to realize the personal potential I've been neglecting all these years. . . . I will say now, however subjectively, that human teleportation—molecular decimation, breakdown and reformation—is inherently purging. It makes a man a king! All I've done is say to the world, 'Let's go! Move! Catch me if you can!'" Later, he attempts to muscle Ronnie into the telepod, telling her that after she's been disintegrated and reconstituted—purged, in Nietzschean terms, of her "all too human" qualities—they'll be "the perfect couple, the dynamic duo." She wriggles free, shrieking, "Don't give me that born-again teleportation rap!"

As detailed in chapter 1, minimanifestos very like "that born-again teleportation rap" were a fixture in early issues of *Mondo 2000*. In an early editorial, Queen Mu and R. U. Sirius proclaim that "Eco-fundamentalism is out"; so, too, are "finite possibilities." Noting that "we are living at a very special juncture in the evolution of the species," the authors close with the Nietzsche-meets-*The Revenge of the Nerds* assertion that the masses must place their destiny in the hands of "a whole new generation of sharpies, mutants and superbrights" not unlike More's Extropian vanguard ("the leading wave of evolutionary progress"). Like the Extropians, the *Mondo* editors celebrate "human/technological interactive mutational forms" and "[b]rain-boosting technologies" and look forward to "[b]ecoming the Bionic Angel." This, they declare, is the "dawn of a new humanism."[248]

To Andrew Ross, who refuses to be dazzled by cyberbole, Mu and Sirius's new dawn looks like the same old, hallowed humanism that has historically concealed its Western, white, increasingly technocratic interests behind high-minded rhetoric about what is best for "mankind." Humanism laid the philosophical groundwork, Ross contends, for European civilization's shameful dealings with the natural environment and the animal kingdom. Needless to say, true species-centrism would be compelled, *entirely by self-interest*, to protect the natural environment on which humankind is so demonstrably dependent. Thus, we are drawn to the inescapable conclusion that much of what passes for posthumanism is in fact egoism leavened with a dash of technocratic elitism, whether it is *Mondo 2000*'s dictatorship of the neurotariat—the "sharpies, mutants and superbrights" in whom we must place our "faith" and "power"—or the Extropian triumph of the overman. The *Mondo* editorial and *Extropy* manifestos reverberate with what Ross calls "a voice that appears to speak the language of unfettered development, heedless of any concern for those who cannot keep up or who are subordinated as a result of the logic of underdevelopment."[249]

The Theology of the Ejector Seat

Since these philosophies owe so much to Hans Moravec, it seems only appropriate that a critique of them be laid at his feet. In a 1993 interview with the roboticist, I attempted to make political and socioeconomic sense of ideas that had always floated, like the "laissez-faire libertarian" Utopias described by Spinrad, "airily unconcerned above a Third World favela called Earth":[250]

> MARK DERY: One of the things that troubled me while reading your book *Mind Children* is that your vision of human evolution is yoked to quantum leaps in technology and seems not to take into account the socioeconomic landscape of your future. I suspect you would argue that such issues are irrelevant to your thinking, since you

think in terms of hypothetical technologies, but I can't help wondering about the fate of those on the lower rungs of the socioeconomic ladder in your world of transmigrant minds and "superintelligent robot bushes."

HANS MORAVEC: Well, I think what you would call the socioeconomic implications of the developments I imagine are—unless you're looking at the interactions of the machines themselves—largely irrelevant. It doesn't matter what people do because they're going to be left behind, like the second stage of a rocket. Unhappy lives, horrible deaths, and failed projects have been part of the history of life on Earth ever since there was life; what really matters in the long run is what's left over. Does it really matter to you today that the tyrannosaur line of that species failed?

MD: Well, I wouldn't create a homology between failed reptilian strains and those on the lowermost rungs of the socioeconomic ladder.

HM: But I would. You see, many cultures are gone; the Maori of New Zealand are gone, as are most of our ancestors or near relatives—*Australopithecus,* Homo erectus, Neanderthal man.

MD: Your position seems rather Olympian.

HM: "Olympian?" I take that as a compliment, in many ways, because I think you can wallow in compassion and really screw up the bigger things, an example being the current U.S. welfare system, which I think had much too much compassion for individual cases and in so doing totally wrecked the inner city family by creating the wrong incentives. My own politics are basically libertarian because I like to see as much happen as possible, and giving people maximum freedom to try things without having to have the approval of everybody else is the most fruitful way to get the most results in the shortest time.

MD: But in the larger sense your politics are less libertarian than Darwinian; the individual ego is of far less consequence to you than it was to Ayn Rand.

HM: Well, individuals (as they exist today) only have a very short lifetime and consequently only have a very small part to play in the big story; if some individual dies—if *I* die—it's not going to affect the whole story very much. I think the view taken by Richard Dawkins in *The Selfish Gene*—that we're Rube Goldberg contraptions which our genes have managed to assemble, whose primary purpose is to make more genes—is a very useful way to look at the nature of humanity.

Of course, the notion of an "I" with motivations and future plans could be abstracted from the living form initially [cobbled] together by its genes and installed in some other machine without the genes having any part in it anymore. And then there's the concept of abstracting the *overall* biological and cultural evolution of a population, which is yet another level of abstraction that goes beyond the pains and tragedies and joys of individual people and has a story of its own. That, too, has a dynamic that can be tinkered with and that's the biggest story that I can comfortably encompass at the moment. To me, it's the most important one, because if the survival of the overall process is jeopardized, then you've lost all the little parts of the story. In time, the really interesting things about humanity will be carried on in a new medium.

Obviously, the discourse of posthumanism that Moravec, the Extropians, and the *Mondo* essayists take literally is bathed in political and philosophical associations. Moreover, its popular appeal suggests that what began as scientific speculation is well on its way to becoming secular myth; the imaginary technologies that would make "downloading" possible are in theory made out of microchips, but for many they function as metaphors and speak to mythic needs.

End-of-the-millennium science fictions about disembodiment through "downloading" and re-embodiment in the "shiny new body of the style, color, and material of your choice" (one of Moravec's factory options) are daydreams that began as nightmares. David Skal theorizes that the space invaders who terrorized earthlings in fifties creature features gave shape to the information anxiety beginning to nibble at the American subconscious. Bug-eyed and bulbous-headed, they present an image of intense and unbearable visual-mental overload, a description that may have more relevance to the unprecedented level of media bombardment (mainly by television) in the '50s, than to any possible physiology of extraterrestrial beings. . . . [T]hese new creatures anticipated not the violent rending of the body but its withering and atrophy. The future was about watching images and processing information; the eyes and brain were the only useful parts of the human form left.[251]

Earlier, in 1948, Norbert Wiener had drawn parallels between organisms and machines. Both, he said, used on-off switches in their information processing (neural in one case, electromechanical in the other) and both used "feedback loops"–circular processes beginning in the nervous system, emerging as output through muscular activity, and cycling back into the nervous system through sensory input–to interact with their environments. By the late sixties, the cybernetic society's definition of humans as information-processing systems had given rise to the creeping fear that computer culture would ultimately reduce human beings to brains floating in nutrients, wired for sensation. The villains in the 1968 *Star Trek* episode "The Gamesters of Triskelion" were brains under glass, sustained by machines; only by titillating and tormenting captive humans could such effete, bodiless creatures vicariously experience long-lost emotions and bodily sensations.

In recent years, the image of the brain without a body–or, better yet, a "downloaded" mind without a brain–has been appropriated by posthumanists, for whom it is a symbol of godlike immortality and power rather than an embodiment of humanist anxiety.

Vinge argues that the infinite, everlasting superminds who inhabit his "post-Singularity world" would be Gods by the physicist Freeman Dyson's definition: "God," argues Dyson, "is what mind becomes when it has passed beyond the scale of our comprehension."[252] Moravec imagines the subsumption of "downloaded" cyberbeings into a "community mind," omniscient and omnivorous, which spreads "outwards from the solar system, converting non-life into mind" through some form of data conversion.[253] This process, suggests Moravec, "might convert the entire universe into an extended thinking entity."[254] In Nerdvana, all is cerebration; the dominant term of the body/mind dualism has vanquished its detested opposite forever.

For many of posthumanism's critics, such images are fatal seductions, glossing over the fact that issues of power are anchored in the physical bodies of the governed, at least for the forseeable future; the abstract calculus of commerce and politics, together with the ethical issues raised by advanced technologies, become personal and palpable when they intersect with bodies, especially our own. Allucquere Rosanne Stone, the director of the Advanced Communications Technology Lab at the University of Texas at Austin, argues,

> There's a kind of rapt, mindless fascination with these disembodying or ability-augmenting technologies. I think of it as a kind of cyborg envy. . . . The deep, childlike desire to go beyond one's body. This is not necessarily a bad thing. Certainly, for the handicapped, it can be very liberating. For others, who have the desire without the need, there can be problems. Political power still exists inside the body and being out of one's body or extending one's body through technology doesn't change that.[255]

In her essay "Will the Real Body Please Stand Up?: Boundary Stories about Virtual Cultures," Stone asserts, "No matter how virtual the subject may become, there is always a body attached," reaffirming the importance of "keeping the discussion grounded in individual bodies."[256]

Vivian Sobchack, a cultural critic and feminist film theorist, needs no convincing on that point. In "Baudrillard's Obscenity," her smart, tough response to the French postmodernist's essay on Crash, she brings us joltingly back from the disembodied rhetoric of posthumanism to her own, intensely personal here and now, where she is convalescing after major cancer surgery. Sobchack calls Baudrillard to account for his "naïvely celebratory" rhapsodies about the penetration of bodies by technology in Ballard's novel, which Baudrillard reads as a cyborg future beyond good and evil in which wounds and other artificial orifices take their place alongside natural ones as possible sites of sexual pleasure and where sex, in turn, is only one of many conceivable uses for such interfaces.[257] Forcing her reader to confront the painful reality of the twelve-inch scar on her left thigh, a memento of the surgery that removed a cancerous tumor, Sobchack notes,

There's nothing like a little pain to bring us (back) to our senses. . . . Baudrillard's techno-body is a body that is *thought* always as an *object*, and *never lived* as a *subject*. . . . [H]e's into the transcendent sexiness of "wounds," "artificial orifices". . . . But sitting here *living* that orifice, I can attest to the *scandal* of metaphor. . . . Even at its most objectified and technologically caressed, I *live* this thigh—not abstractly on "the" body, but concretely as "my" body.[258]

Sobchack bridles at Baudrillard's celebration of the end of what he calls the "moral gaze—the critical judgmentalism that is still a part of the old world's functionality" and the advent of an affectless, postmodern sensibility for which the "incisions, excisions, scar tissue, gaping body holes" left by violent collisions with technology are little more than erogenous zones for cyborgs.[259] "The man is really dangerous," she observes, tartly wishing him "a car crash or two":

He needs a little pain (maybe a lot) to bring him to his senses, to remind him that he has a body, *his* body, and that the "moral gaze" begins there. . . . If we don't keep this subjective kind of bodily sense in mind as we negotiate our technoculture, then we . . . will objectify ourselves to death.[260]

Historically, objectification is often a prerequisite to repression or worse. In Nazi Germany, deportees arriving at Auschwitz were shorn and tattooed with ID numbers whose true purpose was an open secret:

And as they gave me my tattoo number, B-4990, the SS man came to me, and he says to me, "Do you know what this number's all about?" I said, "No, sir." "Okay, let me tell you now. You are being dehumanized."[261]

When we objectify *ourselves*—our own bodies—we enter the numb, neon nightmare of *Crash*, where people are "mannequins dressed in meaningless clothing" and only a violent collision can jolt them back to their senses.[262] The social critic Walter Benjamin foreshadowed just such a world in the early thirties when he noted that mankind's "self-alienation has reached such a degree that it can experience its own destruction as an aesthetic pleasure of the first order."[263]

Posthumanists such as Vinge and Moravec fulfill the premonitions of Benjamin and Sobchack when they contemplate the disappearance of humanity from the assumed perspective of smart machines. It appears that neither thinker has much in common with the Extropians after all, since the sympathies of both men lie not with the individual ego, self-transforming or otherwise, but with the ultra-intelligent machines they believe will render Homo sapiens obsolete. Moravec delights in humanist-baiting pronouncements about the self-assembling automata he predicts will put DNA out of a job, and Vinge suspects humans may not survive his postevolutionary singularity:

> If you do create creatures that are smarter than you, they become the principal actors. . . . . If we got in their way, whether they'd rub us out or use some other solution would probably depend on the expense.[264]

Whether or not the posthuman futures imagined by Moravec, Vinge, and others are likely to come true, and what humankind's fate will be if they do, are brainteasers for AI experts, futurologists, perhaps even chaos theorists. Meanwhile, we might consider (since few seem to be doing so) the immediate social, political, and ethical implications of posthumanism, specifically Homo Cyber's reduction of the body—*his* or *her* body, as Sobchack insists—to an organic machine. As Andrew Kimbrell points out,

> The idea that we are biological machines has consequences. Consider: What rights adhere to a biological machine? What duties and obligations are owed a biological machine? What dignity and love should be given to a biological machine? The whole constitutional system of rights, duties, and respect is based on the old-fashioned idea that we are reverable persons, not machines.[265]

Moreover, he notes, the dehumanization of societal outsiders that has so often been a prelude to their exploitation or extermination has been extended to the natural world, which Kimbrell argues was desacralized "before we moved in to destroy it."[266] In that light, the fantasies of postevolutionary space migration entertained by Stelarc, Burroughs, Moravec, and the Extropians exhibit what Andrew Ross calls the "technohumanist contempt for a planet that, once exhausted, will then be left behind."[267] In a *Whole Earth Review* forum devoted to the question "Is the Body Obsolete?" the computer programmer and cybercultural theorist Yaakov Garb wonders,

> Why . . . are we so eager to disown the material substrates of our lives in a time when the fabric of our world—from soil to ozone layer—does actually feel like it is disintegrating? Why, as toxins and radiation trickle into the most fundamental recesses of our cells and ecosystems, is there such enthusiasm for self-sufficient space colonies, disembodied intellects, and cyborg futures?[268]

Thomas Hine notes, in his discussion of Moravec, that the roboticist's prediction that "self-reproducing superintelligent mechanisms" with our cultural DNA will "explode into the universe, leaving us behind in a cloud of dust,"

> make[s] the unthinkable survivable. It argues that there is life after life. It is reassuring that if humans make the Earth uninhabitable for themselves as organisms, it will still be possible to continue by other means. Nuclear war need not be an obstacle, or death of any kind. There can be lifeboats for our minds.[269]

As Hine hints, it is equally likely that we are not, as the painter and William Burroughs coconspirator Brion Gysin was fond of remarking, "here to go." Perhaps we are here to *stay*, in these bodies, on this planet. The sociobiologist Edward O. Wilson, who holds the Frank B. Baird Jr. Professorship of Science at Harvard, argues that the Earth is "finite in many resources that determine the quality of life" and that, simultaneously, "scientists theorize the existence of a virtually unlimited array of other planetary environments, *almost all of which are uncongenial to human life*."[270] He warns,

> Many of Earth's vital resources are about to be exhausted, its atmospheric chemistry is deteriorating and human populations

have already grown dangerously large. Natural ecosystems, the wellsprings of a healthful environment, are being irreversibly degraded. . . . Earth is destined to become an impoverished planet within a century if present trends continue. Mass extinctions are being reported with increasing frequency in every part of the world.[271]

The sobering assessments of scientists such as Wilson imply that even cyberculture has its limits, and no one likes limits, least of all Michael G. Zey, a management professor and the executive director of the Expansionary Institute in Morristown, New Jersey. In *Seizing the Future: How the Coming Revolution in Science, Technology, and Industry Will Expand the Frontiers of Human Potential and Reshape the Planet*—a book whose title takes corporate futurology to the carnival midway—Zey maintains that

humanity does not have to choose between progress and the health of the environment. . . . As the Macroindustrial Era evolves, society will simultaneously tap the potential of its own inventions and utilize technology to improve the environment.[272]

The gloomy forecasts of Wilson and his ilk, he asserts, are nothing more than anti-growth, anti-technology fearmongering based on "sketchy" evidence: "Humanity is about to overcome scarcity, biological restrictions, and nature itself."[273] Zey, prophet of a hyperventilating "hyperprogress," derides the idea of "living in balance with nature"; he is a diehard defender of the Old Testament article of faith that

humanity, not nature, has ultimate domain over the planet. . . . The species must be willing to accept the responsibility that its unique abilities and superior intelligence have thrust upon it to improve itself, enrich the planet, and ultimately perfect the universe.[274]

Zey's pronouncement "We stand at the most critical juncture in the history of humanity" echoes, nearly word for word, the *Mondo* editors' announcement that "we are living at a very special juncture in the evolution of the species."[275] An ingrained suspicion of the very notion of limits makes strange bedfellows of Zey; the techno-yippie authors of the *Mondo 2000* editorial, who urge an all-out assault on "the limits of biology, gravity and time"; and Andrew Ross, a self-styled "left libertarian" struggling toward "a green cultural criticism."[276] As Ross argues, limits are too often "socially induced for the purpose of regulation, or even repression"; the "language of 'limits,'" he stresses, "can have different meanings in different contexts, some very progressive, some not."[277]

Ross is rightly wary of the use of irrefutable "natural" laws to validate social limits that bound human possibility. A healthy skepticism about limits, "natural" as well as social, is a necessary safeguard against encroachments on individual liberty. But social limits justified by artificially created scarcity are not synonymous with natural limits imposed by the biosphere's interaction with the technosphere. Ross, unlike Zey or the *Mondo* manifesto-makers, concedes that we are in the middle of an "ecological crisis" that is largely if not entirely attributable to the blinkered worldview of industrial culture, with its calamitous ideology of ceaseless consumption, unrestrained growth, and inexhaustible resources—an obdurate refusal, in short, to acknowledge limits of any sort.[278] "The devastating consequences of viewing the physical world as mere raw material make it clear that no livable future is possible if current trends in capitalist production continue," he writes.[279] (Ross never makes clear how he resolves his ecopolitics with his libertarianism.)

Posthumanist visions of the mind unbound, of the Earth dwindling to a blue pinpoint in the rearview mirror, are a wish-fulfillment fantasy of the end of limits, situated (at least for now) in a world of limits. The envisioned liftoff from biology, gravity, and the twentieth century by borging, morphing, "downloading," or launching our minds beyond all bounds is itself held fast by the gravity of the social and political realities, moral issues, and environmental conditions of the moment. Try as they might to tear loose from their societal moorings and hurtle starward, the millenarian science fictions of "transcendental" posthumanists such as Moravec, Vinge, and the Extropians remain earthbound, caught up in a tangle of philosophical problems: Sobchack's contention that we are in danger of "objectify[ing] ourselves to death" versus Moravec's mechanist premise that we *are* objects, that consciousness is the result of wholly material processes and is therefore reproducible by technological means; Donna Haraway's belief that "the Earth really is finite, that there aren't any other planets out there that we know of that we can live on, that escape velocity is a deadly fantasy" versus Zey's conviction that natural resources are the raw material of expansion and that the "movement to the Moon, the planets, the stars represents a transcendent process in which the species fulfills its destiny."[280]

Zey's heady exclamations are textbook examples of what the historian Leo Marx calls "the rhetoric of the technological sublime," hymns to progress that rise "like froth on a tide of exuberant self-regard, sweeping over all misgivings, problems, and contradictions."[281] Verging at their most exultant on almost mystical transports of rapture, these paeans to post-evolutionary apotheosis constitute a theology of the ejector seat. It is a theology founded, like much of the Western religious tradition, on a contempt for the body and the material world. What will become of the body once the mind is "downloaded?" wonders Fjermedal, in his interview with Moravec. "You just don't bother waking it up again if the copying went successfully," replies the roboticist. "It's so messy."[282]

Oddly, for all its reductionism, transcendental posthumanism suffers from a Cartesian confusion of mind and spirit. As Hine has noted, it is passing strange that an unequivocal scientific reductionism should

> have the effect of reviving dualism in yet another form by its presumption that human intelligence can exist separately from the organism in which it evolved. That places intelligence in much the same position in which, for example, Christian thought has conceived of the soul. . . . There are, of course, far more differences than similarities. . . . But there is one important way in which the two ideas are similar: They both tend to devalue the body and the life of human beings on Earth. . . . Both beliefs tend to discount physical reality and exalt the abstract.[283]

According to Fjermedal, the computer scientist Charles Lecht theorizes that

> when the computers and the robotics become sufficiently advanced to carry their human creators to a certain pinnacle, we

may attain a point where "we may ultimately leave even our technology behind us." When that day comes, when we do *become mind,* [Lecht] says we will be given a boost, "out of the physical, and from there into—where else?—the spiritual."[284]

We may be born, as St. Augustine shuddered, "between feces and urine," but we will spend eternity, the story goes, as disembodied demiurges in cyberspace or reincarnated as the superlunary voyagers envisioned by the cultural critic O. B. Hardison, Jr.[285] In *Disappearing through the Skylight: Culture and Technology in the Twentieth Century,* Hardison arrives at the conclusion that "the idea of humanity is changing so rapidly that it . . . can legitimately and without any exaggeration be said to be disappearing."[286] Taking a leaf from Moravec, he imagines human minds "downloaded" into deep space probes fitted with solar sails. Powered by sunlight bouncing off the solar cells silvering their spinnakers, these otherworldly beings drift lazily between galaxies. Ultimately, they sail off our star charts, into the eye of infinity, little less than gods. Perhaps, he suggests, this is

> the moment at which the spirit finally separates itself from an outmoded vehicle. Perhaps it is a moment that realizes the age-old dream of the mystics of rising beyond the prison of the flesh to behold a light so brilliant it is a kind of darkness.[287]

Nonetheless, even the most sublime evocations of the Posthuman Assumption seem shadowed by doubts. The dream of software without hardware—mind without body—runs aground on our profound ignorance of the nature of consciousness and its relation to embodiment. In *The Silicon Man,* Charles Platt's cunningly wrought novel about a cabal of government scientists who have realized the dream of "downloading," a digitized human intelligence living in computer memory tells a fellow cyberbeing about an unfortunate candidate whose scanned intelligence never regained consciousness. "We're still working on it," explains the "infomorph," a woman named Rosalind French. "The peel and the scan were good; his intelligence is intact. It just won't—come to life. The trouble is, we still don't really know what consciousness *is.*"[288]

Indeed, we don't. The neurobiologist William H. Calvin, who decries the "malignant metaphor and rampant reductionism" of the brain-as-computer conceit, believes that brains are "the most elegantly organized bundles of matter in the universe."[289] "Everyone's always underestimating the brain," he maintains, pointing out that the shopworn factoid that the brain contains ten billion neurons is in fact an estimate of the number of neurons in only the cerebral *cortex* of *one* hemisphere, and that, moreover, the cerebral cortex is only "the frosting on the cake"; Calvin will not even hazard a guess about the number of neurons in the entire brain.[290]

The physicist Erich Harth holds that neurobiology and consciousness are inextricably entangled, a premise that renders "downloading" theoretically impossible. In *The Creative Loop: How the Brain Makes a Mind*, he asserts,

> The information we try to transfer is specific to the brain on which it grew in the first place. It cannot just be lifted from one brain and downloaded onto another. To run the stored software of a lifetime of experiences and thoughts, we would need a system that—unlike the general purpose computer—is matched to the stored information, a brain equivalent that not only is genetically identical to the original brain, but contains all the myriad random modifications of its circuitry that occur between conception and maturity. The amount of information necessary to specify this system is astronomical. That even a small portion of it could be extracted from a living brain without destroying it is doubtful.[291]

Of course, the "downloading" adherent David Ross, who concedes Harth's point that the brain is not a general-purpose computer, would counter that even a von Neumann machine, as such computers are called, could support a human consciousness if the emulation "reach[es] down low enough (probably at least to the individual neurons) so that it is emulating systems that are below the essential level of the brain"—that is, the transistors and switches from which "mind" is supposed to arise.[292] But Dr. Richard Restak, a neurologist and intractable "biochauvinist," does his best to dash such hopes, stressing that neurotransmitters and regulatory hormones are not confined to the brain, but are scattered throughout the body, in the intestines, the lungs, even the sex organs. "This ubiquity," he remarks, has stimulated a startling question that is currently haunting neuroscientists around the world: Is it possible that our definition of the brain is too narrow? That the regulatory processes that we now localize within our heads are much more widely distributed?[293]

Acknowledging that a "person is not just brain cells," Ross speculates that "nanomachines invading [our subject]'s body will replace all sensory neurons as well, and then replace all the parts of his body that influence the neurons with programs [that] do the same thing."[294] The infomorph inhabits a cyberspace whose fidelity to reality is so impeccable that the muffled thump of his heart, the wind tickling his sweaty back, the rusty sweetness of red wine, and a universe of other sensations, no less subtle or complex, is virtually indistinguishable from embodied experience.

Assume, then, that the mind could be distilled from the body, that we could follow to its ultimate conclusion the process of bodily extension and "auto-amputation" which, according to McLuhan, constitutes the history of technology, "downloading" our selves after having delegated, one by one, all of our mental and physical functions to our machines. Still, a shadow of a doubt remains, nagging at the edge of awareness—the doubt that once our bodies have been "deanimated," our gray matter nibbled away by infinitesimal nanomachines and encoded in computer memory, we might awake to discover that an ineffable something had gotten lost in translation. In that moment, we might find ourselves thinking of Gabe, in *Synners,* who unexpectedly finds himself face-to-face with his worst fear while roaming disembodied through cyberspace:

> *I can't remember what it feels like to have a body.* . . . He wanted to scream in frustration, but he had nothing to scream with.[295]

A COMMENT ON SOURCES

All unattributed quotes in this book are taken from interviews conducted by the author, who is grateful to the following for willingly submitting to lengthy interrogations:

Guy Aitchison, J. G. Ballard, John Perry Barlow, Glenn Branca, Stewart Brand, Rodney Brooks, Pat Cadigan, Gary Chapman, David Cronenberg, Erik Davis, Maxwell X. Delysid, Eddie Deutsche, Julian Dibbell, K. Eric Drexler, Rhys Fulber of Front Line Assembly, William Gibson, H. R. Giger, Brett Goldstone, Rob Hardin, Eric Hunting, Billy Idol, Greg Kulz, Jaron Lanier, Brenda Laurel, Timothy Leary, Bill Leeb of Front Line Assembly, Chico MacMurtrie, Terence McKenna, Michael Moorcock, Paul Moore, Hans Moravec, David Myers, Orlan, Rodney Orpheus, Marcus Pacheco, Mark Pauline, Genesis P-Orridge, Lynn Procter, Dr. Richard Restak, Trent Reznor, Dr. Joseph M. Rosen, Andrew Ross, Rudy Rucker, Rick Sayre, Barry Schwartz, Elliott Sharp, Jonathan Shaw, John Shirley, Pat Sinatra, R. U. Sirius, Stelarc, Bruce Sterling, David Therrien, Mark Trayle, Shinya Tsukamoto, and his translator Kiyo Joo.

A word about quotes from electronic bulletin board systems: I have attempted, when possible, to observe the YOYOW ("YOU OWN YOUR OWN WORDS") dictum that is a cornerstone of netiquette, securing the written permission of anyone quoted. Unfortunately, as was the case with several contributors to BaphoNet echomail discussions, dogged attempts to track down users sometimes proved fruitless. I can only hope that they will be flattered to find their quotes in these pages.

Responsibility for any errors of fact or misrepresentations must be laid, as always, on the author's doorstep.

NOTES

Introduction

1. Marshall McLuhan and Quentin Fiore, *The Medium Is the Massage: An Inventory of Effects* (New York: Bantam Books, 1967), p. 63.
2. Robert B. Reich, "On the Slag Heap of History," *New York Times Book Review,* November 8, 1992, p. 15.
3. Bernard Weinraub, "Directors Battle Over GATT's Final Cut and Print," *New York Times,* December 12, 1993, International section, p. 24.
4. Michael J. Mandel et al., "The Entertainment Economy," *Business Week,* March 14, 1994, p. 59.
5. Sales figures quoted in the Computer Museum's "People and Computers: Milestones of a Revolution," *Annual Report 1991* (Boston: Computer Museum, 1992), p. 18.
6. Otto Friedrich, "The Computer Moves In," *Time,* January 3, 1983, p. 14.
7. Philip Elmer-Dewitt, "First Nation in Cyberspace," *Time,* December 6, 1993, p. 62; John Markoff, "The Internet," *New York Times,* September 5, 1993, p. V11.
8. Estimate given in Markoff, "Internet".
9. Figure cited in Gareth Branwyn, "Compu-Sex: Erotica for Cybernauts," *Flame Wars: The Discourse of Cyberculture / South Atlantic Quarterly,* ed. Mark Dery, vol. 92, no. 4, (fall 1993), p. 781.
10. Bruce Sterling, *Schismatrix* (New York: Ace, 1985), p. 179.
11. Mark Dery, "Flame Wars," in *Flame Wars,* p. 565.
12. Ted Nelson, "Pain Killer," *New Media,* June 1994, p. 118; John Holusha, "Carving Out Real-Life Uses for Virtual Reality," *New York Times,* October 31, 1993, p. F11; N. R. Kleinfield, "Stepping through a Computer Screen,

Disabled Veterans Savor Freedom," *New York Times*, March 12, 1995, Metro section, p. L39.

13. Frank J. Tipler, *The Physics of Immortality: Modern Cosmology, God and the Resurrection of the Dead* (New York: Doubleday, 1994), p. 1.

14. Terence McKenna, "Psychedelics before and after History," recorded 1987 lecture, available on cassette from Lux Natura, 2140 Shattuck Avenue, Box 2196, Berkeley, Calif. 94704.

15. Leo Marx, *The Machine in the Garden: Technology and the Pastoral Ideal in America* (New York: Oxford University Press, 1964), p. 207.

16. Quoted in Richard Guy Wilson, "America and the Machine Age," in *The Machine Age in America*, ed. Richard Guy Wilson, Dianne H. Pilgrim, and Dickran Tashjian (New York: Harry N. Abrams, Inc., 1986), p. 24.

17. From the song "Re: Creation" by the Shamen, *Boss Drum* (Epic, 1992).

18. Thomas Hine, *Facing Tomorrow: What the Future Has Been, What the Future Can Be* (New York: Alfred A. Knopf, 1991), p. 34.

19. Donna J. Haraway, *Simians, Cyborgs, and Women: The Reinvention of Nature* (New York: Routledge, 1991), p. 153.

20. Quoted in Bryan Miller, "Got a Minute?" *New York Times*, April 24, 1994, sect. 9, p. 8.

21. *Adbusters Quarterly*, vol. 3, no. 3 (winter 1995), inside front cover.

22. Bruce Sterling (bruces), topic 1220: "AT&T's 'You Will' Campaign," in the WELL's telecommunicating conference, June 20, 1993.

23. The resident CIA analyst (amicus) aka Ross Stapleton-Gray, ibid., June 20, 1993.

24. Mitch Ratcliffe (coyote), ibid., June 25, 1993.

25. Gary Chapman, "Taming the Computer," in *Flame Wars*, p. 844.

26. Kelly is quoted in Paul Keegan, "The Digerati!" *New York Times Magazine*, May 21, 1995, p. 42; Zerzan is quoted in Kenneth R. Noble, "Prominent Anarchist Finds Unsought Ally in Serial Bomber," *New York Times*, May 7, 1995, National section, p. 24.

27. Constance Penley and Andrew Ross, "Cyborgs at Large: Interview with Donna Haraway," in *Technoculture*, ed. Constance Penley and Andrew Ross (Minneapolis: University of Minnesota Press, 1991), p. 16.

Chapter 1

1. Eric Scigliano, "Relighting the Firesign," *New York Times*, May 2, 1993, p. 11.

2. *New York Times*, April 4, 1993, p. 17.

3. "The Trip," *Details*, March 1993, p. 128.

4. Howard Fineman, "The Sixties: The GOP's New Strategy," *Newsweek,* March 25, 1991, p. 39.

5. Bruce Sterling, *The Hacker Crackdown: Law and Disorder on the Electronic Frontier* (New York: Bantam, 1992), p. 235.

6. Fractal geometry, a field of study pioneered by the mathematician Benoit Mandlebrot in the seventies, offers mathematical recipes for generating stunningly detailed images reminiscent of snowflakes, inkblots, paisleys, tree branches, coastlines, and so forth; their seeming randomness bears a striking resemblance to "many of the irregular and fragmented patterns around us," in the words of its founder. See Benoit B. Mandlebrot, "How Long is the Coast of Britain?" in *The World Treasury of Physics, Astronomy, and Mathematics,* ed. Timothy Ferris (Boston: Little, Brown and Company, 1991), pp. 447–55.

7. *Inner Technologies* catalogue, fall 1991, p. 21.

8. Smart *drugs,* many of which are controlled substances in the United States, are not be to confused with smart *drinks,* the supposedly brain-boosting blender confections served at raves. Largely a mixture of fruit juice, vitamins, amino acids, caffeine or the caffeine-like l-phenylalanine, and choline, which allegedly nourishes brain cells, the latter are far less potent.

9. Philip Elmer-Dewitt, "Cyberpunk!" *Time,* February 8, 1993, pp. 64–65.

10. Bruce Sterling, preface to *Mirrorshades: The Cyberpunk Anthology,* ed. Bruce Sterling (New York: Ace, 1988), p. xii.

11. Ibid.

12. Camille Paglia, "Ninnies, Pedants, Tyrants and Other Academics," *New York Times,* May 5, 1991, sect. 7, p. 1.

13. Jane and Michael Stern, *Sixties People* (New York: Alfred A. Knopf, 1990), pps. 164, 166.

14. Sterling, preface to *Mirrorshades,* p. xiii.

15. Theodore Roszak, *The Making of a Counter Culture* (Garden City, N.Y.: Anchor Books, 1969), p. 177.

16. James Haskins and Kathleen Benson, *The '60s Reader* (New York: Viking Kestrel, 1988), p. 163.

17. Tom Wolfe, *The Electric Kool-Aid Acid Test* (New York: Bantam, 1969), p. 145.

18. Steven Levy, *Hackers: Heroes of the Computer Revolution* (New York: Dell, 1984), p. 162.

19. Ibid., p. 156.

20. Theodore Roszak, "The Misunderstood Movement," *New York Times,* December 3, 1994, p. 23.

21. *"Playboy* Interview: Marshall McLuhan," *Playboy,* March 1969, p. 66.

22. Frank Kappler, "A Film Revolution to Blitz Man's Mind," *Life,* July 14, 1967, p. 22.

23. Wolfe, *Acid Test,* pp. 60–61.

24. Ibid., p. 123.

25. Todd Gitlin, *The Sixties: Years of Hope, Days of Rage* (New York: Bantam, 1987), p. 207.

26. Arthur C. Clarke, "The Mind of the Machine," *Playboy,* December 1968, p. 293.

27. Ibid., pp. 293–94.

28. Richard Brautigan, *Trout Fishing in America, The Pill versus the Springhill Mine Disaster; and In Watermelon Sugar* (New York: Delacorte Press, 1971), p. 1.

29. Queen Mu and R. U. Sirius, editorial, *Mondo 2000,* no. 7, fall 1989, p. 11.

30. Ibid.

31. Ibid.

32. Douglas Rushkoff, *Cyberia: Life in the Trenches of Hyperspace* (New York: HarperSanFrancisco, 1994), pp. 181–82.

33. Gitlin, *The Sixties,* p. 213.

34. Ibid., pp. 208–9.

35. Throughout this section, I look to the writings and interview comments of the magazine's publisher, Queen Mu, and the erstwhile editor-in-chief R. U. Sirius, for *Mondo*'s deeper meanings. It goes without saying, of course, that it, like all magazines, is the collective brainchild of diverse contributors, most notably its influential art director, Bart Nagel. Nonetheless, it was indelibly stamped in its formative early issues with the ideologies, attitudes, and aesthetics of Mu and Sirius; their manifestos, spoken and written, must play a prominent role in any critique of the magazine.

36. HarperPerennial catalogue, June 1992, p. 48.

37. The Firesign Theatre, "I Think We're All Bozos on This Bus," in *The Firesign Theatre's Big Book of Plays* (San Francisco: Straight Arrow Books, 1972), p. 107.

38. Queen Mu, "Bacchic Pleasures"; John Perry Barlow, "Virtual Nintendo," *Mondo 2000,* no. 5, pp. 46, 82.

39. Queen Mu, "Orpheus in the Maelstrom," *Mondo 2000,* no. 4, p. 131; Andrew Hultkrans, "The Slacker Factor: GenXploitation," *Mondo 2000,* no. 10, p. 14.

40. Queen Mu interviews herself in "Tarantismo and the Modern-Day Rock Magician," *High Frontiers,* annual, 1987; Sirius's girlfriend Sarah Drew is

profiled by Marshall McLaren in "Infinite Personalities, Multiple Orgasms, Cyborgs & Foucault," *Mondo,* no. 4; Sirius's band, Mondo Vanilli, is profiled in *Mondo,* no. 7; Doug St. Clair (aka Ivan Stang) reviews *Three Fisted Tales of Bob,* ed. Ivan Stang, in *Mondo,* no. 2; Durk Pearson and Sandy Shaw, peddlers of Designer Foods and Psychoactive Soft Drinks, were interviewed in *High Frontiers,* annual, 1987, as well as the no. 7 (fall 1989), summer 1990, winter 1991, and no. 4 issues of *Mondo,* all but two of which they advertised in. Their departure from the magazine is coincident with the disappearance of their advertising.

41. R. U. Sirius, "New World Disorder: All Is NOT One," *Mondo 2000,* no. 4, p. 9.
42. D. H. Lawrence, "A Sane Revolution," in *The Complete Poems of D.H. Lawrence,* ed. Vivian de Sola Pinto and Warren Roberts (New York: Viking Press, 1971), p. 517.
43. Vivian Sobchack, "New Age Mutant Ninja Hackers: Reading *Mondo 2000,*" *Flame Wars: The Discourse of Cyberculture / South Atlantic Quarterly,* ed. Mark Dery, vol. 92, no. 4 (fall 1993), pp. 573–74.
44. R. U. Sirius (rusirius), topic 288, "Flame Wars: The Discourse of Cyberculture by Mark Dery," in the WELL's *Mondo* conference, February 21, 1994.
45. R. U. Sirius, "The New Species Comes of Age," *High Frontiers,* no. 4, 1987, p. 6.
46. Martha Sherrill, "Virtually Unreal! A Mag for the Millennium," *Washington Post,* February 19, 1992, p. C2.
47. Richard Scheinin, "Tune In, Log On, Drop Out," *San Jose Mercury News,* May 30, 1989, p. 8F.
48. Norman Spinrad, *Science Fiction in the Real World* (Carbondale and Edwardsville, Ill.: Southern Illinois University Press, 1990), p. 133.
49. R. U. Sirius, "Upwingers: Looking for Solutions in the Solution Box," *High Frontiers,* annual, 1987, p. 26.
50. Alvin Toffler, *The Third Wave* (New York: Bantam, 1981), p. 166.
51. Wes Thomas, "NanoCyborgs," *Mondo 2000,* no. 12, 1994, p. 16.
52. R. U. Sirius, topic 22, "Flame Wars," in the WELL's Mondo conference.
53. R. U. Sirius, "Sirius' Soapbox," *High Frontiers,* annual, 1987, p. 3.
54. Hakim Bey, "Pirate Utopias and the Temporary Autonomous Zone," *Mondo 2000,* no. 5, p. 128.
55. Ibid.
56. Gracie and Zarkov, "An Acid Take on Camille Paglia," *Mondo 2000,* no. 5, p. 118.
57. William L. O'Neill, *Coming Apart: An Informal History of America in the 1960s* (New York: Times Books, 1971), p. 265.

58. Ibid., p. 240.

59. Quoted in Richard Scheinin, "Tune In"; Leslie Harlib, "Alison in Wonderland," *The Monthly,* December 1990, p. 10.

60. Catherine McEver, "Sex, Drugs & Cyberspace," *Express,* September 28, 1990, p. 12.

61. "Homo Technoeroticus," *Mondo 2000* advertising brochure.

62. Ellen Willis, "Let's Get Radical: Why Should the Right Have All the Fun?" *Village Voice,* December 20, 1994, p. 33.

63. R. U. Sirius, "Upwingers," p. 26.

64. Ibid., pp. 26–27.

65. Gitlin, *The Sixties,* p. 227.

66. Rushkoff, *Cyberia,* p. 232.

67. "Laura Fraser (phraze)," topic 266, "Future Sex–the Magazine: Feedback and Discussion," in the WELL's sex conference, June 29, 1992, and July 2, 1992.

68. Rushkoff, *Cyberia,* pp. 21, 37, 59.

69. Sigmund Freud, *Totem and Taboo* (New York: W. W. Norton, 1950), p. 87.

70. Rushkoff, *Cyberia,* p. 7.

71. All quotes this paragraph, ibid., pp. 13, 48, 61, 67, 77.

72. Ibid., p. 23.

73. Ibid., p. 5.

74. Manuel De Landa, *War in the Age of Intelligent Machines* (New York: Zone Books, 1991), p. 15.

75. Ibid., p. 7.

76. Ibid., p. 121.

77. Ibid.

78. Tom Wolfe, *Acid Test,* p. 147.

79. Quoted in Rushkoff, *Cyberia,* p. 7.

80. "*Playboy* Interview: Marshall McLuhan," p. 72.

81. Teilhard de Chardin, quoted in Stephen Toulmin, *The Return to Cosmology: Postmodern Science and the Theology of Nature* (Berkeley: University of California Press, 1982), p. 124.

82. "*Playboy* Interview: Marshall McLuhan," pp. 72, 158.

83. Pierre Teilhard de Chardin, *The Future of Man,* trans. Norman Denny (New York: Harper & Row, 1969), pp. 275–76.

84. Paul Keegan, "The Digerati!" *New York Times Magazine,* May 21, 1995, p. 42.

85. Ibid., pp. 42, 88.

86. Ibid.

87. Gary Wolf, "Don't Get Wasted, Get Smart," *Rolling Stone,* September 5, 1991, p. 60.

88. Craig Bromberg, "In Defense of Hackers," *New York Times Magazine,* April 21, 1991, p. 47.

89. Hugh Ruppersberg, "The Alien Messiah," in *Alien Zone: Cultural Theory and Contemporary Science Fiction Cinema,* ed. Annette Kuhn (New York: Verso, 1990), p. 35.

90. Rushkoff, *Cyberia,* p. 61.

91. Ibid., p. 147.

92. All quotes this paragraph, ibid., pp. 19, 172, 189, 214.

93. Walter Kirn, "Cyberjunk," *Mirabella,* June 1993, p. 24.

94. Ibid.

95. Quoted in Joe Haldeman, *Star Trek: World without End* (New York: Bantam, 1979), epigraph on opening page.

96. Quoted in Margot Adler, *Drawing Down the Moon: Witches, Druids, Goddess-Worshippers, and Other Pagans in America Today,* rev. ed. (Boston: Beacon Press, 1986), p. 368.

97. Because of their common relationship to science and technology, I have fuzzed the distinction between neopaganism and the New Age throughout this section. It should be pointed out, however, that while they share a reverence for the Earth and the spiritual beliefs of indigenous peoples or archaic civilizations, neopagans and New Agers see themselves as polar opposites, representing the earthy and the airy, the chthonic and the celestial, respectively.

98. Erik Davis, "Technopagans: May the Astral Plane Be Reborn in Cyberspace," *Wired,* July 1995, p. 128.

99. Julian Dibbell, "Cool Technology: Toys for the Mind," *Spin,* May 1991, p. 50.

100. Ibid.

101. Lurker Below (ashton), topic 316, "Thee Temple ov Psychick Youth," in the WELL's spirituality conference, December 20, 1992.

102. Neil Strauss, "Tripping the Light Ecstatic: Psychic TV & the Acid House Experience," *Option,* no. 25 (March/April 1989), p. 84.

103. Ambient Temple of Imagination, *Mystery School* (Silent Records, 1994).

104. Quoted in Matthew F. Riley, "Clock DVA: Energy Tending to Change," *Technology Works,* unnumbered, unpaginated issue.

105. Ibid.

106. Edward Rothstein, "A New Art Form May Arise from the 'Myst,' " *New York Times,* December 4, 1994, sect. 2, p. 1.

107. Erik Davis, "Into the Myst: The Miller Brothers' Virtual Tale," *Village Voice*, August 23, 1994, p. 45.

108. Ibid., p. 46.

109. Spinrad, *Science Fiction*, p. 111.

110. William Gibson, *Mona Lisa Overdrive* (New York: Bantam Spectra, 1988), p. 215.

111. William Gibson, *Count Zero* (New York: Ace Books, 1986), pp. 118–19.

112. Erik Davis, "Techgnosis: Magic, Memory, and the Angels of Information," in *Flame Wars*," p. 586.

113. Ibid.

114. Maxwell X. Delysid, E-mail to the author, December 2, 1992.

115. Charles B. Kramer, "Nazis in Cyberspace!" *BBS Callers Digest*, August 1992, p. 28.

116. Ken Kelley, "The Interview: Whole Earthling and Software Savant Stewart Brand," *SF Focus*, February 1985, p. 78.

117. Teilhard de Chardin, quoted in R. C. Zaehner, "Teilhard de Chardin" in *Man, Myth & Magic*, vol. 10, ed. Richard Cavendish (Freeport, Long Island, N.Y.: Marshall Cavendish, 1983), p. 2811.

118. *Tools for Exploration* vol. 4, no. 1 (winter/spring 1994–95), p. 55.

119. *Tools for Exploration* vol. 4, no. 2 (1993 supplement), p. 16.

120. *Tools for Exploration* vol. 4, no. 1, p. A–3.

121. Michael Hutchinson, *Mega Brain Power: Transform Your Life with Mind Machines and Brain Nutrients* (New York: Hyperion, 1994), p. 431.

122. Tony Lane, echo area 30, "Cybermage," on BaphoNet, August 7, 1991.

123. Rossell Hope Robbins, *The Encyclopedia of Witchcraft & Demonology* (New York: Bonanza Books, 1981), p. 190.

124. John Markoff, "The Fourth Law of Robotics," *Educom Review* 29, no. 2 (March/April 1994), p. 45.

125. Aga Windwalker, "Cybermage," August 9, 1992.

126. Maxwell X. Delysid, E-mail to the author, December 2, 1992.

127. Charles Neal, *Tape Delay* (Harrow, England: SAF Ltd., 1987), p. 32.

128. Constance Penley, introduction to *Close Encounters: Film, Feminism, and Science Fiction*, ed. Constance Penley, Elisabeth Lyon, Lynn Spigel, and Janet Bergstrom (Minneapolis: University of Minnesota Press, 1991), p. x.

129. Andrew Ross, *Strange Weather: Culture, Science and Technology in the Age of Limits* (New York: Verso, 1991), p. 30.

130. Godfrey Harold Hardy, "A Mathematician's Apology," in *The World Treasury of Physics, Astronomy, and Mathematics*, ed. Timothy Ferris (Boston: Little, Brown and Company, 1991), p. 439.

131. Rudy Rucker, *Mind Tools: The Five Levels of Mathematical Reality* (Boston: Houghton Mifflin, 1987), p. 223.

132. John L. Casti, *Searching for Certainty: What Scientists Can Know about the Future* (New York: William Morrow, 1990), p. 404.

133. Bruce Sterling, "Cyber-Superstition," *Science Fiction Eye*, no. 8 (winter 1991), p. 11.

134. Gary Chapman, "Taming the Computer," in *Flame Wars*, pp. 830–31, 837.

135. Joseph Campbell with Bill Moyers, *The Power of Myth* (New York: Doubleday, 1988), p. 19.

136. Ibid., p. 18.

137. Christopher Evans, *The Micro Millennium* (New York: Washington Square Press, 1979). p. 233.

138. Ibid., p. 262.

139. Tracy Kidder, *The Soul of a New Machine* (New York: Avon Books, 1981), p. 98.

140. "Is Computer Hacking a Crime?" in *The Harper's Forum Book: What Are We Talking About*, ed. Jack Hitt (New York: Citadel Press, 1991), pp. 256–57.

141. Julian Dibbell, "A Rape in Cyberspace," *Village Voice*, December 21, 1993, p. 42.

142. Farrell McGovern, "Cybermage," *Village Voice*, February 13, 1993.

143. Dibbell, "A Rape in Cyberspace," p. 42.

144. Campbell with Moyer, *The Power of Myth*, p. 214.

145. Barbara Presley Noble, "At Work: Labor-Management Rorschach Test," *New York Times*, June 5, 1994, p. 21.

146. Stuart Ewen, "Pragmatism's Postmodern Poltergeist," *New Perspectives Quarterly* 9, no. 2 (spring 1992), p. 47.

147. Robert B. Reich, "The Fracturing of the Middle Class," *New York Times*, August 31, 1994, sect. A, p. 19.

148. Dibbell, "A Rape In Cyberspace," p. 37.

149. Neil Postman, *Technopoly: The Surrender of Culture to Technology* (New York: Alfred A. Knopf, 1992), p. 71.

150. William Mook (mook), topic 30, "Techgnosis: Computers as Magic," in the WELL's Fringeware conference, January 15, 1994.

151. K. Eric Drexler, *Engines of Creation: The Coming Era of Nanotechnology* (New York: Anchor Books, 1986), p. 63.

152. Robert Pirsig, *Zen and the Art of Motorcycle Maintenance* (New York: William Morrow, 1974), p. 16.

153. Campbell with Moyer, *The Power of Myth*, pp. 19–20.

Chapter 2

1. This chapter is a distant descendant of my cover story "Cyberpunk: Riding the Shockwave with the Toxic Underground" (*Keyboard*, May 1989, pps. 75–89) and my feature "Beneath the Valley of the Ultra-Cybers: Brain-Bruising Soundtracks for Life in Robotopia" (*Keyboard*, January 1992, pp. 69–83).

2. Katie Hafner and John Markoff, *Cyberpunk: Outlaws and Hackers on the Computer Frontier* (New York: Simon & Schuster, 1991), p. 9.

3. Lewis Shiner, "Inside the Movement: Past, Present, and Future," in *Fiction 2000: Cyberpunk and the Future of Narrative*, ed. George Slusser and Tom Shippey (Athens: The University of Georgia Press, 1992), p. 19.

4. Lewis Shiner, "Confessions of an Ex-Cyberpunk," *New York Times*, January 7, 1991, p. A17.

5. Ibid.

6. *Keyboard*, February 1994, p. 3.

7. Ibid., p. 90.

8. Michael Marans, "The Next Big Thing," *Keyboard*, February 1994, p. 108.

9. Tod Machover, "Hyperinstruments: A Composer's Approach to the Evolution of Intelligent Musical Instruments," in *CyberArts: Exploring Art & Technology*, ed. Linda Jacobson (San Francisco: Miller Freeman, 1992), pp. 73–74.

10. Ibid., p. 75.

11. Louis M. Brill, "Mark Trayle: Making Space for Music," *Keyboard*, October 1992, p. 39. Trayle's CD, *Études and Bagatelles* (Artifact) is available from 1374 Francisco Street, Berkeley, Calif. 94702. E-mail: info@artifact.com.

12. Erik Davis, "Wireheads and Cybergunk," *Village Voice*, August 8, 1989, p. 72.

13. Stewart Brand, *The Media Lab: Inventing the Future at M.I.T.* (New York: Penguin, 1988), pp. 108–9.

14. Quoted in a record company biography accompanying the release of *Hack*.

15. Richard Kadrey and Larry McCaffery, "Cyberpunk 101: A Schematic Guide to Storming the Reality Studio," in *Storming the Reality Studio: A Casebook of Cyberpunk and Postmodern Fiction*, ed. Larry McCaffery (Durham, N.C.: Duke University Press, 1991), p. 28.

16. Joe Gore, "Sonic Youth," *Guitar Player*, February 1989, p. 29.

17. Jon Savage, introduction to *Re/Search 6/7: Industrial Culture Handbook*, ed. Vale (San Francisco: Re/Search, 1983), p. 5.

18. Ibid., p. 10.

19. Front Line Assembly, *Tactical Neural Implant* (Third Mind Records, 1992).

20. William Gibson, "Burning Chrome," in *Burning Chrome* (New York: Ace, 1987), p. 182.

21. Mark Dery, " 'We Are the Reality of This Cyberpunk Fantasy': Glenn Branca and Elliott Sharp in Conversation with Mark Dery," *Mondo 2000*, no. 5 (1992), pp. 70–72. This reedited excerpt differs slightly from the published version.

22. John Shirley, *Transmaniacon* (New York: Zebra Books, 1979), p. 13.

23. William Gibson, "The Winter Market," in *Burning Chrome* (New York: Ace, 1987), p. 118.

24. William Gibson, "Cyberspace '90," *Computerworld*, October 15, 1990, pp. 107–8.

25. Elliott Sharp, liner notes to Elliott Sharp/Orchestra Carbon, *Abstract Repressionism 1990–99* (Victo, 1992).

26. All quotes this paragraph: Robert R. Conroy, "For the Airwaves," *Rockpool*, November 15, 1989, page number not available; Gareth Branwyn, "Industrial Introspection: An Interview with Trent Reznor of Nine Inch Nails," *Mondo 2000*, no. 5, p. 62; Robert L. Doerschuk, "Nine Inch Nails: Trent Reznor Hits College Radio on the Head with a Tough, Sharp Solo Album," *Keyboard*, April 1990, p. 42.

27. Kimberly Carrino, "Nine Inch Nails: Gettin' Down in It with Trent Reznor," *Buzz* 6, no. 49 (December 1989), page number not available; Branwyn, "Industrial Introspection," p. 64.

28. *The Downward Spiral* (Nothing / TVT / Interscope, 1994).

29. Ibid.

30. Ibid.

31. *Pretty Hate Machine* (TVT, 1989).

32. Undated "Happiness in Slavery" press release from Formula Artist Development & Public Relations. "Happiness" is currently available only as a bootleg video, circulated among fans, but it may be included in an upcoming NIN video compilation.

33. *Broken* (TVT / Interscope, 1992).

34. Ibid.

35. Georges Bataille, *Erotism: Death and Sensuality* (San Francisco: City Lights, 1986), p. 90.

36. Moon Unit Zappa, "Trent Reznor: The Voice of Reason," *Raygun*, June/July 1994, unpaginated.

37. Samuel Butler, *Erewhon* (Penguin: New York, 1985), p. 206.

38. *Broken*.

39. Kadrey and McCaffery, "Cyberpunk 101," p. 23.

40. William Gibson, "Johnny Mnemonic" in *Burning Chrome*, p. 5.
41. William Gibson, *Neuromancer* (New York: Ace, 1984), p. 148.
42. Larry McCaffery, "An Interview with William Gibson," in *Storming the Reality Studio*, p. 265.
43. Larry McCaffery, "Introduction: The Desert of the Real," in *Storming the Reality Studio*, p. 12.
44. Bruce Sterling, preface to *Mirrorshades: The Cyberpunk Anthology*, ed. Bruce Sterling (New York: Ace, 1988), p. xiii.
45. Lewis Shiner, "Inside the Movement: Past, Present, and Future," in *Fiction 2000: Cyberpunk and the Future of Narrative*, p. 21.
46. Rudy Rucker and Peter Lamborn Wilson, "Introduction: Strange Attractor(s)," in *Semiotext(e) SF*, ed. Rudy Rucker, Peter Lamborn Wilson, and Robert Anton Wilson (Brooklyn: Autonomedia, 1989), p. 13.
47. Jude Milhon, "Coming In under the Radar," *Mondo 2000*, no. 7 (fall 1989), p. 100.
48. Ibid.
49. Takayuki Tatsumi, "Eye to Eye: An Interview with Bruce Sterling," *Science Fiction Eye* 1, no. 1 (1987), p. 33.
50. Ibid., p. 35.
51. John Shirley, "About 'Fragments of an Exploded Heart,'" in prepublication manuscript of *The Exploded Heart* (Asheville, N.C.: Eyeball Books, 1994), pagination not yet complete as of this writing.
52. Michael Moorcock, *The Final Programme*, in *The Cornelius Chronicles* (New York: Avon, 1977), p. 65.
53. Moorcock, *A Cure for Cancer*, in *The Cornelius Chronicles*, pp. 414–15.
54. Tatsumi, "Eye to Eye," p. 36.
55. John Shirley, *Transmaniacon*, p. 15.
56. Ibid., pp. 14, 33.
57. Ibid., p. 33.
58. Ibid., p. 34.
59. Ibid., p. 33.
60. Sterling, preface to *Mirrorshades*, p. xii.
61. Ibid., p. xiii.
62. Ken Tucker, "Rock in the Video Age," in *Rock of Ages: The Rolling Stone History of Rock & Roll* (New York: Summit Books, 1986), p. 595.
63. Mark Crispin Miller, "Where All the Flowers Went," in *Boxed In: The Culture of TV* (Evanston, Ill.: Northwestern University Press, 1989), p. 174.
64. Andrew Goodwin, *Dancing in the Distraction Factory: Music Television and Popular Culture* (Minneapolis: University of Minnesota Press, 1992), p. 185.

65. Miller, "Where Flowers Went," p. 181.
66. Miller, afterword to "Rock Music: A Success Story," in *Boxed In,* p. 196.
67. Miller, "Where Flowers Went," p. 181.
68. Miller, afterword to "A Success Story," p. 200.
69. Goodwin, *Distraction Factory,* pp. 154–55.
70. Sterling, preface to *Mirrorshades,* p. xii.
71. Cadigan, "Rock On," in *Mirrorshades,* p. 42.
72. Ibid., p. 39.
73. Ibid., pp. 36, 37, 42.
74. Ibid., p. 42.
75. McCaffery, "Introduction: The Desert of the Real," in *Storming the Reality Studio,* p. 6.
76. Anthony DeCurtis, *Present Tense: Rock & Roll and Culture,* ed. Anthony DeCurtis (Durham, N.C.: Duke University Press, 1992), p. 5.
77. John Shirley, "Freezone," in *Mirrorshades,* p. 148; all other quotes this paragraph, p. 145.
78. Ibid., pp. 145–46.
79. Ibid.
80. Ibid.
81. Ibid., p. 154.
82. Ibid., p. 157.
83. Ibid., p. 146.
84. Norman Spinrad, *Little Heroes* (New York: Bantam Spectra, 1987), p. 4.
85. Ibid., pp. 4, 7.
86. Ibid., p. 4.
87. Ibid., unnumbered page.
88. Ibid., p. 7.
89. Ibid., p. 8.
90. Ibid., p. 11.
91. Sterling, preface to *Mirrorshades,* p. xiv.
92. Jon Savage, *England's Dreaming: Anarchy, Sex Pistols, Punk Rock and Beyond* (New York: St. Martin's Press, 1992), p. 133.
93. Sterling, preface to *Mirrorshades,* pp. x–xi.
94. Goodwin, *Distraction Factory,* p. 31.
95. Norman Spinrad, *Science Fiction in the Real World* (Carbondale and Edwardsville, Ill: Southern Illinois University Press, 1990), pp. 113–14.
96. Ibid., p. 113.
97. Ibid., p. 116.

98. William Gibson, interviewed by Terry Gross on *Fresh Air*, National Public Radio, August 31, 1993.

Chapter 3

1. The germ of the idea for this chapter appeared as a feature, "The Art of Crash, Hum, and Hiss," in the *New York Times*, March 15, 1992, Arts & Leisure section, p. 12.
2. Rob Hafernik, "Robofest II: Austin, Texas," in *Mondo 2000*, no. 5, p. 18.
3. Glenn Rifkin, "Making Robot Gladiators," *New York Times*, July 31, 1994, p. 8F.
4. *Re/Search 6/7: Industrial Culture Handbook*, ed. Andrea Juno and V. Vale (San Francisco: Re/Search, 1983), pp. 28–29.
5. K. W. Jeter, *Dr. Adder* (New York: Signet, 1988), p. 70.
6. Marshall McLuhan, "The Gadget Lover: Narcissus as Narcosis," in *Understanding Media: The Extensions of Man* (New York: Signet, 1964), pp. 55–56.
7. Ibid., p. 56.
8. Manuel De Landa, *War in the Age of Intelligent Machines* (New York: Zone Books, 1991), p. 3.
9. *Re/Search 11: Pranks!* ed. Andrea Juno and V. Vale (San Francisco: Re/Search, 1987), p. 13.
10. Ibid.
11. Ibid., pp. 13–14.
12. It should be noted that Frankensteinish fabrications such as the Mummy-Go-Round and the Piggly-Wiggly make use of dead animals purchased from slaughterhouses or scavenged from train tunnels. The Mummy-Go-Round, for example, resulted from an amphetamine-addled friend's ravings about a macabre stretch of Pacific Railway tunnel he had stumbled on during one of his late-night rambles. Pauline and Heckert decided to investigate and returned in high spirits with a sack full of mummified animals. SRL's organic robots are featured, along with their heavy metal brethren, in an extensive selection of videotapes, available from SRL, 1458-C San Bruno Ave., San Francisco, Calif. 94110.
13. Howard Rheingold, *Virtual Reality* (New York: Summit Books, 1991), pp. 254–55.
14. John A. Barry, *Technobabble* (Cambridge, Mass.: MIT Press, 1991), p. 185.
15. John R. MacArthur, *Second Front: Censorship and Propaganda in the Gulf War* (New York: Hill & Wang, 1992), p. 161.

16. Quoted by Judith A. Adams, in *The American Amusement Park Industry: A History of Technology and Thrills* (Boston: Twayne Publishers, 1991), p. 93.

17. Howard Millman, "Risky Business," *Compute,* July 1991, p. 88.

18. Margaret Cheney, *Tesla: Man Out of Time* (New York: Dell, 1981), p. 129. See illustrations as well.

19. Quoted by Frank Barnaby, in *The Automated Battlefield* (New York: The Free Press, 1986), p. 1.

20. Quoted by Lewis Yablonsky, in *Robopaths: People as Machines* (Baltimore, Md.: Penguin, 1972), p. xii.

21. Georges Bataille, *Erotism: Death and Sensuality* (San Francisco: City Lights, 1986), p. 15.

22. Claudia Springer, "Sex, Memories and Angry Women," *Flame Wars: The Discourse of Cyberculture / South Atlantic Quarterly,* vol. 92, no. 4 (fall 1993), p. 718.

23. William Burroughs, *The Ticket That Exploded* (New York: Grove Press, 1968), p. 52.

24. Ibid., p. 53.

25. Bataille, *Erotism,* p. 18.

26. Georges Bataille, "Sacrificial Mutilation and the Severed Ear of Vincent Van Gogh," in *Visions of Excess: Selected Writings of Georges Bataille,* ed. Allan Stoekl (Minneapolis: University of Minnesota Press, 1985), p. 70.

27. Seymour Melman, "The Juggernaut: Military State Capitalism," *The Nation* 252, no. 19 (May 20, 1991), p. 666.

28. Kathe Burkhart, "Extremely Cool Practices," *High Performance,* no. 32, pp. 66–67.

29. Elizabeth Richardson, "The Mechanisms of Machismo," *Artweek* 16, no. 30 (September 21, 1985), p. 4.

30. Jim Pomeroy, "Black Box S-Thetix: Labor, Research, and Survival in the He[Art] of the Beast," in *Technoculture,* ed. Constance Penley and Andrew Ross (Minneapolis: University of Minnesota Press, 1991), pp. 292–93.

31. This debt, while acknowledged, has never been repaid, notes Pauline. "The creators of *Hardware* made no attempt to contact me for permission to use the SRL video footage featured in the film and refused to make any payment after the film's release," he writes, in an August 31, 1993, fax to the author. "When pressed, Miramax, the film's U.S. distributor, threatened a lengthy and expensive legal battle which, due to my lack of a Swiss bank account, I declined to engage in."

32. Yablonsky, *Robopaths,* p. 7.

33. Guy Trebay, "Machine Dreams: Survival Research Laboratories' Heavy Metal," *Village Voice*, May 24, 1988, p. 20.

34. Calvin Ahlgren, "Robot Olympics Gets Down to Nuts and Bolts: Performance Artist Puts Iron Men on Display," *San Francisco Chronicle*, September 10, 1989, p. 28.

35. Harry Moss, "The Adventures of a Metalman: Robots Take Over the Palace," *The City*, October 1990, p. 29.

36. An early draft of Rex Everything's "*Negativland Presents the Rex Everything Guides, Vol. 1: Disneyland*" (forthcoming from Concord, Calif.: Seeland Media) proved an invaluable, not to mention hilarious, resource in the writing of this section.

37. Michel Foucault, *Discipline and Punish: The Birth of the Prison* (New York: Vintage, 1979), p. 136.

38. Ibid.

39. Samuel Haber, *Efficiency and Uplift*, quoted in Stuart Ewen, *Captains of Consciousness* (New York: McGraw-Hill, 1976), pp. 105–6.

40. Feature article, *Tri-City Labor Review* (Rock Island, Ill., April 13, 1932), quoted in Ewen, *Captains of Consciousness*, p. 11.

41. Quoted in Ellen Lupton and J. Abbott Miller, "Hygiene, Cuisine and the Product World of Early Twentieth-Century America," in *Zone 6: Incorporations*, ed. Jonathan Crary and Sanford Kwinter (New York: Zone, 1992), p. 504.

42. Ewen, *Captains of Consciousness*, p. 19.

43. Mike Kelley, "Mekanik Destruktiv Kommandoh: Survival Research Laboratories and Popular Spectacle," *Parkett*, no. 22 (September 1989), p. 127.

44. Ibid.

45. Scott Bukatman, "There's Always Tomorrowland: Disney and the Hypercinematic Experience," *October*, no. 57 (summer 1991), pp. 63–64.

46. Isaac Asimov, *The Rest of the Robots* (New York: Pyramid Books, 1964), p. 11.

47. Frederik L. Schodt, *Inside the Robot Kingdom: Japan, Mechatronics, and the Coming Robotopia* (New York: Kodansha, 1988), p. 163.

48. John G. Fuller, "Death By Robot," *Omni*, March 1984, p. 102.

49. Andrew Ross, *Strange Weather: Culture, Science and Technology in the Age of Limits* (New York: Verso, 1991), p. 95.

50. Jon Palfreman and Doron Swade, *The Dream Machine: Exploring the Computer Age* (London: BBC Books, 1991), pp. 179–80.

51. Umberto Eco, *Travels in Hyperreality* (New York: Harcourt Brace Jovanovich, 1986), pp. 47–48.

52. Mark Pauline, "Technology and the Irrational," in *Ars Electronica / BandII / Virtuelle Welten,* ed. Gottfried Hattinger, Morgan Russell, Christine Schopf, Peter Weibel (Linz, Austria: Ars Electronica Festival for Art, Technology and Society, 1990), p. 232.

53. Kevin Kelly, *Out of Control: The Rise of Neo-Biological Civilization* (Reading, Mass.: Addison-Wesley, 1994), p. 32.

54. Quoted in Rex Everything, "Disneyland," p. 115.

55. Judith A. Adams, *Amusement Park,* p. 45.

56. Jane Kuenz, "It's a Small World After All: Disney and the Pleasures of Identification," *The World According to Disney / South Atlantic Quarterly,* ed. Susan Willis, vol. 92, no. 1 (winter 1993), p. 71.

57. Adams, *Amusement Park,* p. 56.

58. Mark Pauline, in the unpublished introduction to his press packet.

Chapter 4

1. Bruce Sterling, *Crystal Express* (New York: Ace Books, 1990), p. 25.

2. Quoted from an archival videotape of Stelarc's lecture "Remote Gestures / Obsolute Desires," at the Kitchen Center for Video, Music, Dance, Performance, Film and Literature, New York, March 9, 1993.

3. Marshall McLuhan and Quentin Fiore, *The Medium Is the Massage: An Inventory of Effects* (New York: Bantam, 1967), p. 41.

4. Stelarc, "Strategies and Trajectories," *Obsolete Body / Suspensions / Stelarc,* ed. James D. Paffrath with Stelarc (Davis, Calif.: JP Publications, 1984), p. 76.

5. J. E. Cirlot, *A Dictionary of Symbols,* trans. Jack Sage, 2d ed. (New York: Dorset Press, 1971), p. 199.

6. John Shirley, "SF Alternatives, Part One: Stelarc and the New Reality," *Science Fiction Eye* 1, no. 2 (August 1987), pp. 57, 61.

7. Ibid., p. 59.

8. Stelarc, "Beyond the Body: Amplified Body, Laser Eyes & Third Hand," undated essay accompanying a performance at the Yokohama International School in Japan, p. 28.

9. Stelarc, press release for a performance of "Remote Gestures/Obsolete Desires: Event for Amplified Body, Involuntary Arm, and Third Hand" at the Kitchen, New York, March 12 and 13, 1993.

10. Simon Bainbridge, "The Body Is Obsolete," *The Crack*, no. 30 (December 1991), p. 75.

11. Quoted in Linda Frye Burnham, "Performance Art in Southern California: An Overview," in *Performance Anthology: Sourcebook for a Decade of California Performance Art*, ed. Carl E. Loeffler and Darlene Tong (San Francisco: Contemporary Arts Press, 1980), p. 399.

12. Thomas McEvilley, "Redirecting the Gaze," in *Making Their Mark: Women Artists Move into the Mainstream, 1970–85*, ed. Randy Rosen and Catherine C. Brawer (New York: Abbeville Press, 1989), p. 193.

13. Quoted in Judith E. Stein, "Making Their Mark," p. 134.

14. Interviewed in *Re/Search 13: Angry Women* (San Francisco: Re/Search, 1991), p. 77.

15. Quoted in Paul McCarthy, "The Body Obsolete," *High Performance*, no. 24 (1983), p. 18.

16. "*Playboy* Interviewed: Marshall McLuhan," March 1969, p. 74.

17. McLuhan and Fiore, *Medium Is the Massage*, pp. 26–39.

18. Marshall McLuhan, *Understanding Media: The Extensions of Man* (New York: Signet, 1964), p. 52.

19. Ibid., p. 53.

20. Stelarc, "Prosthetics, Robotics and Remote Existence: Postevolutionary Strategies," *Leonardo* 24, no. 5 (1991), pp. 591, 594.

21. Stelarc, "Redesigning the Human Body," an essay delivered at the Stanford University conference on design, July 21–23, 1983.

22. Stelarc, "Prosthetics, Robotics and Remote Existence," p. 591.

23. Ibid.

24. Stelarc, "Redesigning the Body," *Whole Earth Review*, summer 1989, p. 21.

25. Ibid.

26. Stelarc, "Prosthetics, Robotics and Remote Existence," p. 594.

27. Ibid., p. 593.

28. Sterling, "Cicada Queen," *Crystal Express*, p. 76.

29. Stelarc, fax to the author, December 1, 1993.

30. Stelarc, "Prosthetics, Robotics and Remote Existence," p. 594.

31. Stelarc, Kitchen videotape, March 9, 1993.

32. "*Playboy* Interview: Marshall McLuhan," p. 66; Stelarc, "Prosthetics, Robotics and Remote Existence," p. 594.

33. Stelarc, "Prosthetics, Robotics and Remote Existence," p. 594.

34. McLuhan, *Understanding Media*, p. 56.

35. Stelarc, "Prosthetics, Robotics and Remote Existence," p. 593.

36. Stelarc, "Redesigning the Body," p. 21.

37. Michel Foucault, *Discipline and Punish: The Birth of the Prison,* trans. Alan
    Sheridan (New York: Vintage, 1979), p. 136.
38. Stelarc, "Prosthetics, Robotics and Remote Existence," p. 594.
39. All quotes in this paragraph are from Stelarc's fax to the author, December 1, 1993.
40. Ibid.
41. Claudia Springer, "Sex, Memories, Angry Women," *Flame Wars: The Discourse
    of Cyberculture / South Atlantic Quarterly,* ed. Mark Dery, vol. 92, no. 4, (fall
    1993), p. 714.
42. Stelarc, "The Myth of Information," *Obsolete Body / Suspensions / Stelarc,* p. 24.
43. Stelarc, "Detached Breath/Spinning Retina," *High Performance,* nos. 41–42,
    (spring/summer 1988), p. 70.
44. Kristine Ambrosia and Joseph Lanz, "Fakir Musafar Interview," in *Apoca-
    lypse Culture,* ed. Adam Parfrey (New York: Amok Press, 1987), p. 111.
45. Ibid., p. 114.
46. Stelarc, "Triggering an Evolutionary Dialectic," in *Obsolete Body / Suspen-
    sions / Stelarc,* p. 52; McLuhan, *Understanding Media,* p. 19.
47. *Obsolete Body / Suspensions / Stelarc,* p. 71.
48. "*Playboy* Interview: Marshall McLuhan," p. 59.
49. McLuhan and Fiore, *The Medium Is the Massage,* pps. 63, 114.
50. Stelarc, fax to the author, December 1, 1993.
51. Mircea Eliade, *The Sacred & the Profane: The Nature of Religion* (New York:
    Harcourt, Brace and World, 1959), p. 207.
52. Stelarc, "Prosthetics, Robotics and Remote Existence," p. 591; Mircea Eliade,
    The Sacred & the Profane, pp. 118–19.
53. Roland Barthes, *Mythologies,* trans. Annette Lavers (New York: Noonday Press,
    1972), p. 72. The italics are mine.
54. Ibid.
55. Ibid.
56. Ibid.
57. Interview with D. A. Therrien, "Man in the Machine," *Nomad,* no. 4 (spring
    1993), pp. 3–4.
58. Arthur Kroker, *Spasm: Virtual Reality, Android Music and Electric Flesh* (New
    York: St. Martin's, 1993), p. 113.
59. Interview with D. A. Therrien, p. 8.
60. Ibid., p. 7.
61. Rossell Hope Robbins, *The Encyclopedia of Witchcraft & Demonology* (New York:
    Bonanza Books, 1981), pp. 57, 497, 509.
62. Ibid., p. 135.

63. *Catholic 1993 Almanac* (Huntington, Ind.: Our Sunday Visitor Publishing Corp., 1993), p. 313.

64. J. G. Ballard, introduction to the French edition of *Crash* (New York: Vintage, 1985), pp. 1, 4–5.

65. Ibid., p. 6.

66. Andrew Sinclair, *Francis Bacon: His Life & Violent Times* (New York: Crown, 1993), p. 134.

67. Ibid., p. 315.

68. Martin Kemp, *Leonardo da Vinci: The Marvelous Works of Nature and Man* (Cambridge: Harvard University Press, 1981), p. 115.

69. Gavin Stamp, quoted in Arnold Pacey, *The Culture of Technology* (Cambridge: MIT Press, 1983), p. 88.

Chapter 5

1. I owe the title of this chapter to a J. G. Ballard aphorism quoted in *Re/Search 8/9: J. G. Ballard* (San Francisco: Re/Search, 1984), p. 164. I first explored the ideas that gave rise to this chapter in "Sex Machine, Machine Sex—Mechano-Eroticism and RoboCopulation," *Mondo 2000*, no. 5 (1992), which was reprinted in *Mondo 2000: A User's Guide to the New Edge* (New York: HarperPerennial, 1992).

2. Marcel Jean, *The History of Surrealist Painting* (New York: Grove Press, 1960), p. 98.

3. Marshall McLuhan, "Love-Goddess Assembly Line," in *The Mechanical Bride: Folklore of Industrial Man* (Boston: Beacon Press, 1967), p. 94.

4. Ibid.

5. Ibid., p. 96.

6. Ibid., p. 94.

7. Ibid., p. 98.

8. Ibid., p. 100.

9. *Cyborgasm* press release, April 1993.

10. Quoted by Simon Frith in *Sound Effects: Youth, Leisure, and the Politics of Rock 'n' Roll* (New York: Pantheon, 1981), p. 243.

11. Chris Hudak, "Head from a Binaural Dummy: 3D-CD 'Virtual Reality' Erotica," *Mondo 2000*, no. 11, p. 124.

12. Rudy Rucker, *Mind Tools: The Five Levels of Mathematical Reality* (Boston: Houghton Mifflin, 1987), p. 287.

13. Henry Adams, "The Dynamo and the Virgin," in *The Education of Henry Adams* (New York: Vintage, 1990), p. 356.

14. MacKnight Black, *Machinery* (New York: Horace Liveright, 1929), p. 15.

15. Robert Short, *Dada & Surrealism* (Secaucus, N.J.: Chartwell Books, 1980), p. 27.

16. Quoted in Short, *Dada & Surrealism,* p. 27.

17. Tellingly, the painting makes a cameo appearance in William Gibson's *Neuromancer* (New York, Ace, 1984) a novel in which a woman's beauty is described in decidedly mechano-erotic terms, "the sweep of a flank defined with the functional elegance of a war plane's fuselage," p. 44.

18. Stephen Bayley, *Sex, Drink and Fast Cars* (New York: Pantheon, 1986), p. 22.

19. Ibid., p. 34.

20. e. e. cummings, *100 Selected Poems* (New York: Grove Press, 1959), p. 24.

21. Quoted by James Mackintosh in "An Ode to Cyborgs," *Adbusters* 2, no. 2 (summer/fall 1992), p. 12.

22. Ibid, p. 13.

23. J. G. Ballard, *Crash* (New York: Farrar, Straus & Giroux, 1973), p. 8.

24. Jean Baudrillard, "Two Essays," in *Science-Fiction Studies* 18, no. 55, part 3 (November 1991), p. 313.

25. Ballard, *Crash,* p. 74.

26. Ibid., pp. 99–100.

27. Ibid., pp. 12, 41.

28. Quoted in *Re/Search 8/9,* p. 157.

29. Michael Crichton, *Westworld* (New York: Bantam, 1974), p. 66.

30. John Cohen, *Human Robots in Myth and Science* (Cranbury, N.J.: A. S. Barnes, 1967), p. 66.

31. K. W. Jeter, *Dr. Adder* (New York: Signet, 1984), pp. 169–70.

32. Ibid., p. 172.

33. Charles Bukowski, "The Fuck Machine," in *Erections, Ejaculations, Exhibitions and General Tales of Ordinary Madness* (San Francisco: City Lights, 1977), p. 44.

34. Ibid., p. 43.

35. Ibid., p. 46.

36. Ibid., p. 45.

37. Terry Eagleton, *Literary Theory: An Introduction* (Minneapolis: University of Minnesota Press, 1983), pp. 164–65.

38. Jacques Lacan, "The Mirror Stage as Formative of the Function of the I as Revealed in Psychoanalytic Experience," in *Ecrits: A Selection* (New York: W. W. Norton, 1977), pp. 2–3.

39. Sigmund Freud, "The 'Uncanny,'" *On Creativity and the Unconscious* (New York: Harper & Row, 1958), p. 143; Jean Baudrillard, "The Orders of Simulacra," *Simulations,* trans. Paul Foss, Paul Patton, and Philip Beitchman (New York: Semiotext(e), 1983), p. 153.

40. Jean Villiers de l'Isle-Adam, *The Future Eve,* quoted by Raymond Bellour in "Ideal Hadaly," in *Close Encounters: Film, Feminism, and Science Fiction,* ed. Constance Penley, Elisabeth Lyon, Lynn Spigel, and Janet Bergstrom (Minneapolis: University of Minnesota Press, 1991), p. 111.

41. Ibid., p. 110.

42. Ibid., p. 115.

43. Steven Levy, *Hackers: Heroes of the Computer Revolution* (New York: Dell, 1984), p. 220.

44. St. Jude, "Woman's Home Companion," *Mondo 2000,* no. 8 (1992), p. 43.

45. Both messages were posted in WELL topic 281, "What Do Humans Really Want from their CYBORG LOVE SLAVES???" on August 8, 1992.

46. Arthur Harkins, quoted in *Whole Earth Review,* no. 63 (summer 1989), p. 17.

47. Gareth Branwyn, "Compu-Sex: Erotica for Cybernauts," *Flame Wars: The Discourse of Cyberculture / South Atlantic Quarterly,* ed. Mark Dery, vol. 92, no. 4 (fall 1993), p. 786.

48. Never Could Leave WELL Enough Alone (susanf), topic 265, "Text Sex," in the WELL's sex conference, July 15, 1992.

49. Ibid., Victor Lukas (lukas), July 11, 1992.

50. Ibid., Gareth Branwyn (gareth), July 13, 1992.

51. Linda Hardesty, topic 299: "Sex in Virtual Communities," in the WELL's sex conference, September 24, 1992.

52. Ibid., Afterhours (gail), September 25, 1992.

53. Ibid., Attractive Nuisance (axon) aka Alan L. Chamberlain, September 25, 1992.

54. *Online Access,* June 1993, p. 92.

55. Frank Browning, *The Culture of Desire: Paradox and Perversity in Gay Lives Today* (New York: Crown Publishers, Inc., 1993), p. 201.

56. Tim Oren, in a private E-mail message to the author, August 17, 1993.

57. Howard Rheingold, *The Virtual Community: Homesteading on the Electronic Frontier* (Reading, Mass.: Addison-Wesley, 1993), p. 150.

58. Anne Balsamo, "Feminism for the Incurably Informed," *Flame Wars: The Discourse of Cyberculture / South Atlantic Quarterly,* ed. Mark Dery, vol. 92, no. 4 (fall 1993), p. 695.

59. Julian Dibbell, "A Rape in Cyberspace," *Village Voice,* December 21, 1993, p. 38.

60. Jerod Pore (jerod23), topic 278, "Kiddie Porn, on America Online?" on the WELL, December 20, 1991.

61. "Computer Porn," *Time,* March 15, 1993, p. 22.

62. Peter H. Lewis, "New Concerns Raised over a Computer Smut Study," *New York Times,* July 16, 1995, National section, p. 22.

63. Brock N. Meeks, *CyberWire Dispatch,* July 5, 1995. E-mailed to the author on the WELL.

64. Tau Zero (tauzero), topic 299, "Sex in virtual communities," on the WELL, March 6, 1993.

65. Suzanne Stefanac, "Sex & the New Media," *New Media,* April 1993, p. 40.

66. Jeff Milstead and Jude Milhon, "The Carpal Tunnel of Love: Virtual Sex with Mike Saenz," *Mondo 2000,* no. 4, p. 143.

67. "Cyberpunk," Philip Elmer-Dewitt and David S. Jackson, *Time,* February 8, 1993, p. 64.

68. Though popularized by Rheingold, the term "teledildonics" was coined by the computer visionary Ted Nelson.

69. Howard Rheingold, *Virtual Reality* (New York: Summit Books, 1991), p. 346.

70. Ibid.

71. Pat Cadigan, *Synners* (New York: Bantam Spectra, 1991), p. 140.

72. Lisa Palac, "The Sugar Daddy of Sexware," *Future Sex,* no. 2, p. 26.

73. Posted by Adam Peake in topic 19, "Dildonics II," in the WELL's *Mondo 2000* conference, October 28, 1991; this was originally posted on the Internet newsgroup alt.cyberpunk, October 23, 1991, by Uutis Ankka on behalf of Pekka Tolonen.

74. Ibid.

75. Rheingold, *Virtual Reality,* p. 347.

76. David Aaron Clark, "Test-Dicking the Force-Feedback Vagina with William Gibson," *Future Sex,* no. 4, p. 24.

77. Spiros Antonopulos and Andrea Barnett, "Brenda Laurel: Talking about That Very Chrome, Way-Dangerous, White-Man Interface," *bOING-bOING,* no. 10, p. 12.

78. Eric Hunting, fax to the author, November 12, 1993.

79. Eric Hunting, "A Discussion of a Cyberporn Device," posted by Paul Lenoue (palenoue), topic 19, Dildonics II, July 11, 1991.

80. *Mondo 2000: A User's Guide to the New Edge* (New York: HarperPerennial, 1992), p. 272.

81. Quoted by Peggy Orenstein in "Get a Cyberlife," *Mother Jones,* May/June 1991, p. 63.

82. John Tierney, "Porn, the Low-Slung Engine of Progress," *New York Times*, January 9, 1994, section 2, p. 18.

83. Peter H. Lewis, "Multimedia (Especially the X-Rated) Stars at Comdex," *New York Times*, November 21, 1993, p. 12F.

84. Tierney, "Porn," p. 18.

85. Milstead and Milhon, "Carpal Tunnel of Love", p. 145.

86. Lawrence K. Altman, "At AIDS Talks, Science Confronts Daunting Maze," *New York Times*, June 6, 1993, p. 20.

87. "Aids Is Top Killer among Young Men," *New York Times*, October 31, 1993, p. L19.

88. Carys Bowen-Jones, "Hi-Tech Sex," *Marie Claire*, April 1993, p. 24.

89. Steven Levy, *Hackers: Heroes of the Computer Revolution* (New York: Dell, 1984), p. 83.

90. Rosemarie Robotham, "Robopsychology," *Omni*, November 1988, p. 44.

91. Ibid.

92. Tracy Kidder, *The Soul of a New Machine* (New York: Avon, 1981), p. 96.

93. Geoff Simons, "The Biology of Computer Life," in *Questioning Technology: Tool, Toy or Tyrant?* ed. John Zerzan and Alice Carnes (Santa Cruz, Calif.: New Society Publishers, 1991), pp. 119–20.

94. Cited by John A. Barry in *Technobabble* (Cambridge: MIT Press, 1991), p. 146.

95. Levy, *Hackers*.

96. Patty Bell and Doug Myrland, *Silicon Valley Guy Handbook* (New York: Avon Books, 1983), passim.

97. John A. Barry, *Technobabble*, p. 123.

98. Levy, *Hackers*, p. 18.

99. Ibid., p. 126.

100. Harvey B. Milkman and Stanley G. Sunderwirth, *Craving for Ecstasy: The Consciousness and Chemistry of Escape* (Lexington, Mass.: Lexington Books, 1987), p. 133. I am grateful to Douglas Trainor, whose post in the WELL's "Computers and Drugs" topic brought this arcane reference to my attention.

101. "*Playboy* Interview: Marshall McLuhan," March 1969, p. 65.

102. Ibid.

103. Susie Bright, *Susie Bright's Sexual Reality: A Virtual Sex World Reader* (Pittsburgh: Cleis Press, 1992), p. 67.

104. Marilyn French, *The War Against Women* (New York: Summit, 1992), p. 159.

105. *Re/Search 13: Angry Women* (San Francisco: Re/Search, 1991), p. 77.

106. Joseph D. Younger, "Novelist Tom Clancy, American Dreamer," *Amtrak Express,* November/December, 1992, p. 35.

107. Cited in James Ledbetter, "Deadlines in the Sand: How the Pentagon Ambushed the Press," *Village Voice,* February 5, 1991, p. 31.

108. John J. O'Connor, "Labeling Prime-Time Violence Is Still a Band-Aid Solution," *New York Times,* July 11, 1993, section 2, p. 1.

109. Quoted by Edwin Diamond, in *Sign Off: The Last Days of Television* (Cambridge: MIT Press, 1982), p. 47. The judgment rendered by Roberts is, admittedly, over a decade old, but a casual graze around the daytime dial will confirm that it is as accurate now as then.

110. Laura Miller (lauram), topic 266: "*Future Sex*—the Magazine: Feedback and Discussion," in the WELL's sex conference, July 4, 1992.

111. Rheingold, *Virtual Reality,* p. 350.

112. Ballard, *Crash,* p. 16.

Chapter 6

1. Earlier, far less evolved versions of this chapter were rehearsed in *Mondo 2000* and the *South Atlantic Quarterly,* and in lectures given at Youngstown (Ohio) State University and the Dia Foundation in New York.

2. Ovid, *Ovid's Metamorphoses,* trans. Rolphe Humphries (Bloomington: Indiana University Press, 1955), p. 3.

3. David F. Channell, *The Vital Machine: A Study of Technology and Organic Life* (New York: Oxford University Press, 1991), p. 129.

4. John Harris, *Wonderwoman and Superman: The Ethics of Human Biotechnology* (New York: Oxford University Press, 1992), pp. 1–2.

5. Gretchen Edgren, "The Transformation of Tula: The Extraordinary Story of a Beautiful Woman Who Was Born a Boy," *Playboy* 38, no. 9 (September 1991), p. 105.

6. William D. Marbach, "Building the Bionic Man," *Newsweek,* July 12, 1982, p. 79.

7. Thomas Hine, *Facing Tomorrow: What the Future Has Been, What the Future Can Be* (New York: Knopf, 1991), pp. 230–31.

8. Digby Diehl, "NeXTWORLD Interview: Alvin and Heidi Toffler," *NeXT-WORLD,* March/April, 1991, p. 14.

9. Anthony Robbins, *Awaken the Giant Within: How to Take Immediate Control of Your Mental, Emotional, Physical & Financial Destiny!* (New York: Summit Books, 1991), pp. 120–21.

10. Ibid., p. 127.

11. Andrew Kimbrell, "Body Wars: Can the Human Spirit Survive the Age of Technology?" *Utne Reader*, May/June, 1992, p. 60.

12. Ibid., p. 62.

13. Anthony Beadie, "Body-Parts Black Market on Rise, Film Says," *Arizona Republic*, November 12, 1993, p. A1.

14. Ibid.

15. Barbara Ehrenreich, "Why Don't We Like the Human Body?" *Time*, July 1, 1991, p. 80.

16. Ibid.

17. J. G. Ballard, "Project for a Glossary of the Twentieth Century," *Zone 6: Incorporations* (New York: Urzone, 1992), p. 269.

18. Linda Hasselstrom, "A Real Workout: Our Bodies Are Designed for More Than Pushing Pencils," *Utne Reader*, May/June 1992, p. 63.

19. Bruce Sterling, *Crystal Express* (New York: Ace, 1990), p. 30.

20. Ibid.

21. Ibid.

22. Laurie Anderson, *Words in Reverse* (Buffalo, N.Y.: Top Stories, 1979), unnumbered page.

23. Ballard, "Project for a Glossary."

24. Quoted in *Cronenberg on Cronenberg*, ed. Chris Rodley (Boston: Faber and Faber, 1992), p. 80.

25. Northrop Frye, *The Great Code: The Bible and Literature* (New York: Harcourt Brace Jovanovich, 1982), p. 19.

26. Rodley, ed., *Cronenberg on Cronenberg*, p. 79.

27. Bruce Mazlish, *The Fourth Discontinuity: The Co-Evolution of Humans and Machines* (New Haven, Conn.: Yale University Press, 1993), p. 218.

28. Jeffrey Meyers, *D. H. Lawrence* (New York: Alfred A. Knopf, 1990), pp. 105, 363.

29. Hans Moravec, *Mind Children: The Future of Robot and Human Intelligence* (Cambridge: Harvard University Press, 1988), p. 4.

30. Transcript of *Nova* program, "Killing Machines," originally broadcast on PBS November 13, 1990, p. 12.

31. R. W. Apple, Jr., "U.S. Jets over Iraq Attack Own Helicopters in Error; All 26 on Board Killed," *New York Times*, April 15, 1994, p. A12.

32. Quoted in Anne Balsamo, "Feminism and Cultural Studies," *Journal of the Midwest Modern Language Association* 24, no. 1 (spring 1991), p. 64.

33. Ibid., p. 63.

34. Leonard Cohen, *Stranger Music: Selected Poems and Songs* (New York: Pantheon, 1993), p. 97.

35. Stuart and Elizabeth Ewen, *Channels of Desire: Mass Images and the Shaping of American Consciousness* (Minneapolis: University of Minnesota Press, 1992), p. 99.

36. Stuart Ewen, *Captains of Consciousness: Advertising and the Social Roots of the Consumer Culture* (New York: McGraw-Hill, 1976), p. 180.

37. Naomi Wolf, *The Beauty Myth: How Images of Beauty Are Used against Women* (New York: William Morrow, 1991), pp. 82–83.

38. Stuart Ewen, *All Consuming Images: The Politics of Style in Contemporary Culture* (New York: Basic Books, 1988), p. 91.

39. Quoted in *Panic Encyclopedia*, ed. Arthur Kroker, Marilouise Kroker, and David Cook (New York: St. Martin's Press, 1989), p. 186.

40. "Brian D'Amato Talks about Art, Writing, and *Beauty*," undated, unpaginated Delacorte press release.

41. Margalit Fox, "A Portrait in Skin and Bone," *New York Times*, November 21, 1993, p. 8.

42. Barbara Rose, "Is It Art? Orlan and the Transgressive Act," *Art in America*, February 1993, p. 86; James Gardner, *Culture or Trash?* (New York: Birch Lane Press, 1993), p. 171.

43. Orlan, undated letter to the author, 1994.

44. Ibid.

45. Wolf, *Beauty Myth*, pp. 266–67.

46. M. G. Lord, *Forever Barbie: The Unauthorized Biography of a Real Doll* (New York: William Morrow, 1994), p. 244.

47. Ibid., pp. 244, 251.

48. Wolf, *Beauty Myth*, p. 267.

49. Ibid., p. 269.

50. The title is borrowed from Donna Haraway's essay "The Promises of Monsters: A Regenerative Politics for Inappropriate/d Others," in *Cultural Studies*, ed. Lawrence Grossberg et al. (New York: Routledge, 1991).

51. Claudia Springer, "Muscular Circuitry: The Invincible Armored Cyborg in Cinema," *Genders* 18 (winter 1993), pp. 95–96.

52. Scott Bukatman, *Terminal Identity: The Virtual Subject in Postmodern Science Fiction* (Durham, N.C.: Duke University Press, 1993), p. 20.

53. Donna J. Haraway, *Simians, Cyborgs, and Women: The Reinvention of Nature* (New York: Routledge, 1991), p. 150. The italics are mine.

54. Ibid., pp. 151, 173.

350   Notes

55. Ibid., pp. 150, 161, 164.

56. Ibid., p. 152.

57. Ibid., p. 174.

58. Ibid., p. 157.

59. Ibid., p. 162.

60. Ibid., pp. 165, 181.

61. J. G. Ballard, *Crash* (New York: Vintage, 1985), pp. 3–4.

62. Joan Howe, "Housebound," *Questioning Technology: Tool, Toy or Tyrant?* ed. John Zerzan and Alice Carnes (Philadelphia: New Society Publishers, 1991), p. 103.

63. Haraway, *Simians, Cyborgs, and Women*, p. 181.

64. Anne Balsamo, "Feminism and Cultural Studies," p. 65.

65. Haraway, *Simians, Cyborgs, and Women*, p. 151.

66. Arthur Kroker, *Spasm: Virtual Reality, Android Music, Electric Flesh* (New York: St. Martin's, 1993), p. 26.

67. Haraway, *Simians, Cyborgs, and Women*, p. 150.

68. Kroker, *Spasm*.

69. Bukatman, *Terminal Identity*, p. 247.

70. David Skal, *Antibodies* (New York: Worldwide Library, 1988), p. 25.

71. (jcourte), topic "Flame Box," on the WELL, February 13, 1993.

72. *Mondo 2000: A User's Guide to the New Edge*, ed. Rudy Rucker, R. U. Sirius, and Queen Mu (New York: HarperCollins, 1992), p. 170.

73. William Gibson, interviewed by Terry Gross on *Fresh Air*, National Public Radio, August 31, 1993.

74. Meyers, *D. H. Lawrence*, p. 103.

75. William Gibson, *Neuromancer* (New York: Ace, 1984), p. 5.

76. Ibid., pp. 5, 51.

77. Ibid., p. 6.

78. Ibid., p. 21.

79. Ibid., p. 10.

80. Ibid., p. 203.

81. Kimbrell, "Body Wars," p. 61.

82. W. David Kubiak, "E Pluribus Yamato: The Culture of Corporate Beings," *Whole Earth Review*, no 69 (winter 1990), p. 6.

83. Gibson, *Neuromancer*, pp. 4, 12, 14, 21, 97.

84. Ibid., p. 46.

85. Ibid., p. 258.

86. Ibid., p. 256.

87. Andrew Ross, *Strange Weather: Culture, Science and Technology in the Age of Limits* (New York: Verso, 1991), p. 150.

88. Ibid., p. 25.

89. Pat Cadigan, *Synners* (New York: Bantam, 1991), p. 232.

90. Cadigan, *Synners*, p. 283; William Burroughs, introduction to *Naked Lunch* (New York: Grove Press, 1966), p. xli.

91. Cadigan, *Synners*, pp. 253–54.

92. Ibid., p. 331.

93. Ibid., p. 234.

94. Ibid., p. 232.

95. Ibid., p. 235.

96. Joseph Campbell with Bill Moyers, *The Power of Myth* (New York: Doubleday, 1988), p. 211.

97. Norman Spinrad, "On Books: Virtual People," *Isaac Asimov's Science Fiction Magazine,* mid-December 1991, p. 171.

98. Anne Balsamo, "Feminism for the Incurably Informed," *Flame Wars: The Discourse of Cyberculture / South Atlantic Quarterly,* ed. Mark Dery, vol. 92, no. 4 (fall 1993), p. 688.

99. Ibid., pp. 692–93.

100. Ibid., p. 703.

101. Ibid., p. 695.

102. *New York Times Magazine,* April 14, 1991, p. 46.

103. Jeffrey Rothfeder, *Privacy for Sale: How Computerization Has Made Everyone's Private Life an Open Secret* (New York: Simon & Schuster, 1992), p. 180.

104. Ibid., p. 181.

105. Ibid., p. 189.

106. Steve Kurtz, E-mail to the author, November 19, 1993.

107. Critical Art Ensemble, *Critical Art Ensemble: The Electronic Disturbance* (New York: Autonomedia/Semiotext(e), 1994), pp. 57–79.

108. Steve Kurtz, E-mail to the author, February 10, 1994.

109. Steve Kurtz, E-mail to the author, March 11, 1994.

110. Quoted in K. G. Pontus Hulten, *The Machine as Seen at the End of the Mechanical Age* (New York: Museum of Modern Art, 1968), p. 11.

111. Hine, *Facing Tomorrow,* p. 174.

112. Ehrenreich, "Human Body," p. 67.

113. Alan M. Klein, "Of Muscles and Men," *Sciences,* November/December 1991, p. 36.

114. Paul Solotaroff, "Living Large," *Village Voice,* no. 44 (October 29, 1991), p. 30.

115. Ibid., p. 156.

116. Erik Hedegaard, "Making It Big," *Details*, October 1993, p. 192.

117. F. T. Marinetti, "Multiplied Man and the Reign of the Machine," in *Marinetti: Selected Writings*, ed. R. W. Flint (New York: Farrar, Straus and Giroux, 1972), p. 91.

118. Ewen, *All Consuming Images*, p. 188.

119. Klein, "Of Muscles and Men."

120. Ross, *Strange Weather*, p. 152.

121. Ibid., pp. 145, 152.

122. Marinetti, Introduction to *Marinetti*, p. 6.

123. Ross, *Strange Weather*, p. 162.

124. *The Beacon Book of Quotations by Women*, ed. Rosalie Maggio (Boston: Beacon Press, 1992), p. 14.

125. Hunter Thompson, *Hell's Angels* (New York: Ballantine Books, 1985), pp. 116, 119.

126. Quoted in Naomi Wolf, *Fire with Fire: The New Female Power and How It Will Change the Twenty-first Century* (New York: Random House, 1993), p. 283.

127. Klaus Theweleit, *Male Fantasies*, vol. 2 (Minneapolis: University of Minnesota Press, 1989), p. xix.

128. Ibid., p. xix.

129. All quotes this paragraph from Margot Dougherty, *Entertainment Weekly*, no. 74 (July 12, 1991), sidebar to cover story on *T2*, p. 18.

130. 1988 spring supplement to the Loompanics Unlimited Main Catalogue, p. 2.

131. Claudia Springer, "Sex, Memories, and Angry Women," p. 726.

132. Mark Dery, "Black to the Future: Interviews with Samuel R. Delany, Greg Tate, and Tricia Rose," *Flame Wars*, p. 777.

133. Tony Rayns, "Tokyo Stories," *Sight and Sound*, December 1991, p. 15.

134. Ballard, *Crash*, p. 5.

135. Bukatman, *Terminal Identity*, p. 20.

136. Ibid., p. 308.

137. Ibid.

138. J. Hoberman, "Reanimators," *Village Voice*, April 28, 1992, p. 51.

139. Undated press release.

140. "*Tetsuo:* The Iron Man/Synopsis," undated program for a screening of the movie at London's ICA artspace.

141. Ballard, *Crash*.

142. William Bohnaker, *The Hollow Doll (A Little Box of Japanese Shocks)* (New York: Ballantine, 1990), p. 121.

143. Unbylined editorial, "Exhibit Hall A: Alien Art," *Tattoo Flash*, no. 7 (February 1995), p. 14.

144. Anonymous futurist, quoted in Angelo Bozzolla and Caroline Tisdall, *Futurism* (New York: Oxford University Press, 1978), p. 81.

145. David Levi Strauss, "Modern Primitives," in *Re/Search 12: Modern Primitives*, ed. V. Vale and Andrea Juno (San Francisco: Re/Search, 1989), p. 158.

146. Herman Melville, *Moby Dick or The Whale* (New York: Vintage Books, 1991), p. 53.

147. Ibid., p. 537.

148. *Re/Search 12: Modern Primitives*, p. 4.

149. Ibid., p. 153.

150. Rosalind Coward, *The Whole Truth: The Myth of Alternative Health* (London: Faber & Faber, 1989), p. 197.

151. Ibid.

152. Mary Douglas, *Re/Search 12: Modern Primitives*, p. 195.

153. Ibid., pp. 4–5.

154. Rodley, ed., *Cronenberg on Cronenberg*, p. 65.

155. *Re/Search 12: Modern Primitives*, p. 36.

156. Ibid., p. 5.

157. Ibid.

158. Marshall McLuhan and Quentin Fiore, *The Medium Is the Massage* (New York: Bantam, 1967), p. 63.

159. "*Playboy* Interview: Marshall McLuhan," March 1969, p. 64.

160. Ibid., pp. 62, 64.

161. Ibid., p. 70.

162. Gibson, *Burning Chrome* (New York: Ace, 1987), p. 18.

163. Richard Kadrey, *Metrophage* (New York: Ace, 1988), p. 3.

164. Walter Jon Williams, *Facets* (New York: Tor, 1990), pp. 69–70.

165. Queen Mu and R. U. Sirius, editorial, *Mondo 2000*, no. 7 (fall 1989), p. 11; Bukatman, *Terminal Identity*, p. 302.

166. William Gibson, *Virtual Light* (New York: Bantam Spectra, 1993), p. 220.

167. Dr. Fritz Billeter, "H. R. Giger's Environments," in *H. R. Giger's Necronomicon* (Zurich, Switzerland: Edition C, 1981), p. 74.

168. Cliff Cadaver, "How to Make a Monster: Modifications for the Millennium," *Outlaw Biker Tattoo Revue* 6, no. 31 (December 1993), unnumbered pages.

169. Haraway, *Simians, Cyborgs, and Women*, p. 179; Cadaver, "How to Make a Monster."

354Notes

170. Ray Bradbury, *The Illustrated Man* (Garden City, N.Y.: Doubleday & Company, 1951), p. 11.

171. F. T. Marinetti, "Multiplied Man," p. 91.

172. *Cyberpunk* (VHS, 60 minutes, available from ATA/Cyberpunk, P.O. Box 12, Massapequa Park, N.Y. 11762).

173. Gibson, *Burning Chrome*, p. 14; Gibson, *Neuromancer*, p. 59.

174. *Cyberpunk.*

175. Ibid.

176. Burt Brent, "Thoracobrachial Pterygoplasty Powered by Muscle Transposition Flaps," in *The Artistry of Reconstructive Surgery: Classic Case Studies*, vol. 2 (St. Louis: C.V. Mosby Company, 1987), p. 967.

177. Ibid., p. 959.

178. *Cyberpunk.*

179. *The New Hacker's Dictionary* defines a "wirehead" as a hardware hacker who concentrates on communications systems; Gareth Branwyn notes that the term "specifically applies to techies who hack LANs (office networks), ToasterNets (cobbled-together Internet sites using cast-off PCs and shareware), and telecom hardware hackers in general." But in *Schismatrix*, Bruce Sterling refers to the prosthetically enhanced, electronically interconnected Mechanists as "wireheads," and the term is loosely used in cyberpunk circles as a synonym for "aspiring cyborg." It is in this sense that it is used here.

180. Gareth Branwyn, "The Desire to Be Wired," *Wired*, September/October 1993, p. 65.

181. Ibid., p. 62.

182. Gibson, *Neuromancer*, p. 56.

183. John Leonard, "Gravity's Rainbow," *Nation*, November 15, 1993, p. 585.

184. David P. Snyder, "Repairing the Mind with Machines: The Supernormal Possibilities of Prosthetics," *Omni*, September 1993, p. 14.

185. Ibid.

186. Janice M. Cauwels, *The Body Shop: Bionic Revolutions in Medicine* (St. Louis: C. V. Mosby, 1986), pp. 208–9.

187. Snyder, "Repairing the Mind."

188. Ibid.

189. Ibid.

190. Darrell E. Ward, "Gaze Control," *Omni*, December 1988, p. 30.

191. Andrew Pollack, "Computers Taking Wish as Their Command," *New York Times*, February 9, 1993, Section D, p. 2.

192. Branwyn, "The Desire to Be Wired," p. 113.

193. Ibid., p. 65.

194. Ibid.

195. R. A. Chase and Joseph M. Rosen, "Microsurgery: The Future," in *The Hand and Upper Limb Series*, vol. 8: *Microsurgery Procedures*, ed. D. E. Meyer and M. J. M. Black (New York: Churchill Livingstone, 1991), pp. 261, 264, 265.

196. Bruce Sterling, "Swarm," in *Crystal Express*, p. 15.

197. Sigmund Freud, *Civilization and Its Discontents* (New York: W. W. Norton, 1961), pp. 38–39.

198. Jude Milhon, "Coming In under the Radar: Bruce Sterling Interviewed by Jude Milhon," *Mondo 2000*, no. 7, p. 100.

199. Hine, *Facing Tomorrow*, p. 43.

200. Jeffrey Deitch, *Post Human* (Hamburg, Germany: Deichtorhallen Hamburg, 1992), second page of introductory essay (not numbered).

201. Ibid., unnumbered pages.

202. Michael Murphy, *The Future of the Body: Explorations into the Further Evolution of Human Nature* (Los Angeles: Jeremy P. Tarcher, 1992), p. 28.

203. Michael Hutchison, *Mega Brain Power: Transform Your Life with Mind Machines and Brain Nutrients* (New York: Hyperion, 1994), p. 429.

204. Stewart Brand, *The Media Lab: Inventing the Future at M.I.T.* (New York: Penguin, 1988), p. 200.

205. K. Eric Drexler, *Engines of Creation: The Coming Era of Nanotechnology* (New York: Anchor, 1986), p. 234.

206. Grant Fjermedal, *The Tomorrow Makers: A Brave New World of Living-Brain Machines* (Redmond, Wash.: Tempus Books, 1986), p. 8.

207. Scott Bukatman, "Who Programs You? The Science Fiction of the Spectacle," in *Alien Zone: Cultural Theory and Contemporary Science Fiction Cinema*, ed. Annette Kuhn (New York: Verso, 1990), p. 203.

208. Rodley, ed., *Cronenberg on Cronenberg*, p. 79; Scorsese is interviewed in Chris Rodley's 1986 documentary on Cronenberg, *Long Live the New Flesh*.

209. Pat Cadigan, "Pretty Boy Crossover," in *Patterns* (Kansas City, Mo.: Ursus Imprints, 1989), p. 129.

210. Jean Baudrillard, "The Precession of Simulacra," in *Simulations*, trans. Paul Foss, Paul Patton, and Philip Beitchman (New York: Semiotext(e), 1983), p. 11.

211. Ballard, *Crash*, p. 1.

212. Ibid., p. 39.
213. Bruce Sterling, "Sunken Gardens," in *Crystal Express*, p. 89.
214. Bruce Sterling, *Schismatrix* (New York: Ace, 1985), p. 237.
215. Ibid., p. 183.
216. Ibid., pp. 282–83.
217. Ibid., pp. 286–87.
218. Ibid., p. 287.
219. Vernor Vinge, "Technological Singularity," *Whole Earth Review*, no. 81 (winter 1993), p. 89.
220. Ibid.
221. William Burroughs, "Dinosaurs," *The Dial-a-Poem Poets / Better an Old Demon than a New God* (Giorno Poetry Systems GPS 033), LP.
222. Ibid.
223. Ibid.
224. Terence McKenna, *The Archaic Revival* (New York: HarperCollins, 1991), p. 230.
225. Ibid., p. 231.
226. Ibid., p. 232.
227. Ibid.
228. Hans Moravec, *Mind Children: The Future of Robot and Human Intelligence* (Cambridge: Harvard University Press, 1988), p. 6.
229. Ibid., p. 102.
230. Ibid., p. 107.
231. Ibid., p. 112.
232. Ibid., p. 114.
233. David Ross, "Persons, Programs, and Uploading Consciousness," *Extropy* 4, no. 1 (9), p. 14.
234. Ibid., p. 16.
235. Max More, "Technological Self-Transformation: Expanding Personal Extropy," *Extropy* 10, pp. 17, 20.
236. Norman Spinrad, *Science Fiction in the Real World* (Carbondale and Edwardsville, Ill.: Southern Illinois University Press, 1990), p. 133.
237. Ibid., p. 127.
238. More, "Self-Transformation," p. 17; Stelarc, *Obsolete Body / Suspensions / Stelarc* (Davis, Calif.: J. P. Publications, 1984), p. 76.
239. More, "Self-Transformation," p. 16; "Join Us on the Leading Edge of the Evolutionary Wave as We Build a Better Future!" undated flyer from the Extropy Institute.

240. "Sacred or For Sale?" in *The Harper's Forum Book: What Are We Talking About?* ed. Jack Hitt (New York: Citadel Press, 1991), p. 307.

241. Barbara Branden, *The Passion of Ayn Rand* (Garden City, N.Y.: Doubleday & Company, 1986), p. 140.

242. Max More, "Transhumanism: Towards a Futurist Philosophy," *Extropy*, no. 6 (summer 1990), p. 8.

243. Ibid.

244. Ibid., p. 23.

245. More, "Self-Transformation," p. 23.

246. Ibid., p. 24.

247. Max More, "Extropy Institute Launches," *Extropy* 9, p. 9.

248. All quotes this paragraph from Queen Mu and R. U. Sirius, editorial, *Mondo 2000*, no. 7, p. 11.

249. Andrew Ross, *Strange Weather*, p. 163.

250. Spinrad, *Science Fiction*, p. 129.

251. David Skal, *The Monster Show: A Cultural History of Horror* (New York: W. W. Norton, 1993), pp. 251–52.

252. Vinge, "Technological Singularity," p. 95.

253. Pamela McCorduck, *Machines Who Think* (San Francisco: W. H. Freeman and Company, 1979), pp. 354–55.

254. Ibid., p. 355.

255. Gareth Branwyn, "The Desire to Be Wired," p. 62.

256. Allucquere Rosanne Stone, "Will the Real Body Please Stand Up?: Boundary Stories about Virtual Cultures," in *Cyberspace: First Steps,* ed. Michael Benedikt (Cambridge: MIT Press, 1991), p. 111.

257. Vivian Sobchack, "Baudrillard's Obscenity," *Science-Fiction Studies*, vol. 18, no. 55, part 3 (November 1991), p. 327.

258. Ibid., pp. 327–28.

259. Jean Baudrillard, "Ballard's *Crash*," *Science-Fiction Studies*, pp. 313, 319.

260. Sobchack, "Baudrillard's Obscenity," p. 329.

261. Michael Berenbaum, *The History of the Holocaust as Told in the United States Holocaust Memorial Museum* (Boston: Little, Brown and Company, 1993), p. 147.

262. Ballard, *Crash*, p. 205.

263. Walter Benjamin, "The Work of Art in the Age of Mechanical Reproduction," in *Illuminations,* ed. Hannah Arendt (New York: Schocken, 1969), p. 244.

264. Michael Synergy, "Hurtling towards the Singularity: Vernor Vinge Interviewed by Michael Synergy," *Mondo 2000*, no. 7 (fall 1989), p. 116.

265. Hitt, ed., *The Harper's Forum Book,* p. 317.

266. Ibid., p. 322.

267. Andrew Ross, *Strange Weather,* p. 70.

268. *Whole Earth Review,* no. 63 (summer 1989), p. 53.

269. Moravec, *Mind Children,* p. 102; Hine, *Facing Tomorrow,* pp. 155–56.

270. Edward O. Wilson, "Is Humanity Suicidal?" *New York Times Magazine,* May 30, 1993, pp. 26–27.

271. Ibid., p. 27.

272. Michael G. Zey, *Seizing the Future: How the Coming Revolution in Science, Technology, and Industry Will Expand the Frontiers of Human Potential and Reshape the Planet* (New York: Simon & Schuster, 1994), p. 45.

273. Ibid.

274. Ibid., pp. 45, 368.

275. Ibid., p. 369.

276. Queen Mu and R. U. Sirius, editorial, *Mondo 2000,* no. 7, p. 11.

277. Ross, *Strange Weather,* p. 5.

278. Ibid., p. 12.

279. Ibid., p. 191.

280. Constance Penley and Andrew Ross, "Cyborgs at Large: Interview with Donna Haraway," *Technoculture* (Minneapolis: University of Minnesota Press, 1991), p. 16; Zey, *Seizing the Future,* p. 109.

281. Leo Marx, *The Machine in the Garden: Technology and the Pastoral Ideal in America* (New York: Oxford University Press, 1964), p. 207.

282. Fjermedal, *Tomorrow Makers,* p. 5.

283. Hine, *Facing Tomorrow,* pp. 154–55.

284. Fjermedal, *Tomorrow Makers,* p. 202.

285. Quoted in Camille Paglia, *Sexual Personae: Art and Decadence from Nefertiti to Emily Dickinson* (New York: Vintage, 1991), p. 17.

286. O. B. Hardison, Jr., *Disappearing through the Skylight: Culture and Technology in the Twentieth Century* (New York: Penguin, 1989), p. 347.

287. Ibid.

288. Charles Platt, *The Silicon Man* (New York: Bantam Spectra, 1991), p. 232.

289. William H. Calvin, *The Throwing Madonna: Essays on the Brain* (New York: Bantam, 1991), p. 59.

290. Ibid., p. xvii.

291. Erich Harth, *The Creative Loop: How the Brain Makes a Mind* (Reading, Mass.: Addison-Wesley, 1993), p. 131.
292. David Ross, "Persons, Programs, and Uploading Consciousness," p. 15.
293. Richard Restak, M.D., *The Brain Has a Mind of Its Own: Insights from a Practicing Neurologist* (New York: Harmony Books, 1991), p. 119.
294. David Ross, "Persons, Programs, and Uploading Consciousness," p. 16.
295. Cadigan, *Synners*, p. 406.

INDEX